Scatterlings—A Tapestry of Afri-Expat Tales

Eve Hemming

To order additional copies of this book, contact:
Xlibris Corporation
1-800-618-969
www.xlibris.com.au
Orders@Xlibris.com.au
503880

CONTENTS

For my beloved Ant, and to our cherished family—Kate and Nick, Justin and Lisa, Paul and Stacey—and grandchildren Toni, Gabrielle, Emma, Dylan, Daniel and Aliyah. You are the centre of my world.

There are two great days in a person's life—
The day we are born
And the day we discover why.

William Barclay—theologian (1907-1978)

On Joy and Sorrow
Kahlil Gibran
"Your joy is your sorrow unmasked.
And the selfsame well from which your laughter
arises was oftentimes with your tears.
And how else can it be?
The deeper the sorrow carves into your being,
the more joy you can contain . . ."

Acknowledgements

You know who you are! My own beloved 3-D family and my 'online family' who held me up through thick and thin.

To my beloved husband, Ant, who had to live the journey with a wife manically burning the candle and eating, sleeping, dreaming this book . . .

To my mentors who believed in me.

To Carol Champ who morphed my book cover design into a reality.

To my Emma and Dylan for the gorgeous tree designs for the book cover.

For Lisa and my Toni and Gabi for your treasured poems.

To all the renowned writers and wonderful contributors (too many to name individually), who bravely shared their articles and personal stories.

Without you, there simply would not have been this book! You made it . . .

To Kerry Engelbrecht, for your editing support and empathetic identification, and to my publishers for your patience!

"I prefer to be a dreamer among the humblest, with visions to be realized, than lord among those without dreams and desires." Kahlil Gibran

Preface

"The tapestry of life stitched together by a unifying knowledge manifested from joy."

Bill Levacy

I never in my wildest dreams thought that I'd be writing this book. Of course part of me wishes I never had to, while half of me is glad that I am. As a child I had dreams about being an authoress, much as most imaginative children love to fantasise about achieving possibly the impossible. It was perhaps sparked by Anne Frank's diary, but of course like any idealistic child, my book wouldn't require me to be in hiding behind a bookcase for an inimitable period, finally to die a terrible death in a concentration camp. Mine would surely be a happy-ever-after-after story.

Someone once asked me how my stories germinate. I replied, "Something triggers an idea, like a seed that suddenly ripens and sends out a little shoot. After that it grows into a robust bean stalk." One can never create an authentic story. It creates itself. One can't lie in the bath contemplating one's navel and beseech the words to flash across the bathroom tiles, or lie under a tree squinting at sunrays through filigreed leaves, waiting with miserable hope.

Ideas for my stories and for this book have often popped into my head at the most inopportune moment, like when I'm idling in a traffic jam or in the process of falling asleep. I simply think, "Oh . . . . I hope I don't lose that light-bulb thought before I can scribble it down."

When creating and typing one's story, one takes the hand-scribbled notes of reminders of one's past, together with the moments when one actually indulged oneself to have 'me time' to write. These snippets then start to cohere. And as one writes, one's own life and the world around are happening in parallel to one's written life. As John Lennon said, "Life is what happens to you, while you're busy making other plans."

My story is not an autobiography, but rather holds some snippets about my life from which, like a wash-line, I can hang up some embellishments, thoughts, philosophies, memories and some of my published articles with colourful pegs to form a wash-line of my life world.

If one has not had an extraordinary life, WHICH I HAVEN'T, it lacks the lustre to engage the reader. For people are in essence voyeurs. Thus, it is more the thoughts hanging from each peg, that create the imagery, and they in turn create the flesh and the bones of one's story. For in the end, a story is a gathering of words on a page. And there are thousands of permutations of how to paste the words into a coherent journey. But a journey doesn't have to have a timeline. It can wend its way back and forth to yesterday, to tomorrow and back to today. Because a story is just the thoughts of the mind. And the mind is never static. In *Scatterlings* . . . my story and others' stories, thoughts and contributions are interwoven to offer you a tapestry of tales.

'Scatterlings' has become a well-known word in South Africa; its popularity amplified by Johnny Clegg's *Scatterlings of Africa*, a song that today can still evoke me to cry . . .

> *And we are scatterlings of Africa*
> *On a journey to the stars*
> *Far below we leave forever*
> *Dreams of what we were*
> (Lyrics from Johnny Clegg's *Scatterlings of Africa*.)

A 'scatterling' is defined as someone with no fixed abode. In many ways migrants are like scatterlings—genetically scattered into Southern Africa by our forbearers, to then become globally scattered. In essence like vagabonds—with memories fuelled by a pulsating heart in Africa, intermeshed with a three-dimensional existence of adapting, morphing and residing elsewhere.

It is the word that best defines me. I never ever feel entirely complete and wonder if I ever will feel totally whole again. Oh, there are moments, like family reunions. But generally speaking I feel as though there is a schism of my soul, as though I have agnosia, wherein I cannot draw myself as a total entity, but with arms, legs, head, heart, soul severed, flailing and disconnected.

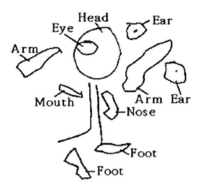

I more than ever feel as though I breathe for my cherished husband, children, children-in-law and their children, and that my purpose in life is to love them unconditionally. Nothing else has quite the same tangible substance in my soul anymore. Maybe that is the beauty, tragedy and paradox of emigrating. When one is away from some of the people one most loves, possibly only then is one truly able to know the depths of one's own love for them. It is in bearing our children that my husband and I have a purpose. Of course this isn't exclusively accurate—we have had the purpose of contributing to society too, having both worked to serve the South African community for the major part of our lives. But, now in the aftermath of emigration, the lights of passion for my family burn brighter, the pain for those afar cuts deeper and the joy of those close by is greater. Everything else loses an element of its patina. Things that were important have faded into a paler washed-out hue.

I've previously written about the world being a merry-go-round. I conjure up the image of the steel-eyed, nostril-flared, colourfully adorned horses, rhythmically yet monotonously moving in a never-ending circular motion, mounted by laughing, innocent children. The children's futures are unbeknown to them . . . they start on that merry-go-round not asking or wondering where their life journey will take them. Will they remain on the merry-go-round or will they climb off it to fly to unknown realms?

Why a tapestry of tales you may wonder? With a surname Hemming, it seemed apt and humoured me. The tales could figuratively be hemmed together to create a rich, multi-hued rainbow tapestry that would be reminiscent of some of the rainbow nation's peoples' lives. Also because the sense of collectivity has always strongly resonated for me. The idea of sharing a *potpourri* of many lives made my heart pound louder. I had listened to people's stories, but here was a chance to chronicle them into the textile of colours, textures, patterns and designs to make the fabric that much richer.

However, as one writes a book it undergoes a metamorphosis as new inspirations serendipitously confront one; it starts to weave its own tale, adds more patterns and fibres to the tapestry; develops a life of its own, as though one's tangential thoughts allow it to rearrange itself by creating new nuances into the luxuriant tapestry.

I do not support all the views, contributions and excerpts in this book. I have, however, attempted to incorporate a cross section of others' points of view and have attempted at all times to retain the integrity of the book as far as possible, and to reflect a respect for all of humanity. There is a strong difference in disliking a person or disliking his or her actions or opinions.

My life is a mere blip on the planet. Its shout gets lost in the fragmentation of all existence and in the temporality and mania of life. But in incorporating others' stories and in being the mouthpiece for others, our collective voices will hopefully be heard in more places.

Existence
Eve Hemming 2011

Galaxies of light
Above
The scatterlings of humanity.
We are mere portals that turn our faces to
Kiss the sun,
Catch a moonbeam,
Wish on a falling star.

Mere mortals
Co-existing through the dirty bathos
The aching pathos.
Or basking in the futility of
Shallow hedonism
Oblivious of life's
Chaos;
Or of other's terrible loss.

Existence.
Each has an aspiration,
Maybe being jolly
Or grabbing a moment of
Folly.
Each breathes the breath of myriad emotions
Of life with its plans, its dramas
And its unplanned
Sagas.

It is cyclical . . .
Like seasons changing
With spring blossom and autumn gold
Or windmills rotating in the wind
Clanging again
And again
Gloriously bold
Anciently old.

But
Time is the leveller.
Pouncing unwittingly on good, bad
And sad.
It grabs at the jugular
It sucks with visceral greed
Tightening its squeeze
To scatter our lifeless forms
Into a galaxy of storms.

Disclaimer: *All the information, views and articles published in this book are not necessarily representative of my personal views.*

The Universe Intercedes

Life isn't about finding yourself. Life's about creating yourself.
—George Bernard Shaw

Africa is a hard place to leave. In the words of Alexandra Fuller, *Cocktail Hour Under the Tree of Forgetfulness*, now married and living in the USA: "We see our lives as fraught and exciting, terrible and blessed, wild and ensnaring. We see our lives as Rhodesian, and it's not easy to leave a life as arduously rich and difficult as all that."

It is July 2009. A chilled Antarctic wind whips up to chase me indoors from where through a large expanse of unfettered window, I can view several aeroplanes, like pregnant bellied giant fish, almost static, slowly one after the other descending across the Manukau Harbour to the airport. As always, I feel a surge of desire, wishing that it was the aeroplane that belched my children and their children from its gaping wound, to touch down on my terra firma. But again, it's just filled with anonymous souls who will kiss others with arms outstretched.

It's a year since I arrived here. Alone. And still the tears flow. Life steadily pulses with the constant ticking of the clock, but tears still flow at the most inopportune moments. Ironically though, there is always an element of happiness. There's the happiness of adventure, of the birth of a new era, of the joy of living, imbibing, discovering, and assimilating. I'm blessed with *joie de vivre; or* else I think I would have 'crashed' by now.

But never far from the edge are the tears. Anything can trigger them to flow. And, as easily, anything can cauterise them. It's all in one's thoughts, one's memories and in a million *Déjà vu* moments.

Children are genetically engineered to fly away; to disembark from the cosy nest where parents held them maybe too suffocatingly through the formative years. As children of the universe, we are inherently questers who seek to explore beyond the familiar landscape, to taste the curiosity of a sun-drenched romantic dream.

It may be propelled by a passion to actualise or nudge oneself out of the comfort zone, or it may be to follow some innate drive for that elusive goal-driven adventure, for an extension of the self, for riches or a spiritual awakening. And that makes sense.

But ours was a reverse scenario. That came as an insane awakening to my, and everyone else's, psyches. So here I am; wife, mother, grandmother—still reeling from the shock of flying on three aeroplanes across the planet—from my comfortable, well, feathered nest . . . Quintessentially I left my husband and our three children and their families behind. And I am besotted about them. They are the breath that I breathe. It makes no sense whatsoever to me. But that (in part) is the way it is, (or was, at that moment). And ah, my crystal ball's reflection has faded and the future's not mine to see . . . *Que Sera, Sera* . . .

An African Childhood

It is November 2011. Something clangs in my head . . . you know the way one starts to review one's life towards the end of the year and starts thinking about 'what next?' for the following year; about setting goals, having resolutions and defining some direction. The little clang becomes a loud clang bouncing in my brain. All the newspaper articles I write and my blog seem to recede into the background as the name of the book is born. That in itself is satisfying. Now it is time to start cobbling the tales together and to gather others' tales to add to mine.

It's a balmy Saturday and Ant, Paddywag (our Kiwi doggy) and I, plus our Kate, Nick, Emma and Dylan have enjoyed a beach and natural vegetation walk in a protected bay near our Auckland home. Walks are times of bitter sweet poignancy, the deliriously evocative surroundings—now the *Pohutukawa* trees, emblazoned in crimson are highlighted against the soft ocean silvery reflections—and the gratitude of having our daughter and her family so close by, yet my heart feels the empty space in it waiting for tonight's Skype call to our SA family and grandchildren.

I drift into my thoughts and return home to reminisce about my own childhood . . .

I was born in Africa. And every child born in Africa somehow has the outline of the African continent imprinted as a tattoo in the mind's eye, whether they're conscious or oblivious of this. *Africa!* It is depicted as the centre of the planet on the world map. It shouts out its stupendous shape. It squats proudly between immense oceans and is severed from Asia only by the Suez Canal—a little incision between the Mediterranean and the Red Sea.

It all started a long time ago. I was born and bred on a farm on the Lesotho border in South Africa, where my life's vista was encapsulated by voluminous Freestate clouds, shale grey dolomite topped *koppies* (hills) and archaic windmills with rotating metallic fingers pointing skywards. African straw-roofed mud huts, acres of golden wheat fields and heavily fertile, red dusty earth were part of the world which I was born to understand and deify.

The Maluti Mountains of Lesotho, known as God's Kingdom, became the edge of my childish world. They were a startling cobalt blue some days and snow-covered in the winter. I had no idea what world lay behind that mountain range.

There was stoic, earnest, gentlemanly Dad, donned in khaki—a farmer who played the occasional game of polo until he had a nasty fall and broke his nose. I only knew a man with a skew nose as my father. I didn't know the dad with a straight nose and laughed at him when he shaved as his reflection in the mirror made his skew nose look the wrong way round to me. And there was flamboyant and elegant Mum, a dance and drama teacher, who staged ambitious theatrical productions in the nearby *dorp* (town), in which I loved to participate. Their lives were full of the 360-degree circle of events dictated to and symbolised by the cyclical rhythm of seasonal changes and the weather. Mealie (maize) crops destroyed by a malevolent hailstorm could be juxtaposed against a magnificently fertile wheat crop the following season.

There would be glorious sun-kissed days when cumulonimbus clouds hovered high above the sun baked *koppies*. Rain would pelt down to nourish the crops. Autumn would emerge with its exquisite gamut of autumnal hues, munificently decorating the trees, *veld* grasses and *vleis* (field grasslands and valleys) then the harsh winter. There'd be bitter frost on crunchy, dead, white grass, the snow-capped Maluti Mountains framing our chilly vista. Then cherry blossoms would burst open in the spring.

Children were born and celebrated. I was the last born, being second born of twin girls, which surprisingly created a family comprised of four children. I was delivered breech and was unexpected—the bonus child. The doctor was allegedly scrubbing up after delivering my twin sister so as to dash off to a cocktail party when the midwife bellowed, "*Dokter daar's nog 'n een*" ("Doctor there's another one").

And so began my 'unexpected life'.

Home was in robust stone under an iron roof, on which rain lyrically cascaded down on to the sturdy corrugated iron roof and could mesmerise one when tucked up in bed. And there were laughing siblings and beaming, shimmering teethed nannies who spoke in clucking voices.

My twin's Sotho name was Ntswaki and mine was Mphoneni. Her nanny was Jacina, mine was Mantona. Our older brothers' Sotho names were Lefa and Thabo. My childhood memories of our brothers are hazy. They were the 'big' boys whom we revered, who went away to school on a Monday and came home on a Friday. Then they were bigger boys who went away on a train in uniform with a red Wyvern symbol on the badge and only came home a few times a year from boarding school in Grahamstown.

Ntswaki and I each had a nanny as the farm policy was to employ as many of the farm labourers' wives as possible, as it was too far from the local *dorp* (town), nestled next to the Caledon River on the Lesotho border, for them to travel to seek employment. And what type of employment could many folk find in a small European *dorp*? It also meant that Jacina and Mantona were in good spirits, as they could cluck away in their agreeably captivating native Sotho tongue to one another whilst they tended to us as we played and explored in the never-ending garden. Our father would have been up on the land crop planting, threshing corn or checking on the livestock. Our mother could have been in the home writing her plays, planning her concerts, baking, cooking, or else outdoors gardening or maybe in the *dorp* buying the groceries or, later, teaching elocution and ballet to her students.

I was a tomboy, particularly attached to my father, who was nicknamed Miller. I'd accompany him on sorties in his ancient truck along with the fox terriers, Frisky and Houdini. The bizarre things stand out in my memory. I watched him shoot a dying cow. I saw the Sunday dinner rooster dancing around headless, after being *slagged* (slaughtered). I would shield my eyes and peep between my fingers in disgusted fascination. I helped him rescue lambs that were orphaned at birth, which I bottle fed in the kitchen beside the comfort of the warmly crackling old cob-fuelled stove. Once I gouged my leg badly on a barbed wire fence as I crawled through to then unsuspectingly have a face-to-face encounter with a puff adder. I still have a rather splendid scar. Life and death were things one was exposed to as a farm child.

I don't remember my siblings being bad, so I'm not sure where I inherited the bad gene from. I was without a doubt the most recalcitrant and probably the most impetuous of the four kids. I recall cutting my teddy bear's hair off when I was about four. I also cut the cat's whiskers. How the hell was I to know that cat's whiskers are their 'antennae'? When I was five I fiddled with Aunty Maisie's knitting and dropped the stitches, which I vehemently denied. I puked my stomach empty out the car window aged six when we drove home from a wedding in Lesotho, as I'd smoked several *stompies* (cigarette butts) picked up off the lawn. I disfigured my big brother's leather bound books he'd won as prizes at boarding school by proudly writing his name on them when I'd just learned to read and write. I used his razor to shave and of course nick my legs when I was ten. I must've been a real pain! I also nearly *vrekked* (died) a few times, like the time I took a short cut to the wash line by scaling up a wall, dislodging a clump of large rocks that tumbled on to me so that I couldn't breathe. I guess every family has one of those sorts of kids.

We loved the abundant Christmases which started out by sharing time with the African staff on the farm; with Christmas carols and prayers, followed by presenting them with gifts of food, clothes, goods and kitchen ware. They in turn, danced, sang and gave us elaborately handcrafted brooms made from dried grass. Our wonderfully wacky and eccentric relatives would descend on us from various cities or farming communities for Christmas dinner served on a laden table stretched out in the sunroom that opened on to the veranda. As kids we didn't understand about filial politics, but there were conspiracy theories about our permanently slightly pissed uncle unceremoniously plonking himself in his unlaced '*tackies*' next to moth-balled, prickly chinned, less-than-amused grandmother with her thick bifocals and silver hair pinned up in a hair net contraption.

In later years, my father developed motor neuron disease and was confined to a wheelchair. He refused to surrender his passionate work ethic and his wizened form was carried in a wicker chair by two of his labourers, so that he could oversee the daily farm routine. Mum's many creative pursuits ceased so that she could nurse him.

And now they are long dead. We, their offspring, are adults. I am a grandmother. One day our children will reflect on our lives while peering at old browned craggy-edged photographs captured in a split second. Each photograph may be the starting point of an elaborate narrative . . . I still reminisce about my parents and celebrate the cyclical nature of life.

*   *   *

Wherever one is born must surely become the epicentre of one's own universe. A child's universe begins with its mother's face and her breasts as she connects with and suckles her young. This universe slowly enlarges in ever concentric circles which Bronfonbrenner refers to as the Ecological Theory of Development. The child's universe starts with family, followed by peers and neighbours and school; these being the areas which most shape the child's personality and development. Later systems interrelate with one another, like school and home, and permeate outwards to the culture, religious beliefs and ideologies one is born into; the mores of one's society, followed by chronological events, historical factors and environmental transitions. When one throws a stone into a pond and it creates a circle beyond a circle and another beyond that circle . . . such are the ripple effects in one's life.

Being born in South Africa in 1950, of predominantly Scottish decent and from a Christian, English-speaking background, are some of the factors which formed who I am and contributed to my personal journey. If I'd been born an Inuit, my world impressions would have impacted on my life vastly differently. For a start, I would not have the connection to Africa but rather to snow; I would not feel as though Africa was embedded in my bone marrow, in my soul and in my psyche. Ask any person born in Africa about feeling it in their bones . . .

Sixty something years later I reflect on all these things and wonder how in any ways it could have been different; partly wishing that it was, and yet sensing that we do seem to have some kind of inexplicable destiny. Some of these more esoteric facets are beyond my comprehension. Where does free will begin and where does preordained destiny converge with it?

'Immigration is not a cosmic mishap—it's a destiny or a dream realised.'

A wonderful quote I found but regrettably don't know who wrote it!

My earliest memories as a small child become blurred where true memories and old frayed-at-the-edges black and white photographs, held in place by small black triangular edges in our mother's large photograph albums, merge. The photographs show my twin and me as infants, one held by our father, the other by our mother, and our two older brothers standing awkwardly with 'smile at the camera' grimaces. One delves into the labyrinths of the mind and somewhere tucked into fuzzy cerebral popcorn is a conglomeration of sounds, vistas and images; of laughter, a sense of safety, of family and African staff, fox terriers, the black and white cat and pet lambs, scruffy farm clothes and church best with white gloves and socks, of burnt grass, spring with its buzzing bees and blossoms, and Summers festooned with fruit-bowed trees, of expansive land and endless skyscapes.

Early memories are always imprinted with the windmills, the dolomite *koppies* and the majestic Freestate clouds—pregnant, multi toned in whites and greys, and at sunset in golds, pinks and magentas. Colours and textures dominated my visual perceptions; the autumn shades of the golden poplars, the ochre soil contrasted against an expanse of verdant green mealies, or of softly golden hued wheat. To this day I marvel at windmills—they have a poignant symbolism for me connected to the rhythm and seasons; that circular motion of existence, to do with water being drawn up to sustain life. If I had to be an inorganic object, it would be a tall, steel windmill, with an omnipotent sense of overarching nurturance.

My other senses were tantalised by the sounds and odours of Africa. My world was mostly out of doors. Indoors was for meals, bathing and sleeping. I was a free spirit, learning to drive a John Deere tractor and firing a .22 gun at targets at the age of 12. The drone of a tractor signified 'home' to me. I loved the sensation of sitting between the two vast tyres on the John Deere with their deeply indented designs which left their yawning impressions in the earth behind me. I loved the engine's putter putter and the sense that there was no need to go anywhere specific and that time was inconsequential. I miss that African farm time, only controlled by seasons and the weather. Going to sleep at night, tucked in my warm bed, the sounds of nature and the creaking contractions of the corrugated iron roof were sensations which for me encapsulated a sense of security, spellbound by the repetitive symphony.

Oh and the birds! The *Piet my Vrou* and the cooing doves always signified home, as did a distant sheep bleating, a herd of cows mooing in unison, the echo of agitated dogs barking in the valley, the poultry stirring. For a farm child this was the norm and it's only when one is away from it that one realises what a charmed life it is to grow up in the country. African clicking sing-song voices made a child feel nurtured. They were there; part of the place called home.

I loved the smell of the *veld* burning and would watch the strong African men silhouetted again a red sky hitting the flames with wet hessian sacks, as they burnt firebreaks in the winter. Later on once the fire had died, walking on the burnt grass as it crunched under foot, was an almost delicious sensation, as was the heady smell of rain on dry dust. There were the pungent odours of animal manure up at the sheds and when the sheep were sheared my twin and I would curiously peep as the men deftly used sheep shears, snipping away layers of grimy wool to reveal unsoiled fresh layers of wool beneath. Afterwards we would jump into the massive bales of wool and roll around in the woolly greasiness; much to our mother's vexation as afterwards she'd wash us from head to toe, in case of lice. We'd also jump into the silo and roll around and bury one another in the fermenting foliage once the mealies had been picked and their stems and leaves stashed into the silo by some kind of spewing out machine for winter fodder for the cattle.

The warmth from the kitchen was welcoming in the winter, where there was the smell of burning mealie cobs in the fire mingled with coffee aromas from the old chipped enamel coffee pot on the stove. There was an old iron crook that one had to dexterously use so as not to get burnt. Using this, one could lever out the metal plate on the stove to throw more cobs on the flickering flames. The kitchen was always warm and a place where I bottle-fed my adopted orphaned lambs. Sometimes our broad beamed, jovial maid, Jemima, was stirring *putu* porridge on the stove, and I would go in to the kitchen to taste it, or the 'samp and beans' with a pinch of curry. I loved eating the African staff's food with them in the kitchen. It felt collegial and more fun than eating at the table set for my twin and me in the hallway adjoining the adult's dining room.

Dad used to make *biltong* (dried spiced meat) in the winter. We had to stand with our hands behind our backs when he sliced it. It was a warm pinky-brown colour, salty and scrumptious. Once you're brought up on *biltong*, you can't imagine life without it. Dad also used to make wheat beer. We would sit in the dimly lit green painted pantry and watch it fermenting, the wheat seeds dancing up and down in the golden yeasty liquid. It had an interesting bitter sweet taste that's difficult to describe, partly because it's possibly 50 years ago since I tasted it. Mum was the great baking mamma and we adored her Afghans, Crunchies and Gypsy Creams. My twin and I were each given a wooden spoon to scrape every last bit of biscuit mix till the bowl was empty. Mum was generous about leaving the mixture thick on the sides for us to lick and devour.

In the harvesting season we'd go on the large green harvester with dad and watch as the machine lopped off the tops of the wheat with its sharp edged blades and blasted out the chaff. It was a gargantuan, raucous contraption that dwarfed us. But with dad holding us we felt safe. We watched as the wheat was mechanically bagged and once we got back to the farm sheds, the African men helped dad sew the bags up with enormous twisted metal needles and rough brown twine.

Children didn't need television in those days. We had a generator and dim yellow lighting at night and no appliances that required electricity. It was the norm for us—that life—and I loved it with a heartiness as I knew no other life. Dad would go out in his overalls and crank up the generator as dusk loomed. All I recall was that it was a big smelly and cumbersome looking piece of machinery in a dark shed which was out of bounds without supervision. Once started, it made a spluttering, vibrating noise. We were considered quite privileged. When I went to my best friend Lynette's farm for sleepovers, there were paraffin lamps, candles and a long drop toilet outside.

The fridge was another story. My dad would wear his oldest, stained khaki farm clothes whenever the fridge needed to be refuelled and lit. This necessitated him to get into some sort of contorted horizontal position on the pantry floor, his long legs under the white enamel pantry table. After adding paraffin to a container under the fridge, he'd strike a match and light the wick. He would have to use a spirit level to ensure the angle was perfect, or else the flame would peter out and he'd utter a "blast" under his breathe, before purposefully attempting the wick-lighting process again. Blast was the worst word Dad ever used. And Mum never said anything worse than the occasional "bloody hell". Sadly that linguistic self-control didn't rub off on me!

My twin and I had been bundled off to weekly boarding school at the tender age of seven, having been home schooled by mum when we were six. We were driven to town on Monday mornings, and fetched on Fridays—our oversized suitcases in the boot of our dad's old blue 50s-something Chevy.

I don't ever recall my twin or me crying or being homesick. Possibly it was because we had one another and our best friends, Anne and Lynette. Or possibly it was because it was the only life that we knew. All the farmers' children were bundled off to the same place, and this was the life doled out to us. And possibly it did instil in us the deep awareness of collective living, of sharing and of co-existence.

Vague memories have become patched together with faded photo images, so that it feels as though it's someone else's life that I'm piecing together. Bells rang to wake us up. Bells rang for roll call, for meals, for prep and for bedtime.

The kindergarten classroom seemed spacious—little people at little desks. I remember a poor railway child (they were called the 'onderdorpers'—the people who lived in the lower socio-economic area on the edge of the town) who ate white lumpy margarine on his stale bread. It was rumoured that his toes on one foot had been amputated by a train. I shared my apricot jam hostel-made sarmies with him sometimes; partly out of compassion and maybe partly out of curiosity about his peculiar foot. We could not communicate though, as I spoke English and he spoke Afrikaans, and at that stage we were only being taught in our mother tongue. There were no African children in our school, as those were the days of Apartheid. As a seven year old I had no clue about any of this. To this day I still feel the guilt for not comprehending any of this and having no early awareness of the abhorrence of such a callous and inane system.

One remembers some things while some of the everyday minutiae can become intertwined and lost with the fading of time. I find it strange that I was so observant about some things and that other larger and more critical forces that were being played out were completely below the radar to my naïve childish mind.

After school we would walk from the kindergarten across the senior school's courtyard, flanked by stately red brick buildings renowned for their Pierneef murals, of which I was then childishly oblivious. We'd have to traverse a vast playing field and then cross a road to arrive at the hostel.

The playing field seemed an endless, flat, desolate place where boys flicked marbles around in the dust and girls jumped over skipping ropes, tripping on sashes tied around their waists over black-pleated pinafores. The toilets were at the far side, quite a distance to walk to on a winter's morning with frost embedded in dead clumps of grass. The Mimosa trees on that verge were smothered in yellow blossom in the summer. Today I still find their odour repugnant.

The *koshuis* (hostel) consisted of six-bedded dormitories, the beds separated by small cupboards. Weekly dormitory inspection was a terrifying ordeal. Our beds and the interior of our cupboards had to undergo the rigorous inspection of what can only be described as army specifications. A placard with a big black circle hanging on the door denoted detention, a red circle meant "okay" and a silver circle meant a reward. Being very much a minority English speaking group meant that our 'dorm' tried really hard to achieve and to comply.

Mondays were a treat as we'd walk to 'Monday School' at the Anglican Church right across town from the hostel and stop off for koeksusters at Lynette's *ouma* (grandmother),'Tannie Lettie's house. We each had sixpence to spend at the OK Bazaars as our weekly pocket money too, and 'Oom Mike' subsidised us with a further ten pence each! We also used to go to '*nagmal*' (The Lord's supper) at the Dutch Reformed *Kerk* (church) occasionally, although we didn't understand a word of Afrikaans at the age of 7. At school it was compulsory to be taught *Volkspele* (Afrikaans folk dancing), which I found quite fun, dancing to songs like '*Jan Pierewiet*'.

I shudder now about those days, because I realise how oblivious I was to any other type of childhood. As I witness the lives of my cherished grandchildren, I realise what my childhood lacked. With my own children I was too busy rearing them to make such a clear distinction. I watch my grandchildren splashing happily in the bath. At boarding school this was a regimented affair, children lined up on a wet concrete floor to grab a bath slot. I watch my grandchildren sharing tasty meals with their parents. Our meals were reduced to scoffing down colourless, runny stews, a housemother's eyes scorching the back of our necks.

I reflect back that at that age that we weren't kissed and cuddled into bed, that there were no bedtime stories, just a clinical gong declaring that the lights were being extinguished and that the blackness of night would then cloak us till dawn. A sinister apparition with a hairy mole on her firmly set jaw stalked the corridors. Our nights would echo with the snivelling of homesickness reverberating from the surrounding beds. But I did not cry. I was born into and knew no other existence.

I find that those years of collective living have probably contributed to me treasuring my space and welcoming some solitude as I've aged, but also contributing to my having a gregarious nature. I'm discerning about whom I spend time with and I still crave parental affirmation, although they're long gone.

Growing up meant many years of suitcases and boarding school, with its own set of complex social structures. But there were always parents to fetch us and take us back home. Our childhood was marked by the peculiar polarity of our treasured freedom on the farm compressed against the more cloistered boarding school life.

Adulthood meant responsibility from a carefree childhood, which had embraced us so effortlessly. With it came defining the self through student years, pushing the limits to discover one's identity, peer pressure and social constraints. A narrow pathway filled with obstacles that no safe childhood could prepare one for. Then it was marriage, motherhood and a profession and the perennial studying. Mine stretched over thirty years and was in the field of education of children with disabilities and special needs, followed by psychology and drama.

One looks back at one's life and it feels as though it can be compressed into a series of fleeting memories; into one page in a book, or a yellowed dog-eared photo album.

I sometimes wonder how a different childhood would have altered me. But one thing's for sure—boarding school teaches one to survive. It's also made me endlessly loving and tolerant towards my own children and grandchildren.

And even though one's children suddenly emerge into mature adults, as though time escalated past all those years from the wretched pangs of childbirth, through to the dissonance of acne faced youth and then abruptly catapulted into cherishing their own infants, and one's own skin feels as though it convincingly reveals the secrets of one's age, one still feels the same child within; the one that still needs a mother when one has a bad bout of flu.

If I did elongate my life, it would feel rich and intricate, like a multi-hued tapestry with configurations depicting the passions, pains, ecstasies, successes, challenges, monumental cock-ups and disappointments of life.

Being born on a farm in Africa, surrounded by endless landscapes, contributed to my feeling that I was a child of the universe; somehow connected to the spacious vistas and the cyclical nature of the seasons. It made me a soul with a passion for life, space, wide open vistas, raw beauty, animals, nature and family. The external social world and boarding school connectivity stimulated me to see more broadly and to define myself, while only time taught me to be more discerning and less emotionally volatile and to establish what resonated for me and what didn't.

I learnt very quickly that to be a survivor in life one had to excel in one's study and work ethic, have enormous self-belief and marshal one's self—where and when necessary. Maybe the early boarding school existence paved the way for me to see life as a challenge to be tackled. I think much of this process work and defining the self is subconscious and takes years, as one is moulded by genetics and environment—extraneous and internal factors. On reflection one learns that one did play a part in being who one is; that we have choice, self-discipline and motivation. One doesn't buy those ingredients over the counter . . . one needs to cultivate some of it and having good role models and a stable foundation helps enormously.

I adhere to the Darwinian evolutionary model of survival of the fittest and believe in utilising one's personal resources to better the world for self and others. Combine this with the external persona we develop that represents the inner us. We define our individuality through our dress, personality, image and body language. I am an exuberant and compassionate extrovert, but also a person who is sensitive, hurts easily, hates rejection and wants to love and be loved. I think boarding school made me a tad needy but hey, those early years do mould us and are hard to reformat. I've made a myriad mistakes in life due to my passionate, headstrong persona and am finally at an age where I have had some of the crap rubbed off and am maybe reaching a level of sensibility, feeling more in tune with who I am, what I've achieved/have failed at, more comfortable about who I am; not having to prove anything . . . just at a stage of BEING in an existential way. I think I am more forgiving of self and others now and am finally ready to write about the pain of migration.

Too many Farewells

Sadness is but a wall between two gardens

—Kahlil Gibran

Living out our frightfully secure rural childhood with solidly functional loving parents with old world values meant that it would have been an impossible concept for my siblings or me to project to our current lives.

In the normal, or rather predictable unfolding of events, if the world had not spewed us out as by-products of a global village, we'd have in all probability stayed close to the immediacy of that existence. My brothers would have become farmers driving large Ford utility trucks with robust children and dogs attached to wagging tails hanging out the back, my twin and I, farmers' wives with snotty-nosed, red chafed-faced infants and chicken shit on our gumboots.

But life is never predictable. It's as changeable as the cold breeze blasting the windowpanes outside as I write this in New Zealand . . .

I glance up and see myriads of photographs on our yellowwood dresser—precious memorabilia that came across the ocean in our container. The smiling faces glue me together, but in the same breath tear me apart. We were blessed with three children, each unique and filled with a passion for life and remnants of the missionary zeal genes.

Missionary zeal did I say? In around 1880 missionaries and farmers settled in the Freestate, intrepid spirited adventurers from Scotland and Prussia who were the ancestors from our children's matriarchal side, together with the gene pool of British and French descendants from their patriarchal side, who settled in the Transkei, the Cape Province and Zambia (then Northern Rhodesia). Rumour has it that my Prussian grandmother, Caroline, was leaving on a train when Scottish grandfather Percival stridently rode his horse alongside the train, proceeded to stop the train, asked Caroline for his hand in marriage and whisked her off on his stead. They settled at 'Sevenfountains', the family homestead, where they bore six children. My father, Archibald (Miller) was the fourth child. Our mum Joan's parents arrived from Perth, Scotland and settled in Pietermaritzburg, where they bore four children and were more urban than rural, although it was a small town way back then.

Each of our children have married, so that now our yellowwood dresser is cluttered—the gaze from the portraits of the toothless grins of our six adorable grandchildren seem to follow me. As I write this I glance at them and again have moist cheeks.

My twin followed her great love, a musician, to Britain. I was 21 at the time. In hindsight I went through the most traumatic sense of loss. She'd been my other half my entire childhood. For years after she'd left, I'd look up to see someone that resembled her; even seek out her familiar form on busy pavements. Life wasn't meant to allow vast oceans to sever twins apart. Even now I notice women's hands that look like her lovely compact creative hands.

Later on my brother left for Australia. His departure never seemed as sad. Maybe one gets immune to sad farewells. But more likely it was that it never had that finite feeling about it—and two years later he returned home. Although we infrequently saw one another, his presence nearby was sufficient solace to settle my heart. And when we did meet for birthdays and celebrations, it was always like a hand slipping into a glove; so much so that I regret not making more effort to truly know him. For knowing someone's innards isn't necessarily imperative. It's sometimes enough to just be joined by the same genes.

Around the same time my older brother, his wife and their five children left to make the USA their homeland. We bid them farewell at the airport in Johannesburg. My body felt as though a thousand knives were cutting into it. I cried all the way back to KwaZulu Natal; a 500 kilometre trip home from the airport.

My husband and I were the last to leave our heritage behind. It seemed as though bidding farewell was indelibly engraved in the script. My husband, too, bore the brunt of wandering intrepid soul syndrome—his precious older brother chose to follow his first love to Argentina.

There is not a sense of bitterness about these farewells. There was never anger; only a sad acceptance that this was the essence of all existence—that loving anyone meant the possibility of deep loss or separation, which started for me at the age of seven.

Later in life it was time for our own children to start their own nest exoduses, first to study in different cities, and later to do the world exploration thing or to start work elsewhere. When our eldest child left, I climbed into bed next to her the night before her flight to London and cried all night. We both woke worn out and yet we both knew that this was the inevitable way of the journey.

Later my best friend, Molly, died of cancer . . . this was a significant factor as it later galvanised the diversion I orchestrated which I alluded to as my 'metaphorical death' when I migrated.

*   *   *

Ant and I met way back in 1969. It was the year of psychedelic colours, flowers in one's hair, bell-bottoms, moustaches and sideburns, and flower power.

We met by sheer chance, fell in love and now 40 plus years later we are living together in the Waitakere Ranges of Auckland. The only constant in our lives at this moment is one another. Without the other, we'd never have had the courage to fly across the Indian Ocean to reside on an island remote from our African heritage, neatly tucked between the Tasman and the Pacific. The one small comfort was that being in the Southern hemisphere we'd still see the same sky and that the bath water would still rotate down into the bowels of the underbelly in a clockwise motion. A consolation was that it was a land with some commonality, like English and rugby and bacon and eggs. Additional succour was knowing that a million South Africans had done it as part of the global Diaspora before us, and that another million or more would do it subsequent to us. We hoped that soon we would feel like *fundis* (from *'umfundisi'*, meaning an authority or expert), and be able to walk tall in our adaptation.

The three of us—Ant, Paddywag and I—initially resided in our 'virtual reality home'. When the harbour lady called to say that "our ship" (with our container aboard) would arrive soon it was an off-the-Richter-Scale thriller. We were euphoric as it meant that we would then have a home with real furniture in it.

Meanwhile, the best (and only) throne in the house was the loo. From the loo was a spectacular view across the Manukau Harbour. It was also a terrific vantage point from which to watch every international jet's bulbous belly impossibly hanging in suspended animation before each landed across the bay.

From the loo throne I wrote in my diary:

"The tree that scrapes against the window ledge is the spring home to a pair of New Zealand pigeons. These are the most robust bellied of the pigeon species. A bit like the jets, one feels awed at how these rotund chaps actually acquire the art of ever becoming airborne and how they manage to suspend themselves upside down in the delicate filigree-leafed branches to devour wads of sprigs. If one obliquely squints in the general direction of the tree, one would wonder why some lunatic had planted two rugby balls up there. Below the tree is a pastoral scene, where four horses graze contentedly, their blankets, which have protected them from the wet, cold winter, newly removed.

The land of the long white cloud is indeed just that. Bulwarks of clouds scurry, build up to a crescendo and vanish with the click of a celluloid frame, to reveal a fabulous rainbow arched from one end of Auckland to the other. There are generally four moments in a day—sun, clouds, rain, then the rainbow. One dresses accordingly. It's the land of layered garments.

It's three months that we've lived here; hence we are still in the honeymoon phase! I've grown to love the place. I love the quirkiness juxtaposed against the orderliness. In so many ways it's similar to home, yet it's diametrically opposed.

Talking of rugby balls, there's the same rugby mania here, with cars adorned with little black flags, the way the blokes at home have their Springbok and Sharks banners out. And talking of rainbows, believe me, it's as bold a multi-hued rainbow nation as South Africa is. In my work organisation alone, there are over 10 different cultural groups and/or nationalities.

On the converse side from home, it's a land that's receptive to its constant metamorphosis. There's a constant flux as people come and go. Some go to big brother, Aussie, and some arrive from the UK, South Africa, Canada, USA, China Korea and India, among others. Helen Clarke, the previous prime minister, talked about a brain gain as skilled immigrants arrive, whereas South Africa used to bemoan its alleged brain drain.

New Zealand is spectacularly beautiful, no more nor less than South Africa—just utterly different. NZ only has 4.5 million people in its entirety, so one never feels crowded, pushed or rushed by the maelstrom of humanity. It's a quieter, more ordered, tidier place, yet equally florid with immigrants from far and wide, plus the *Pākehā* (NZ Europeans) and the indigenous Maori.

Everything works pretty well. It's thrilling when one is phoned to say the garden furniture will be delivered at 10.07 am and, oh boy, at seven minutes past, there's a knock at the door. It's a zero-tolerance country on law and order, and having hailed from a more laissez faire system, one truly has to learn to dot the i's and cross the t's to ensure not getting into trouble. It's a skill being an accomplished Kiwi and I'll take ages to get there as I'm an untamed spirit . . . (*In retrospect I'd like to put some ingredients from Africa and New Zealand into a melting pot together—add some of Africa's free spirit here and add some of New Zealand's orderliness there . . .*) After being in Africa with remnants of circular time, here the linear time at its extreme requires some adaptation. Don't ever believe that Kiwis aren't hard working. They work arduously and fearlessly. There are companies one can even call through the night if emergency repair work is required, and women drive buses and bulldozers and chop wood, though don't carry large bundles of wood on their heads like the African women do back home.

Although it's a blissful place, there's no Nirvana. Globally speaking it functions impressively away from the hot spots on the planet (other than the potential volcanoes and earthquakes). It's generally egalitarian, democratic and non-fundamentalist. Being part of the global village, though, sadly means that negative social influences and the global recession have infiltrated this otherwise gloriously pristine place. But it has a rich heritage and a titillating metamorphic vibe.

It's blissful not living behind a high wall. I love the freedom of wide expanses of glass—unfettered by burglar bars, the freedom of no gates or electrical gadgets, security guards, two-way radios and panic buttons. I sleep peacefully except for my occasional early a.m. tea. It's difficult to imagine that once we slept in a permanent state of high arousal. We were always waiting. Waiting for the dogs to bark that heralded a possible property invasion and the possibility of one's personal space being violated.

Yet without our children, this perceived bliss is coloured by that pulsating void. *Hope* seems to be the intangible ingredient, which propels people to survive. It is the intangible heart beat which pulses through our survival genes. Hope comes in many forms. It is, I think, linked to the individual's value system and personal circumstances. Some people hope for survival in the midst of a holocaust, others for a meal to hold those nagging hunger pangs at bay. Some hope for a material object.

My hope on an egotistical level is to be reunited with my children. But on a more altruistic and universal level, my hope is for the unattainable nirvana—that place we all wish existed; the place where no one suffers, where no one manifests any form of injurious behaviour to self or others.

Ant and I never envisaged embarking on such a crazy journey. Like all good South Africans, we declared that Africa was in our bones and we were confident that we'd grow old in our current home, retire there, have some ducks and chickens and a veggie patch and collect the brown speckled free-range eggs and cut a few spinach leaves daily, water the plants, feed the wild birds with grain, and sit and contemplate life with dimming eyes from our rocking chairs.

Sometimes things don't happen the way one has mapped it out and there is no definitive explanation. Possibly it's a bit of a Pandora's Box and will unfold for us some day—that enviable third eye in which one can see the future. For now it is blurred with no definition and no instruction manual about how to live it.

Deaf Ears; Blind Eyes

I've always been intrigued by politicians maniacally campaigning before an election, primarily because I think that some people make their decisions based often on prejudice or arbitrary reasoning instead of on functional judgement or persuasive campaigning. Possibly a few fence sitters could be swayed by an appropriate smile or wink as they walk to the voting booth.

The same applies to religion. People are born into a religious belief system and only a few people will make a fundamentalist swing from one extreme to the other. Others may change a religious allegiance at a symbolic rather than spiritual level for the sake of marriage to a partner from a different religious affiliation.

People, I believe, don't revel in the idea of making a conscious life-altering choice or decision. They are generally happier to remain in the comfort zone in which they are familiar; be it politics, religion or their geographical environment. There are exceptions to the rule, but in any survey, there would most probably be a reasonably well-proportioned bell curve, with the majority at the centre point and the extreme views represented at the two opposing ends of the bell.

Generally change is difficult and, as the saying goes, 'better the devil one knows'. Humanity likes familiarity, routine and a sense of connectivity to the environment, surroundings and roots, rather than opting for the road less travelled . . . at whatever cost, even one's safety in some cases.

Research has shown how different people react in different situations. One can never truly know how one will react in a situation of extreme threat until one is in it. Some run, some fight, some hide and others freeze. How would you respond in the event of an earthquake or a tsunami, or to a brutal encounter with a raging wild animal, or being confronted by a group of aggressive human beings? Does one respond differently in different situations? If one freezes, could this in a way equate to denial? Or one can hide in the safe, confined corridors of one's constructed perceptions of where it is safe, avoiding where it is unsafe, else fight and lash out at the perpetrators or the perceived threat. In the same way as one may wish to fight, hide or be in denial, one may wish to seek shelter elsewhere, or in essence, as some may like to allude to it, as run. Maybe this is my analogy about emigration. Would one be called a coward if one ran up a hill to avoid the path of a raging tsunami, or to climb a tree to escape from an angry rhinoceros? I don't think so!

I remember well the delightful film *Shirley Valentine*, which I think I watched three times and could happily watch again. People generally like going back to the same eatery to order their standard fish and

SCATTERLINGS—A TAPESTRY OF AFRI-EXPAT TALES

chips or curry and rice. We are creatures of habit and our spots don't change. Not easily. We cut our cloth accordingly; whether we're the ones eating/drinking the caviar or the bunny chow or the yak's milk. We prefer what we're accustomed to—most of us.

Thus for people to decide to just 'up and off' into the vast unknown without a reason, is almost insane and somewhere on the bizarre spectrum. People don't do it lightly, although they may make a quick decision, but it's probably been a slow process; a simmering in the subconscious mind before the actual decision to leave home is galvanised. It's not like getting a new hairstyle that can be altered. It's a colossal life-altering choice.

For some, the choice is non-negotiable. Something triggers it; sometimes an horrific incident either as the victims or being emotionally or geographically close to the people who have been violated. For others it happens with less definition.

My book is not about promoting emigration, nor is it about promoting people to return to, or stay in Southern Africa! It is more about people sharing their own real or perceived truths—that South Africa is a country whom many people love and yet some possibly hate or fear simultaneously and which people leave with deep sorrow, due to various factors (First wave—anti apartheid, Second wave—the new 'democracy', and in the last five years, including ourselves, the Third wave—mostly due to untenable levels of violence), but that in leaving, they discover not only that emigration is a harrowing journey, but how deeply our African roots are entrenched in the soul. As people say 'Emigration is not for ninnies'. If one has a choice (which many don't have) and opts to emigrate, it is hoped that the contents of this book will be of some assistance; as a way of solace, identification and where advice can be offered by those who have walked the road less travelled before.

No one can make a choice for someone else. If someone tried to sell one something one didn't want, one would focus on the negatives and the anomalies instead of seeking out the positives. If one migrated under duress, one would dislike anything and everything from the weather, the local quirks and different humour, the people, the accents and different sayings, the dress code and tattoos, or the barbeques instead of *braais*. One would possibly not even appreciate the safety, cleanliness and functionality because one would be caught up in the 'blame game.'

That's the irony of life. If one chose the polka dot dress against everyone else's advice who had said 'Buy the striped one', one would live with it come hell or high water, so as to justify that one had made the right choice. However, if one was forced to buy the polka dot dress, one would hate it and possibly hide it in the wardrobe. Same principle.

Any amount of persuasion will fall on deaf ears or blind eyes. It's about one opening one's own eyes to view the world in a new light, opening one's ears to realities, else opening one's mind to the truths that one has been ignoring or denying. Only then can one truly be ready to make one's own fundamental choices in life; to stay or leave . . .

Seek not to change the world, but choose to change your mind about the world. What you see reflects your thinking. And your thinking but reflects your choice of what you want to see. (From A Course in Miracles.)

Epiphany—*the aha ka-ching moment*

Anne Townsend: *"Life,"* she wrote, *"is just too short to spend it all in one place."*

After we had lived here in New Zealand for about a year, Ant and I were walking along the beach with our little dog one evening when we heard a lady saying, *"Kom seun, dis nou tyd om huis toe te gaan . . ."* (Come son, it's now time to go home . . .). We greeted her in Afrikaans, *"Aangename kennis"* (How do you do?). She and her small son seemed forlorn and alone, and our hearts reached out to them. "We came the month after my husband was murdered" she said. That moment, with the waves lapping on the beach sand, kissing the seashells, the luminescent clouds scudding along the ocean's horizon, spoke volumes; the heart broken mother and her little boy courageously walking away to their fractured new life.

No one's going to leave home in a hurry. It's where we experience that inner sanctum. One never knows if one will have that 'Aha moment' until it hits one. One can't orchestrate it, but I think within our blue print we have a conscious or unconscious search for something better or safer; maybe as part of the existential search for the 'meaning of life' and also in the genetic make-up of human survival.

Ant and I had felt as though we'd 'just arrived' in life—as though all our life's labours were bearing the fruits, after many years of working and serving the South African community. We both had excellent professions; my husband as a design engineer designing roads and I as a school principal of a special needs' school with fantastic staff that embodied the 'rainbow nation'; the school predominantly comprised of African children, many from disadvantaged environments.

Our three adult children were happily married, busy with their own vocations and their child rearing. Life was in many ways idyllic, with regular family get-togethers, *braais* (barbeques), frolicking in our swimming pool and family meals and outings, camping in the *Berg* (mountains) or at the beach, trips to Cape Town etc. I was a besotted granny, who adored and still adore my grandchildren. Our home was a place where the children played and could literally dismantle the house in their creative and noisy fantasy playing, with a massive garden to explore and a motley menagerie of dogs, ducks, geese, guinea fowl and two pet Chinese pot-bellied pigs named Bubble and Squeak.

All would have been perfect if it had not been for the years of incidents to people we knew and to a lesser but still impactful degree to ourselves, which had insidiously worn the veneer paper thin.

And then the epiphany!

My epiphany was waking up to the reality that we felt that there would be no safe future for our grandchildren in South Africa. When one has been exposed to violence and can count people (on both hands and feet), whom one knows well, who've been either murdered, highjacked, attacked or violated, then one finally hauls one's head out of the denialistic sledge and awakens to reality. We personally felt on a gut level that life wasn't going to get any better. That was the hideous reality that confronted us.

Ant's epiphany differed from mine; sure the safety aspect was a concern, but for him it was more about the grandkids possibly not being able to get the secondary and tertiary education they would need to guarantee them a decent future, and the fact that our whole family had had many a dialogue over breakfasts out, where the general consensus was that emigration should be done sooner rather than later.

It was a horrid revelation! We had been soooo optimistic about our country, and life for us was so good (although in reality it was an illusion, as one can't live happily having so much when others have so little . . .)

An epiphany doesn't come to all of us, and even if it does, we have this built in self-preservation which is loaded with wonderful defence mechanisms that includes the Theory of Justification (which endorses our beliefs, ideas and actions).

Half of humanity will justify why they chose to do something. The other half will justify why they chose not to. In this way we all feel better about the choices we make, irrespective of whether to quit smoking, to eat that forbidden piece of decadent chocolate cake or to emigrate.

The epiphany is that amazing '*ah ha*' moment. It can be sudden or a slow process which one has subconsciously been suppressing. It can suddenly surface and '*ka-ching!*'—one has that intuitive perception hitting one rather robustly between the eye balls. 'Eff&&!' shouts in one's head. Reality stares one in the face and one almost feels as though a shining light bulb has been switched on somewhere in the mazes of one's mind . . . almost like the sound of money deafeningly spitting out of a casino machine.

That is possibly the finite moment that can trigger change, though I think we may have the epiphany and then subconsciously struggle with the logistics of it, desperately shoving it under the mat, proceeding to stamp it down into the depths of the subconscious mind, as though wrestling with it to stay put. 'Stay down!' our inner voice shouts. We proceed to draft up a myriad justifications why it isn't feasible. I'm sure I did that for a good five years or more. I recall saying 'Oh well we can't even contemplate it . . . we can't possibly afford to', when several friends of ours left South Africa . . . . even though we'd never so much as done any homework or calculations as it was '*sommer*' (just) dumped into the far-too-hard basket and the horribly uncomfortable discomfort zone. It was a given with a nonchalant shrug of the shoulders, whilst we jovially laughed about everyone 'Packing for Perth' and were even stupidly entertained by the silly South African jokes such as "The last one to leave the country switch out the lights . . ."

I think back now to the profound complexity of South Africa and her people, and continue to wish and in my own feeble way pray for her to heal, for poverty and disease to drastically reduce, for unemployment to decrease, for violence, crime and corruption to stop, for racism to be cauterised for once and for all, for people to respect human life and to stop the futile killing fields . . . because it is and always will be home.

An epiphany happens when one least expects it. Maybe it's about synchronicity—when one reads a paradigm altering book (mine spanned the Russian Revolution through to WW2 and its impact on vast parts of the planet with refugees and immigrants aplenty), simultaneously to experiencing a conglomeration of happenings on already shaky foundations. This included having stones thrown at us during the 2007 Cosatu strikes, evacuating the school staff and children, and as the school principal, being personally violated and screamed at on the telephone in a blood curdling guttural tone of voice by a militant African unionist; 'We are coming to get you now, you $%^&* *umlungu* (white person) . . .' which in a difficult-to-define way battered my soul and destroyed my belief in Africa that day. It was a defining moment of the futility of my existence. It was a very understandable reaction after the Apartheid era, which I had, in any case never supported, and was surprised that we weren't exposed to more verbal abuse. But something tore in my heart; its raw blood seemed to feel the bruising of truth; of being told I no longer belonged and was no longer welcome in my own country of birth. It was a moment of what heralded for me a sense of undiluted rejection and others' resentment, after years of devoted service to the underprivileged. This was followed by the murders and hijackings of people we knew, and a few months later witnessing a mother's inconsolable grief, after the accidental and utterly futile death of her game ranger son. I suddenly summoned up the courage to acknowledge that emigration was a long shot from the permanency of death of one of my children, and that if they chose to leave, I would try to be strong and give them my blessing. And so the story began . . . the kindling of an idea which transposes another idea . . . after a series of psyche'-bludgeoning events.

The series of events seemed to synchronistically fall into place, adding to the sense of skating on delicately thin ice. After several years of other incidents; atrocious and hideous events that happened to people whom we knew and hearing gun shots at night, experiencing people throwing things around in our one home (while we were locked in the bedroom waiting for the police to arrive), and on another occasion a man standing at our bedroom door at 3am (who had quietly removed a window pane so that he could squeeze his arm in to unlatch the door and stolen various items plus a bunch of keys) but was thankfully startled, as at that moment my husband awoke and climbed out of bed, having woken to some movement or light. The dogs did not bark that night. That remained a mystery . . . and we stayed awake till daybreak, exhausted and worn out. The perpetrators returned at 11 pm the following night while we sat and watched TV and audaciously attempted to unlock our front door with the keys they'd stolen . . . but thankfully we'd changed the locks after the detectives had been round in search of finger prints.

Once, while parked in line at a red traffic light, I was left scratched and bleeding by a youth with eyes black with hatred, who almost levitated and lunged from nowhere with lightning speed to attack me though my car window for my mobile phone, which I held onto for dear life. No one came to the rescue. Time became frozen and elongated into a chasm of nothingness. The silence was deafening in my ears . . . The traffic lights turned green and cars moved on. I drove off shaking. One does not know how one will react under ambush. I must have shouted "Eff you!" at least 22 times and developed an overpowering strength which I had no idea that I possessed. On another occasion I gave a man wearing a dark hood, who was hobbling on crutches, a lift (yes the '*ubuntu*' {Ubuntu is an African humanist philosophy focusing on people's allegiance with one other} spirit of African goodwill!), to then have to fend him off as he attempted to stroke me between my thighs, while asking for my address and telephone number. I calmly and politely told him that Jesus would be inexplicably unimpressed and asked him to get out the car, which he did as I ensured that I dropped him at a busy bus stop. (I was aware that being calm was paramount to my safety . . . I was proud of myself for having sustained an aura of calm detachment.) Shaken up I went home and told Maria, our dear employee. She threw up her arms and shouted in her deliciously theatrical way, "Jesus-God-Angels . . . How-how-how . . . *Howbabo bloody shitttt!*" The man was allegedly a convicted rapist who was on crutches as he'd been shot by the police before serving his sentence, she said. (True or untrue, it prevented me from being able to be vaguely 'godly' by offering anyone a lift on the road ever again, crutches or no crutches).

In more recent years, having to live behind electric fences and gates with a two-way radio, security guards patrolling our suburb and solar panels, alarms and burglar bars, which still didn't safeguard us 100%, meaning disturbed sleep and fatigue, had over time worn us down, leading to my experiencing anxiety and even panic attacks and my husband's poor health being exacerbated.

Mike Dooley in *Infinite Possibilities* states that one is never thrown into anything, and that one creates experiences and situations when one is ready to face the consequences and see things from a new perspective. His philosophy is that if one is unsure one should wait until one reaches a point of awareness . . . Maybe that is what an epiphany is. He alludes to one needing to look beyond the material world to see the world more clearly in its entirety away from expectations based on material needs, comforts and desires. He is possibly alluding that the answer lies within, and that our thoughts facilitate us to create our plans for the future. In this way when we are ready to have an epiphany we are open to the possibility.

Letting the locals know my emigration intention—2008—*Leaving South Africa on a jet plane*

The world's a strange place. People migrate from one land mass to another. It's connected to humanity's free will and desire to conquer or explore new territory. My ancestors landed on this continent from the Outer Hebrides of Scotland and a few missionaries from Prussia. Now it's my turn. I'm heading off on a jet plane. And no, it won't be easy.

I love the sensory evocation of Africa — the smell of rain on dusty earth and the piercing prehistoric timbre of those sycophantic *Hadedas*. I love the bold autumn hues and crunching on frosty dry *veld* grass. I love waiting for a purple Jacaranda flower to drop on my windscreen while I'm driving and slowing down for cows in the road.

I love buying Wilson's toffees in a trading store and smelling the African-print fabric, the aromas of incense and pungent Durban curries, and the ornate oriental artefacts in the Indian markets. I love the thumping sound of African music emanating from that car parked down the road and the prayer chants wafting across from a mosque.

I love the banter of indigenous languages that flow like a song that I can't quite understand after all these years, yet that sound as familiar to me as a mother's bedtime lullaby.

I love the smell of a veld fire, of sizzling chops and *boerewors* on a *braai*, the salty aftertaste of *biltong* when my body has shouted for salt, and the Sharks. I love the sounds of yacht stays tinkling in the wind along Midmar Dam's shore and the crack of a melodramatic thunder after a humid day.

I love our memorable family holidays—watching a golden orb setting across a gorge of silhouetted thorn trees, gathering handfuls of pebbles and shells on a south coast beach, the sounds of the Indian Ocean singing in my head, camping and picnics, and wide-open spaces.

I love the sounds and vistas from my childhood—the soothing coos of a rock pigeon, the sandstone farmhouse architecture, my Free State clouds, windmills and *koppies*. It's strangely comforting to think that if other things change, they'll remain constant for billions of years.

Loving so much has enriched my life beyond measure. The staff and children I work with are embedded in my soul. And I love my own precious children and grandchildren; even those chaotically noisy family suppers at 'Spur' with that rather dire Happy Birthday song.

Where I'm going there won't be any of this. Instead, there are volcanic craters, magnificent, but alien vistas, geological delights and long winters. There's the Treaty of Waitangi and a whole different political arena. And there's the All Black's *haka*.

Why am I going if there's so much I love here? Because, that's why. I love so many things from my rich life here that I want to cherish them in my mind before they morph into something that's no longer precious or familiar to me. I want to explore a new chapter because life's transient and unpredictable. I can live with periods of no electricity, with exasperating delays and even some disorder and disintegration in infrastructure. But I can never condone the prevalent, heinous and inhumane criminality and violence.

People like me may be searching for a Nirvana that's non-existent. We're all born with free will, but not necessarily all with the opportunity to create change. I have the choice. It may lead to material impoverishment, but then some of us are dreamers.

Nothing will be able to replace the passions which are at the core of my psyche. No new acquaintances will be able to reminisce about the "remember whens". But there will be enticing new chapters. And despite currently waking up each morning feeling gutted, I'm enormously optimistic. I feel a profundity of abundance in what I've tasted in South Africa and absolutely no one can ever take that away from me.

When my article "Leaving South Africa on a jetplane" was published in *The Witness* in May 2008, it created a reaction in our little city, once dubbed 'Sleepy Hollow'. But, if one is a writer (even small-time like me), sooner than later one's going to piss on some one's battery. One can't please all of the people all of the time, and one needs to be true to oneself, and not just try and say what makes people purr ecstatically, while ensconced in their comfort zones, nor remain forever silent, quietly and conscientiously tending one's own cabbage patch . . . That's not going to push the envelope one iota, and that's what writer's do! We nudge to get people to think, debate and reflect. I had attempted to share my feelings and emotions, and WOW . . . it opened a can of veritable worms . . . As a writer one attempts to share with others about joy, pain and reality; in this context it was about the deep emotions which such an undertaking had evoked in me; just one of a million migrants . . .

Leaving South Africa on a Jet Plane
Dear Eve and Ant

Well done Eve for a truly moving piece on the country we all love so much. We are going to miss you so much and we hope you have a wonderful adventure and the career you deserve in NZ. We are shouting for you and look forward to hearing how things are turning out in NZ.

Love you lots! Merry and Bruce

That jetplane . . .

Oh Eve, you've got a big heart and your words are powerful. I know you will remember us when you have gone away to that other land. Africa is part of what you are. Keep on writing! *Hamba kahle*. You will be missed. *Renee Alcock, 12 May 2008*

Leaving South Africa on a jet plane

Beautifully written, Eve, and so true. Every happiness in your new home and hope we get to hear about your life in that exquisite country. *Vren, 12 May 2008*

Emigrating

Nirvana does exist—in the head. Emigrating is hard, physically because you are cut off from all networks to help when you need to move furniture for example, and emotionally because you have to make new friends and build a life in a society very different from the one you left. But it is, for most people enriching, if not materially then emotionally. In the bad old days I once hitched a lift with an Afrikaner who poured scorn on the idea that "We Afrikaners will fight to the last because we have nowhere else to go." At the time, he said his son was living in Jamaica and loving it. As soon as South African passports were recognised, Afrikaners were the first to travel and some to stay overseas, like tens of thousands of their Zulu, Xhosa and Sotho countrymen. And of the three million Zimbabweans who have emigrated, how many of them will return home?

Enjoy and make the most of your new life and do not regret the past, treasure the good parts, but realise they are part of the Nirvana in our heads. *Brian, 12 May 2008*

Pretty punchy and emotional, because I'm half way there—living here and still with a foot there. Well put! *Rory, 12 May 2008*

Leaving

We left about 18 months ago. Africa is in our blood, we are Africans—you can't just let it go. But here in the Land of the Long White Cloud we've found what we all long for in SA—peace & safety. NZ is very different from SA, but there are so many similarities. The British heritage instilled that. There are many places with the same names—Ashburton, Howick, Hilton Ave, etc. In my part of NZ the countryside is very similar to the Midlands. I call it the Midlands on steroids. There are bold autumn colours, frost on the grass and Jacaranda flowers. There is all the rugby you can watch (including SA rugby) and cricket (SABC Sport) and you can have the sizzling chop on the braai (BBQ), but thankfully there are no Hadedas as shouting outside the window at 4:30am; there are the Indians Mynas though. The winters are ok—a lot better than I expected—wet, but not depressive like the UK. Yes, there are things we miss and it is the hardest thing to do, but there are enough similarities and with a pioneering spirit it is an amazing adventure. You'll love it—all the best. *Steve, 13 May 2008*

One should always look at new adventures as a fresh start to one's life. Living in a new country is hard. However, being South African and the fantastic memories of a truly fabulous country will never depart from one's heart. Good luck—A true South African. *Anonymous 16 May 2008*

Not leaving   *Geoff Caruth, Pinetown*
19 May 2008

Eve Hemming may be leaving SA on a jet plane (Witness, May 12) but what does her article seek to convey? We all know that crime is bad in South Africa and we all love the things she loves, but surely in this time when our country needs its educated people, true patriotism dictates she should stay?

The United States is noted for its high rate of college massacres. Do all the victims' parents emigrate after these events?

While the decision to emigrate or not is a personal one, Hemming must realise that the loss of every talented émigré puts more pressure on those who decide to remain.

Sorry Eve, I wish you well for the future, but I for one can do without your self-indulgent sentimentality. Rather leave quietly and let us get on with the business of true love.

Leaving a legacy
22 May 2008   *Shirley Gault, Pietermaritzburg*

I TAKE strong exception to Geoff Caruth's mawkish generalisations about the departure of Eve Hemming (The Witness, May 19).

For a start, I refuse to be included in those he terms "we" or in his use of the bland verb "love". How does he know that I love what Hemming loves? I find vigour in experience. My responses to what I encounter are diverse. I resist pigeonholing them into enfeebling mass value judgments. I found Hemming's leave-taking to her readers poignant in essence. Reading her lines and the meaning between the lines one identified with the fear, sorrow, heartbreak and courage entailed in loss and change.

To evoke emotion with both subtlety and symbolism is the skill of a writer worth her salt. If she only leaves this lesson as a legacy (and I know she leaves many more) she has left more than enough to lift any burden from Caruth's smart ass decision to stay—provided of course that he is sufficiently enabled to drink deep from her maxim.

As for his intended true love business that we must indulge in, can he provide examples from his own life of what he means me as an individual to do?

Our country needs us
28 May 2008   *Geoff Caruth, Pinetown*

SHIRLEY Gault (The Witness, May 22) misses the point of my comment on Eve Hemming's much self-heralded departure. I was trying to make a distinction between a superficial "biltong and Karoo sunsets" love of country and the business of real love and true patriotism. Scott Peck in his best-seller 'The Road Less Travelled' describes such a love. It consists of unselfish giving, of hard work with perhaps little reward, to achieve a difficult end. In this instance I was referring to our beloved South Africa and its current difficulties. Our country needs us now more than ever; in the words of Dylan Thomas, "Rage, rage against the dying of the light".

Auckland is an easy option. The choice is entirely personal and I do not judge those who go this route. What I do judge is those who publicly seek absolution for their decisions; those who shouted the loudest for our new democracy and, when the going gets tough, cut and run; and those who patronise us and rub our noses in it with their condescending self-justifications.

Rather give me the young man who I bumped into in the *thornveld* recently. He wore a *Vierkleur*-emblazoned T-shirt that said: "*Ek is 'n boer en ek is hier om te bly*". (I am a farmer and I am here to stay.) I didn't agree with his politics, but I loved the sentiment.

True Love   *Shirley Gault, Pietermaritzburg*

Mr. Caruth what a stupid silly little man you must be. Please write a follow up to this article when your sister, daughter, wife, mother, gran, aunt and even yourself have been hijacked, beaten up mugged or raped. I wonder then how fast it will take you to consider getting out. Your comments to Eve are an insult to anyone who has left this country. I have had seven members of my family leave this country, with another four on their way out this year. I have no friends in this country as they have all left. I will also be leaving this time next year and I promise you I will not be singing the praises of S.A. So I raise a glass to you for staying, may you live long enough to enjoy it. That will be true love.

Don't go quietly!

9 May 2008   *Colleen Webb, Florida, USA*

Who exactly is Geoff Caruth to judge anyone for deciding to leave South Africa? With one of the highest crime rates in the world, deciding to stay is decidedly risky and I wouldn't want anybody's blood on my hands (literally) for persuading them to stay. Leaving has been one of the most difficult things I have ever done; something that has ripped my family apart and the families of thousands of other South Africans like me, so to call Eve's expression of pain 'self-indulgent sentimentality' is base ignorance and utter disregard for the gut-wrenching heartache that comes with leaving behind everything familiar and beloved. Leave quietly? No sir! Make as much noise as you can, Eve. Too many have left quietly. We should make a great clatter of noise about it so people pay attention to the problem rather than sanctimoniously condemn Africans like Eve who can no longer bear the pain of living in Africa. True love can mean making tough choices to put family before country! I would like to think that when people like Eve, who has made it their life's work to uplift the disadvantaged in South Africa decide to leave, the outrage will grow and something will change. But perhaps that is just too optimistic!

Jet Plane 27 May 2008   *Merry Torr, Caversham*

Eve, your friends and colleagues know you and love you for what you have achieved and stood for in your life in the Pietermaritzburg educational field.

You are a devoted wife and granny, perpetual student, hard working headmistress of a disadvantaged school and (unpaid!) counsellor to so many, and an all-round, fun loving and most of all very caring person.

Remember Eve, as you start your career in NZ, in life it's not the accolades from Pietermaritzburg society that are sweet, but those tiny simple moments that you have had with all the people that you have helped.

You know what I mean, the look, the hug, the smile, the tears—those intangible "things" that no-one can take away from you . . . . ever. That's the field we as caregivers/professionals of the people are in, we don't get paid enough, we are unappreciated, but we go to bed knowing that we have helped people and that is what we do and go to sleep happy doing.

You are such a special person, you have achieved more than most of the people I know and you are appreciated by so many voiceless people. People who have no access to papers, computers or time for comments in the daily newspaper, because they simply can't afford it.

Just remember all those people that you have touched and smile with pride, my darling. Enjoy the last part of your career, I know exactly why you are going to NZ, and for those of you who don't, tough tacky hey? (Hint: it's got a lot to do with Love of family). Love Merry

Request granted
10 Jun 2008   *Geoff Caruth, Pinetown*

I CRAVE the Editor's indulgence for a few last words on the Eve Hemming saga to wish her all the very best for her future in New Zealand. She seems to be a kind and well-loved woman and it was never my intention to insult or demean her. Go well, Eve.

Request Granted
10 Jun 2008   *A non e mouse*

Too little too late, you did insult her and a great many others that have left their families for an unknown hard but safer life; something that is not easy to do and also heart breaking for the ones left behind. Next time you pick up your pen think before you scribble, once in print it can almost never be erased. Anyway, who cares about what you think, just keep it to yourself.

Thank you for the apology!
10 Jun 2008   *Eve Hemming*

Thanks Geoff—Much appreciated—Life's too short for anything less than mutual respect . . .

*'And here is the shock—when you risk it, when you do the right thing (*or the wrong thing*), when you arrive at the borders of common sense and cross into unknown territory, leaving behind you all the familiar smells and lights, then you do not experience great joy and huge happiness.*
You are unhappy. Things get worse.

It's a time of mourning. Loss. Fear. We bullet ourselves through with questions. And then we feel shot and wounded.

And then all the crowds come out and say, "See, I told you so."

In fact they told you nothing." Jeanette Westerson

Emigration

Emigration, forced or chosen, across national frontiers or from village to metropolis, is the quintessential experience of our time.

John Berger

Emigrating is a profound and impactful journey. Those who haven't taken the plunge can't remotely identify with what is essentially a life-altering paradigm shift. The decision may arise due to being affected by violent crime, seeking an employment opportunity, looking for adventure or for a variety of other reasons. Once the decision is made, its equivalent to crossing the great divide to plunge into a life forever altered whereby one forever views the world differently.

Thousands of Zimbabweans, South Africans and people from neighbouring countries can identify with the incredible journey; not just because it's across an immense ocean, but because it's an immense journey of the soul.

After our daughter and son-in-law made the decision that New Zealand was their choice and my husband and I had had our epiphanies, it was comforting acknowledging that NZ was on the same planet. But my desperate efforts to rationalise what I was doing (being the one who was going ahead alone, having acquired a job after a telephonic interview) lead to an inner sense of chaos and reactive over justifications. The scenario was exacerbated by well-meaning souls who yacked on about The Global Village and "Oh well, there's Skype . . ." Sure, the cyber spectrum shrinks the planet and technology creates a sense of immediacy compared with eons ago when letters written with quills dipped in ink took ages across boundless oceans carried by sailing ships, followed by another year anticipating a response.

I kept saying, "It's already inhabited by thousands of '*Saffas*' (South Africans Far From Africa) so it's just like moving to another South African province." But just prior to leaving I felt a sense of hysterical madness. It was impossible to comprehend what this great leap into the unknown was all about. I was heading off to 'The land of the long white cloud', and may as well have been going into a different dimension; not just another time zone. I was about to vanish into a different space, as though I was falling through Alice in Wonderland's looking glass and waking up an extra-terrestrial in an alien landscape.

Family and friends responded along the optimism-pessimism trajectory. Some patted me on the back exclaiming how courageous I was. Others were disparaging and accused me of being a traitor by abandoning the great African continent. I was both supported and beleaguered in the media.

Others who were uncomfortable about seeing me, conveniently bustled out of sight in the supermarket to hide behind mountains of tinned dog food, as though I was highly contagious . . . ooh sod it! They could catch the virus and would have to start 'Packing for Perth' I thought, as I pushed my grocery trolley back to the car.

The world's a roundabout with intrepid humanity continent-skipping ever since time immemorial. But when it's Africa that one's exiting, abuse is hurled. Others called me 'lucky', which it was in part, as one has to qualify in specific criteria, including one's health and credentials. But it requires more than that; it also requires undiluted guts and perseverance. People who haven't undertaken the 'emigration thing' invariably seem to lack an understanding about what monumental obstacles one goes through to get to the other side, and then what deep bereavement it entails. For me it was like my personal summit climb and descent from Mt Kilimanjaro.

A friend commented that I love the paradoxical roller coaster ride in Africa and that life in a quieter place would be too mundane for me. I felt that that was the captivation of life. For me it was about having the courage at my age to try and bravely ride a different roller coaster without knowing where it was headed and what the bumpy road ahead held. I thought at the time that the emotional roller coaster of emigrating to New Zealand, and with it the re-identification of the self, was probably as equally tough as the mayhem roller coaster if one stayed in South Africa. Staying or departing would both have jagged upsides and downsides. Maybe that was what I needed to come to terms with—that there was no right or wrong choice. It was something which belonged in one's own moment and possibly even in a strange way was part of one's destiny.

Emigrating is a personal choice and odyssey. I, too, have Africa under my skin. But that didn't mean that I had to remain entrenched. We're creatures of the universe, with options our birth right. Life's transience should revere exploration and new horizons. I felt that it was plucky for Ant and me (at our age) to climb out of our comfort zones, to aspire to seek more security as trailblazers for our family—to transform pastel daydreams into a reality and to actualise a challenge through seizing the moment.

Maybe it was a naive notion. Maybe we shall never know. But at the time we fervently believed that we were doing the right thing; were making a supreme sacrifice for our children and grandchildren's futures. We believed that they would follow with their extended families one day, if we stoically paved the way . . .

For Ant and for me, the justification to go was as strong as someone else's justification to stay. In the final analysis we each have to write our own script.

A major life-change brings with it trepidation. It's bloody painful shedding the gut-naked stuff in one's soul. It's not about hedonistic pleasure or gratification. It's usually about making sacrifices for others . . . It's in our blueprint to gravitate to safety for our offspring at whatever cost; pangs of loss of roots, identity, material comforts and all that is familiar. It would be a new chapter with character-building adversity and numerous hindrances. After several years of adaptation it was hoped that it would be a celebration of courage to cross the symbolic and real boundaries of life.

Epiphany

Standing in the humble kitchen
Chatting trivia
We busied ourselves
Preparing the tea
When
She bellowed at me-
'Wake Up and See!'

And proceeded to draw
A mental time-line
About the journey of our life

And
Our precious lands'
Strife
From way back when,
To then

I felt the resounding clang
Shouting in my brain-
A rude awakening!
A stabbing Pain
And suddenly it all seemed
Miserably in vain

A flash moment of thought
So vividly bright!
A candle burning
A flower slowly
Turning
To seek the light

A curtain ripped apart
Torn from my hand
To open my blind eyes
To expose my naked
Heart
Under a bleeding land.

Eve Hemming 2011

Logistics—between the devil and the deep blue sea . . .

Your daily life is your temple and your religion. When you enter into it take with you your all.

Kahlil Gibran

If you are familiar with the phrase 'a logistical nightmare' then that is probably the most accurate description of what the emigration process entails!

It's about unpacking the contents of one's own life. Some of us may have done that for someone else—for me when my beloved mother died in 1996. It's that unravelling a person's entire life and then packing it away, putting it into boxes and categorising it. It's like cataloguing a human being into a filing cabinet. It is unreservedly heart rending. When my mum died, her almost 80 years of life was reduced and compartmentalised into boxes; a box of goodies for Hospice and for the SPCA and things for various other charities and things to turf out, things to sell and things to share amongst the four siblings, including one in the USA and one from the UK. Slowly but surely all that remained were a few arbitrary items and a casket of ashes, as though 80 years could be concertinaed and compressed into almost nothing. It reminds me of the film *21 Grams*. That is allegedly the weight of the soul.

Moving country is different, but feels the same. We had boxes for this and boxes for that. It was the biggest spring clean of our lives—kitchen appliances, linen, furniture and clothes for our loved domestic employee and friend, Maria, some furniture and household goods to my SA brother, items for the kids, for friends and charities, and stuff to sell. What remained was for the container to be shipped across the ocean.

Other logistics included retiring from my position as a school principal. I was given a series of ceremonious send offs, which astounded me. I was amazed and humbled by the love and generosity bestowed on me. That place and its 'family' will always have a special place in my heart.

Logistical nightmares included the closing of accounts, sorting out income tax and the cancellation of policies and contracts. The logistics of getting our NZ work permits included our fingerprints being sent to Pretoria for Police Clearance, combined with several trips to Durban to have blood tests, X-rays and a raft of medical check-ups, and emails and telephone calls back and forth to the New Zealand Embassy. I also had to get University transcripts, testimonials, original documents and screeds of paper work to apply for my registration as a psychologist in New Zealand. The endless waiting for documents to arrive was agonising and it felt impossible to enjoy the last months in Africa, already fraught by the family tensions and dynamics, which were becoming increasingly unbearable for us all.

One major stress was regarding having our passports renewed. We stood in queues in the late March heat, sweat pouring from our brows, feet swollen and achy. It felt as though the entire planet was applying for passports and identity documents simultaneously. The documents were sent off and thankfully we eventually arranged to have them collected and couriered back. This was to my great relief as The Department of Home Affairs in Pretoria, to whom we made countless telephone calls, had in fact addressed the envelope to the incorrect address, in which case without the courier, I could have missed my flight . . . I received my passport five days before my flight! It had taken almost three months to obtain it.

It is strange that after four years as a migrant, telling the story is still acutely painful; sending shivers down my spine. One is filled with poignant regrets, and yet when one looks back over one's shoulder, into the recesses of one's brain where memories are lodged for easy access, one dusts them off, peers into them as though looking at one's reflection in the watery abyss and slowly acknowledges why one left. It's a Catch 22 situation, there is no denying it. Being stuck between the devil and the deep blue sea.

We had to put our treasured home, which we thought we'd live in for the rest of our lives, or until we were too decrepit to manage staying there, on the market. Vehicles, a caravan and a motorbike were sold. Slowly our material world was diminishing and made us realise that we had far too much stuff anyway.

Pets

One of the most hard-hitting parts was finding good homes for pets and sending our beloved bit ailing thirteen year old Staffie, Gyspey Queen to heaven. My darling husband had to take her to the vet which was traumatic for him. I am ashamed to confess that I didn't have the courage to go. I sat on the slate veranda with her in the dappled morning sunlight before I left for my school. It was one of those moments that will remain in my memory long after other memories fade into oblivion. One of those moments when time seems to stop in its tracks and the world becomes deafeningly still. I spoke to her softly, salty tears dripping into my mouth; softly thanked her for being the most loyal pet that we had ever had and gently stroked her, smelt her warm fur and caressed the velvet coat under her neck. Her precious face looked at me and licked my hand and my tears . . .

Pooch was a different story. (He and Scallywag and Paddystix stayed until just before I flew, before they went to their prospective homes in Hilton, to caring people whom we remain indebted to.) However, Pooch was the self-appointed kingpin of our diabolical doggy brigade, which lent itself to us experiencing high-voltage mayhem in an otherwise serene sanctuary. He was our besotted, idiotic Staffie with mascara-lined brown soppy eyes that have the ability to make me melt. He would get away with murder, like sneak into our bed in the middle of the night. We'd wake up in the dark hours hanging 10 on either side of the bed, while Pooch had centre stage with his four paws skyward, airing his balls to the nocturnal world. He was also couch potato, not a rabbit hunter. *Jock of the Bushveld* would totally disown him. When we watched a movie on the box he got the best seat.

I was going away and Pooch had smelt a rat. Okay, well there were a few suitcases around and some boxes that he was tripping over. It was a bit of a giveaway, but heck, I could swear that he was psychic. I did talk to my dogs and was inclined to ask Pooch advice about deep existential stuff, like—"What do you think, Pooch?" He'd tilt his head to one side and give a nonsensical response, which completely satisfied my need for a profound opinion.

Once Pooch suspected that something was cooking, he would come and sit at the side of bath, while I was bathing, climb up and doggie-groan at me, as though to ask if he could jump in, too. He hated water. He also took to climbing into my bedroom cupboard and sitting on all my shoes, making them squashed and misshapen. When on the computer, he would come and sit on my feet. It was like having the FBI trailing my every move. I would not have been surprised if he had tapped my phone and had a far better knowledge of English than I have given him credit for.

We did make our lives difficult by being animal lovers. Besides the dogs, we had seven resident guinea fowl, two geese, two Muscovites and two Mallards. It meant that every time we went anywhere we needed animal sitters. That required a page of instructions of who to feed what to, in what containers and at what venues, as each pet had acquired an impressive CV of eccentricities. Life would have been dull without our menagerie, but the down-side was leaving them. We were going far away . . . for how long I didn't know, and we couldn't take them with us. That made for a bitter-sweet sort of poignancy about our time left together. Pooch seemed to have surmised all that and was seriously miffed . . .

Grandchildren

My deepest and most profound pain is connected to my 'Far Away Grand Children'—which reminds me of one of my favourite childhood story book, Enid Blyton's *The Faraway Tree*.

I am, what could be termed, a 'besotted granny'. My intention was to never leave them behind. It was all an awful misinterpretation, as our elder son and family were at the time contemplating and talking about moving, too. Ant and our elder son had even booked a camper van to do a New Zealand 'look-see' trip. He'd shown their two daughters, then aged 6 and 7, books with the majestic scenery of the country in it and had said to them 'Shall we go there, too?' But clearly it wasn't meant to be, for numerous reasons, primarily I believe that it wasn't meant—well not then anyway, and the future remains unknown. However, by that time (and with a rather osmosis sort of assumption that they would join us) I'd been offered a position in Auckland, leading to our home being put on the market . . . the wheels suddenly rapidly in motion. Their camper trip was cancelled, the deposit lost and the pipe dream gone pear-shaped; which something of such magnitude can often can tend to do . . .

I had never intended to leave without them! If I had known what I know now, I'm convinced that we would never have left—at that stage anyway—and hence not been able to be trailblazers for them, if ever they desired to join us.

One of the hardest moments of my entire life was sitting on the settee in our living room with my eldest grandchildren, Toni, then going on eight and her sister, Gabi, going on seven. Toni looked at me with imploring large brown eyes and asked, "But Granny, why are you going away if you love us so much?" Now, four years later, I'm wiping my tears as I type this and clearly envisage it as though it was yesterday. It still cuts right into my chest like a sharp knife.

At that time, my heart shredded into a million pieces, my eyes hurt, my chest exploded, my breathe was lost in its tightness. I could not muster a reply, only tears, and to hold and rock them. How could

I tell them that our intention was in fact to leave for our children and grandchildren's futures too, when they weren't coming anymore?

Since leaving South Africa, our younger son and his wife have had two babies born in South Africa. We have returned a few times to meet them and to be at various celebrations. My heart breaks daily for being relegated to a role as the celluloid granny that smiles and wipes tears away on Skype. When we first started Skyping, our grandson, Daniel, used to be fascinated. Later he got curious and used to look behind the computer to try and find us! Now our baby granddaughter, Aliyah is getting quite interested in being entertained by us 'two old farts', too. Ant and I sing 'Clap Handies' 'Twinkle Twinkle Little Star', 'The Wheels on the Bus Go Round and Round' and 'Old Macdonald had a Farm' . . . and hold up cars and puppets, carrying on with our antics as though we are presenters on a kiddies' TV programme in our endeavour to engage them and keep them amused, while they sit in their high chairs nibbling breakfast toast, watching us . . . Daniel used to say that we lived on an aeroplane. He can now say with theatrical articulation that we live in 'New Zealand' . . . but it may as well be on the moon!

Thankfully we have two of our grandchildren, Emma and Dylan, here. They moved to New Zealand with our daughter and her husband two years ago. They live two and a half kilometres from us and we are the little NZ family, which helps enormously. But none of us truly feels a sense of totality severed from the remaining family in SA . . . and I guess visa versa . . .

From my treasured eldest grandchild who turned 8 just after I emigrated . . .

Dear Gran here is a poem for your book.
It is called 'I Miss You'   *Toni Hemming* (12)

I lie in my bed and think about you,
I love you so much I don't know what to do,
Impatiently I wait for the day,
I don't have to see you go away.

Years have come and gone,
Yet our love has held on strong,
I miss you.

As I am saying goodnight at the end of the day,
And you are not here,
But miles away.
My heart is so empty and so lonely inside,
As I wipe away a tear I am trying to hide.

I MISS YOU!   Love from Toni

*From my beloved second grandchild, Gabi who was 6 when I left SA . . . She has a
wonderful way of shielding pain with her wit!*

Saturday mornin'   *Gabrielle Hemming* (11)

One lonely Saturday mornin'
I woke up in my bed.
I looked up at the ceiling,
But then I bumped my head.
Then I looked up again and saw a bunch of stars
I tried to snap myself out of it, but then I flew to Mars
From there I saw New Zealand,
It looked so, so cool
So then I flew back down again
And landed in someone's pool
But up the stairs I climbed and climbed until I reached the top.
Right then and there I noticed I was in a Chinese shop
This was getting weird,
Too weird for my liking
So I jumped down to the floor and saw a zombie Viking
She started running after me I nearly screamed to death
She chased me all around the world but she ran out of breath.
Now I'm in New Zealand,
But how will I get home
I have no money, no penny, no dollar
All I've got is this comb.
I'll have to walk or swim,
Of course I can't fly
Unless . . . .
Unless I learn to, and everything will be mine
I'll rule the world for ever

And nothing shall go wrong
My rules would never fade: Don't dance! Die quietly! Stop singing that song!
Wait—I feel something tugging on me,
Stop! Stop! Stop!
And everything was spinning round,
I think my brain just popped
I landed in my bed again,
And felt quite cross and mean.
I thought that I was finally king
But *that* was just a dream.

Love Gabzzz

Goodbyes—No one ever told me it would be like death . . .

And ever has it been known that love knows not its own depth until the hour of separation
—Kahlil Gibran

After Molly, my best friend of many years, died and missing her sea of tenderness I thought that losing a special friend would equip me for emigration. I was wrong, but possibly it did help to a degree. She went to heaven. I went to New Zealand . . . I used that as my yardstick that reminded me that 'my white cloud place' was still on this planet.

We were best friends, the way children have a best friend living next door. It may sound childish, but I felt it strongly, possibly because my twin sister had emigrated to the UK. Molly embraced the role with sentient sensitivity. She was there for me through crises and euphoria, tolerating my quirky personality without judgment, when others couldn't. We were unconditional friends. That was a priceless gift.

I took Molly to her first chemotherapy session. She was matter-of-fact about it, but inside she was suffused with terror. She had to semi-recline in a massive chair with drips and attached things and insisted that I come back later. Molly never wanted others to witness her anguish and ceaselessly displayed a brave veneer, saying,

"I'm absolutely fine . . ." She vomited copious bile on the ride home, apologising for soiling the upholstery. And I said, "What for?" That's the way we were.

But Molly's ordeal remained brutal. She'd always been the robust pragmatist, me the scatter-brained dreamer. She'd cared for me. Now the tables were turned, although she was proud about appealing for assistance. Molly combatted the cancer, but never seemed to regain her sparkle. I'm sure that if one trudges along an oblique path feeling suffocated by pending death it alters everything.

As the cancer spread, we'd talk about the painful reality as the afternoon sun filtered into her room. "I don't want to die!" she'd say. She wanted to be around for her children's weddings, for grandchildren and oodles more living. But one can only hold up the wall for so long. Molly matter-of-factly described the wretched decay wreaking havoc inside her body. I sat next to her skeletal form, rubbing her back with scented oil, her bones protruding from her once-gracious form.

I wrote her a poem. It was the end of October. I took it to her and lay next to her in the room warmed by child art on the walls, painted by children at the school where Molly had taught. The view on to the Lion's River was restful.

I read her the poem . . . "It's called *Ode to Mollerita*," I tell her. She conjures up a weak smile. This is my name for her. Molly, reaching out for my hand, huskily whispers, "Thank you. And I'll write poems for you in the sky." I lightly touch her skeletal frame. Her morphine pump makes a whirring swish. This is not a dream—I couldn't remove us from the certainty.

In February 2003 Molly slipped into a coma. There is a time when one finally has to say goodbye. It wasn't easy walking out of her bedroom, pausing at the door to immortalise the moment; her, fading, tiny, crumpled form, balancing between life and death. It was Thursday night when I said goodbye. Molly slipped away quietly on a Sunday in the presence of her family. It was a still day in the summer. The washed out sky was shockingly empty. When I received the news, I felt wrenched out, bereft.

Every day there's a poem in the sky from Molly; a sunrise over the sea, a beguiling cloud formation, a mesmerising rainbow or sunset, even a blazing comet. Each time a palpable sense of peace washes over me as I revere the immutability of existence.

The loooooong goodbye

Among the top stressors in life include changing homes, jobs, cities or countries. Human beings simply don't like change. We're sticklers for constancy! Maybe we're all a little bit on the Autism spectrum!

Moving to another country is a conglomerate change that encompasses multiple losses—loved ones, home, job and country, roots and identity. It's like a total reconstruction of the self. Before I left I was told that New Zealand didn't favour "tall poppies" and that one must quietly blend and merge with the landscape and avoid being conspicuous.

I thought that it could possibly be challenging for someone like me with my burgundy hair, clanging bangles, scarves and gypsy paraphernalia. I decided that I'd try (being the operative word . . .) to arrive gently, hover under the radar and be a silent observer. I was also told to avoid "just now" or "now now". It's interpreted as immediately, not as *'net nou'* from the direct Afrikaans translation. It is a South Africanism that we understand only too well. It is these subtle nuances that one has to learn by osmosis.

I looked at the world map and tried to conceptualise being on a little dot on the North Island, itself a mere dot on the sea-scape. It seemed so remote. Somehow, the way the flat world map has been created makes Africa seem like the centre of the planetary universe

One internalises that concept into one's personal mind map. Going down there, to a little dot; an after-thought midget landmass near Aussie seemed quite disquieting. It would require a complete reorientation. The most bizarre concept would be the time difference. When my fellow South Africans are awake I'd be asleep and vice versa. That would create a complication for nano-communication. But it still felt strangely comforting staying in the southern hemisphere. I'd still be able to see the Southern Cross and it would still be winter in July and summer at Christmas time.

The most difficult part of going anywhere is the getting there. That's when one realises what a mammoth journey it is. For the intrepid souls who are taking a plunge into the unknown, there are just no short cuts. But one can learn the procedures from the folks who have done it and who've banged their heads in exasperation waiting and sitting in queues; from the medicals, police clearance, passports, work visas, international driver's licences, certified copies of everything, the packing up and finally the distribution of the contents of one's life. I called it the "*deconstruction phase*".

It was like peeling an onion; one peeled off layers disposing of one's objects and collectibles, and at the core were the wet-eyed, emotional, heart-wrenching goodbyes to family and the re-homing of precious doggies.

At the epicentre, saying goodbye to family at the airport was going to be the biggest nightmare and I had planned to have my Rescue Remedy on hand. Being a born optimist means that after the deconstruction phase the reconstruction phase emerges. I had the belief that with some flexibility and a sprinkling of chutzpah, that acclimatising to change was possible . . .

Hamba Kahle from SA, *Haere Mai* to NZ
Lisa Hemming (my beloved daughter-in-law)

You seek the season
You've been missing
Your winters dim and grey

The homeless sun
Remains uplifting
The gloom will go away

Remember that this rock
Will stand
A beacon, if you will

Fly safely
To your place of safety
And know we love you still.

But let there be spaces in your togetherness and let the winds of the heavens dance between you. Love one another but make not a bond of love: let it rather be a moving sea between the shores of your souls. Kahlil Gibran

The Airport

May the road rise up to meet you,
may the wind be ever at your back.
May the sun shine warm upon your face
and the rain fall softly on your fields.
And until we meet again,
may God hold you in the hollow of his hand.
Irish Blessing

This is the part that I keep avoiding writing—the hardest part—forever like a giant wound deep in my fractured heart . . . their sobbing etched on each of their precious frighteningly loved faces . . . . And my own wretched sobbing . . . like I've never sobbed before, all the way from Durban to Johannesburg, so much so that the plane must have lurched a few times! I wanted to get on the next plane back to my ENTIRE beloved family, (my husband, three kids, three kids-in-law and at that time four grandchildren), whom I said goodbye to at the old airport in Durban, and just ditch the entire sodding plan—the door 'out' for everyone 'if the shit hit the fan . . .'. Somehow I willed myself on to that plane to Hong Kong and sat next to a silent Chinese man who slept the whole way and then after 8 or what felt like 14 miserably lonely hours in the airport, walking up and down long walkways, sleeping on a hard-as-hell bench clinging on to my camera, laptop and luggage for dear life . . . departed for Auckland . . . and another endless flight . . . . But I did it as so many others have and also survived!

Your children are not your children. They are the sons and daughters of Life's longing for itself. They came through you but not from you and though they are with you yet they belong not to you.
Kahlil Gibran

Arriving in The Land of the Long White Cloud

I arrived in NZ on the 14th July 2008 after an endless period of time in transit; jettisoned into space in a time capsule full of strangers, to emerge from the deep belly of the plane, exhausted and wrung out from sobbing. I laid my feet on to the soil of my new life—NZ terra firma. I must have looked an abomination and I felt a complete wreck!

I was eternally grateful to be welcomed and fetched from the airport by my husband's cousin and wife, who'd been living in NZ for many years. A glorious soaking bubble bath, a tasty meal and a magically large soft bed helped, plus a phone call home to SA so say I'd arrived, were a godsend . . . But in truth the jetlag, jelly legs, nausea, dizziness and fatigue lingered for three weeks.

Once I'd had some sleep all I had to do was get the basics sorted, which they helped me get done at their local mall; opening a bank account and laying my hands on a NZ compatible mobile phone, GPS and Internet modem. Next step was to drive an automatic (which Ant had bought for me on the Internet), an old but snazzy little Z3 sports car as his way to cheer me up!) In SA I'd driven a manual my entire life. That was followed by us finding my accommodation on the complete opposite side of this sprawling city using the GPS, and to finally get settled. I commenced my new job a few days later, still jetlagged and shell-shocked.

Living here was still a surprise. One simply cannot read a guidebook to assimilate one's self into a new lifestyle. About the only things that were familiar to us from photographs and calendars were the Auckland Sky Tower and the Auckland Bridge. The rest was unknown, unchartered territory; a country with snow-clad peaks, aquamarine oceans, squeaky green rolling hills and sheep. That was my naïve perception before my arrival . . . The nightmare process re the myriad logistics the few months before departure had kept my mind so preoccupied that I hadn't found the time or the energy to do any research on a crash course in becoming a Kiwi.

What does it take to become a Kiwi? Arriving here was a startling revelation. Arriving two months before Ant added to the absurdity. In a way it was the first time I'd been truly alone. I'd never done the 'gap year' after boarding school and being a twin meant that I'd even had company 'in utero'. I'd never experienced my own company as I'd plunged into marriage as a teenage bride, then into studies, a career, and motherhood. So, here I was in my late 50s going to the effing far edge of the world by myself.

New status quo = new country and large sprawling city, after my somewhat protected existence living in a more insular, middle-class, predominantly white village in South Africa. The rolling hills and sheep concept wasn't exactly blown out the back door, as it is a reality, but it became underplayed by my urban existence. Reflecting back I experienced a sense of schism—severed from my roots. Survival was by immersing myself in a new career and by playing the symbolic death and rebirth game, which I will expand on later in the book.

I learnt to drive according to the new road rules in my automatic sports car and kept wondering where the clutch and back seat had vanished to. You may be shaking your head, but I do think that one initially goes a little insane. One is in a state of undiluted shock, with one's world being tipped upside down and emptied out into little pieces like coloured marbles scattering from a hole in a frayed old pocket. Undeniably I heard the Kiwi accent on the radio. I read the words New Zealand on my mobile phone screen. My mind knew that it was as a reality, but my psyche felt three steps behind, as though it simply couldn't assimilate this surreal scenario. Maybe it was a subtle form of post-traumatic stress disorder. My mind map had to totally alter, also my biorhythms. Even the texture of my hair and fingernails altered and I could swear that I even smelt different for a while.

I started to learn the wacky linguistic nuances and tried to plug into the different mind-sets. I soon discovered that I was perceived as idiotic and naïve, as my life experiences, studies and acquired skills were irrelevant in NZ and mattered little to others. Having been known and respected in my previous vocation felt like a previous life and were inconsequential. It made me realise what a leveller death is and that I wouldn't be taking my CV and my various degrees and my summa cum laude (my one and only astounding moment of brilliance) with me to any afterlife. Afterlife shrouds don't have pockets.

In a way it was actually cleansing being back at square one. There is something exhilarating and philosophically challenging about that. It was a brand new fig leaf for Eve—how symbolic was that? A clean page, a new book . . . the onion peeled to the core . . . many tears flowed . . . often!

Then the rebuilding had to commence . . . tiny steps . . . *Tiny*. I developed a list of quirks and foibles, routines and perseverations . . . One was the work car; yellow Car 13. One was Classic Hits Radio. You get accustomed to driving a specific work car or listening to a specific radio station and don't want to change these or other things for a while. Why was that so hard for others to understand? For frig sake, you've had to be reformatted in every single minuscule detail after 58 years of living with the old mother board! Throw out the old brain. Insert a new hard drive! Change . . . new change . . . tiny steps. They thought I was barmy at work. I really didn't care. If they had only known; taken the time to try and analyse what it was like . . . "Please can I swop with you? I must have Car 13" . . . And when the novelty of the sports car had worn off, Ant bought me a red Alfa on an auction on Trade Me, which he had to take to the garage to expand the band range, as I simply had to have 89.4 Classic Hits en route to and from work. After all, the DJs voices—Jason et al—were my very first companions from Day1! (People out there—please understand; migrants can be a delicate and eccentric breed and need to be understood.)

One's journey of rebuilding travels in concentric circles from a diminutive inner circle outwards to the next circle and the next like a ripples from a stone in a pond; first explore this shop or this street or drive this route and slowly expand one's repertoire and become more adventurous as one orientates and discovers shops around the next corner, a new road, a new route. I guess I felt like a blind woman with a white stick inching my way forward and stumbling along on untravelled, unsteady terrain.

Despite the idiosyncrasies one may develop as coping mechanisms while adjusting to change, it is revitalising starting that new page. A *Tabula Rasa* adult. No one has a clue of one's past achievements (or failures), or knows that one's great uncle was the mayor or that one's grandfather-in-law was a parliamentarian in the pre-apartheid old Union of SA, or that one's cousin played the cello in the London Philharmonic orchestra. Nor about the fecund skeletons in one's family's cupboard. More so that one has close friends and an entire full-blooded existence on another continent. New people in one's life either cannot assimilate this, or else it's too complicated for them to conceptualise how different one's past life was. I may as well have come from an undiscovered planet somewhere between Venus and Mars. Or better still, I may as well have fallen through a computer screen on to the floor, stood up, tidied my skirt, coughed a little cough and arrived—a rather odd and eccentric cyber creation that automatically morphed into a fully-fledged breathing being.

One is gauged by the immediacy of that moment when one walks into one's new work environment with overwhelming trepidation, nonchalantly peppered over with a ridiculous smile to camouflage one's inner sense of absurd ignorance and apprehension, all exacerbated by exhaustion, shock and jetlag.

There are days when one has little time to reflect on all this and one is merely attempting to exist, to adapt and to survive. It's really a case of 'fit in or . . .'

But when I was in bed with uninvited flu, the respite of bed-dozing meant a moment to pluck my thoughts, examine and distil them. It was a year since I had moved to a new country. Maybe this had been sufficient time for me to do a mini-review of all the pros and cons, the swings and roundabouts of migration, I pondered.

It was a crisp, sun-filled day. A little cold crept into my hand as I wrote down my thoughts. This necessitated intervals to pause and hide my hand under the bedcovers. Paddywag faithfully lay next to me. He was named to commemorate two of our South African dogs that we'd sadly had to re-home; Paddystix and Scallywag. (On a recent visit to South Africa we'd avoided seeing our ex-dogs as we felt that it would be too painful for us, too confusing for them, now ensconced in their new lives.)

Paddywag is an illuminating light that delights us. He's brought a new meaning to the word 'watch dog'. One doesn't need a watch dog for protection here. Instead, he is a watchdog because he watches us. We wake to his scrutiny. I bath to the same scrutiny as he pushes the bathroom door ajar. He seems mildly amused by our every move.

Moving country remains the hugest thing we've ever experienced/ accomplished/ drowned in. It's an act of seemingly utter insanity, which negates all one's most primal connections to the cosmos. I find myself quoting Keats more often, *'Happiness is sharpened by its antithetical elements'.* Experiencing a new chapter of life is life-altering and isn't given enough credence. Each day we are grateful to taste a figuratively different menu, yet simultaneously we miss the staple diet stemming from our roots. I recall emailing a psychologist colleague of mine a few months after my arrival here, "Am I experiencing a schism of the self?" I asked. She replied, "No, just re-inventing the self." I kept that pinned on my notice board at work for the first year to reflect on.

I never feel anxious driving here because I know that Johnny Soap won't push me off the road, although, 'yeha right', Kiwis can be impatient on the curvy roads. Kiwis have an internalised holistic respect and I was actually wondering whether Kiwis could possibly have a more diluted version of the survival gene that "Saffas" have had to develop. They haven't had to walk on the same edge of the precipice of life. Maybe they haven't experienced loving and hating their land simultaneously as some Saffas have done when they have lost a loved one to violence. They possibly aren't exposed to such a wide spectrum from exhilaration through to primeval threat.

Living Alone in Titirangi—*written at a pavement café after a month in NZ!*

I love it! I come here to get my canine therapy. I miss my dogs back home. If I don't get my own pooch soon here, my soul will simply start curling at the edges.

Oh and there are plenty of babies, too, and toddlers in gumboots and teens in miniskirts and leggings. People don't care about the weather. It rains so much we call it 'liquid gold'. One adapts. Knitted hats, skullcaps, scarves and gloves, and babies with plastic pram covers to face today's chill wind off the Manukau Harbour. Kiwis are far from dull; they sip massive mugs of coffee, tuck into eggs and bacon wrapped in muffins and laugh around tables on the pavement, their chilled breaths spilling into the air.

I've been living alone for a month now. It's an entire new life experience for me. Yes, and it's true, people who live alone do talk to themselves, like Shirley Valentine. But it also means that one's observations are sharpened. One watches more closely, observes life from one's own fringe.

Back at my pad on my own I've had some laughable experiences. Trying to open a bottle of wine without a corkscrew. Result—red wine decorated the kitchen wall, which was seriously sanitised before the veggies got fermented. I've also had some adventures in my sports car. The things a woman learns to do without their man around! There I was standing in the pit under my car, in high heeled boots beside a greasy acne-decorated youth in his blue overalls, diagnosing what the rattle was in the vague vicinity of the exhaust pipe. And twice around the time of the reportedly worst deluge in NZ in ten years, having to demurely smile at muscled joggers to rescue my cab out of the muddy morass.

As my spouse is the remote control *fundi* (authority) and I'm a techno–disaster, since arriving on my own I've had to learn to change channels, and to operate the DVD and video machine myself. I've also learnt to navigate my way around this sprawling city using my GPS, to Skype and to put petrol in the tank. For a self-confessed twit on such matters, I'm constantly amazed at my ability!

As for trying to master a new job and trying to decipher so many accents . . . The other day, my waiter said his name was 'Bin'. I said "As in rubbish bin?" Wry response, " No Bin—B—E—N . . ." Get my point. In hindsight, I should've asked for a Gen and Tonic.

Each day new uninvited adventures mean that I hit the ground running. I've discovered that parts of my brain that were dormant have had to go on a rapid march. My senses have sharpened. I listen more intently; watch more carefully, process with deeper illumination. On another level, my subconscious mind is no longer on high alert. I find that I relax more and my vibrations are calmer. I sleep more peacefully. The other night the back door blew open in the wind and it just didn't matter. I woke up and laughed when I discovered it wide open.

I also enjoy the sense of anonymity—the invisible voyeur—the dude at the table next to mine is on his mobile—"Hiya mate . . . are we gonna link up?" And always an acute awareness of a palpable sadness of being so far from 'home', contrasted against my wonderment at my new world. And I count the days till my spouse arrives and opens the next bottle of wine . . .

First published in The Witness 2008

'Another Saffa expat bites the dust'

I was thinking the other day when I read that 1 million or more South Africans had emigrated, how immigration impacts on the individual. If each of those million folk knew 20 people really well 'back home' that would hypothetically amount to 20,000,000 people in South Africa being affected by emigration.

When Dee, aged 5, moved to New Zealand 20 months ago, his little best friend at pre-primary school in KZN, South Africa, was deeply traumatised, as of course was Dee. They had been inseparable at pre-school. They hadn't learnt to read and write so writing emails to one another wasn't viable after Dee left. One or two chats on Skype took place, but the time difference made it difficult and life inevitably moved on. Dee has a new best friend in NZ, a little boy who emigrated from the UK, at the same time as Dee did from SA. And hopefully the little boy in KZN has a new best friend by now too, which I'm sure he has.

Irrespective of if one is a grandparent, parent or a child, one is going to leave either a massive or a small ripple effect back home. Someone is going to be affected. It's now four plus years since we left. People in SA seem to write more seldom, despite my initial religious flow of emails, pictures and updates . . . and so the gap insidiously closes over like a fine but tightly meshed shield across a gaping chasm. The shield is penetrable by the closest loved ones, who keep talking on Skype, emailing or face-booking. But for the rest, life goes on and one becomes a forgotten entity—another expat that may as well have 'bitten the dust'.

Of course when one goes back to SA to visit one does reconnect, but I find that this gets harder as folk really are resistant and there is this sense of 'us' and 'them' . . . or is it my imagination ? From the reaction I'd received in the media on my departure, I don't think so. There was a definite sense of anger and of being 'abandoned'. And now I'm bemused as to why people are angry when one is following one's choice to seek a safer option at great emotional and financial sacrifice; not just for the self, but for one's loved ones and family. After all the expats don't throw a tantrum at those who wish to stay in SA. I'm acutely aware that the majority of South Africans simply CANNOT leave and for those of them who would desire to, I deeply empathise. As for the many folk who wish to stay regardless of talks of nationalisation, land grabs, and ongoing atrocities, that is their choice and I totally respect that as part of the spirit of human freedom of choice.

I still wonder what it feels like 'back home' when yet another close friend departs. As incredibly hard as it is to leave and wave goodbye to one's entire past life, loved ones, identity and connections, it must be equally hard for those at home when yet another good connection vanishes across the great divide into a life beyond.

I belong to a forum where expats chat to folk planning to migrate to New Zealand to offer them support. Daily there are 'newbies' who come on to the forum to announce that they are applying to immigrate to New Zealand. One is a woman whose family survived a highjacking and decided to stay in SA . . . until their second highjacking. Then they decided "How much more can we take?" and are on their way.

We know oodles of folk in SA who contentedly retort about 'Another glorious day in Africa' as they sip their cocktails under a setting sun, looking out at a majestic panoramic vista . . . and it does feel gloriously dandy and sugar candy. I'm sure if one is in the right place at the right time it can be idyllic. And those are the moments every expat dreams of and envies like hell!

But it's only idyllic until one is in the wrong place at the wrong time. And please don't get me wrong, one can be in the wrong place anywhere. A South African expat woman was traumatised in Auckland recently when an idiotic inebriated woman with road rage followed her and then proceeded to open her car door and slap her around. Now she wants to move to Aussie. Maybe she still has to discover that the truth is that there's NOWHERE where zero shit hits the fan . . .

My wish is that Saffas, expats and wannabes all continue to support one another in the spirit of *Ubuntu*; respecting personal choice and endeavouring to make South Africa a safer place for those who stay, whilst supporting and lovingly releasing those who opt to leave in search of a new land.

Bouncing off Planet Africa

There's so much constantly to react to in the world in which we live, and in a country like South Africa, that can become a full-time occupation André Brink

"A nomadic people learn to take their homes with them—and the familiar objects are spread out or re-erected from place to place. When we move house, we take with us the invisible concept of home, but it is a very powerful concept. Mental health and emotional continuity do not require us to stay in the same house or the same place, but they do require sturdy structure on the inside. And the structure is built in partly what has happened on the outside. The inside and the outside of our lives are each the shell where we learn to live." *Jeanette Winterson*

Resilience

Your living is determined not so much by what life brings to you as by the attitude you bring to life; not so much by what happens to you as by the way your mind looks at what happens
Kahlil Gibran

Before talking about the Process of Migration, it's worth a mention that everyone responds and adapts differently. This can be part of one's inner determination, staying power, personality, health, age, personal circumstances, skills and resilience. People don't all react in the same way to traumatic or stressful life events.

"Resilience is that ineffable quality that allows some people to be knocked down by life and come back stronger than ever. Rather than letting failure overcome them and drain their resolve, they find a way to rise from the ashes. Psychologists have identified some of the factors that make someone resilient, among them a positive attitude, optimism, the ability to regulate emotions, and the ability to see failure as a form of helpful feedback. Even after a misfortune, blessed with such an outlook, resilient people are able to change course and soldier on." *http://www.psychologytoday.com/basics/resilience*

Factors in Resilience

A combination of factors can enhance one's resilience. The primary factor is in having considerate and supportive relationships with family and close friends. If one has access to being loved, encouraged and reassured in life, one's capacity to develop resilience is increased.

Resilience is developed if one has the ability to make realistic plans and to implement them, if one has a positive outlook on life, has self-belief in one's abilities and self-confidence, as well as communication and problem solving skills. One also needs to be able to self-regulate one's emotions and to harness one's subjective impulses.

Strategies to help one build Resilience

Developing resilience is an individual journey; characterised by cultural differences. Some cultures encourage people to externalise their feelings, while other cultures discourage it. Some strategies may be found on the following website. *http://www.apa.org/helpcenter/road-resilience.aspx#*

Ten Ways to Build Resilience—*Find what works for you!*
- Make connections with family and friends
- Avoid seeing crises as insurmountable and unable to be solved
- Accept that change is a part of living
- Move toward your goals
- Take decisive actions
- Look for opportunities for self-discovery
- Nurture a positive view of yourself
- Keep things in perspective

- Maintain a hopeful outlook
- Take care of yourself

Learning from your past

It may be helpful to reflect on one's personal life and look at past experiences so as to establish what one's strengths are. One can identify what events are the most stressful and look at ways to reduce, avoid or minimise stressors, as well as reflect on who helped one and what strategies or processes were the most effective for one personally. One may also see one's self in a new light and be quite amazed at discovering inner resources and qualities that one had never before had put to the test. In this way it can enable one to build new faith and trust in one's own ability to manage challenging situations.

Managing one's state of resilience requires one to have a flexible outlook on life and to learn to honour one's emotions. One needs to know when to ask for help and when to avoid stress and reenergise one's self with quality time with those one feels safe with. One should also take time out to nurture one's self.

Adjusting As a Migrant in a New Country   *Doris Schöneberg*

Moving to a new country, for whatever reason, can be either easy or difficult. The difference is your attitude and your ability to cope with change . . .

My husband has always wanted to spread his wings and work in another country, but having a wife like me put paid to those ambitions. You see, I resisted change like a lioness protecting her cubs! I was in a comfort zone. We lived in our dream home, on a big property in the countryside, with family and friends not too far away. Why on earth would I want to move and leave that all behind? He always said that there was no point in pursuing those dreams if I wasn't on board with the idea, because the whole family is affected if the wife is unhappy!

Later, I began to realise how much I was limiting my family and myself with my fierce resistance to change, because of my fear of change. At the same time I came across a quote, "Change the way you look at things, and the things you look at change" and a light bulb went on in my head. This is now my mantra, which I apply constantly in my life. I have stepped out of my comfort and into the magic!

There are moments in every person's life when a decision is necessary, a big decision and a major choice. Once the decision has been made to move, stop focusing on what you are leaving behind and start focusing on all the opportunities that your new country will present, and all the doors that will now open for you. Sometimes, visa applications can take a long time to be approved, but instead of getting impatient with the process, see it as an opportunity to organise and plan the many things it takes to get your house in order, and ensure the move is a smooth and uneventful one! Do you see the pattern here?

No one really wants to leave the country of their birth, their family and friends and everything that is familiar, but instead of resenting your experience and "having to make the choice", embrace the changes and all the excitement and wonder it brings with it. Get rid of the irritation and anger, and instead see the beauty of your new surroundings. Welcome and appreciate each new experience as it presents itself. We all have choices, and we can either choose to be a victim and wallow in self-pity, or rise above our circumstance by changing our attitudes, and emerging as stronger and well-adjusted human beings.

Many people do not realise that happiness can be a choice. When our mental state is calm and happy, it is easier to deal with whatever life throws our way. Most of what we believe is real, is actually created by our thoughts, which determines our emotional state, which determines how we behave and therefore produces our results. This means that when we are unhappy with the results in our lives, we have the tools and the power within us to change them and create a new reality!

Whenever you start experiencing feelings of anger, fear, guilt, or sadness, ask yourself how having those feelings are working for you. You will find they are not, and can even make you ill! Wouldn't the logical conclusion be to make the choice to change them? What you choose today makes you who you are, and who you choose to be, and that is what determines your quality of life.

Having, and applying this knowledge to my life, has made the transition of migrating to the other side of the world, and thousands of kilometres away from my precious family and life long friends, that much easier.

You have the power within you to control your thoughts and change your results, and there is where you will find the key to freedom . . . !

Makes you think, doesn't it?
Much love and wishing you every success in your new life!
Doris Schöneberg
Master Life Coach at Self and Beyond Life Coaching

SA people are trauma victims   *Anonymous*

I went to see a doctor who informed me that all SA people are trauma victims, not necessarily because of what we experienced, but because of the way of life we had to lead behind bars. Stress points are: Immigration, buying a house, moving, changing jobs, death, divorce etc. I wonder how many of us can press these stress buttons . . .

I must say though, that we love it here and will never move back to SA. We miss the family and wish they could all come over here, but it is just not possible for some of them, so we count ourselves very blessed and will always feel grateful. When we moved here we decided to give ourselves two years and if after two years we were not happy, then we would go back, but we were happy right from the start. We have been here for five years now and we look forward to the day we can become citizens.

This is not my husband and my first move. We had to do this once before when we left Zimbabwe in 1982. We are both Rhodesian born. They say third time lucky. I will say though that Africa will always stay in my heart, and we do long for the 'good old days', but life goes on.

"I saw this great billboard—"Wherever you go, there you are". I must admit that it took me a long time to 'get it'. And one day the light bulb switched on; No matter where you are, you're still the same person—happy, sad, or whatever. The place doesn't make you or define you. Who you are makes what the place is for you!" Amanda Stapelberg Trent, Washington, USA

The Process

W'é'd probably all benefit from some 'survival tips' if we bounced off planet Africa; moved from that achingly familiar place and space which we call 'home' to what is quintessentially an alien space . . .

The truth is that it's uncomfortable confronting reality. We'd all prefer to have a broken arm swathed in Plaster of Paris than confess to feeling anxious or depressed. We've been brought up to suppress our emotions (especially men) and to put on a heroic face.

Bull shit!—on being Heroic . . . We need to acknowledge how we feel; try to comprehend these emotions welling up inside of us; honour them and accept that these emotions are perfectly normal. And . . . if we didn't have these powerful and sometimes overbearingly agonising emotions, then we would NOT be Normal! As we all know, emigration is a frenzied process and to be sad or mad doesn't mean that one's a ninny. Migration usually takes real guts and body parts of steel, and with it comes the reality of the emotional, physical and material costs. We are led to believe that South Africans and Zimbabweans are a tough bunch. We are! But under the veneer—the fearless and defiant front we display, the tough and rough 'don't mess with me, my China' image that we portray, we're all human and mere mortals ~~~

Some folk have no blinkers and know all the pros and cons to staying or migrating and elect to stay in Africa. To those of you, I venerate your personal choice. However, some folk want to display such a tough image that they don't want to concede that migration is an option (that is if it is, as we all acknowledge that it isn't an option for everyone.). They'd rather put on the bravado image at any cost or risk with their '*'n Boer maak 'n plan*' (a farmer makes a plan) boldness, whilst denigrating any brave soul who makes an alternative choice. If one chooses to migrate, it's about making an intelligent, well-formulated decision, based on the data at one's disposal.

This section of the book discusses the various emotional states that one may encounter or experience due to the traumas, fears, stress and anxiety one may have been exposed to in Southern Africa, (or elsewhere), leading to migration, combined with the massive adaptation and acculturation process of migrating and settling in a new land. Please take from it what you need and return to it as a resource again . . . and again—as or when you need a 'top up'!

Sometime in my life I discovered Elizabeth *Kübler-Ross*. My interest in her was possibly compounded by my disenchanted discovery of life's transience. I went through that juvenile egotistical phase in which I was shattered to discover that during the first half of life one is attempting to invent one self, whilst the latter half one is merely endeavouring to come to terms with that persona. I enjoyed coining phrases like 'Life isn't a full dress rehearsal, so get on with it and grab it by the balls' . . . or John Lennon's 'Life happens while you're busy making other plans' . . .

With some introspection, possibly the type one has when catching five minutes in the bath, I made the personal deduction that every single life-altering event or change of circumstances embraces the principles which *Kübler-Ross* formulated about the death process. It could be a tiny or an epic change, with the process being more moderate or intense on the continuum, like an infant being weaned from his dummy though to dealing with one's own or one's dearest loved one's terminal illness or a loved one's unexpected death.

Kübler-Ross, an American psychiatrist, pioneered the theory of thanatology (which comes from 'Thanatos', the god of death and mortality in Greek Mythology.) She introduced the five stages of loss in her renowned 1969 book, *On Death and Dying* Her book offered the earliest model in which she proposed that people experience stages in their grieving process, which included:-

- Denial
- Anger
- Bargaining
- Depression
- And finally Acceptance.

Kübler-Ross emphasised that these stages, which she had identified were normal reactions to a tragedy. They are normal defence or coping mechanisms which people apply when confronted by trauma or a significant change of circumstances. In the perfect world we would not have to deal with tragedy. It would be ideal if all sufferers could reach a level of acceptance. However many people may get 'stuck' and have difficulty in progressing to a stage of complete inner peace and acceptance regarding an intensely sad event or process.

My objective in presenting these (and additional stages) in this book is to emphasise that it's normal for people to experience various coping mechanisms when confronted with a life-altering scenario. People can experience several of these emotions or states of mind simultaneously and not necessarily in the same sequence. They may regress back to an earlier stage due to additional stressors, for example.

The reason that I've brought this pioneer's work into a book on emigration is self-explanatory. I'm alluding to what I called a 'metaphorical death'. And in knowing about this process in advance, it better equipped me for my personal journey of the soul.

Metaphorical Death

When I emigrated, I decided I'd play a game as my coping mechanism. It was a colossal help. I'd lost two of my best friends, Rose and then 'Mollerita' to cancer over the years in South Africa, and Ant had lost two close mates, Phil and Glen, from strokes. We'd both lost various other friends and colleagues from illness or accidental death.

With this in mind, it was relatively easy for me to pretend that I'd died. In moving from Africa I was going to a 'metaphorical after life.' It was my own personal game. At times when I was shocked, numb, lost (yes, even with a GPS), confused, scared, sad or mad, I'd do the rebirth into the 'afterlife' game.

In my mind's game, it's like Alice in Wonderland stepping through the looking glass. I enter a tiny narrow door and slide down what feels like a never-ending cascading tunnel. Finally it opens into sunlight. On the other side I find an astonishing place with hills, trees, flowers, water, birds, sky and beauty, and I say out loud to myself, "Wow! They have trees and flowers here too . . ." (when no one was in earshot as I didn't want anyone to either run a mile or have me certified for substance abuse detox). That was the way I coped when I was all alone and so far from my family, my roots, My Life! This was my teeny new after-life island and I was going to rejoice and celebrate my after-life come hell or high water!

I've inserted facets of the different stages related to grief below; It could be the grief a reader may have experienced before they left their homeland, due to an atrocity, or the loss of all that is familiar, combined with the new grief of loss of the homeland once in a new land . . . *Please don't abandon the book just yet ~ the grief process is a mere part of the book! ~*

My Heart
I call it 'shrapnelled';
Splintered into millions
Of sharp piercing shards
Of silver blue glass
That cut into my veins
Spilling my hot visceral
Globular achingly red
Blood
All over the place
So that it pours
Drips
Squirts
Leaks
Messes
And stains
My world.

Eve Hemming

Denial

What is it that makes people go into denial and what is it that we deny? It is a defence mechanism, first postulated by Sigmund Freud. It's really about pushing a reality factor under the carpet and avoiding its truth because it's either too difficult or painful to come to terms with. Instead, one pretends that it's not true, despite the fact that the evidence is glaringly obvious.

People may completely deny the truth, else they may minimise the severity of a situation by underplaying it. Alternatively one may acknowledge the facts, but avoid taking responsibility by blaming others for the way things have panned out.

In this scenario, we may take cognisance of the multi layers of denial on the migrant topic. Firstly, people may be in denial that there is a reason to emigrate from a situation, despite the possible deterioration of their life world, regarding safety, security or circumstances. People around the world become desensitised to circumstances which become the norm—so much so, that they become accustomed to living in the symbolic "killing fields." If the situation is a slow and subtle process they may detach themselves from witnessing a deterioration of circumstances, despite continually 'upgrading' their security systems, for example. It's a subconscious way of avoiding reality. Secondly we may be in denial that we are too fearful to emigrate, or alternatively that we are bereft and homesick once we do emigrate.

A multitude of defence mechanisms come into play, with denial leading to blaming others and casting aspersions, because we are all cerebrally wired to want to believe that *our* decision and life view or perspective is the correct one and thus that others must therefore be misguided.

Elizabeth *Kübler-Ross* referred to denial taking place when one is given a diagnosis of being terminally ill. It is a stage of shock and numbness or of blocking out the patently obvious facts. Having lost two of my closest friends to cancer I was able to share the journey of denial and with time witness the shift to acceptance in one friend and the denial right up until she slipped into a coma in the other friend. We also use denial if we hear the awful news of a beloved family member's tragic or unexpected death. It is as though the brain grapples with the truth and initially denies it as *bona fide* fact. "It must be a terrible mistake" . . .

I, for one, was in denial for a long time—denial that my physical and spiritual life-worlds were being eroded away due to indisputable threat, that my life was being marginalised, that my sleep was being deprived and that my mental wellbeing was being undermined. We had over the years gone from an arbitrary countrified hedge—to a wire fence and then to a sturdier fence, followed by an electric fence and gate, to solar panels and alarms and interior padlocked gates, neighbourhood security guards and two-way radios. That is how long it took for the denial to slowly seep into my state of awareness. Years.

In life if we're able to 'bluff' ourselves that the decline in our health or our safety and wellbeing isn't happening, and we keep the facts at arms' length, it may just quietly dissipate into the ether . . . It is the typical ostrich syndrome and I lived it and breathed it so very easily.

Likewise, those who emigrate want to put on a brave face, even though for the first two years or so they may think "Oh shit I have made a terrible mistake . . ." They try to save face as don't want the folks back home to say "I told you so" . . . that too is a form of denial combined with justification.

Anger

I'm not sure how many of you have experienced deep anger due to migration. It was an emotion which my entire family seemed to experience. The ones that elected to emigrate were angry, as we felt that Africa had in essence betrayed us by letting us down. This was our birth place and we felt that it was untenable and non-negotiable to continue to live in a place where life was so cheap, where cold blooded and ruthless violence was conspicuously present, where criminality was endemic and where corruption meant that insufficient progress and healing were evident or expedient enough. It felt as though we were living in a place with our bleeding fingers fiercely pushing into the burgeoning holes in the dyke, as floods of torrential violence poured in, leaving us in a miasma of confusion, anxiety and fear.

People whose choice was to stay in Africa were angry with us for electing to leave, whilst we were angry that they elected to stay. We were 'traitors'. We were 'cowards'. We were idiots forsaking our land. The bitterness between us and some of our family and friends was harsh, deep and raw. But through it we never stopped loving one another. In hindsight I know it is because of the exceptionally deep love which we have for each other that it felt as though the passions and sentiments were running so very deep and were etched in our blood, as it coursed and spewed and stained the African soil with indelible magenta.

In their book, *Letting Go of Anger—The 100 most common anger styles and what to do about them*, Ron and Pat Potter-Efron remind us that anger is a relevant emotion. It is a reaction which is triggered by our painful thoughts. What we think actually triggers what we feel and that triggers how we behave. I use it as a graphic triangle when assisting people with 'Rational Emotive Therapy'. Deep emotional pain can lead to angry thoughts, which can then lead to angry and hurtful confrontation. In dealing with anger and channelling or redirecting it constructively, as well as in reflecting on what the anger is being triggered by, can lead to the prevention of damage and hurtful reactions to those whom we love so deeply.

The raw emotion does serve a purpose and if bottled up, intense emotions can be detrimental to one's health. I think of the body as a pressure cooker. It simply needs to give off steam. Playing sport and physical exertion are far healthier ways to release fuming steam than by using wounding words and aggression.

The Potter-Efrons recommend that there is a healthy way of letting off the steam if one is able to acknowledge ones anger as a normal emotion and as a signal that something is burning one up inside. Taking action such as reflecting about the causative factors and triggers of one's anger is helpful, as this prevents one having an uncontrollable outburst. One needs to have a goal to attempt to solve the problem. It won't go away on its own and anger won't resolve the issue either, hence problem solving is the most constructive and proactive approach. Of course in expressing the anger in a controlled way, it allows both parties to listen and articulate without shouting each other down. It doesn't take away the problem, i.e. in this case a fractured family due to emigration. But it can better facilitate respect for the choices made by one's loved ones; honouring these without mudslinging.

It is recommended that once one has articulated the angry emotions in a calm and self-restrained way, that one needs to then 'let the emotions go'. This is probably the most difficult part, which does not come easily to people. We tend to mull, ponder, ruminate and agonise over things which we have no control over. Letting go is hard!

Anger can be directed at one's spouse, family, friends and often at God. People tend to blame the economic climate, the political-historical milieu, the government, one's work environment and singular events which may have acted as a catalyst. Shifting the blame doesn't remove the anger, but taking responsibility does.

Bargaining

"Please just let me live long enough to see my daughter get married . . ." or "I'll do anything, God. Please just don't let me die just yet . . ." These are the bargaining responses of people who are terminally ill. We would all want to postpone something hideous from stealing away the natural progression of our life. We would feel incalculably cheated. It's a natural phenomenon to desire to fit a colossal chunk of living into our allotted time. We don't want to be robbed of our goals and our desire to actualise our dreams . . . none of us do, unless we are so deeply depressed that we wish to terminate our own life.

Part of the attempt to postpone an event is to bargain. We may bargain with God and make promises. "Please forgive me God. I will change. Please just don't let me die . . ." I watched one of my friends bargaining when she discovered that she was terminally ill and yet she had been an amazing wife and mother. It wasn't like she could say to God, "If I make more effort, will you please take this bloody tumour in my uterus and shrink it please?"

Where does bargaining come into play about migration? Maybe one could pray to God and ask him, "Please God won't you stop the violence and the atrocities because I don't want to leave my country . . ." I'm fairly sure that that came into my thoughts or my prayers in some or other way. Likewise family at home may pray to God, "Please let them come back" or those who have left may pray "Please let them come too . . ."

Blame

It's so much easier to blame someone else when the going is tough . . . "It's all your fault . . . that we were at the wrong place at the wrong time . . ." if we land up being caught up in a nasty experience. We may even become self-righteous and judgmental. We blame others for our unhappiness. The stage of blame is often seen as the height of one's unhappiness before healing can begin.

Blame seems to be a primary defence mechanism regarding emigration. We are able to blame the hideous things happening—the corruption, chaos and mayhem. People blame the government, historical factors in Africa; blame different cultures, political leaders or circumstances. People are also inclined to blame the ones who elect to emigrate and literally crap on them . . . "How dare you leave . . . !" may be tossed at one. Likewise, the people who do elect to emigrate blame their family members for not coming too. "It's your fault that we can't be together . . ." The fragmented family syndrome can create the most immense levels of pain and anguish for families, severed by migration.

Forgiveness

How to let go of the anger? That is the next question! I would say that forgiveness is a key component. It is a great antidote that can dissipate deep feelings of anger. If one has rage in one's soul it becomes toxic and must surely eat away at one's psyche like a cancer of the mind. One needs to forgive the world for whatever it has doled out, whether it arrived invited or uninvited—maybe one would have preferred to never have to emigrate and leave home, and most certainly no one would ever wish to be violated or attacked, or witness loved ones hurt. This type of hatred and anger festers and one can't move forward if it's lodged inside one's body like a heavy weight. One ultimately has to work through and process the pain, anger and all the associated emotions. Only you know when you are ready to actually forgive. No one can expedite the process for you. With it comes an inner sense of cleansing and healing.

The forgiveness also has to be in forgiving one's self, as we can be harsh with ourselves and feel ashamed of maybe some of the choices we've made. If we can't let go of the self-loathing, we are in fact sabotaging our capacity to heal. Trying to minimise pain, anger and deep hurt by drowning in substance abuse is really being self-destructive. It may temporally numb the pain, but this is temporary until one starts relying on the next 'fix'. This is really escapism and not confronting one's truth and one's reality. Once one can feel forgiveness and a sense of lightness of being one can move forward in the process.

Sadness

I value Karen Masman's take on Sadness in her book *The Uses of Sadness*. Masman reminds us that as humans we are tuned in to an understanding of the cyclical nature of life and the seasons, of the tides, of breathing and of sleeping. Everything animate, as well as inanimate has a season. Think of the day and night cycle and how each day we awake to a new day and each new year we awake to the concept of a new year, a new page and a new year's resolution! Within each cycle there is a beginning and an ending. Masman argues that the same can apply to sadness.

As in my mention of Elizabeth *Kübler-Ross's* ground breaking work, we are able to learn to understand the journey, process and flux of our sadness and pain. In understanding one's grief and honouring it, one is able to know that tomorrow it will be easier and different.

I use the moon as my emotional landscape. It waxes and then wanes. I am emotionally far more vulnerable and sensitive when it's Full Moon. I wasn't as acutely aware of this until our emigration. I found myself weeping inconsolably sometimes, and finally fathomed out that my highest acme of undiluted pain was at Full Moon. For a while I dreaded the moon until I learnt to make it my friend and know that at that time I would be more alive in some ways—my pain was sharper, but so was my love for my far away family and for life in general. I knew it would pass and that at the following full moon it would be easier. And so it has . . . so many moons later!

Grief

Your pain is the breaking of the shell that encloses your understanding
—Kahlil Gibran

Mike Dooley in *Infinite Possibilities* cheers me up as his book endorses my belief that as sentient beings we have amazing potential. We face life's array of prospects and can then develop our personal odyssey. He adds that it is vital that one takes ownership of one's own pain and bereavement. It stems from within one's self and only the individual experiencing the pain can alter the inner state by working through the pain and discharging it. This may take considerable time. With emigration, people generally refer to the two year mark. For some it may take longer. For others it merely lessens, but is an almost endless mild sense of dis-ease. This too is grief.

How would one define grief? It can come in many forms and is powerfully associated with many emotions and sensations. With grief we may feel the trauma of severance and separation, the way a child feels separated from his parents. We may feel abandoned by the ones who leave. We may experience any one of or a combination of emotions such as sadness, depression or regret.

'I feel like there's a hole inside of me, an emptiness that at times seems to burn. I think if you lifted my heart to your ear, you could probably hear the ocean. The moon tonight, there's a circle around it. Sign of trouble not far behind. I have this dream of being whole. Of not going to sleep each night, wanting . . .' (From the film *Practical Magic*).

That's how I felt for the first few months, although I put on a brave face, loved the sense of adventure and all the newness around every corner . . . and felt truly emancipated. When had I ever been on a life-altering adventure on my own before?

I was excited and proud of myself for taking this plunge, yet I was in a state of deep bereavement, combined with a sense of adventure, shock and numbness.

What grief also brings are some positives. It is important to know and acknowledge this. Through the grief encountered when one emigrates, one discovers many qualities one never knew that one had. One needs to draw deeply on this maxim; on these inner strengths and to dig and delve into a part of one's soul previously relatively unscathed (if one's fortunate), or else not yet fully tapped into. For those with a scathed soul, they miraculously seem to have a reservoir of additional mettle to pluck strength from.

One learns humility by seeing the world through different eyes and by the world seeing you as foreign through its eyes. By starting life again as though *tabula rasa*, one's many years of foundation have been erroneously erased from the visible eye of one's new colleagues. One starts out as a vulnerable shell with no tangible or visible history attached to one's new world. They don't know it, fully comprehend it, or always understand it. You aren't one of them and never will be.

One also learns to discard unimportant matter and clutter. Materialism loses its allure. For many, they may develop their spirituality though such a journey. For others their relationships become strengthened, though sadly, the converse is also true and relationships may break down. One has new vistas, newly found knowledge, vocabulary and life experiences added to one's new life. One sees the world differently. It's part of crossing the vast idiomatic Rubicon of enlightenment from which there is no return, but which is accompanied by the dark journey of the soul.

Depression

The migration process includes depression for many people for various reasons. Some may have been depressed having experienced trauma which triggered the decision to emigrate from their home country. For others there may be a sense of depression arriving in a new and foreign landscape, already stressed and hyper aroused, which can then become magnified by the myriad new stressors encountered.

People are often in denial about depression. They may even view it as an ugly word. I think, 'For heaven's sake—we take our car to the garage when the engine is 'missing' . . . so why the heck not go and have a consultation with the doctor when it feels as though one isn't ticking over smoothly on all one's emotional cylinders?'

Depression can be a scary and deeply lonely state of being. All seems dark and dismal. One may feel that bed is the best place and wish to hide under the covers. One's sleep may be disturbed, and one's appetite and libido non-existent. I think it's no small wonder why a titanic journey such as migration can lead to relationship discord or break down. Both partners need to be particularly sensitive, nurturing and patient, so as to pace themselves to deal with the obstacles and challenges. It's imperative to acknowledge that within a partnership, people respond differently. One person may be quite resilient and manage the process better than the other, who may be more vulnerable, exacerbated by factors such as possibly having had to sacrifice more in leaving the homeland, and may have more difficulty in finding employment or in adapting and developing a circle of friends in the new country.

I believe that the largeness of this journey simply cannot be over-estimated. I am one of the fortunate ones. Emigration has made my beloved husband and I grow stronger and closer in our relationship. We buffered the storms together and for this I am deeply grateful. This doesn't mean that we have not been depressed. We have! We have in our mature years been severed from our roots, our identity and from our two sons and their families. Migrating later in life, as we did, isn't as easy as when one is younger and can create a new life, dig down some new foundations and forge new friendships.

It's important for people to recognise that one can heal from depression and that there are different types of depression, such as clinical and reactive depression. The latter depression is the type I am alluding to where one's depression is a reaction to one's extraneous world rather than to internal chemical factors. Melissa Deitz describes in her book, *My life as a side effect*, that in feeling depressed one feels trapped and consumed by what she refers to as an 'impending doom'. I think that the person suffering from depression, as well as the care givers would benefit by reading books written by people personally suffering depression rather than only medically written books. In this way one is able to say " Ah . . . that is exactly how I feel", so that one can identify with someone else's depression and not feel alone or remotely crazy. There is also the 'Beck Inventory' which is a test that can be conducted, which can assist one to establish which are the areas of one's life that are affected, and which are the best treatment options towards healing and recovery.

The most important factor, I believe, is to acknowledge that one is permitted to feel this way, that there is no stigma and that with the correct support—medical, emotional and spiritual, the majority can reach a level of inner peace . . . With the correct approach and mind-set you can—and hopefully you will!

Dr Steve Ilardi discusses ways to combat or reduce one's feelings of depression. One can take Omega-3 fatty acids, which can facilitate brain function and reduce depression. We all acknowledge that physical exercise and activity reduces depression. But the paradox is that when we feel down, we want to climb under that duvet and nibble chocolate. Does that ring a bell? When one is depressed one's mind is filled with toxic thoughts and one gets stuck in negative thought patterns. Getting up and going out is the best option, as it can blow the cobwebs of negativism out of one's mind. Exercise switches little light bulbs on in the brain. It is as though the brain is being oiled with dopamine and serotonin so that the little brain cogs and wheels start to crank up and the rust is removed.

Sun lovers will be delighted to know that sunshine has healing properties against depression. I'm convinced that I'm a SAD (Seasonal Affective Disorder) sufferer, if there aren't enough sunny days. For this reason I've ensured that my office desk is in a bright corner with glass windows to the floor, which allows the light to generously pour in. My mood at work has conspicuously improved since finding a sunny light space. Sunlight manages our rhythms which regulate our sleep, appetite and energy levels. I'm told that the melatonin from sunlight also reduces the effects of jetlag, which upsets one's circadian rhythm. As migrants, we are inclined to fly back and forth and hence need lashings of melatonin!

Sleep is imperative and when we suffer from sleep deprivation or disturbed sleep, it becomes a vicious cycle. Sleep heals one and yet when one suffers from depression, or depression combined with PTSD, one's sleep patterns are severely affected and disturbed. I found that the first three months as an immigrant my sleep was severely affected. My circadian rhythm was '*deurmekaar*' (Back to front.) I wanted to drink tea at 2 a.m. and I was sleepy at 3 p.m. My body was still in tune with the African time zone.

Socialisation is vital when one is feeling depressed. Being surrounded by caring friends and family can help one to remove oneself from one's inner world of sadness. The irony is that when one is sad one withdraws. I remember our very first Christmas as immigrants. We'd declined a few invitations as we were both miserable. I cried a lot that day but felt that we couldn't impose our sadness on others on a day when families are cheerfully together. Here sat my husband and me, whilst at the time (before our daughter and family emigrated), we had three children, their spouses and all our grandchildren in South Africa. It felt like lunacy. Thankfully we can tick that day off and not have to relive it.

Laughter . . .

As we know is medicinal. It may be helpful to watch a humorous film or to listen to cheerful music. I find that when I'm sad I tend to dislike gloomy music and a depressing film is a total no-no. Invariably one can listen to one's self and establish what helps one to shift out of a melancholy mood. One thing that helped me was to take photographs of scenic places in my new land, or to write poems or words—respecting my tears and to then move on. Shopping—need I say more? Even a new warm toned lipstick makes a sad woman cheer up . . . Sensory things assisted me; colourful art, vibey music and tasty food. Another tool which helped me was to think of the people who had experienced an incredibly tragic life and to pray for strength and forgiveness for having the audacity to feel any self-pity. I'd chastise myself and give myself a firm talking to. One can't easily do that if one is in a deep depression. Healing is a process and requires patience and nurturance from self and others. We can all find methods and tools which can be helpful as we dredge our way through the hard times of either losing beloved family to crime or emigration, else being the migrants severed from the loved ones 'back home'.

"Live, so you do not have to look back and say: 'God, how I have wasted my life'." Elizabeth *Kübler-Ross*, M.D. (1926-2004) www. change-management-coach.

Assisting adolescents to overcome depression

When an entire family migrates, they may each be taken up with their own emotional process and adaptation. I'm told that in some cases the youngest children are supported while a family may assume that the older, more independent siblings are managing 'just fine'. Teenagers are complex creatures at the best of times.

I recall sitting under a tree mulling about the universe, and in a typical adolescent way had the egocentric perception that I was the centre of my little planet and that any pending doom was seen as inconsiderate of the universe to cruelly flick in my direction. My dad had been diagnosed with a tragically debilitating disease, Motor Neurone Disease and was confined to a wheelchair for his last few years of life. I was a devastated 15 year old who felt cheated of a dad.

Books have been written on adolescence and its psychological mind set. Suffice to say that we all know that adolescents are vulnerable, with one foot in adulthood and the other in childhood. They are wavering on shaky ground and may arrive in a new land which has different adolescent norms, expectations and pressures. They may become influenced by a drug culture. They may suddenly be permitted to drive a car at a much younger age on winding roads which are unfamiliar to them. The educational system and curriculum may be vastly different. They may speak a different language or have a strong accent. These things can all stack up against a kid with a susceptible ego, low sense of morale and to add insult to injury, possibly even a fresh outbreak of acne or orthodontic braces.

Parents need to listen to the signs; watch their kid's body language, notice the peer group that their child gravitates towards, and at all times be available to lend a listening and non-judgemental ear. I used to say to my three teens long ago; "I may not like what you've done, but that doesn't mean that I love you any less." There's a strong difference between loving your child and disapproving of the poor judgment or bad decision he or she has made.

Teens are emotionally impulsive. Their bodies are rattling with hormones. They're easily influenced by their peers. They want to be accepted and to do so, may go to the most drastic steps to achieve this; whether it's an outlandish 'pants on the ground' bum-baring fashion statement or a run in with the law. Being new to the group could mean that a kid has all the more reason to have a strong need to feel acceptance and to 'prove himself'.

In South Africa, teens in certain areas been protected due to various factors such as the risk of being violated or hijacked, for example. In other countries where they move to, there may be a new found freedom and what I allude to as the necessity for internal self-regulation, rather than external regulation. This requires maturity and the capacity to make healthy choices.

The primary concern for any parent is when an adolescent suffers from suicidal ideation. In their fragile ego state and sense of not belonging, they may start contemplating and developing ideas about suicide.

Manassis and Levac in their book *Helping Your Teenager Beat Depression* discuss a problem-solving programme called L.E.A.P, which can support one's depressed adolescent. It is based on a cognitive therapy approach and the acronym stands for:-

L—Label (as in Labelling; identifying the teen's thoughts and emotions.)
E—Empathise (as in being Empathic to one's teen by exploring ways to respond and to listen with empathy, rather than being the judgemental unapproachable parent.)
A—Apply (as in Applying alternative ways to respond to the teen, which may be perceived as more appropriate to him or her.)
P—Plan (as in Planning ahead with professionals and family and picking suitable times for this.)

I liked this acronym and saw it as a proactive Leap of faith in supporting teens suffering from depression.

Trauma

Some of the following disorders associated with Trauma are included. This is not a medical, but a layman's model and should serve as a guideline and not as a means of diagnosis. *Please don't abandon the book yet! There is light at the end of the tunnel!*

Anxiety

There are various theories about what triggers anxiety. It can, for example have a biological basis, due to a chemical imbalance or a psychological genesis stemming from trauma. Anxiety can precipitate a panic attack. If one experiences a panic attack, one will experience symptoms such as heart palpitations, perspiration, shaking, and shortness of breath, combined with chest pain, nausea, dizziness, light-headedness, fear and numbness. A panic attack may be triggered by a memory, or a specific situation or place, which may consciously or subconsciously be reminiscent of previous traumatic events. In some cases the trigger is non-specific and may stem from a subconscious association.

I used to have panic attacks when we were nearing the electronic gate of our home when we returned from a function at night. The electronic gate had to be deactivated and the fear used to crawl into my skin and close up my throat as we paused in the darkness, shadows and shrubs dancing in the misty breeze. It felt as though my husband was fumbling and taking too long to hit the remote control button to activate the electronic gate, which created massive anxiety for me. My pupils dilated, my heart pounded, I became ill with nausea and I wanted to run away. I have never actually put two and two together until this moment. It was possibly due to being attacked through my car window some months before this . . . in broad daylight in traffic in the city where I worked, which triggered these panic attacks at the gate. I expected to be attacked and was trapped in a car with a safety belt pinning me down. It would then take at least two hours for my hyper arousal state to reach a calmer plateau.

Stress

Dr Katie Richard has written on the topic of *Coping with Immigration Stress*. She alludes to how a foreigner can feel in a country that is not home. Alienated feelings can lead to anxiety and depression, which can in turn lead to the consumption of alcohol, cigarettes, food and drugs. I have a Recipe section in this book for the precise reason that familiar 'home' recipes and food is part of one's need for comfort. We comfort eat. We gain weight. And so what!

Richard recommends developing a social network, which can include a sporting club, a church or a migrant group from one's own country. I absurdly tried to 'wing it alone' when I arrived in New Zealand. Other than a relative of Ant's across the city and an ex work colleague also across the city, but in a different direction, I knew no one in Auckland on my arrival. No one! Oh, I stupidly thought that with my effervescent personality it would be easy. I forged friendships with work colleagues, but with no history, it was as though they had befriended someone with amnesia. I may as well have wiped out my entire memory and life of 58 years. Maybe they didn't all comprehend why I opted to have a busy work corner with photographs of my childhood, siblings and parents, my wedding photograph, husband, children and grandchildren. At one stage I was asked to minimalise my space station as it could distract me from my work. I was dumfounded. This was my only identity. Who was I to them? Where was Africa? Was it just a big heavy land mass with lions and elephants to the West of their island across a massive ocean? Whatever it was to others, for me the photographs and memorabilia were my life force and I needed a part of my identity to swathe me and comfort me. My pictures still remain in my cheerful sunny corner and bring me great joy.

It took a few years after my husband and daughter, son and law and two grandchildren and another couple we'd known for years had arrived, but who also lived hell and gone, before I realised that I needed more than that. That is when I decided to reconnect with the South African community in New Zealand, which gave me a sense of belonging again as well as the emotional springboard to work on my previously abandoned efforts at writing my book.

Richard reminds the immigrant to acknowledge that it is stressful and tough, and to acknowledge that the difficult times will pass and ease. It's imperative to not throw in the towel and run home when one feels tempted to. One needs to rather 'sit it out' as in the height of emotional trauma one is unable to think rationally. By creating goals for one self, one is able to focus on each new day. However Richard does recommend that one may wish to see a psychologist if after goal setting and persevering one is still suffering from immense stress, feeling directionless and floundering.

Ways to reduce Stress

- Allow yourself to cry
- Practice deep breathing
- Try yoga, meditation or visualisations
- Eat a healthy diet
- Exercise in a way you enjoy, like dancing
- Spend some time gardening and feeling the earth between your fingers
- Get plenty of rest, not just sleep
- Take up a hobby
- Indulge in a hot bath or shower
- Enjoy affection from loved ones
- Keep a journal
- Laugh
- Make a to-do list to still your mind
- Go for a massage
- Use positive self-talk
- Read interesting literature
- Realise your own limitations
- Share your stress with family, friends, support groups, counsellors, social workers, churches and/or help lines
- Spend some time alone just respecting one's own state of being
- Volunteer at a church, hospital, the SPCA, or an old age home
- Try something completely different, like ice skating or if an oldie, bird watching, stamp collecting or scrapbooking
- Get a pet or volunteer to walk a neighbour's dog.

http://www.sadag.org/ (The South African Anxiety and Depression Group.)

Ways to be Happy!

- Be part of something bigger—if one has a sense of purpose in life, like belonging to a group, one feels a collective meaningfulness about existence, which in turns reduces anxiety and lifts one's mood.
- Do things for others—Help someone cross a road or even a smile is a gift.

- Connect with people—Reach out to others who may be feeling alone too.
- Take care of your body—Spoil and pamper yourself with a perfumed body cream, a neck massage or a jolly good night's sleep.
- Notice the world around you—Notice how many shades of green you can see in nature, or look carefully at colours and textures when walking down a road.
- Keep learning new things—Try to learn something new each week; whether a new word, a new fact about your new country or even tackling a new crossword.
- Have goals to look forward to –Get the calendar out—plan a weekend away and if too costly, then a free outing somewhere new, even if just around the corner . . .
- Find ways to bounce back –Make a list of things you enjoy that are attainable and then draw from this list for a 'bounce back tonic' when you need one.
- Take a positive approach—I like to think of that song "Always look on the bright side of life"—only you can pick that moment . . .
- Be comfortable with who you are—Love yourself as you are; warts and all!

From http://www.actionforhappiness.org/10-keys-to-happier-living

Truth

You have your ideology and I have mine

—Kahlil Gibran

Jeanette Winterson, in her book *Why Be Happy When You Could Be Normal*, talks about truth. She states that it is complex. "For a writer what you leave out says as much as those things you include beyond the margin of the text. The photographer frames the shot: writers frame their world." So is it with the individual's story of staying, going, choices and each of us creating our own reality.

Migration, cultural bereavement and cultural identity

Dinesh Bhugra and Matthew A Becker's abstract titled *Migration, cultural bereavement and cultural identity* offers an immense amount of information which migrants can identify with. They argue that emigration creates multiple stressors for the individual such as it impacting on the individual's wellbeing, including religion, culture and social system. One has to redefine one's identity as well as one's self-concept. The authors report that migration increases the chances of mental illness and that medical professionals need to be sensitive to the vulnerability of the migrant and refugee populations.

The authors report that people migrate for various reasons which can include political, socioeconomic and educational reasons. They concur that migration is a stressful process. Cultural bereavement and identity are major factors which require sensitivity and understanding.

Migration is about relocating from one country to another, in which the authors report that often migrants represent ethnic minority groups within a new country. Whilst immigrants have a choice, refugees do not have a choice and relocate to avoid being persecuted. They add that migration is comprised of three stages.

Pre-Migration

This is the stage which I allude to as 'the epiphany'. It involves making the decision to move and requires loads of logistical preparation, selling items, dismantling one's life and over and above that a massive amount of psychological preparation. For some people this can be a long term plan which may span several years, whilst for others it may be quick and spontaneous.

Migration

This requires the actual relocation; bidding farewell, getting on that plane, the long journey and the arrival.

Post-Migration

The authors allude to this phase as when one is absorbed into the social and cultural context of the new environment.

A migrant's adjustment will largely be dependent on factors such as the age when one migrated, the similarity between one's own culture and the culture of the environment one relocates to, language and what support systems are accessible (such as an expatriate community), the mind-set and attitude towards migrants by the primary culture, employment opportunities and housing.

The authors argue that if a migrant feels isolated from his/her culture, is not accepted by the primary culture and has limited social support, he/she may experience feelings of alienation and a poor sense of self.

Factors which will predispose the migrant to adapt or develop mental illness include the individual's personality combined with the level of trauma experienced prior to migration.

The authors mention bereavement, culture shock, inconsistency between a migrant's expectations and what he can achieve and how well he is accepted by his new country as 'vulnerability factors', combined with the individual's personality, capacity to adapt, flexibility, resilience and biological/psychological make-up.

Cultural Bereavement

It is a very real aspect of migration, due to the loss of one's social structure and culture. One loses all that is familiar including one's colloquial language, as well as the norms, values and traditions one is accustomed to.

The authors argue that grieving is a healthy and natural response. They add that if the symptoms create on-going substantial trauma and dysfunctionality, that psychiatric intervention is recommended.

A valid factor is that Western concepts of bereavement may lack a full understanding of the way grief is expressed, experienced or ritualised in other cultures. For example in the Western culture, Bolby's attachment theory discusses the four phases of mourning, which include being numb, anger, disorganisation, followed by reorganisation.

Cultural Identity

The authors state that our cultural heritage, beliefs and values are assimilated and inherited from previous generations. They are what connects us to others, whereas our identity is the way we perceive ourselves and incorporates our race and culture. Our identity alters if we migrate and assimilate a new culture into our framework. Within our cultural identity we share a common history, as well as values, religion, food, interests (such as music, sport, and literature) and language with others who share the same culture. All these factors foster a sense of connectivity and belonging with others.

Food is a powerful part of one's cultural identity. (For this reason there is a chapter in this book dedicated to the culture of food!) Food has a powerful symbolism, as it nourishes and is part of daily life, of ritual and of social interaction.

As migrants we experience psychosocial adaptations through assimilating a new cultural identity. Acculturation takes place when migrants integrate with various cultural groups and in so doing their various cultures assimilate facets of each other's values and traditions. This can lead to some cultural 'cross pollination'—to a sense of universality and what we allude to as the 'global village culture'. Psychologically migrants may experience either assimilation of a new culture, a sense of rejection, else integration or deculturation.

The authors state that post-migration stress may include either culture shock or cultural conflict. Feelings of confusion, alienation, isolation or depression may be experienced. Much depends on the host culture's attitudes towards migrants, as well as if the migrants can find employment, suitable housing, schools for children and a support system.

The authors argue that acculturation may be beneficial to assist migrants to combat bereavement at losing their own culture and possible feelings of guilt about leaving their home country, as through acculturation the migrant starts to assimilate a new culture and to feel a sense of acceptance and belonging.

Cultural Congruity

Migrants hail from various cultural backgrounds. To develop cultural congruity, the migrant needs to have a good support system, self-belief and self-concept, as well as the ability to integrate into the new culture, so as to combat feelings of alienation, loss of identity and cultural bereavement, as well as economic stressors and a loss of empowerment and status.

"Where you are born—what you are born into; the place, the history of the place, how that history mates with your own—stamps

who you are, whatever the pundits of globalisation have to say."
(Winterson) This is who you are and moulds the choices you make . . .

Post-Traumatic Stress Disorder

I am convinced that there are significant numbers of immigrants
who suffer from Post-Traumatic Stress Disorder (PTSD). This has
been well documented in refugee populations. Regarding migrant
populations who are not refugees, it would be dependent on the level
of trauma which they had experienced before their departure from in
this case, Africa, and after their arrival in their new country. For this
reason I am including PTSD in my book, as it may be beneficial to
people who experience some of the symptoms with regards to them
then being able to take proactive action to gain the necessary medical
and psychotherapeutic support required.

"PTSD to me is an echo that seems to follow me wherever I go. It is
a solitude that embraces my everyday. A battle that at times I think it is
over until I realize it is effecting me again in yet a different way. It is as
though the person I once was has vanished and those that surround me
do not understand where I have gone. Clouded by misunderstandings,
frustration, and a battle that I want to win. Daily life can be a challenge
and one day I know that in the end the battle will be worth the
journey." *http://healmyptsd.com/education/how-survivors-define-ptsd*

If one was exposed to an extremely traumatic event (e.g. a natural
disaster, an accident, man-made or life-threatening illness) one could
experience PTSD.

Herman in *Trauma and Recovery* argues that Psychological Trauma
is what happens to one when rendered helpless. "Traumatic events
overwhelm the ordinary systems of care that give people a sense of
control, connection, and meaning."

In other words, if one is exposed to a situation of being under
violent attack by other human beings, one is rendered helpless with no
opportunity to be in control of the outcome, which could result in one
sustaining a severe physical assault and associated emotional trauma.
If a person who emigrates due to a direct attack on them, or due to
an atrocity inflicted on a loved one, they will have experienced intense
fear and helplessness combined with terror and feelings of incapacity for
self-preservation. PTSD may then manifest.

When one is attacked or witnesses an extreme atrocity, the sympathetic nervous system responds to the signal of threat one experiences. This releases adrenalin. The individual's heightened arousal means that he or she will have an altered state of attention, perception and emotion. The surge of adrenalin permits one to run faster, or to fight with strength that one never knew one was capable of. We often refer to this as the 'fight or flight response.'

When I was attacked through my car window in South Africa, I had no idea how I would react. I obviously could not run and was buckled in, so the next best thing was to fight; to shout and swear like there was no tomorrow. That was my survival instinct which kicked in and took over. It was guttural and came from deep inside me. I also recall how everything seemed to go into slow motion, the stillness of everything else in that moment burned in my ears and a sense of isolation gripped me, despite the fact that there were motorists in their vehicles all around me at the red traffic lights. We are genetically engineered to fight for survival of self, loved ones and particularly our children.

What occurs after experiencing trauma or a series of traumas is that one develops what is referred to as 'hyper arousal.' This results in one easily being startled. One may be more reactive to little things, sleep restlessly and lose one's appetite. One may also experience poor focus, agitation, restlessness, poor concentration and memory. One is more easily startled by noise, movement and sound.

Although I emigrated four and a half years ago, I still experience startle responses, though they have greatly reduced and are less easily triggered. If one has been exposed to a battery of traumatic experiences or one extreme traumatic event, one's baseline for anxiety and arousal is raised. It is as though one's brain and nervous system become rewired to be on high alert more easily. In psychology we refer to this as a change in the 'organicity' of the brain whereby the chemical make-up of the Central Nervous System may alter and be more easily adrenalised through the release of cortisol. Prolonged cortisol levels in one's blood stream due to chronic stress can affect the body negatively:-

This can include poorer mental processing, under active thyroid functioning, blood sugar imbalances, poorer bone density, increased hypertension (blood pressure), poor immunity leading to health problems and an increase in abdominal fat which can lead to bad cholesterol, heart attacks and strokes.

Intrusion is when the trauma continues to recur within the individual. This can in some cases continue for years. It is as though the trauma is encoded in the memory and cannot be erased, as hard as one tries to shut it out. If one does sublimate it by pushing the thoughts out of one's conscious mind they resurface again and again in one's dreams and one's conscious and subconscious mind. They simply want to play themselves out again and again as part of the healing process to eliminate the toxicity from the psyche'.

The dreams which perseverate are described as being 'frozen in time'. They are stuck in the memory and replayed like a stuck record. They are thus encoded more as sensory experiences and imagery, rather than as narrative dialogues. It is thought that mind and body functions become suppressed so that the fight-flight response has priority; hence speech is taken over by sensory memory and visual imagery.

People who have been exposed to terror feel compelled to re-enact it over and over again in an obsessive way. In children this is reflected in monotonous play patterns which lack spontaneity. It is thought that in reliving a traumatic event, that it may possibly be the conscious and unconscious mind's way of attempting to develop mastery over one's emotions and overwhelming feelings; hence to be in control of one's life again.

When a person is unable to pursue a fight or flight form of survival, they may instead freeze. Rape victims may freeze and feel utterly paralysed. This is the mind and bodies' other survival strategy when fight or flight does not seem possible. It is as though one dissociates one's mind from one's body, as though one is omnipotently watching oneself being attacked from some levitated position above. Time is said to stand still and reality to alter. It is as though the mind anaesthetises itself as a form of protection from the horror it is exposed to.

Dreaming

I often had nightmares when I lived in South Africa. They were gruesome with large petrol tankers imploding into flames on our pavement, or floods that left one hanging on for dear life, or falling off precipices, crawling through tunnels, grotesque hands opening windows and entering and always a need to run and to shut and lock windows and doors. I had dreams of small deformed children and little furry animals—and always trying to save them and rescue them from drowning or starving. Else a recurring dream of a banquet and having a deep anxiety if the people arrived before the preparations were completed, if there was enough food for the masses and having to clean up all the dishes after everyone left me to clean the mess . . . always trying to clean up like 'Little Mrs Tittlemouse' in Beatrix Potter. I often also had recurring 'washing machine dreams', finding piles of laundry in the attic or basement and having to attempt to stuff it all into several rather decrepit washing machines.

They say that one's dreams are ways in which the subconscious mind processes one's anxieties and that while one sleeps, the brain does a route march in an endeavour to problem solve. Often one may wake feeling as though, with the new day, the problem seems less complicated or that one has a solution. I never fully understood the chaos of my dreams, but I am sure they were telling me that all was not well within my psyche', and that I needed to seek inner peace to find some harmony in my existence.

My dreams are more peaceful now, exotic and creative in softer hues; else they are ones where I am back in an earlier chapter of my life with my children still young, the days when I had a spare dummy in my handbag. I also have confusing dreams where the past and the present merge and I am in both countries at once, with old fears juxtaposed against new freedom. I do still have the banquet dreams with not enough food for the hordes that converge, as well as having to protect children and animals.

Human beings have attempted to understand and interpret their dreams since time immemorial. In some ancient civilisations "dreams were considered a sacred communication with the divine that could deliver omens of the future." Thousands of years later Freud and Jung believed that dreams depicted our unconscious fears and desires. Modern scientists argue that dreams are a form of survival. This theory is called "threat rehearsal". In a dream one is able to confront primordial threats which then better equip one to confront these challenges in one's daily life. *www.lifed.com.*

Dreams may also serve the purpose of stimulating one to achieve, to explore, to reach one's full potential and to make definitive decisions. For my doggy it may be dreaming about chasing his 'bunny rabbits' (his supreme favourite past time) and for humans it may be to climb the highest mountain, or for a person recovering from a life threatening accident, to take his first step . . .

"I have been having recurring nightmares for nearly a month now—always same theme. I'm back in SA and can't leave, either lost passports, or being in danger, or fearful, always that same feeling of "stuck in fear" and not being able to get back to NZ for whatever reason, I think I'm going to stop following any SA news as its making me paranoid."

Carol Champ NZ

"For the past few months I have been having bad dreams every night; all involving burglary, murder etc. and all in SA. Perhaps it's just delayed PTSD?"

Jurgen Schirmacher Oz.

"I've been having a few home invasion SA style nightmares lately; woken up in a cold sweat and it was far too real for comfort and always worrying about family back home. I've considered that it may be spurred on by our sharing on websites; however I will not give up sharing with amazing folk for all the tea in China. I love our Internet group and empathise with almost each and every post and have shed a tear here and there, but mostly I laugh myself silly and that is a very good thing! It just feels right and I know this is my home away from home."

Linda Fetting USA

"I used to wake up in the morning and have to think where I was, sometimes feeling lost as it was all so unfamiliar."

Liezel Buckenham Oz

"Back in SA, my husband used to have nightmares that our daughters and I were being "attacked" and he was lying in bed paralysed. Since we moved to Oz, he hasn't had one nightmare."

Beryllu Zwaanenburg Oz

"For a year after we arrived in NZ, I had really awful nightmares about being attacked—I would wake up shaking and in a cold sweat. I also had a short spell of sleep paralysis which was quite disturbing. But thankfully all that disappeared after a year."

Janet Rogers Musto NZ

"Before we migrated, hubs used to frequently dream about being attacked. After we migrated I often dreamt of family and friends back home, and it was quite distressing. Now I very seldom remember my dreams, due to a lack of Vitamin B, I'm told."

Debbie Leigh Van der Meulen OZ

THE PURPOSE OF DREAMS: I think that we dream as a way to * unlock riddles in the mind * resolve unfinished business * sequence and order areas of confusion * problem solve * seek a resolution* and find closure. As we sleep, the brain goes into 'computer mode' and tries to 'clean' the brain disc by trying to resolve issues that the mind revisits in the subconscious . . . these can recur for years if they are deep seated enough and there will be triggers from conversations, memories, foods, odours, flavours, places and d*éjà vu* scenarios that will ignite the brain to revisit and re-attempt to find a solution . . . we also dream in metaphors and riddles. *Eve H*

The Consequences of Truth: Post-traumatic Stress in New South Africa
Lynn Burke

"JOHANNESBURG—For years her sleep was plagued with visions of that night, and when she woke up in a cold sweat, she could still see the four white men, running toward her, grabbing for her, spreading her legs across the cold floor, reaching out, strangling her . . ."

Burke shares Thandi Shezi, aged 26's, story. A group of policemen had barged into her home in the night, beat her and dragged her off to a jail cell, whilst her two small screaming children watched in horror. The four white policemen then covered her head with a wet sack, attached electrodes to her to shock her body, chained her feet to a table and proceeded to take turns to rape her.

Ten years later she is a counsellor for victims of abuse and says that the physical scars from her torture are still visible on her chest and thighs.

Shezi shares her story with Burke. She was targeted because she worked in an underground movement against apartheid. The police had been misinformed that she was a trained terrorist. Shezi was imprisoned for a year without trial before she was released. She became withdrawn, fearful of men and extremely angry. She felt violent emotions and utterly broken. Shezi bottled up her massive well of emotions, being too ashamed to disclose the rape. Her own child became the victim of her anger, whom she adds she used to beat due to her own deep pain and confusion. This is a symptom of Shezi's post-traumatic stress disorder.

Burke adds, "She is not alone. Many people in this country have suffered great emotional and psychological harm because of apartheid. Many have developed post-traumatic stress reactions, and they need counselling. But South Africa is a country with limited resources, and therapy is a luxury here."

The Truth and Reconciliation Commission which was formed by the new government gave people affected by apartheid the opportunity to tell their stories as part of the healing process, with the then President Nelson Mandela selecting a group of commissioners to serve on the TRC, with Archbishop Desmond Tutu as chairman.

"Victims of past acts of political violence and torture were encouraged to come forward to document the human rights abuses they suffered between March 1, 1960, and May 10, 1994, within or outside South Africa, and perpetrators were invited to apply for amnesty, which would be only granted for full disclosure of crimes proven politically motivated" states Burke.

For some, this process brought a degree of healing. For others it brought old pain and anger to the surface, thus intensifying their emotions. Burke states that it reveals "the degree of ambiguity inherent in reconciliation and the trauma involved in seeking the truth."

Burke reinforces that PTSD is not a phenomenon that is new (or unique to South Africa.) Though the diagnosis of PTSD was only officially introduced to the Diagnostic and Statistical Manual of Mental Disorders and adopted by the American Psychiatric Association in 1980, the condition has been around from time immemorial. Burke reports that in the American Civil War it was called "soldier's heart" or "melancholia," in World War I, it was referred to as "shell shock" and in World War II, it was known as "combat neurosis." These labels were attached to soldiers returning home from combat, especially ones who witnessed or were exposed to catastrophic violence, who became withdrawn and depressed, and who were likely to panic and react to the sound of a loud noise. Today the diagnosis of PTSD includes the after-effects of stressful events other than war, like rape and violent crime.

In 1997, the World Health Organization issued a study on the Global Burden of Disease. It was found that mental disorders are second after infectious diseases. The consequences of disorders like PTSD are the cost in terms of human productivity and quality of life. Of the thousands of Vietnam War veterans diagnosed with PTSD, 33 % became alcoholic. Many were unable to ever function well enough to pursue a career after the war, so severe were the long term effects of PTSD.

Burke reports that there have been limited epidemiological studies of trauma disorders in South Africa. However, research suggests South Africans, especially blacks struggling to make sense of the tragic and complex historical factors, may suffer from the disorder in numbers far greater than the average.

Burke states that Michael Simpson, a psychologist at the National Centre for Psychosocial and Traumatic Stress in Pretoria, South Africa, has said that PTSD is not accidental, specifically with regards to political prisoners. In November 1997, Simpson reported at a National Health Workshop that torturers deliberately traumatised their political prisoners.

"(If) your cohesive and abusive interrogation (didn't) force somebody to tell you what you wanted to know, at least you could return them to the community . . . sitting shivering in the corner and awake with nightmares all night and no darn use to further the cause that he or she had been fighting for," he said.

Burke states that experts have reported that although a vast number of people who were marginalised due to apartheid currently suffer from few symptoms, others have been so brutalised by the atrocities that they cannot work nor have a meaningful life. Their lives are filled with night terrors, pounding hearts and alarming flashbacks. Other symptoms include a poor short-term memory and severe mood swings. Others turn to glue sniffing or alcohol in an endeavour to drown out the pain. South Africa reportedly has one of the highest rates of alcoholism in the world.

Thandi's Story

"In July 1997, the TRC held a women's hearing in Johannesburg. The hearing began with mournful songs and poems that ended in a burst of applause. Archbishop Desmond Tutu, clad in his signature crimson robe, thanked the reader, saying "we are grateful for whatever it is in our culture that has produced someone like you so that we can talk about our pain, share our laughter and our sadness as well." It was a sentiment Tutu would repeat often throughout the hearings, and revealed his underlying philosophy of reconciliation in South Africa. Blacks, Tutu believes, have a special capacity for love and forgiveness. Tutu then introduced Thandi Shezi. "Mama, thank you for coming today," he said. (Quote Lynn Burke).

Shezi had to share her story with all the gruesome details into the microphone in front of her. When she was finished, she was asked about how the rape made her feel about her womanhood.

Lynn Burke reports that Shezi said that as she was she deeply hurt . . . "There's nobody I've been able to relate the story to. My mom is hearing this for the first time."

"When you lock your past inside your brain and mind, when this thing explodes, your life would be in tatters, like mine for the past ten years," she added. However, the testimony reportedly left her feeling hollow. "You rip open the closed wounds and you are left with a gaping wound."

Post Traumatic Stress Disorder does not have a cure. Sufferers may take anti-depressants, such as serotonin re-uptake inhibitors or tranquilizers, which can reduce anxiety as well as insomnia, prescribed by their medical practitioners. Eye Movement Desensitization and Reprocessing (EMDR) has been used for PTSD.

Healing Memories

Burke reports that it was a few weeks after Nelson Mandela was released from prison when the Anglican priest, Michael Lapsley, opened his mail in the home where he resided in Zimbabwe on April 28, 1990. "He was immediately blasted by a letter bomb hidden inside the pages of a religious magazine. The explosion took out the ceiling of three rooms of his house and ripped a huge hole in the floor. It was a bomb designed to kill. But Lapsley was sitting down when he opened it, and survived the blow, though his life would never be the same. Both his hands were blown off, one eye was permanently destroyed, and his eardrums were shattered."

Lapsley was expelled from South Africa in 1976 by the National Party reports Burke. "He was a white priest ministering to black students at the University of Natal at the time, and became increasingly vocal in his opposition to apartheid after the killing of black schoolchildren during the Soweto uprising."

"In my own view, in the end it was my theology which was a threat to the apartheid state, because my contention was that apartheid was a choice for death carried out in the name of the gospel of life, and therefore it was an issue of faith to oppose it," Lapsley stated.

In 1992, the exiled Lapsley left Zimbabwe to return to live in South Africa. "It was a natural instinct to return and be part of a new phase of struggle, the phase of creating a different kind of society, and my particular contribution was to be a part of the healing of the country."

In 1993 Lapsley co-founded the 'Trauma Centre for Victims of Violence in Cape Town'. He later founded 'The Institute for the Healing of Memories', which provided a platform from which people in trauma can share their stories as part of their healing. Burke believes that small organisations like Lapsley's have played a pivotal role in what she alludes to as 'the emotional clean-up process left by the legacy of apartheid'.

In 1996 Lapsley reportedly shared his story to a packed audience at a TRC hearing.

"I remember pain of a scale that I didn't think a human being could ever experience," he told the commission" I remember going into darkness—being thrown backwards by the force of the bomb" Lapsley reported.

Lapsley reportedly holds former President F. W. de Klerk responsible for his bombing, stating that the bomb could only have been sent with his knowledge. Burke reports that Lapsley wanted an apology and wanted to know what the Nobel Peace Prize winner was doing to assist in the healing of the nation.

"I have not heard from de Klerk; not one word of remorse," an angry Lapsley said, reports Burke.

"The truth commission was like a giant mirror put in front of the country. Like never before in history, the past of a nation was center stage," Lapsley said. But according to Burke . . . "the mirror revealed a country whose wounds have yet to heal, and it revealed the complicated process of reconciliation and forgiveness." . . .

A Specific Mandate

Burke states that although The Truth and Reconciliation Commission had several duties, trauma counselling services was not among them.

Brandon Hamber, a clinical psychologist reported that speaking about the truth at The TRC did not automatically heal one. It was not that simplistic.

"One of the problems with the process is that I think in the beginning we basically spoke the language in which the country had a psyche, and that a country is the same as an individual . . . in that the truth about the country will help heal in the same way we might say that dealing with your own personal truth in therapy might heal you." "The real bottom line is it's very unlikely that your individual healing process, no matter how useful the testimony is to you, is going to correspond with the national process." Hamber reported to Burke. Burke adds that Hamber concurs that repressed pain may in all eventuality lead to later harmful emotional and possibly physical consequences. However confronting the past rather than suppressing and repressing it is crucial.

Burke feels that the mental health profession in South Africa is coloured by racism. She reports that "During the apartheid years, people who were detained by the state went untreated or mistreated for psychological illness. In some cases, psychologists and psychiatrists assisted security police in developing torture methods and psychological warfare. Traditional psychoanalytic thought equated blacks with a rampaging id that threatened to spin out of control without the whites, the superego of South Africa."

"Prime Minister Dr. Hendrik Verwoerd, a psychologist obsessed with the psychiatric eugenic theories developed in Nazi Germany, intensified the system of apartheid. In the 1960s he encouraged scientific societies like the South African Psychological Association to split along racial lines. The resulting segregated organization, the Psychological Institute of South Africa was an active proponent of apartheid until its dissolution in the early 1980s. Indeed, the horrible acts committed under apartheid were, except in rare cases, never part of the country's psychological agenda."

Lynne Burke reports that "The Truth and Reconciliation Commission endeavored to link truth with reconciliation by sifting through a mountain of atrocities committed in the name of politics, picking out the worst ones, and allowing a national audience to learn about them." She states that The TRC sent a strong message throughout the country as well as the world. In this way the 'cloak of denial' was vehemently ripped away. The reality that some people were living in luxury, juxtaposed against others, who were severely impoverished and under extreme threat became amplified.

She added that at the hearings, no one could escape facing hideous truths; about a security officer burning black bodies as he swigged his beer at the fire, or witnessing Desmond Tutu sobbing . . .

Burke reports that it came at a price. "The Truth and Reconciliation Commission was created in December 1995 for political reasons, to bridge the sudden transition from a white, minority regime that reigned with brutality to a black majority democracy that wanted to avoid a massive civil war." Through it, the TRC uncovered many painful memories. For some this brought closure by voicing previously silenced stories; for others deeply entrenched hurts resurfaced. When a nation is under siege though political inequalities, it does not heal overnight. *The ripple effects can take decades.* This is the aftermath of the legacy of apartheid; lifting the lid on a suppressed mass of humanity. SA is a fractured country, almost twenty years into post-apartheid due to a combination of factors.

Burke adds that a developing country like South Africa, when posed with unemployment (exacerbated by illegal immigrants pouring in through the borders to seek a Nirvana in a new democracy), poverty, the HIV/AIDS pandemic, amongst the highest crime rates in the world and on-going political tensions, far too little has been spent on mental health, wellbeing and healing. A nation where more than half the population have had the negative impacts of apartheid affecting their mental well-being have produced a future generation, which does not bode well. Add into the mixing pot . . . greedy newly empowered and liberated leaders with the lack of insight or self-restraint and a lack of generosity of spirit for their fellow man and it spells out what the current status quo is presenting. A nation with a malady. By neglecting the psychology of a disquieted people in a transformative state, the country is now paying the price. As Burke states, South Africa is seeking "the elusive goal of reconciliation."

"There is no easy solution for a country in the midst of rebuilding its foundations, for the past is inextricably intertwined with the present" adds Burke. Social, economic and psychological disparity remains a reality for many. For those who dreamt of a promised rosy future, this has long been dashed. Years of cumulative trauma cannot be arrested or healed overnight. With it has come a country in violent crisis, in which the vast majority of all cultural backgrounds and socio-economic status are impacted.

'The romanticised 'rainbow nation' is but a murky mess of smudged colours on a stretched and buckled canvass . . .' http://journalism. berkeley.edu/projects/southafrica/news/traumaprinterfriendly.html

Hope and Acceptance

Once one knows that one cannot alter the situation and one has travelled the road of grief, one may reach a point of acceptance. One may inwardly psych oneself up by saying, "It's going to be Okay . . ."

Acceptance doesn't necessarily bring happiness with it. It is more a feeling of acknowledgment that it's no longer any use to "rail against the machine". It's a period when one may start reflecting and facing one's predicament, although it may seem unclear, like walking into a dark room and fumbling for a light switch.

It may be a time of needing to problem solve and refocus, while exploring options. It may be equivalent to accepting that one is well and truly stuck on an island and that there is no boat. "Okay so now what . . . ?" The survival instinct kicks in . . . "Well, I may as well build a shelter of twigs and leaves and try and find something edible . . ." Acceptance is like proceeding in life with a Plan B. It's about not giving up and requires immense courage!

Kübler-Ross does not include Hope in her stages. Yet without Hope people are inclined to give up. It is Hope that is a strong force that I know propels me forward. It is about knowing that I cannot see the future and how it will pan out and in not knowing what lies ahead, there is always Hope instead of resignation. If one has no hope then one can become stuck in a state of despair in which one is not yet ready to move towards acceptance. Through Hope we, as survivors, believe in our minds that there is learning to be acquired from this journey, that there is purpose, light and adaptation at the end of the tunnel, and that it is not about utter hopeless futility.

Once one is able to reach that 'aha' moment, it is that empowering instant, like taking charge of one's life again; of taking hold of the steering wheel tiller to navigate one's future across the rough seas, unknown obstacles, new challenges and adventures.

A great proponent of Hope is Viktor Frankl. He wrote the following excerpt while he was in forced labour in a Nazi concentration camp:

We stumbled on, over big stones and through large puddles, along the one road running through the camp. The accompanying guards kept shouting at us and driving us with the butts of their rifles. Anyone with sore feet supported himself on his neighbor's arm. Hardly a word was spoken; the icy wind did not encourage talk. Hiding his hand behind his upturned collar, the man marching next to me whispered suddenly: "If our wives could see us now! I do hope they are better off in their camps and don't know what is happening to us." That brought thoughts of my own wife to mind. And as we stumbled on for miles, slipping on icy spots, supporting each other time and again, dragging one another on and upward, nothing was said, but we both knew; each of us was thinking of his wife. Occasionally I looked at the sky, where the stars were fading and the pink light of the morning was beginning to spread behind dark bank of clouds. But my mind clung to my wife's image, imaging it with uncanny acuteness. I heard her answering me; saw her smile, her frank encouraging look. Real or not, her look was more luminous than the sun which was beginning to rise.

A thought transfixed me: for the first time in my life I saw the truth as it is set into song by so many poets, proclaimed as the final wisdom by so many thinkers. The truth—that love is the ultimate and the highest goal to which man can aspire. Then I grasped the meaning of the greatest secret that human poetry and human thought and belief have to impact: The salvation of man is through love and in love. I understood how a man who has nothing left in this world may still know bliss, be it only for a brief moment, in the contemplation of his beloved. In a position of utter desolation, when a man cannot express himself in positive action, when his only achievement may consist in enduring sufferings in the right way—an honourable way—in such a position man can, through loving contemplation of the image he carries of his beloved, achieve fulfilment. For the first time in my life, I was able to understand the words, "The angels are lost in perpetual contemplation of an infinite glory".

In front of me a man stumbled and those following him fell on top of him. The guard rushed and used his whip on them all. Thus my thoughts were interrupted for a few minutes. But soon my soul

113

found its way back from the prisoners' existence to another world, and I resumed talk with my loved one: I asked her questions, and she answered me in return and I answered . . .

My mind still clung to the image of my wife. A thought crossed my mind: I didn't even know if she were still alive, and I had no means of finding out (during all my prison life there was no outgoing or incoming mail); but at that moment it ceased to matter. There was no need to know; nothing could touch the strength of my love, and the thoughts of my beloved. Had I known then that my wife was dead; I think that I still would have given myself undisturbed knowledge, to the contemplation of that image, and that my mental conversation with her would have been just as vivid and just as satisfying. "Set me like a seal upon thy heart, love is as strong as death."

Viktor Frankl—Man's Search for Meaning (ww.amazon.com/Mans-Search-Meaning-Viktor-Frankl)

Healing

Bronwyn Fox in *Working Through Panic* discusses understanding one's condition as part of the healing process. I call it taking ownership of one's reactions, honouring the feelings and being gentle with one's self.

Other tools include meditation, including breathing techniques and various mind games. In my drama therapy, I use visualisation techniques with my clients, which can facilitate one to visualise a safe, beautiful and tranquil place, to breathe deeply whilst listening to gentle soothing music. Clients are able to reach a point of extreme relaxation close to a state of sleep. Metaphysical healers suggest wrapping oneself in 'white light'.

My other techniques include puppetry, mask making, collage work, journaling, singing, painting, movement to music, role play, colour therapy amongst others. These techniques can be found in my book, "Painting the Soul—A Process of Empowerment."

For more severe trauma it is recommended that one makes an appointment with a doctor and to receive the support of a therapist. It is vital for the client to acknowledge that it is a journey and that time for healing is imperative. A broken arm takes six weeks to heel when swathed in Plaster of Paris. Regrettably one cannot put one's emotionally tattered psyche into POP for six weeks or longer. It is a process with stages, which I refer to it as 'the unpeeling of the onion' . . . with it comes the tears as layer after layer is stripped away to reach the core.

Part of the process of healing is to go through the mourning process, to honour it and understand the genesis and journey of one's deep and sometimes almost bottomless dark pit of pain. One needs to work towards reconciling with one's pain, accepting it as part of one's expression and as part of the 'current self'. Part of the reconciliation process is to be able to respect the pain, embrace the present and plan for the future.

When one is an immigrant one may have left and be in a state of trauma due to being exposed to crime and trauma. Furthermore one mourns the loss of one's country, one's friends and family, one's previous life, the familiar places, routines and one's identity. It is as though one has lost almost every facet and fibre of one's existence. One is essentially stripped down to the naked shell. One has one's inner resources and one's history, one's learned skills, talents and resources removed, and it is as though one has emerged from the chrysalis into a butterfly. One is in an altered state which can either build one up into a deeper being that has evolved and survived the adversity, or else it can break one down into a lesser part of one's former self.

When I first moved to New Zealand mid 2008 I thought that one could literally 'do it alone'. I had the attitude that I had plenty of survival attitude and chutzpah. Four and a half years later I have learnt how connection to others in the same predicament is profoundly powerful. No one can identify with what I allude to as 'the schism in one's soul' expect another who has walked the same arduous road fraught with obstacles: physically, emotionally and logistically. No one else can fully comprehend.

For this reason I developed a strong connection with those whom I could identify with and relate to—other immigrants—and that lead to the tapestry component of the book. It became more of a shared tapestry than of a one dimensional journey of the soul. It has been through the compelling, transparent and sometimes heart-wrenching sharing of others that I have had the incentive and the courage to make my screeds of notes and pieces of poetry in my pockets a reality. In our sharing, we've been able to support one another's low moments and offer immeasurable support, humour, light hearted banter and sometimes ridiculous humour with one another across planet earth in various ways.

Reflecting, journaling and blogging are excellent ways of keeping tabs on one's emotional state and being able to monitor that healing is taking place. If one has been exposed to severe trauma or suffered deep grief leading to migration, and/or due to emigration, one will be travelling the journey towards the light. Most people do. Some find that there is one too many an obstacle or challenge and return 'home'. Immigrants have generally said that it has taken them two to three years to feel settled and to establish a new sense of belonging. Some may take longer and some may never feel a true sense of integration. I am still learning to feel that sense of totality or inner integration. Despite loving my new land and with it the enormous sense of safety and inner peace which greatly reduces my feelings of anxiety, my psyche remains severed in two. I have children and grandchildren in both countries separated by a vast ocean. I am sure that if one leaves with all one's children, one far more easily integrates.

Kabta-Zinn's book *Coming to our Senses* highlights the fact that we are sentient beings and that in embracing our place within the world we need to be in touch with our senses. I discovered that in my healing from the grief of leaving a life behind and by entering a new life, that my senses were vibrantly alerted as though I had a new awareness of everything around me. As I mentioned this was part of my 'metaphorical rebirth'. I noticed colours and textures in a new way. I noticed a myriad greens—the ferns nestled against the volcanic outcrops. I heard new sounds—the call of the Tui and living close to the sea for the first time ever, the calls of seagulls became a familiar part of my new sensory repertoire. I listened to new accents and found myself misinterpreting what others said if I didn't pay close attention to their intonation. I smelt new odours. These become imprinted in my new memory bank. The smell of A New Zealand coffee. The smells of the ocean—different from the odours of the African ocean, new smells, but not the delirious smell of rain on dry dust. I tasted new flavours that I had never tried before—Fejoa fruit and Surimi . . . I played a game with myself which I do to this day "Notice something new today that you didn't see yesterday" . . . it heightened my awareness. It taught me to see a new world with new eyes, to drink in a new chapter. I noticed a lack of barbed wire, high fences and gates. I noticed the horses had horse blankets on to shield them from the cold and the wetness. I noticed different things and still do each day that I live here.

"I have been very blessed—but a lot of the time it is what you make it—there came a point where I decided I didn't enjoy being sad and longing for a past life, and the only person that could change that was me, so I changed the mind-set, and took each challenge with open arms, and each obstacle became a stepping stone to success! It is what you make it, and of course sometimes there are things that will try to break you and sometimes even things that can't be overcome—but it's how we deal with it that counts and shows and builds true character."

CB—New Zealand

Spirituality

One's religious beliefs or spirituality are powerful tools as part of one's healing from trauma. Irrespective of whether one's belief system is invested within the principles of Buddhism, Christianity, Hinduism, Islam, Judaism, or other, one will be able to find some strength and happiness through the investment of one's spiritual being.

Richard Schoch's book *The Secret of Happiness* discusses various religious paradigms which can assist the individual in pursuit of happiness. Moreover, he invites one to discover enlightenment by understanding philosophical and religious journeys by exploring and respecting others' belief systems, not only one's own. In this way the mind is broadened and one is able to better understand the world; others and the self.

I believe that immigrating offers one the opportunity to remove oneself from one's possibly previous parochial mind-set and to recognise that one may, in moving to a new land, be immersed in a new environment which embraces other religions. It is thus best to understand these, rather than to shun, judge or fear them.

As I write this, it is the Chinese Festival and the celebration of the Year of the Dragon. Having many Asians in my newfound country means a respect of them and an attempt at better understanding their belief systems, language and culture. New Zealand is termed a bi-cultural society comprised of Maori and *Pākehā* (NZ Europeans). Within that framework, it is a richly diverse and multi-cultured land, made up of people with many different religious affiliations, languages, cultures and backgrounds. It is a land of many migrant souls all seeking spiritual sustenance in one way or another, whether consciously or unconsciously.

I do believe that in this day and age too much emphasis is on material wealth; being in the comfort zone and having immediate hedonistic gratification, which may be interpreted as superficial happiness. I have spoken to many immigrants. Many feel that in migrating they changed their value systems, were less influenced by material existence and became more focused on family quality time and on their spiritual growth, often due to the adversity which they encountered along the journey, with its pitfalls and obstacles to overcome en route, combined with the deeper need to rely on the family infrastructure as a support system, partially due to a degree of alienation from the wider community. Many migrants have shared with me that they've learnt to have patience and to have hope, and that they became emotionally stronger and more resilient once they'd overcome their personal anger, grief, shock and sense of deep loss.

Whatever our symbolic or real journey is comprised of, whatever knowledge or enlightenment we seek, and whatever our personal experiential quest is, we finally strip off the layers and discover the naked inner self. It is in knowing, accepting, loving and forgiving the self, in assisting and empathising with others, and in having optimism and spiritual stamina to face challenges with courage and fortitude that we may find the alchemy of happiness along the course of the journey; whichever course, pilgrimage or odyssey we opt for and pursue.

A man asked Lord Buddha "I want happiness."
Lord Buddha said first remove "I" that's ego.
Then remove "Want" that's desire.
See now you are left with only "Happiness".

Forgiveness

I find it interesting that world religions all have forgiveness as a central tenet, and yet forgiveness is what humans have so much difficulty with. In Buddhism, emphasis is made of loving kindness, compassion, sympathetic joy and composure to avoid experiencing resentment in the first place. In Christianity, forgiveness is part of peace-making, as well as reconciling with God and humanity. In Hinduism reparation for wrongdoing can result after asking for forgiveness. Prayaschitt, which is similar to karma, is the effects of one's deeds on one's own and on others' lives. Islam teaches that forgiveness needs some repentance from those asking for forgiveness, while Judaism teaches that if the person is sincere in his or her apology for hurting one, one is obliged to forgive. From a medical perspective, it is proven that people who forgive are healthier than those who hold on to anger. From a psychological perspective, forgiveness is perceived to be a process. It cannot happen instantaneously as it requires emotional healing to occur.

I believe that forgiveness is the only positive outcome of any two-way conflict. There are wise people like Nelson Mandela who have the capacity to forgive after being imprisoned for half his life time for fighting for the freedom and emancipation of the people who were subjugated due to their skin colour. Burdens can more easily be lifted when both parties review their egos. An inability to forgive is a tragic indictment on the self, which I imagine can only reflect elements of fear, prejudice and vulnerability. *What a great world it would be if we all trusted and forgave more, and shook hands more often!*

Uncertain Identity

Spellman's book of the same title *Uncertain Identity* is about international migrations since the mid-1940s. He refers to Africa as '*The Displacement Continent*'. In reading Spellman's book it is astounding to discover that although the population of Africa is a mere 13 % of the global population, some 30% of refugees in the world hail from Africa, plus 60% of its displaced people. Africa thus has the largest 'mobile population,' as well as the most people who can be termed 'involuntary immigrants'.

A combination of problems can be highlighted as contributing to the tragedy of Africa. Years of European colonialism, which dislocated traditional blueprints was followed in various countries by independent mismanagement. These factors have been cited as contributing to Africa being a fractured continent in so many ways.

The scourge of HIV/Aids is believed to have had its genesis in central Africa. "Aids is caused by the human immunodeficiency virus (*HIV*), which originated in non-human *primates* in *Sub-Saharan Africa* and was transferred to humans during the late 19th or early 20th century" (Wikipedia). Refugees and displaced people, migrant labour, the move from rural to urban areas, war torn areas and human trafficking have all contributed to the spread of the pandemic. One of the ways of spreading the virus has been due to highway prostitution from Central Africa to the harbours along major transport routes.

Seventy percent of the world population infected by Aids is reportedly in Africa. Spellman argues that despite massive efforts to uplift Africa by many economic and health organisations, that the pandemic creates a struggle for the continent's predicament to inspire hope.

Demographics
South Africa

1950—Europeans constituted 21% of the South African population of 12 million.

2011—The population of South Africa had grown to approximately 49, 900 million with the African population making up 79.4% of the population, the remainder being made up of the other cultural groups (European 9.2%, Coloured 8.8% and Indian 2.6%).

2012—Demographic data:

Population 48,810,427 (July 2012 est.)

Note: estimates for this country explicitly take into account the effects of excess mortality due to AIDS; this can result in lower life expectancy, higher infant mortality, higher death rates, lower population growth rates, and changes in the distribution of population by age and sex than would otherwise be expected. **Net migration rate:** 6.22 migrants/1,000 population

Note: there is an increasing flow of Zimbabweans into South Africa and Botswana in search of better economic opportunities (2011 est.)

HIV/AIDS—adult prevalence rate: 17.8% (2009 est.)

HIV/AIDS—people living with HIV/AIDS: 5.6 million (2009 est.)

HIV/AIDS—deaths: 310,000 (2009 est.)

Ethnic groups: African 79%, white 9.6%, coloured 8.9%, Indian/Asian 2.5% (2001 census).

Languages: IsiZulu 23.82%, IsiXhosa 17.64%, Afrikaans 13.35%, Sepedi 9.39%, English 8.2%, Setswana 8.2%, Sesotho 7.93%, Xitsonga 4.44%, siSwati 2.66%, Tshivenda 2.28%, isiNdebele 1.59%, other 0.5% (2001 census)

http://www.indexmundi.com/south_africa/demographics_profile.html

"South Africa's population grew by 15.5%, or almost 7-million people, in the space of 10 years to reach a total of 51.7-million in 2011, according to the country's latest national census. The results of census 2011, released in Pretoria on Tuesday, show the country's population standing at 51 770 560 in October 2011, when Statistics South Africa

deployed over 150 000 enumerators, co-ordinators and supervisors in the country's third population count since democratic elections were first held in 1994. The 2001 census had counted 44.8-million South Africans, a 10.4% increase over the 40.5-million counted in 1996."
http://www.southafrica.info/about/people/census-301012a.htm

Zimbabwe

Spellman reports that Europeans made up 5% of the population of Zimbabwe in the 1950s. Zimbabwe had European minority rule in which many Africans were displaced. In 1980 Rhodesia held elections. Robert Mugabe became the country's leader under The African National Union Party. Thousands of Zimbabweans of all cultural groups have fled from Zimbabwe due to Mugabe's dictatorship and associated political repression.

2012—Demographic data:
Population 12,619,600 (July 2012 est.)
Note: estimates for this country explicitly take into account the effects of excess mortality due to AIDS; this can result in lower life expectancy, higher infant mortality, higher death rates, lower population growth rates, and changes in the distribution of population by age and sex than would otherwise be expected.
Net migration rate: 23.77 migrant(s)/1,000 population *note:* there is an increasing flow of Zimbabweans into South Africa and Botswana in search of better economic opportunities (2011 est.)
HIV/AIDS—adult prevalence rate: 14.3% (2009 est.)
HIV/AIDS—people living with HIV/AIDS: 1.2 million (2009 est.)
HIV/AIDS—deaths: 83,000 (2009 est.)
Ethnic groups: African 98% (Shona 82%, Ndebele 14%, other 2%), mixed and Asian 1%, white less than 1%
Languages: English (official), Shona, Sindebele (the language of the Ndebele, sometimes called Ndebele), numerous but minor tribal dialects.
http://www.indexmundi.com/zimbabwe/demographics_profile.html

Weaving the Tapestry . . . Expats' Tales—*Migrants-Refugees-Rootless and Rooted*

A tapestry can't be rich and exotic if it isn't embroidered and lovingly stitched together to incorporate rich hues and textures. The best tapestries are the ones with errors in the stitching, the design or pattern, to reveal that they are handmade and not mechanically produced and replicated in thousands on a production line . . . this is a tapestry of shared tales, each portraying a personal story as part of the Diaspora odyssey from Africa.

I don't believe that one can leave a country one was part of for sixty odd years and ever really settle to the newly adopted land

Ant Hemming

My footprints were left in the sands of South Africa . . . winds and tides have physically removed them . . . they are still there in my mind's eye and may be trodden on unknowingly by our children and their children.

It was a sacrifice for us oldies, as our family were deciding on a new Life. Some have moved, some haven't.

I have underlying feelings of guilt and sadness. On my odd visit back I have bumped into many friends and colleagues which become very treasured events . . . doesn't happen here where I am a stranger to all.

'I float above myself,
In the mall an elderly man wearing a sad mask;

Is he lost I ask?'
I couldn't express my thoughts better than has Barry Levy;

> 'So, yes, I am convinced we who have left South Africa . . . have become a "tribe" who will never truly know ourselves, never truly be whole, never truly know our land—except perhaps in death when, despite the coldness of the soil that we never really came to know, we may yet, at last, be warmed by the spirit as it returns home.'
>
> Barry Levy

The Passion and Pain of Africa

As I write this book; read others' 'scatterling tales' and patch the book together, my emotions dizzily spin 360 degrees. There are days that I almost loathe Africa, feeling as though she put a spell on us—betrayed us by imploring us to leave, yet tried to beguile us back with her magnetic vortex. There are days where I'm fraught with guilt, anger or pain. There are days I miss home and all that it signified for me; have a cavernous yearning to be back in my 'regular life' like turning the clock back with the click of a switch, closing out any of the truths that chased me away in the first place. That is the life of a migrant. Until the next tragic story which galvanises why one left, or at any rate makes one feel one isn't insane to have made this choice as a pathfinder.

Leaving—Ikey from Canada states in *Expat Confessions* that "The reason why people decide to leave South Africa and become expats is often inextricably linked to a particular event in the country's history." He adds that if one asked any expat what had 'pushed them over the edge' there would have most likely been a 'tumultuous' event.

Returning—As Tom from Johannesburg, South Africa states in *Expat Confessions* "Some expats just weren't made to be expats forever. At some point they decide to go home, for reasons that are either good or bad, profound or not well thought out at all, impulsive or drawn out."

I am back in Africa to babysit my precious grandkids when I write this . . . June 2012

There's a stillness hanging over the day. Nature's way of being in repose and reflecting until spring's burst of renewed life of blossoms and stormy skies.

Today the sky was a stone-washed hazy translucent blue, with insidious patches of pinky-grey winter smoke. The golden grass basked in the frozen moment; static and brittle. The miasma from burning *koppies* shrouded the vista from any brilliance. Otherwise nature felt endlessly still . . . I soak in the luminescent sunlight, the pastel sky and winter caramel—gold's and biscuits. A shockingly red poinsettia, a vibrant amber berry, or the orange on a statuesque aloe in flower, adds depth and contrast to the washed out hues of the hazy day.

It's a good time to visit Africa; to imbibe the sun's rays arching across opaque sky, while relishing the winter blandness after the rich greens and azure blues of New Zealand . . . Contrast! Ah, we thrive on it. That's what is offering me pleasure—the bits of Africa we yearn for when we are so far away—the balmy winter sunshine over dry ancient earth . . . It is dusk now. The Hadedas bellow as they fly to their nesting grounds. Then the electricity dances, flickers and dies. I find my trusty box of Lion matches next to the waiting candle . . .

I am in love with Africa's winter sun and hues, and with my sons and their families, which largely cancels out some of the negative elements I've witnessed. I ponder and come to my own conclusions . . . when here as a tourist or an expat, one can so effortlessly revel in the African-ness of Africa. The messy verges, the broken roads, pavements and shoddy buildings, dangerously bent over electricity poles, broken cars with malfunctioning lights, crowded malls, unsavoury ablutions and traffic light vendors who foist themselves at one are part of the package of the landscape. One can see past it to newer buildings being erected and positive initiatives like volunteers who pick up the garbage and take on the task to maintain the pavements outside their shops, and many caring organisations who are engaged in astounding gestures of tireless and dedicated service to care for abandoned and dying children, the fragile, ill and elderly, as well as animal rescue, notably 'Save the Rhino.'

Shouting pedestrians sauntering on littered pavements to queue at taxi ranks, high fenced enclosures, unkempt vistas creates the notion that some of it needs to be rescued as it's precariously held together by a thin veneer. Each time I return I see areas of deterioration and decay encroaching like a slowly moving glacier and other areas which signify attempts at salvaging, or which indicate progress. But then I wonder, is it true, or just my imagination?

It's a funny thing, Southern Africa. It's the type of place one can't make predictions about. It's a place that has backbone, people of amazing fortitude and a hardy resilience. I, for one, can't even start to speculate 'what will happen next' . . . there are so many variables to ponder on. All I know is that both Zimbabwe and South Africa have been presented with multitudes of historical and political challenges over millennia. There remains a mixture of reality, fiction, predictability, miracles and unexpected surprises.

Knowing that mine is a brief encounter means that I can cherish the sunshine along with the idiosyncrasies, without trying to comprehend what a quick solution would be. I don't feel the same gut fear I encountered living here 4 years ago. In the small area I've frequented this past month, all has felt relatively safe, though when I read the newspaper I feel as though I'm wrapped in an illusion; the comfort zone of my mind . . .

For the Love of Africa—Not Going Anywhere in a Hurry—
Amos van der Merwe

When we hit that sandy patch just north of Savuti, I just know that we are in trouble. It is an unbearably hot day and I have to keep the old Defender's revs down to the minimum: the temperature gauge keeps on rising towards the red line all the time. I know I should have checked the oil in Maun, but we had to make up time after I had to shop for the socks I forgot to pack.

Of course, the trick is to keep momentum, follow the tracks and allow the front wheels to find the direction of least resistance. To do that, I can't afford to slow down.

Not even half-way through the sand, I slow down. More accurately, the vehicle comes to a halt, wheels spinning while the chassis sighs to rest on the high wall of sand between the tracks. Not all the lights on the dashboard still work, but those that do, glare accusingly at me. The needle is on the other side of the red line, but I don't have to look at that—the steam from under the bonnet is proof enough.

"You should have kept momentum." My wife is an expert on such situations. "Why did you stop?" Sometimes I think she would have had an excellent career as an interrogator; maybe even a forensic expert. She has 20/20 vision in hindsight and her sarcasm can rust the paint off a tanker at fifty paces.

"I suppose you could have done better?" Not the right approach under the circumstances, but I'm desperate not to let her win this one. After All, we did run out of ice last night and half of the wine bottles broke on the way from North Gate. A man can only take so much . . .

"You shouldn't have geared down." It's a flat statement delivered with the conviction of a nuclear physicist about to split an atom. "It's a matter of simple logic: you slow down, you create a little wall of sand around the wheels. Allow that to accumulate, and you've got a mountain to climb. You should have known that."

Of course I knew that.

"And driving on this stupid road in the middle of the day is crazy. We should have gotten away earlier." I know what is coming: I should have packed up last night. While I was considering doing that, I found the bottle of Jack hidden behind the spare wheel. I think my singing irritated her. "If we got up with first light—and Lord knows I tried waking you up—we could have been over this bit long before the sand became so warm. But no! Mister Hangover insisted that we were on daylight saving time. 'Everybody does it in Botswana', you said. We were the last to leave the camp. You allowed the others to trample this grotty piece of road to powder before we had to pass this way! Now get out—and get us going." She folds her arms like the time I suggested we send her mother away for a long trip to Siberia.

I get out, knowing it is useless. While I was looking for the Jack, I realised I had forgotten the jack. I know it is my mistake. She made a list of essentials, so when I ticked off 'Jack', I packed the one most important to me. I should stop allowing her to make these lists. I mean, who would have guessed 'pegs' meant the things to keep the tent upright, and not the washing on a line? And try to tell her that in the middle of the night, when the tent comes crashing down for the sixth time? She can be very unreasonable sometimes.

Trying to seem busy getting us unstuck, I peek below the Land Rover. The vehicle may as well have been on the lift at Tiger Wheels:

the tyres are suspended above the sand, with the chassis resting happily on the soft sandy bed.

"I'll need a bit of help," I say lamely. "Maybe you can push?"

I get the same reaction as when I told her I forgot to pack the chairs—absolute disbelief.

"Me? You're talking to me? You get us stuck in the middle of nowhere, and you expect me to solve the problem? No way, mister, you caused this . . . this . . . es-aich-one-T. No go make a plan before I get fed up." She's really a mild-mannered, kind person; once you get to know her. Never swears. Never. Maybe she'll spell it, but she won't say it. And I've seen her being this fed up only once before, which was rather scary. That was last holiday, when I forgot to bring the tent.

The funny thing about this part of Botswana is that you have an abundance of wild life and a scarcity of rocks. After my initial search for something to wedge in below the wheels, I find refuge on the roof rack. The lone lion seemed mildly interested in an easy meal until my wife started shouting at it. Cats are hugely intelligent. They sense the mood in a specific situation quite accurately. This lion chose the open *veld* above my wife's use of English. Wise lion . . .

Knowing that the lion got off lightly and I might be next in line, I renew my search for suitable wedge material. The dry wood under the trees would have to do.

About an hour later, I am ready to initiate Operation Unstuck. With all the wheels propped up with branches of varying sizes, I give myself at least a sixty percent chance of survival. Giving my wife one of my attempted overconfident smiles, I start the engine release the clutch—and watch in utter amazement as the pieces of wood get scattered all over the veld.

"Thank you, Einstein." I'm not sure where she gets these quotes from—it must be genetic. I know better than to tell her it's no problem.

It takes another half-an-hour to collect the wood again, stack it under the wheels, and be ready for Attempt Two. This time, I've got the advantage of experience.

"L-l-listen," I say firmly, "y-you have to get out and push. But you won't be alone, see? I'll put the Landy in low-range, diff-lock, 4x4. I'll start the engine with my right hand, while standing outside the vehicle and holding down the clutch with my left hand. When the engine idles, I'll release the clutch and help you push. I-I'm sure it'll work."

Hell, everybody knows that an idling Land Rover can climb mountains in low range. Once these vehicles get a grip on any surface, they keep on going. It must have been my pleading voice, but she makes a *harrumph* sound, gets out and takes up position behind the vehicle.

"Ready?" I shout to make sure we coordinate our efforts.

"Get on with it, you moron!" I take that as a yes.

Starting the engine, with my left hand depressing the clutch, is easier than I anticipated. Now, applying all my weight against the open door, I release the clutch.

For a while, nothing happens. I push with all my strength, shouting at the wife and cursing the bloody sand. And then . . . the wheels grips and my trusty Landy starts moving forward—at an alarming rate. Now, if you haven't travelled through that bit of Botswana, you won't understand about that sand. It not only traps vehicles—it tends to slow people down, as well. My wife falls forward, spoiling her mascara in the sand where the hot and oily differential rested only a few seconds before. I try running after the vehicle—I swear I do—but the thick sand slows me down to a pace most tortoises will find amusing. I watch as my Defender slowly winds her way down the road, steadfastly on track to reach Kasane by nightfall.

Being a considerate husband, I sit down next to my wife to offer my commiserations. I know how much cosmetics cost these days. She's wonderful: she proves that the mix of oil and sand doesn't have to have an effect on the flow of words. She can be rather eloquent if she puts her mind to it.

There's nothing I can do. With a lion that considers this to be part of his territory, it'll be a question of time before he'll want his dinner served. Quite frankly, disappearing down the cat's throat might be a nifty way to escape the dismemberment my wife is describing. I let her ramble on a bit—it's good for her to get the aggression channelled.

"What now, you imbecile? You're going to phone somebody, or what?"

You expect me to tell her my phone is in the Landy—and that there is no reception in this area? You think I'm completely stupid?

So I get up to walk back to the camp. It's only eight or nine kilos through lion infested veld—what can I lose?

And then the miracle happens. From the Kasane side of the track, my dear, beloved, trusted Land Rover comes trundling along. At first I think she's taken pity on me, but then I notice the khaki-clad driver.

"I couldn't believe it," the ranger says as he hops out, "a Land Rover driving itself! Wow! So I stopped my vehicle, allowed the Landy to pass, and sprinted after it. I reckoned there must be some people back here, desperately wanting their vehicle back?" If I wasn't so relieved, I would have felt bad at him laughing so much.

The Chobe River Lodge offers comfortable beds, great food and warm water in the showers. We sit under the big trees, watching the boats on the river as the sun sets. I'm on my third Zambezi Lager, waiting for the guillotine to drop.

"We can cancel the camp at Kalizo," My opening move is to prevent further damage. "From here on, we can stay in lodges, eat in restaurants and if you want, we can fly home."

The intricacy of the female mind is a puzzle most men never unravel. She has just had a bath, smells of shampoo and girly stuff, and has put on the new Chobe T-shirt I just bought her. The mascara-and-oil mix had a bad influence on her temperament, but the recent change in scenery obviously improved the situation.

"What? Cancel camping? Restaurants? Fly home?" She eyes me critically. "You have been taking your malaria pills, have you? Are you feverish? We go camping for the fun and the adventure, and you want to stay in lodges? Have you completely lost that tiny little thing you call a brain?

No, tomorrow you get the pegs, fill the Landy with oil, buy some chairs and be back at the room—with breakfast—at nine, sharp. You know I love camping; I'm not going to let you spoil this trip . . ." I grin happily. "You do understand English, don't you?"

Sometimes my friends express amazement at my tolerance. They think I'm crazy to go camping, take all the flak, and still remain the kind and loving person I am. If they knew me better, they'd be queuing up to tag along. Of course, I'll never allow that.

They're just not reliable enough.

Cowboys don't cry   *Alf Hutchison*

My old and dear friend Frank Du Toit always used to remind me "Alf, cowboys don't cry; not in front of their horses anyway".

We had just disembarked from the chopper after a sortie into Mozambique; a police Land Rover had been blown to Hell by

some natives at Kanyemba. The mood back at base cam
sombre. Suddenly I remembered that one of our 5th Ba.
had brought his bagpipes.

After a few words in the chopper pilot's ear he was again
airborne, this time with our lone Piper. The pilot was the best,
as all Rhodesian pilots were, and he dropped our Piper on top of
'Cleopatra's needle', a huge needle like granite monolith towering
many, many meters above the beautiful autumn leaves of the
M'sasa trees. The helicopter was silent a few meters from us as the
Pilot came to join the entire compliment of soldiers to witness the
spectacle from our hilltop base.

As the sun touched the horizon, silhouetting our lone Piper (about
a kilometre away), the haunting melody of 'Amazing Grace' drifted
across the entire valley on the cool evening breeze.

I had just returned from the Edinburgh Tattoo, August 2006,
and the lone Piper there was unbelievably brilliant, but he couldn't
hold a candle to our Piper; on that unforgettable eventide he played
magnificently. If cowboys don't cry, as Frank insisted, I can tell you for
certain that battle weary and hardened Rhodesian soldiers do; even in
front of their horses.

My very dear friend Frank died on his farm in Raffengora some
time ago, but I will remember that day we shared with that piper as
long as I live; the day when we wept openly for all the friends we had
lost; for a country we loved; for a war we believed in, but which tore us
apart inside.

The Day Rhodesia Died   *Alf Hutchison*

A man stood on the pavement in Main Street, Bulawayo; across
the wide road from him were hundreds of people all anxiously waiting.
The man's son had his young arms wrapped around his father's bare
leg; dressed as he had for many years in camouflage shirt, shorts and
'*vellies*'.

Suddenly there was a deathly hush . . . they were coming. A faint
methodical crunch, as hob-nailed boots striking the tarmac surface
with exacting precision became audible. With every precise step the
crowd's anticipation grew. But no band, no singing . . . people looked
quizzically at one another . . . what was happening?

The sound of their boots on the hot tar echoed off the buildings. It seemed unnatural as the band appeared followed by the banner bearers and the troops.

"Dad!" the little boy cried out "Why aren't the soldiers singing like they always do?"

The words had not left the young lad's lips when a rich baritone voice sang out the opening introduction to their famous song 'Sweet Banana' *"OOH, EHH, EE, OH, EE, OH"!!*. And as the base drummer beat the pace the entire battalion burst forth in song **"A-B-C-D-HEADQUARTERS, I WILL BUY YOU A SWEET BANANA"**

The man stooped down and lifted his son onto his battle weary shoulders. "Don't ever forget this sight my boy; these are some of the finest fighting men in history".

They marched past singing their now famous regimental song for the very last time; the Rhodesia African Rifles was no longer . . . the legacy of their fighting superiority gone . . . but a legacy which will live on in the hearts of all Rhodesians forever.

There wasn't a dry eye on the streets of Bulawayo that day as they marched past singing **"BURMA, EGYPT AND MALAYA . . . .** *IT WAS THERE THAT WE FAUGHT AND WON"*

"Why are you crying Dad?" asked the young lad, truly alarmed at seeing his soldier father in tears.

"Oh my dear son" he answered, as he pressed him close to his chest; choking back his tears, "You are just too young to realize what is happening here; I fought shoulder to shoulder with these men; they are proud Rhodesians, they are fearless Rhodesians; they are the greatest fighting force ever to come out of Africa, and now they are history."

Within a few minutes the streets were back to normal and the man walked back to his car with his son on his shoulders; his head bowed to the ground, reflecting on the certain fact, that this day, the day that the R.A.R handed over their colours and disbanded . . . was the day that Rhodesia died.

The Love and Hate of Africa   *Claire Gifford, NZ*

Where to start?—Maybe an apology if I offend anyone in telling my story. True feelings and thoughts are what are required, so here goes . . . I was born and bred in the Transvaal. I married Gary in

1990 and moved to Newcastle, KwaZulu-Natal where we lived until we immigrated to New Zealand in November 2000. We have two children, Greg, 21 and Andrea, 18.

Gary was born in Chipinga, Rhodesia now Chipinga, Zimbabwe, in 1965. His great grandfather Alfred Samuel Gifford, the leader of the Edenburg trek, which left South Africa in 1894, had led them to Melsetter in Gazaland. The family had three farms, Wolf's Crag, Wolverhampton and Halvetia in the Chipinga District, which is in Manicaland, Zimbabwe.

My first fear of Africa would probably have started way back in little old Volksrust in 1977 when terrorism was rife. I remember being at school and having "bomb" drills in class. Boys were to fall to the left of the desks and girls to the right—good old Volksrust High School! Feelings which still conjure up unease and sticks with me today were the words "*Rooinekke sit voor!*" (Rednecks sit in front). Volksrust was an Afrikaans town and we were only a handful of English kids. We were given English text books but almost all our classes were conducted in Afrikaans.

I remember in about 1982, a young boy heading to school had his legs blown off by a landmine detonated by his vehicle at the farm gate and sirens in town with a bomb going off at the local hardware store, *EZ Handelshuis*. The magistrate's court was cordoned off and the bomb squad blew up a "strange" package. I remember the police walking up and down the roads with mirrors on long handles searching under cars for bombs. A story told by a policeman was about a man being stopped at a road block. From the stress of this interrogation, he'd forgotten the combination code to open his suitcase, and had to sit there until he remembered the code so that they could do their search. The same policeman landed in hospital after shooting a hole in his foot while accidentally discharging his weapon at another roadblock. Scary stuff I thought at the time, but I was to discover a lot worse a few years later.

In the middle eighties I met Gary. I was intrigued that he came from Zimbabwe—me being a country bumpkin! Gary went to South Africa to get a trade to fall back on if things in Zimbabwe 'turned to custard'. He'd studied at Durban Technikon and took a job at Iscor in Newcastle. After dating for a while, I was taken on a road trip to *Zim* to meet "the parents".

A few kilometres from the farm one night we got a puncture—Gary was very uneasy; got out, fixed it in record time and we sped off . . .

On asking him what that was all about, I got a cool "A few years ago the terrorists would hide out in the trees there and ambush cars as they slowed to go through the corners and narrow road." Okay, so maybe this visit wasn't quite what I was expecting.

A couple of days later—noises and lights were seen on the farm at night. I was alone with Gary, his dad and brothers. I was told to stay put, stay away from doors and windows and not move around. They took off with guns and disappeared into the night. That sick fear in my gut still haunts me today. They grew up with it and knew no different.

Later on when I could get Gary to talk, he would tell me about when he was little and they drove to school in convoy with army trucks and soldiers escorting them. This little boy of no more than seven saw a soldier shot and killed next to the road. The same little boy jumped from their Landover and rolled into the dirt because that's what you had to do, or else suffer the consequences if your vehicle was blown up. He laughs now and talks about the thorns he had to pluck from his arms and legs. Usually he won't talk. I think it hurts him too much.

Gary's Uncle was shot and killed by terrorists on the family farm while working on his tractor. His Aunty was killed when she drove over a landmine on the road; a farm where they still had to stay on and a road they had to drive on.

Later Gary would tell me about lying in bed at night while at boarding school in Umtali and hearing rocket launches and rockets flying over the school and hearing the explosions as they hit into the surrounding hills; seeing the flashes of light, listening to the sounds. How they were never hit still remains a miracle and I thank God for that.

On one of our subsequent trips up to *Zim*, Gary's mum, Pat and I went to a neighbouring farm for a function. On arriving back home in South Africa we got a phone call from Mum to say how lucky she and I were. Apparently the day after we left to return to SA, they had some very heavy rain and the soil around the cattle grid at the farm gate that we went through, got washed away, only to reveal a landmine! Somehow it makes a Lotto win not that important anymore. We had a very generous portion of good luck on that day methinks!

Moving on—the lull in Zim, Mandela's release and not much change happening all started the thought process. Should we move to somewhere safer, or should we return to Zim to be with the family and try and make a go of it there? Our future? What future ?

Things slowly started getting ugly with the farm take-overs in Zim. It was getting too dangerous to go for visits. Our home in SA was broken into, the police didn't even bother with finger prints. I was almost mugged. I bent down to show my four year old and baby a puppy in a pet shop window and a thug decided to grab my purse out of my hand. I held on and yelled at him. He slowly started walking away, staring at me and laughing; the fear and anger boiled up in my throat.

Gary used to work night shifts when we lived on a farm for a while. When he left for work I'd barricade myself in with the windows, doors and gates locked, load the revolver and feed, bath and put the little ones to bed, the revolver at my side. I'll never forget waking one night, hearing heavy footsteps outside—damn horses had got out. I don't think I ever forgave them. My heart never stopped racing all night!

On moving back into town, I was watching the news on TV one night while Gary was at work. They showed footage of a farm take-over in Zim. The animals were hacked with *pangas*. Those dogs eyes, filled with pain and fear with pieces of raw flesh hanging off them shocked me. I phoned Gary and said, "That's it, we're going". That was the defining moment. Decision made. From there on we started planning our new life.

We had never been to New Zealand and didn't have the money for an LSD ('look, see and decide') trip. We just did it! I downloaded the paperwork and we got all the police clearances and did our medicals. Gary was offered a job in Morrinsville and that was that. Gary came out in October 2000. I stayed to do the last bitty bits, only to have the house sale fall through the day before Gary left. Somehow I managed to get it sold and the kids and I followed a month later.

That gut wrenching feeling when your every last little possession goes down the road in a container on the back of a truck is something I can't describe. Even worse, the heartache of handing over our beloved pets. Noo Noo, our darling Labrador and Sammy the cat—our family broken into bits. I still feel guilty leaving them.

Andrea, our little girl contracted chicken pox a week before we were due to fly. I thought we were doomed, never to see Gary again! Fortunately an acne cover stick sorted out that little problem.

I was terrified to leave. I'd never been on a big plane before and had no idea how immigration, customs and airports worked. A lovely lady befriended me at Jan Smuts (now called Oliver Tambo Airport). I think she saw my desperation and literally took the two little ones and me under her wing and escorted us all the way to NZ, only leaving our sides when she went down the "NZ Citizens only" queue, after placing us in the "other passports queue" at Auckland International Airport.

On arrival at Auckland airport my dear old SA passport's barcode decided to unstick itself and have half on one page and the other on the opposite page. Just great for scanning! *Not!* After numerous phone calls and me very close to tears, we were finally allowed through to customs. Smooth running—never!

Darling little Max beagle decided to pay us a visit and promptly sat down next to me. I'm convinced he had superglue stuck to his bum because he wasn't going to budge for anything! The lovely handler asked if I had anything to declare, which I didn't. She then asked if she could search our bags—which she did. Nothing was found and she put it down to the kids having kept their little kiddy meal containers, which encouraged Max do his duty! I was beginning to think it was an omen that we should never have come to NZ.

Once we arrived in Morrinsville the truth was revealed. Andrea, the seven year old, snuggled up to Dad and said "Look Daddy I brought you a present!" and out came the little butter and jam thingy's off the plane! Max beagle, you have a damn good sense of smell! To this day, whenever we fly anywhere, I double check that our darling daughter hasn't stashed something in her luggage!

After arriving a lot is a blur, though I do remember house hunting. Gary was adamant that we bought straight away or else I'd want to go back, he said. Anyway, someone should have told us you have to take your shoes off when you go into a house. The amount of times we had to untie and tie shoelaces on that first day was horrendous!

Something that struck us was the cleanliness in the streets and no littering. Everyone was doing something. Every time we drove somewhere Gary had to stop so that I could take photos. Roadside goats were my favourites and still are. But house hunting and schooling were first on the agenda.

The kids started school at a local primary school a few weeks before the end of the year. The Headmaster is an angel in disguise. He welcomed us with open arms and made Greg and Andy feel like they had been there all their little lives. Three days in and Greg got chicken pox! When I think back now I laugh, but I remember crying about my little girl not being able to read and me being so scared for my babies. What those poor teachers must have thought of this hideous South

African mother who had lost the plot. Whatever it was, they never said. All they did was listen, encourage and support.

Back to the house hunting! Remember one of my first encounters in Zim—being told to stay put and stay away from windows and doors? Unbeknown to the rest of the family, when looking at houses I always checked that there was somewhere to hide and I'm proud to say I can fit into my pantry and walk-in wardrobe together with a few members of the family—even if it is a tight squeeze!

Finally we found a lovely home and moved in before Christmas. Our container arrived soon after that and what a glorious feeling to see one's "life" arriving on the back of a truck and coming down the driveway! Our trailer, however, was still stuck in Auckland and Gary was sent on his merry way to retrieve it two days before Christmas, because there was no way that we were having Christmas without our tree and decorations!

A humorous story comes to mind. While unloading the container, my eyes nearly popped out of my head. There were two huge characters doing the job, one wrapped a broad strap around him and our fridge/freezer and just casually picked it up, walked inside and asked where to put it! A few boxes later and one asks Gary, "What the f@#ks in this box?" With language like that we thought to respond quite quickly. We checked the list and discovered it was the box with all the *potjies*, cast iron pots and pans and cast steak plates. Knowing the fella wouldn't know what a potjie was, Gary proceeded to tell him it was "African pots". The response was "Don't know what the f@#k that is mate, but it's bloody heavy!" Just love it! Thanks NZ Van Lines—you were awesome!

Another happening that I remember quite vividly—after a week or two of living in our new home, the kids asked if they could go for a walk. I was pretty apprehensive myself, but with a smile and fingers crossed, I sent them on their way. About five minutes later they returned. On asking why so quick, I got the reply "We were too scared Mum". Now, we can't keep them at home!

Never mind that I couldn't sleep at night, either. No burglar bars, no big gates on the doors, no huge locks and even worse, no fence or walls around the property! Now I forget to lock and sometimes find the ranch slider open when I get up in the morning and much to my husband's disgust, more than once have I returned from work at the end of the day to discover that I forgot to push the remote button to close the garage, which in on the road front and jam packed with every last tool, camping equipment, boat, fishing gear etc.

A few years ago we brought Gary's parents out for a visit, hoping they would fall in love with the place and come out and join us permanently, but to no avail. They came, loved the place and went back home. Presently neither Gary nor my family are considering following in our footsteps.

Over the subsequent years, my in-laws have been thrown off their farm in Zimbabwe so many times I can't even count. Their title deeds were "taken" by lawyers, the court cases have been numerous and all to no avail. Kevin, Gary's brother built a cottage on the farm for himself and his family. They never got the chance to move in. It was taken over and stripped of windows, doors and corrugated iron to build "other" houses. Gary's dad was thrown into jail for refusing to leave on another occasion and so it went, year in and year out. There were endless phone calls, worrying about what was happening over there, followed by weeks of not being able to get through and not knowing if they were dead or alive. How we ever got through all that I'll never know, but we're still doing it and somehow you learn to live with that strain, which remains in the back of your head.

Sadly in August 2007, Gary's mum, Pat was killed in a car accident in Pinetown, SA, while she and my dad-in-law were visiting family there. Some idiot skipped a red light. While dad-in-law was recovering from his injuries and arranging the cremation (because Zim didn't have any electricity for cremations!) the bast@#*s once again moved onto the farm, but this time decided to move into the home as well. Dad-in-law was distraught at losing his wife of so many years and just had no fight left in him anymore and let them have it. He never returned to Zim.

From a prosperous farming family and 117 years of living on the land, the love of the soil, the heartache, the blood, sweat and tears, the heritage and history of the Gifford farms are no more, with the family now scattered all over the world. Dad continues to hover between Zimbabwe and Mozambique. Kevin is farming in Mozambique, Wayne is in South Africa, Tammy in the UK and Gary and I, here in New Zealand.

The sadness is our kids have no family here in Kiwiland. The time delays on the phone have meant that that from when they were little they didn't like talking and now being older they feel they have nothing to say, because the family have become like strangers. A few years ago while on a camping trip up North, I found Andy crying in the tent. On asking why, she said that everyone around us had family and we had none. It was something I felt very difficult to deal with and still do. Deep down I know we made the right decision in coming here and giving them a safe future but at what cost? Family after all is everything.

The kids can't remember much about South Africa and have no desire to go back. I would love to go for a visit but even Gary isn't keen. He says there is nothing to go back to. The family aren't interested in coming over either so it's just the four of us. Greg doesn't mind people knowing he is from SA and has numerous SA friends. Andy on the other hand absolutely hates people knowing. I guess we all have our ways of dealing with it. Me—I can't be a proud South African. What is there to be proud of? Eleven years on and I still feel bitter, hurt, angry, betrayed and deceived by a country I once loved.

Andrea used to get most upset and ended up having arguments with new SA immigrants at school because of the continual, "This is better in SA and that is better in SA." Greg, on the other hand just loves people and the whole world with all its people are his friends. Once again just showing how we all handle the big immigration thing differently. As for me; I'm just a fruit loop as you may have picked up by now! I almost feel offended when people pick up on my accent and realise I'm from South Africa. I just want to be a Kiwi so that I can move on and stop looking backwards.

Cape Town Church Massacre

Ozzie and Ian Forsyth emigrated from Cape Town, South Africa with their two year old twins in 1995. One of the primary triggers was the notorious church massacre.

About the Massacre-

The Saint James Church Massacre took place during the evening service on the 25th July 1993 in Cape Town. It was perpetrated by four cadres of the Azanian People's Liberation Army. I remember this monstrous event only too well, although we lived in KwaZulu—Natal, far from Cape Town. Eleven innocent members of the congregation were killed and 58 wounded, whilst they were in prayer.

The four assailants had entered the church armed with M26 hand grenades and R4 assault rifles. One of the congregation who has written a book about the event returned fire with a .38 revolver wounding one of the attackers. Fortunately this led to the attackers' hasty departure, instead of throwing the petrol bombs as planned, which would most certainly have incinerated the entire congregation. Amongst the dead were four Russian seamen who had joined the church's outreach programme.

Several of the church members who were injured or who lost family members in the attacks, as well as Charl van Wyk, who had returned fire on the attackers, later met and publicly reconciled with the APLA attackers. In 1998, the four attackers were granted amnesty by the Truth and Reconciliation Commission. However some of the group were rearrested and imprisoned for ATM heists and a spate of murders.

For Ozzie, what was truly hard was having close friends who attended St James Church, and knowing that it was a congregation of 'left wing' South Africans who were anti-apartheid folk, who were instrumental in building multi-cultured bridges towards healing and reconciliation. On the aftermath of this tragedy, they experienced further murders and attacks on friends, which cemented the decision to leave the country in the best interests of their twins' futures.

Losing Zimbabwe   *Kt Grubb, UK*

I am tired. So tired, so cold. I unlock the front door and look down the hallway into our tiny kitchen. I can't stop my tears. The house seems so claustrophobic; dark, cold, unwelcoming. Despair seeps through me. The sunshine has gone. This is my reality now. I've just returned to England from yet another trip home, and of course it's always hard, saying goodbye and readjusting, but this time its worse; something inside me has broken. The warmth, the sounds, the smells, the smiles of home . . . . All gone. I leave the bags in the hall, pull myself upstairs and lie down on the bed. How did I allow such unhappiness into my life? I think back to when I was a child listening to the grown-ups talk . . .

"The shops! The clothes! You can get anything in England! The daffodils! Primroses, green, rolling hills . . ." "Queues? You won't find them there . . . this place is so *backwater* . . . tssk so annoying! I can't wait to leave Africa and go overseas!"

And leave they do—in their droves. But we stay. This is home. It's the late 70's and I listen to the endless virtues of England—as I grow up in the dichotomy of a war-torn, unrecognised Republic and then a transitional, new African State, and as I take for granted the luxury of domestic help, the swimming pool in my enormous garden, and the endless, warm, sunny days. Despite all these good things, there's a faint sense, even as a small child, that something sinister lurks beneath this charmed life; after all—we are at war—with bad people . . . terrorists! I don't really understand it, but I'm frightened that the terrorists will come to my house. I listen to the news "Security Force Headquarters regrets to announce the deaths of three soldiers in action . . . ." Some of my friends lose their fathers, brothers, uncles to this war. Politics, war, racism, secrets, and hatred—all lie like a carpet of filth under my barefoot, carefree, sunny childhood.

When I am 15 the country becomes a new independent State . . . lots of change. But still people talk of 'overseas' . . . the promise and the abundance of Great Britain. Friends my own age boast of holidays there . . . the UK hovers in front of me like an elusive carrot that I may one day be able to taste!

I plan my trip overseas with a friend. I sell everything for my ticket. My friend backs out at the last minute. I'm on my own. I'm not backing out. I'm going to do this. I need to experience this amazing place for myself.

A week later I'm walking back to my tiny digs in north London, the wind stinging my face like an unrelenting entity that wants rid of me. I am enveloped by disappointment. Is there something wrong with me? The shops and the daffodils are all lovely . . . but . . . it's so bitterly cold; London is huge and impersonal. People look through me. I'm alone so I feel alien; disjointed and a bit frightened, but I try not to show it. I stand under an umbrella staring at the graffiti on the walls by the train station . . . I think of the warmth, the golden light dappled through the trees, the hot, red earth, the wood-smoky smells of Africa. I'm hurrying back to my room for my daily dose of Australian TV soap; I only watch it for the images of sunshine and swimming pools; a break from my grey reality! On the underground I feel lost. I search for something familiar. I naively smile at a black man because he reminds me of home. He does not smile back. At home everyone smiles, despite all kinds of hardship. I decide that English people are all miserable, and it must be because of their weather. I long for the colours and the comforting warmth of home. I am the personification of misery, yet I have another 10 months before my ticket says I can return home.

I flee London for the relative security of my distant Irish family. So now I'm even farther north—Belfast. At least it's a war zone—something familiar! I attempt to embrace Irish life. I get a job at the University. I work in a tiny grey-tiled room with no windows. The IRA plant a bomb at the police station at the end of my road; I have to spend the night in a stranger's house as I can't get back to mine. Another bomb blast nearby while I'm at work and on my way home I pass a row of huge houses with every single window shattered. A week later I miss the warnings on the radio and walk home from work in a hurricane later known as 'the Great Storm of '87'. I spend half an hour clinging to a tree with a stranger, both of us soaked to the skin and utterly terrified. Days later a bomb goes off a mile away when I am going upstairs to bed and the stairs shake underneath me. I sit down on the landing and laugh hysterically. I can't believe I left my beautiful home in Africa for this! What was I thinking?! Ten months inch slowly by and I return to Zimbabwe, vowing never to leave again; never! Africa is home, it's where I belong.

Never say never . . . Ten years later I marry a British man and find myself back in England *only for a year*. We will return to settle in Zimbabwe. Things are different this time. I'm not alone, and it's not forever! But the 'return to settle' never comes . . . It's 1997 and my father writes that things have taken a bad turn. The economy is crumbling. Violence is rife. I have children now, so we are better off in England. I return home to pack up the remnants of my past life. Everyone seems to be leaving. I need to adjust my attitude. I'm looking forward to my new life in England. I'm still Zimbabwean, right? It's for the best. I will embrace the change! I am positive and determined, this time, to be happy out of Africa.

And I try so hard. I give this new life everything I've got. I return home as often as I can, but each time the pain of leaving gets harder. The pull is too strong to ignore. My heart still beats to Africa's rhythms, not my own.

I fly home for the Millennium New Year. Three weeks later, the goodbyes are unbearable. Before the hot January sun has risen, we are driving away and I look back to see my parents inconsolable, as they wave goodbye to their children and grandchildren; travelling thousands of miles away yet again. I realise we are just another family torn apart by political circumstances. Scattered like seeds in the wind . . . . I don't know when we will all be together again.

This is how I reached this point . . . I am lying here desperate to find a way to return home for good. I'm trapped. I feel like I'm serving a prison sentence. Family circumstances dictate that I cannot leave England. Every day is a struggle to beat homesickness. My unhappiness affects my work, my family, my whole life, until it becomes a constant dull ache deep within me. Claustrophobia enshrouds me. I close my eyes every day and I can hear the *msasa* trees whisper in the breeze and feel the sun on my face and hot, red earth beneath my bare feet.

I am told I'm ungrateful; I should appreciate my life in England and stop longing for home. Perhaps it's true; home is not what it once was, it's a different place now; shattered; broken; changed. Most of the people I grew up with have left. I am British now; I have the passport to prove it. I am not a black African, my parents are Irish, so why do I not relate to England and settle here as others do?

The BBC news tells me about the hatred growing in my country. Friends flee for their lives. People shake their heads and commiserate when I tell them where I'm from. The mention of the country's name is synonymous with violence. The country is in turmoil. There is a new carpet of filth in my land. I feel terrible guilt for abandoning my land, my people. I am safe while so many Zimbabweans suffer. It's not right. I travel to London every Saturday for six months to protest outside the Zimbabwean Embassy because it is the very least I can do. It is all I can do.

I quit my job and go to university. I do the degree I have longed for since I was 20. I pour my passion, and tears for my lost country into my work. My research and my art become a kind of therapy easing the frustration and pain of loss. A further degree allows me to explore issues of identity, Diaspora and exile. I find comfort in the research, tiny details; the science of homesickness. I slowly realise how many people in the world face the same loss. I'm not alone, I never have been . . . . I watch other countries in turmoil and feel enormous empathy for the people that have to flee; for the families that are torn apart by dictatorships and war . . . for the millions of people on this planet who struggle to get home and be where they feel they belong. Social networking reunites me with old school friends . . . still so much in common; we all have that special bond that comes of growing up in a unique land—under unique circumstances. My studies and my reunions cement what I have always known deep down—how lucky I am to have had the experience of a childhood in Africa; to be Zimbabwean; and despite everything—I haven't lost Zimbabwe . . . my beloved land is still there, ailing, but not gone. My plans to return will become a reality, and what I have experienced outside the country of my birth has enabled me never to take a moment spent there, for granted. That's got to be a blessing!

The Souls From Nowhere   *Barry Levy, Oz*

'There is no spirit that does not come home'
—Zulu saying.

MAYBE IT'S JUST ME, an old hard-headed South African who used to think he knew all the answers, but after twenty-five years in The Great Land of Oz, The Lucky Country, 'Strailia, the Sun-shining Civilised New World—Australia—news, any news, especially positive news, about South Africa still excites and energises me like hell. Most of all I love to hear of and see our national teams winning.

This might come as a shock to anyone who knew me when I emigrated back in the '80s—it still shocks me sometimes—because I was part of the generation that vehemently supported sports, cultural and political boycotts of all things South African; who hated what we'd become; who spat on foreigners who visited the country. But then along came 27 April 1994, probably the greatest day in South Africa's history, and everything changed overnight. It was like I too, even here in hot and humid Brisbane, was liberated. Where once the country of my birth had been an embarrassment, a great source of shame, I too felt free. Suddenly, that unmistakable South African accent that you encounter from time to time in Australia was no longer grating; it had become something songful and warm, welcoming to the ears. And when I saw South African sports stars taking the field again after decades in isolation, something in my heart became unshackled and soared. It was one of the most satisfying feelings I have ever had: from seemingly detesting every achievement by South Africans to suddenly feeling my heart beat in rhythm with every pulsing movement of my country's sportsmen and sportswomen. I felt like Icarus, only I had wings that could actually fly.

My anti-South African sentiments were, along with the boycotts, one of the unfortunate (but absolutely necessary) drawbacks of the anti-apartheid era. In retrospect, seeing it as a sickness, I was eventually able to give my affliction a name: I diagnosed myself with "Repressed Patriotism Syndrome". I—and, I suspect, many others—had suffered for years from this political disease without even realising it, and when the first fully democratic South African elections took place I was suddenly cured and free. I had become what I secretly was all along: a South African patriot.

When the Springboks took the field in the 1995 World Cup, despite it so obviously still being such a white Afrikaner sport, it took me back to those wonderful primary-school days when I was innocent enough not to question these things and always felt the butterflies mushing in my stomach before any big test match. Without wanting to sound jingoistic about it, I think I had just discovered—or rediscovered—what it was to be a normal human citizen of the world who expresses love for his country. That "we" won in 1995 was an added bonus of deep jubilation; that Mandela, in his Springbok jersey, handled that day with such aplomb and diplomacy was just heart-wrenchingly and profoundly good.

At the same time that my inner patriot emerged from hiding, I became aware, more acutely than ever, of the type of South African who had immigrated to Australia, claiming to reject the apartheid politics of his homeland, and immediately reinvented himself as a Wallaby-supporting Aussie. It was something I had—and still have—major difficulties coming to terms with, and I found it just a little bit funny to hear these ex-South Africans, often not more than "a few months old" in their new country, hollering in their still heavy Seffricen accents, "Go Aussie, go!"

The reality is that Australians being Australians couldn't give an eff who these newly arrived South Africans supported. No matter how much they may scream their heads off for their adopted country, Australians, if they even bother to talk about the game at all (Aussies have a way of remaining absolutely reticent about even the most heart-raising events), will still take the Mickey out of these "Austrailiophile" South Africans for the result—especially if the Boks or the Proteas have lost. A truth I've learnt from 25 years' experience is that you never lose the place you're from, not in the eyes of those who claim the birthright in your new land. Believe me, they will quickly remind you, and keep on reminding you of that place from where you hail. It's an attitude that dismays the hell out of immigrant South Africans, both new and old. "I kept telling them we were Wallaby supporters but they didn't seem to hear" is a frustrated refrain I've heard over and over down the years.

Most quintessentially, to me, both the Australian and wannabe-Australian responses underlie a spiritless limbo-land that many ex-South Africans have entered into. They try to be what they are not, and they receive no recognition for their efforts. Of course, they would never want to admit to it, but I see and hear these souls flying at me from Nowhereland, trying desperately to be something and somewhere they cannot be.

Worst of all, as I quickly found when I first arrived on these famous shores, most Australians aren't even interested in talking about the "old country"; that is the country you came from. They barely talk about their own country, as politics and religion are forbidden languages here. (Which keeps the peace, I think. Or at any rate they think.)

That for me was one of the most frustrating discoveries when I arrived: working with journalists, people who are meant to be interested in and have a curiosity about the world, who had next to no questions about South Africa—not even to ask me my feelings about the country I had just left, despite it being at the time the fiery centre of world attention.

It was only in the middle of the continued violence being inflicted on each other by Inkatha and ANC supporters in the early '90s, when it looked like there was a real revolution taking place, that the editor of the paper I worked on asked me to put together a feature on my old country. 'What's it all about?' he wanted to know. Even the Aussies were beginning to ask questions.

So keen was my interest that I compiled a three-part series, which to the editor's credit he ran every word of. But afterwards, my enthusiasm was quickly brought down to earth by the subdued response: a couple of letters to the editor and a "Nice one, mate" from fellow journalists. End of story.

When I first arrived in Australia, I was unsurprisingly uncertain about my future. After a brief stint as a subeditor on a daily newspaper, I decided to take advantage of Australia's free tertiary education system to complete the BA I had dropped out of all those years ago at Wits University. I also decided to gain a second career option by studying to be a high-school teacher. It was the best decision I could have made. Without realising it, I had extended by three years the usual one-year honeymoon period most immigrants have when they arrive in their new country, feeling a little like they are on holiday as they discover the novel and exciting ways of their new and safe hideaway.

I was lucky in another way, too. Because of my political steadfastness, my membership of an anti-apartheid group, and possibly because I had chosen a smaller country university, I was perceived by the locals as a kind of symbol of welcome rebellion. I was treated with respect and even, dare I say it, some reverence. The rebel South African! Very quickly too, from studying Australian history and literature, I came to know more about Australia than most Australians, which always made me feel good—and seemed to be something they admired. Then, after four years, I found a proper job and it all changed.

For most new immigrants the real shock of emigration comes when they enter the Australian workplace. Many South Africans find, as I so quickly did, that while Australia may be a very tolerant and democratic country on the surface, when it comes to the workplace—where it counts, where you spend most of your waking and thinking life—the mechanism of rule is, paradoxically, a massively iron-clad authoritarian one: a structure of at times naked command-control. No consideration for the junior's point of view; no "Let's discuss this together in my office"—just full-on command from the top down at the behest of the company CEO or whoever is in charge. One quickly discovers why there is a need for strong unions in the country.

This all seems to be, you might say, a lot of criticism for the place that has taken me in, given me a degree of sanctuary, a free second go at university, and ultimately afforded me a reasonable and very secure living. At the very least it is criticism that I am well aware necessitates an obvious question: Why the hell did you leave South Africa in the first place and go there? And this is probably for me the most anguishing question of all to answer.

In some ways leaving South Africa during the apartheid years was an easy and obvious decision. Living under such morally reprehensible rule in a backwater where everything was banned . . . why would you want to stay? But having left and returned a couple of times as a young man for just those reasons, I had enough sense to eventually realise that the place I felt most at home was, for good or bad, apartheid South Africa. With the experience of travel guiding this revelation, there came a time when I decided to dig in my heels and make a go of it. Despite all the political negatives, I chose to really commit myself to my country, not just to dreams. Life was, of course, taking its own twists and turns at the time, and at my side now was my Australian fiancé, who had been seeking in Europe her own solutions to a better, more liberated future for herself (having "escaped" from a draconian Queensland state governed by the then infamous National Party premiership). South Africa seemed for us the most important priority at that stage. And if I needed any further justification, I really felt that as a journalist I could actually do something positive and constructive for my country. This wasn't just a dream; it was commitment, a reality.

After a few years I found myself with a wife, two children and a managing editor position at Drum magazine. Yes, Drum, the legendary magazine aimed at blacks, run by the late eccentric pro-Africanist Jim Bailey, who for all his quirks and foibles gave 'lefties' like me a chance to encourage political input into a magazine that otherwise could easily have drifted into a kind of British tabloid "stories of the bizarre" for black readers.

Drum brought me right up close to the constituency I supported ideologically—not just thinking about it, but living, eating and drinking (a lot of drinking) with it. As a result I spent more time in the townships, particularly Soweto, in a couple of years than most lefties ever did in their entire lives. But the reality had started to shift.

Away from the work and politics and social pressures, I found I also had to give more consideration to something that was growing at my side: my family. Especially important, of course, were my children, suddenly aged two and four. Another factor underscoring our South African existence was the constant shadow of that most niggling and frighteningly realistic of political affronts: compulsory army service. I had been conscripted for nine months in the early '70s, and we had subsequently been forced to change address many times to avoid my being called up for mandatory annual camps. At the time, 1983 moving into 1984, a very hard-to-swallow reality seemed to be crystallising: seven years after the infamous Soweto riots and despite all the external pressures on the apartheid government, it was beginning to look more and more like nothing was going to change; not, at any rate, in my lifetime.

The nagging questions returned, this time augmented with paternal concerns. Why should I remain? Why should my children have to grow up here and endure apartheid, albeit the white privileged end of it? Why should my Australian wife have to suffer this soul-damaging lifestyle, fighting an oppressive system that isn't getting anywhere? Why should I have to serve in an army that I intensely opposed? Was I—were we all—hitting our heads against a brick wall?

Ultimately, there seemed to be only one solution for my family: to go; to pack our bags and get out of that nefarious, oppressive place, and return another day, when—if—a real change took place. We emigrated in June 1984.

Some may find it hard to believe, but after twenty-five years away I still feel that South Africa is the skeleton beneath my flesh, the blood that runs through my veins. Despite my four-year honeymoon acclimatisation, it was something that I realised early on, and it is a feeling that has, ironically, grown with time. I feel it more now than ever. A large part of me is South African, as simple as that.

On the other hand, after so many years away there can be no denying that a part of me has become distinctly alienated from the spirit of my birthplace, the place that made me what I am. Things can never be quite the same—here or there.

The Fact (with a capital F) is it took me more than twenty-two years to even begin to develop warm feelings towards the Australian flag or national anthem. At the same time, even though it did take me a year or so to get used to South Africa's new flag when it was introduced in the '90s, I now love to see it flying. And right from the beginning I have loved to hear my country's new anthem (it was a song of the revolution, remember?). But this is the surprising part: even the Afrikaans bits—especially the Afrikaans bits—send a longing chill of "home" down my spine.

In my time here since emigrating I have gathered around me a coterie of South Africans, mostly early leavers like me who were genuine anti-apartheid advocates. But on the fringes of this group, I now find myself, to my increasing annoyance, coming into contact with immigrant South Africans who loudly and frequently declare that the "old country" can do nothing right; that it's going down the proverbial toilet and will end up a basket case just like Zimbabwe. They're grateful to be in a country that (fanatically) adheres to the laws of the land—and, I suspect, which looks so much like their suburban First World back home.

Yet strangely, you may think, you will sometimes hear these same Seffricens, especially the new arrivals, saying things (when they are being absolutely honest) like, "It's bizarre, man, everything looks so much the same here, but it's different. I look at myself and I only see some of the person I was. It's like not all of me is here."

Of course, this is not strange to me. And so I am without doubt that the "Aussie, Aussie! Oy, oy, oy!" cry of these ex-South Africans masks a blatant lie. There is nothing I like to do more in the company of these people—and I do it at every opportunity—than mention something positive that is happening in South Africa.

"You know gay marriage isn't even an issue there."

"My sources tell me, despite what everyone says that all is well and on target for the Football World Cup."

"Boy, have you seen that new rapid Gautrain transport system they're putting in place? Pretty amazing!"

I love telling them that I'm optimistic about South Africa's future or describing why I think Cape Town is the best city in the world or reminding them how for security reasons the Indian Premier League T20 competition was moved to South Africa.

I love explaining too, to those who've forgotten, or perhaps never even realised, that South Africa pulled itself into the black (no pun intended—well, maybe a bit) only a few years after the white-ruled apartheid government had bankrupted the country. I love to see the curl on their lips as I say these things, watching them hold back a spray of words and thoughts that they would never dare say to my face.

There is a terribly strong sense among these fellow South Africans of mine—a sense so strong you can almost see it up their noses whenever you're with them—that it is possible to simply dismiss the country of your birth, the country that gave you your wealth and privileges, most of the good times in your life (your first Campari in Benoni . . .), and even the education and money to migrate abroad. More than that, though, this sense includes the notion that South Africa has suddenly become something worse than evil, something somehow Satanic, to the point that it not only has no redeeming qualities left, but it is like a poison. (Never mind the end of apartheid that everyone claimed to have looked forward to . . .)

And this for me is very hard to swallow. I choke on it actually. And I think they do, too. You can see an emptiness floating in their eyes, a gap in their souls, that in their banter around the *braai* (except now it's a "barbie") is translated into an almost tragic cry about their new Australian mates: "They have no sense of fun, no sense of life! They ask no bloody questions—about anything!" Yes, I feel that emptiness and that gap too. Only, I openly admit to it. I feel it closely. I admit to it.

It is only deep down in their souls, or late on a Saturday evening after a good hearty meal when the truth is found at the bottom of a bottle, that many of these expat South Africans will concede the point: "Jesus, I miss that place. Hell man, I do!"

And when they do finally say it, I feel it even harder—the lameness of not being able to do anything about it.

And yet there is more to it than missing home. There is this tendency in Australia among the well-off to ignore or even deny the extent of problems that people at the bottom of society face. To them, the homeless and poor barely exist—and this is something that many expat South Africans relish. "There is no poverty here," they'll tell you simply, choosing to ignore the evidence, which can be difficult to see from the affluent suburbs many of them migrate to. Another let-off for the conscience: no more starving black hands to avoid! They have arrived in heaven. (Well, minus a bit of soul, but who cares about that?)

On a more personal note, the social problems here have affected me differently. As a journalist writing about poverty, family dysfunction, domestic violence, incestuous rape—all of these being huge issues in Australia—I have found that I cannot connect with the victims in the same way that I did with similar (usually black) victims in South Africa, despite their stories being equally sad and tragic, and demanding as much attention.

Writing in Australia is like going through the motions for me, whereas writing of these things in South Africa used to instil feelings on a profound, almost inexplicable, blood-level. I felt that what I was writing about was vital, that it made a difference, that it concerned people who lived in my own house. Their stories brought a heaviness with them that dug into the chest. Without that feeling, that essence that belonged to home, and despite gaining journalistic success here and publishing a book about life on Australia's streets (yes, life on Australian streets!), I have felt the spirit wane and a kind of apathy, common among Australians, set in.

As I fought that feeling over the years, of not really being here, of not being totally the person I thought I was or wanted to be, the dream of returning home and rediscovering that person began to steam in my blood. It reached a point where I started calling Brisbane, the city of Brisbane where I have lived since coming to Australia, "Joburg". And Sydney often became "Cape Town". Slips of the tongue? No. I am sure it was the heart speaking to the head. There was only one solution, I decided: it was time to return home. In 2006 I began to plan. I set about convincing my wife, and even our now-adult children, of my rationale. I set a date to put our house on the market and made arrangements with the shipping company to carry our furniture. My wife and I were going to set sail for "home", my real home. But what I found was that once again life had conspired against me, perhaps even punished me, you might say.

I have recently completed a book, *Dark Holes In White Paradise*, in which a young character speaks of a visit to South Africa with her South African father. She talks of seeing the country, despite the closeness to death and poverty in which people live there, in terms of bright, vivid colours; it is a place that is brilliantly intense, stirring, full of creativity and inventiveness, full of life. By comparison, despite the often-exquisite brightness of the sunshine in Australia, those same colours are seen as no more than variations of grey over here, so robotocised are Australians by their laws and their disinterest in the world around them. Only there's a problem: that grey has become the girl's world, what she knows and calls home, and because of this the father finds he cannot leave it to return home.

What can tear a parent from a child? To a father of this sort, maybe only war.

There is another equally relevant passage in the book, which forms its introductory epigraph and echoes nicely the epigraph of this particular piece. It is an Aboriginal saying that goes like this: "We don't really know who we are until we understand the place we are in."

So, yes, I am convinced we who have left South Africa, more than a million of us since 1994, have become a "tribe" who will never truly know ourselves, never truly be whole, never truly know our land—except perhaps in death when, despite the coldness of the soil that we never really came to know, we may yet, at last, be warmed by the spirit as it returns home. *Barry Levy*

When the windmill vanished . . . *Eve Hemming*

As a child raised on a Freestate farm on the Lesotho border, windmills were my symbolic edifice—they loomed high, were stalwart and rotated hypnotically. They brought water to the surface, glinted in the sunlight and offered some sort of omnipotent benevolence.

We're back in South Africa for a brief visit and my windmills come to mind. They're my Eiffel Tower, my Sydney Opera House, my Auckland Sky Tower.

We arrive after a marathon journey, fatigued and grimy after hours in transit. The desire to soak in a warm bath beckons. Now 28 hours later, it's still effectively the same day, having flown from east to west.

It's all so *déjà vu*—the evening bustle at the airport in Durban—stepping out into a humid autumn night, taxis hooting and the sounds of an African language. We've climbed though Alice in Wonderland's looking glass—and with astonishment plummeted down the rabbit hole back into Africa.

Here we are, bathed and sipping coffee with family, as though we've never been away. The old familiar sounds are welcoming—we wake to the shriek of the archaic *Hadeda* and later listen to the soothing coo of doves, reminiscent of my Freestate childhood.

It's astonishingly effortless being lulled back into a state of near ecstasy; the indolent sun shedding afternoon rays across gold and green hues. We nibble *Biltong*, because no other *Biltong* is quite as good. And sip a mellow Cape Merlot, its vintage ironically pre-dating our immigration.

We breakfast or dine out with family and friends at favourite haunts. Wherever we go we bump into 'old mates', ex-work colleagues and acquaintances. Folk say to me, 'Hey, we miss your articles in the paper . . .' It's a sharp reminder that in Auckland one can walk the length and breadth of a shopping mall and possibly only bump into one or two acquaintances. Here it's someone in every shop—folk way back from boarding school or whom I studied or taught with.

A family weekend in a Berg cottage snuggled below Rhino's Horn caresses my soul into a state of euphoria. The mountains, skyscape, customary sounds and odours taunt me. A soft breeze whips my hair across my face. I close my eyes and imbibe faraway sounds and breathe in Africa's essence. I want the moment to freeze and to eclipse it into my own eternity.

We drive down to the family cottage and enjoy an idyllic few days—bathing in the Indian Ocean and allowing one's self to float in the swells, feeling as though one is transported back to the past; as though the new life in New Zealand was a mere ethereal dream. We listen to the waves crashing on glacial rock which reinforces the antiquity of this continent. And from my window there's a stooped coral tree, its sharp orange blooms emblazoned against the shimmering azure backdrop.

Some ghastly reminders impinge on what's otherwise my metaphorical heaven. I reflect from my room with its resplendent view. I watch my sun kissed grandchildren splashing in a tub under the shade of the tree. I hear their joyful banter.

On our arrival we received news that a close friends' son was senselessly killed in a high jacking in Johannesburg that day. It feels one too many when one has insufficient fingers to count the names of innocent folk one knows, who've been senselessly exterminated.

And whilst I floated in the waves under a balmy African sun, I'd already almost erased this tragedy from my conscious mind, was playing contortionist tricks about how we could stay longer with our beloved family . . . But a moment later it was again reinforced. We bump into old friends on the water's edge. He was recently high jacked, they've had three vehicles stolen, their son has been attacked and 'cleaned out.' Their fences are being cut apart and removed, the cattle stolen on a regular basis. And . . . he had been hospitalised after being stabbed by intruders in his home whilst he slept. It's reminiscent of J.M Coetzee's satire, *Disgrace*, in which a woman impregnated from a violent rape and utterly demoralised refuses to budge from her land . . . Then the other day their neighbour's entire windmill had vanished—dismantled and removed in the dead of night for scrap metal. Gone was my African symbol . . .

It highlighted for me the paradox of our land—its agony and ecstasy. Its profundity pulls one back, like the moons pull on the waves, but always the waves lash against and erode away at the landscape, where violence has insidiously become engrained.

"What I want does exist if I dare to find it . . ."
From 'Oranges'—Jeanette Winterson

Emigration—Then . . .
Then—1962
Dick Knight, NZ

'You are going back to NZ? . . . Why for goodness sake? It's at the end of the world. What is wrong with SA?' Questions I was asked time and time again.

After a three year working holiday in NZ, I returned to my beloved SA and family. Isipingo Beach was my home and I was very happy to be back.

Then my world fell apart. My Ma died and Isipingo was declared Indian residential only; two extreme negatives that were to have a profound effect on my life.

These events, particularly the rezoning of 'Pingo triggered some serious lateral thinking, and to the fore, was how much I enjoyed NZ and Kiwis. My Dad knew what I was thinking, "Go son, this place is going the wrong way". He was a lot wiser than I gave him credit for. So I left, telling myself, 'just another look at NZ', but surprisingly comfortable with my decision and eager to get back to NZ.

NZ in the 1960's was a very different place compared with now. Life was very simple and easy, no unemployment to speak of, no major divisive politics, and no real class distinction, at any level. I did struggle more than I had anticipated; mainly the lost family and friend contact. One corresponded, but that lack of physical contact gnaws away and I did consider returning. Age is obviously a factor in the equation of immigration success, and accordingly being single and twenty two, I assimilated quicker and easier. I coped best by doing as the Romans do, immersing myself in my new life, moving on.

South Africa became a place where I grew up, would forever love, and where I would frequently visit with my Kiwi wife and daughters, then happily return to New Zealand.

My immigration story started some 47 odd
years ago!
Maria Chinn, NZ

My family left Spain when my mom was still pregnant with me, and went to settle in Brazil where I was born and we arrived in Durban when I was two years old.

155

I have always told people 'I'm a Child of the Universe' and had a very confused childhood, never knowing where I belonged, what language to speak and never fitting in anywhere. I struggled to learn English when I first started school as I came from a home where Spanish was the first language and Portuguese and Italian were second.

When I finally mastered English (in one year), my parents decided it was time to go back home to Spain. Unfortunately for me, my parents sent me to a Catholic School run by some seriously strict nuns! English had been drummed into my head, the grammar, phonetics and alphabet, and now Spanish was a distant past. So now instead of English, it was Spanish that was literally "smacked" into me by the nuns.

But, if my parents thought that I wasn't being tortured enough, they decided that life in Spain was not that grand, and hey presto . . . we came back to South Africa after two years . . . And so the vicious cycle started . . . Learn English all over again!

All things considered, I survived pretty well. I may have had a difficult time fitting in anywhere because I wasn't South African or Spanish enough, because I spoke Spanish with an accent. All of this has made me who I am today and I am proud that I am a Spanish, Brazilian, South African Kiwi.

My husband, Russell and I had decided that immigration was not an option for us. Hence we chose to accept the situation in South Africa, make the most of life and not grumble about what was happening by focussing on the positives.

It was about 5 years ago that I received a phone call from Spain that my Mom was on her death bed and I had to get there as soon as possible. Russell and I were on a plane within 24 hours. The good thing is that my Mom lived to see another 4 years. However, while we were in Spain we both realised how the "other half lived"; the freedom, the safety, the peace, quality of life etc. We had not realised this before because of the blinkers we had been wearing for some time. When we arrived back in SA, we made the decision that 'come hell or high water' we were going to GET OUT while the going was good. But again, the blinkers came back on and life was not really that bad in SA; a bit expensive to live, but what the heck.

A couple of months later my daughter decided that she and the grandkids were going to join my ex-husband in Australia. She had been held up a couple of times (at knife point) for her cell phone, had not been able to find work and wanted her children to have a better life. It broke my heart but I knew that this was in her and my grandkids' best interests, and that I had to let them go.

It was shortly after they left that I received a phone call one afternoon from a policeman. My world fell into small pieces—to say my heart came out of my throat is putting it mildly. The policeman kindly told me that Russell was all right, just a little shaken as he and a colleague from work had just been in an armed robbery. I later learnt that as Russell had been the person at the end of the queue at the till, he'd had an AK47 held to his head. The armed robbers were caught, but I doubt whether they have spent any time behind bars, going by the proceedings in court up to the time we left SA.

One day, after this had happened, all hell broke loose in Kenya. We were sitting watching the news and all we saw were hundreds of white people at the airports, some with one little suitcase and some with nothing at all waiting patiently for flights to take them back to their respective countries. That was my wakeup call—had seen it in the Congo, Rwanda, Zimbabwe and now Kenya.

I could see that this is what could possibly happen to us one day, and there was no way that I would want to ever be in that situation. I would rather leave SA of my own free will than be forced out of my home and country. We made the decision there and then that we were going to leave South Africa for good.

We weighed up our options and we were one of the lucky few with the choice of three countries—Spain, Australia or New Zealand. While we were still deciding where to move to, Russell had applied for a position in Fuji Xerox, Dunedin. He had been working for Xerox in SA for 18 years. Luckily for us, he was offered the position. It had taken us 6 months from that night watching the news till we arrived in Dunedin, New Zealand.

We are truly blessed and lucky, as we have seen first-hand how difficult it has been for so many families that have made the move to New Zealand; how they have struggled and battled financially and with finding work, how many have had their visa's turned down and how many families are still sitting in SA just wishing and praying that they could leave.

My most trying part of immigrating to SA and NZ has been my name . . . . In Spain women never take on their husband's name and the children born of that marriage will have a different name to that of their father and mother, and to add insult to injury all girls are given the first name of MARIA, although we never use it as we are given it at birth from the Catholic church.

When we arrived in SA, Home Affairs decided this was all just a bit much for them to manage. So my Mom, my sister and myself had our full surnames taken away and we were given a single surname. My Dad had his surname shortened as well so that we all had the same surname. The girls in the family were all known as *Maria*.

When we filled in our visa papers for NZ, again my name/names surfaced. My Spanish passport has one name (back to the women retaining their maiden name) and my South African passport had another name. To satisfy NZ Immigration I had to obtain a letter from the Spanish Ambassador in Wellington to explain the whole name saga of women in Spain. Now you know why I had a confused childhood and still do . . .

I can't say it has been plain sailing for us since we've arrived, but I still consider myself fortunate that we managed to buy a house in Dunedin within 6 months of arriving (even though I didn't have work and we were on a work visa). Russell has had two promotions since arriving in NZ. We have moved to Auckland, own two cars, have a beautiful home and I have a wonderful job and have managed to go to Australia twice since arriving to visit our family. None of the above would have been possible had we still been living in SA.

I also know that if it hadn't been for my confusing childhood that things would have been a lot different. I have adjusted to living in NZ with a great amount of ease, simply because I had experienced it so many times. I have learnt that it is better to go with the flow, accept change not fight it, and have learnt that we are all different, no matter if we have the same colour skin, believe in the same God or even eat the same food.

I know that this makes it look like my life is, and has been, all "peaches and cream", but I have had ups and downs and have had moments when I have wanted to just pack it all in. My confused childhood has often made me wish for a totally different life and there have been many troubled moments in Spain, SA and New Zealand, but through all of those times I am 100% happy that we have made the right move. We are happy to be living in Auckland and this is going to be my last immigration story . . . . a Spanish, Brazilian South African Kiwi buried in New Zealand.

I finally have found a place where I feel I truly belong and know that I have finally come home and love my new-found Kiwi family.

My migration story started thirty years ago

Cathy Barnard Schwartz, NZ

Thirty years ago I moved from Zimbabwe to South Africa for a better life. It was not easy for us ex Zimbabweans. We were called all sorts of names and I still remember one of them being "when we's" because we often used to talk about the times we had in Zim and it was only because we missed what we used to have. We missed our home towns where we grew up, we missed our friends and we missed our families. It was a difficult time in our lives and we were told that we had just come to SA to take all the jobs.

Five years ago I had to do the whole move all over again. We moved from SA to NZ, and yet again we have had to go through all the emotions all over again. We miss what we called home for the past 25 years, our friends, our family and again we have to go through the whole thing about us immigrants are just here to take all the jobs. But do you know what? I will do it all over again for my family. Rhodesia will always have a very special place in my heart; it was where I was born and grew up. It is no longer the country we knew back then. It has a few places that I guess you could still visit like Kariba, Zimbabwe ruins, etc. But to go there will just be to remember the good old days. Our country died many years ago. Mugabe took our country away from us, but there was one thing he could not take and that is our memories. They still live on to this day. Even though it all turned sour 30 years ago, we still remember those days like it was yesterday.

South Africa will always have a special place in my heart, too. It is where I got married, had my children, schooled them there and all my family is still there. It is a beautiful country, but a lot of the places are not the same anymore. Things have changed, just like they did in Zimbabwe. It is sad to watch your home town so run down and there is nothing you can do about it and I found the more I longed for the 'good old days' the more I missed it, so I had to turn my focus on where my life is now. It is not easy but to keep my sanity I had to.

One thing I am very grateful for is the internet! Without it I would never have got in touch with all my old friends and family. We would never have had these wonderful sites where we can chat with fellow South Africans and Rhodesians and to reminisce about 'the good old days'—keeping in mind that it was then and not now, so as to remind me that I do not want to go back.

I wanted to share my story because my heart aches for all those who are really struggling to adapt to the change and the big move. You may not think so now, but believe me, as time goes on you will find that it does get a lot easier to cope with. It is almost like mourning. You go through a lot of emotions and it hurts, but just give yourselves time. My prayers go out to all those who need it. I pray God gives you the strength to keep going for your family's sake.

Migratory Tales—*UK, SA, Zim, NZ, OZ—1967-2012*   *Ange Baldwin, Oz*

It was November 1967. We caught the train from Glasgow—a great big black steam engine, which hissed, chuffed and billowed black smoke, as it steamed out of the station. We were heading for Southampton Docks. When we arrived, the weather was bitter and grey—not untypical in November. I remember seeing big cranes and huge ships with smoke stacks and a massive building with many windows. I suppose now that I think about it, it must have been the transit terminal where customs and immigration officials ensured that all our documents were in order. At the time, for me as a small child, I was consumed by the excitement of it all and overawed by the largeness of everything—the train, the ships, the buildings. For my parents, however, it must have been daunting knowing that this was the last time they would be in their homeland for a long time; leaving the friends and family they had known all their lives, a lifestyle they were familiar with and jobs they had been secure in. They must have been terribly brave to undertake such a huge voyage to the other side of the world with two small children, aged nearly five and ten months old.

The ship was called the Windsor Castle. Built in 1959, she was the last flagship of the Union Castle Lines. She was the largest passenger/cargo mail ship of the line's Cape Mail service to South African ports. She was also known as the 'lavender lady' with lavender coloured hull, a white top and a big red and black smoke stack. I saw her again in the Port of Durban in 1973. She was sent to the scrap yards in 2005.

Our tourist class cabin had four beds in it. We had a children's hostess on board who entertained us with games, films and interesting activities. One night there was a fancy dress competition. My mum dressed me up as the Queen of Sheba (using one of her nighties) and I won the competition! I also recall King Neptune coming on board the ship when we crossed the Equator. That was rather scary and he threw the ladies into the swimming pool. He was green and covered in seaweed, with a crown on his head and carried a trident in his hand. I also recall us experiencing a big storm. (I asked my parents about this some years later, and it occurred in the Bay of Biscay). It was a force 9 storm and half the crew were down with seasickness. I remember getting an injection from the nurse on the ship for my seasickness. I had a toy elephant called Nellie which I had been given by my dad's workmates when I was born. She went everywhere with me. Somehow one of Nellie's ears had come loose and one day her ear fell off while I was on deck and the wind blew her ear into the sea. I was devastated! I still have my little one-eared Nellie.

The ship docked in Cape Town harbour, where we caught a steam train to Port Elizabeth, where we spent a year there. My dad didn't like it because he said he got teased every time he tried to speak Afrikaans. In 1968 we moved from Port Elizabeth to Bulawayo in Rhodesia by train. My dad had a job with the Rhodesian Railways. The house we had in Bulawayo was made of 'pole and dagga' (mud and thatch). They were called *pied-a-terres*. The *mud* was probably a mixture of *dung, mud and grasses.* The roof was thatched and with thick walls which made it cool in summer and warm in winter.

I don't remember much from our early days in Bulawayo, but I do remember visiting Centenary Park and going on the mini train and seeing the wonderful Christmas displays and lights in the park. They had life size figures of fairy tale characters and it was beautiful. My brother used to play on the big yellow bulldozer in the park. I also remember the beautiful Jacaranda trees in full bloom down the main road into the city centre; a profusion of purple.

Growing up in Rhodesia was a wonderful experience. Those years were the best years of my life. Even though we were in the midst of a war, you wouldn't know it. As a child one was probably sheltered from the nastiness of it, but was made well aware of the politics. We learned that walls have ears and to be careful what one said and to whom. When I think back now, it must have been like living in a spy novel—all espionage and counter espionage! We learned to shoot big guns—FN rifles, 9mm pistols and 38mm revolvers. Mum and dad were both seconded to the Police Reserve and did duties in the charge office and the signals room. Dad did regular call ups to the bush for two weeks at a time. And mum slept with a STAR pistol under her pillow when dad was away. There were curfews on travel and convoys when travelling between certain towns. There were farmers murdered and Africans murdered in their villages by the terrorists. But life continued as normally as it could for the times. For all that, it was an amazing childhood, and although it sounds odd, we had so much freedom.

Once the war was over and the new government came into power, many people left the country. We stuck around. I met my husband when I was 19 and we were married by the time I was 21. We moved around the country a bit; from the midlands (Gatooma) to the Lowveld (Triangle) back to the midlands (Chegutu, Gatooma and Martin Spur) and then to Matabeleland (Bulawayo). We had our first child, Audrey, when I was 24 and our second, Stuart, when I was 27. Things seemed to be progressing better than expected for the first ten years, and then with the expiration of the Lancaster House Agreement, Mugabe's evil plan began to hatch. By 1994 we had decided it was probably time to move on and go somewhere that our children were assured of a future. I would have loved to move back to Scotland, but my husband, a fourth generation Rhodesian refused on the grounds that it was too cold! So, we ended up moving to New Zealand in May of 1995.

The move to New Zealand was not an easy one to make. I realised then what a hard decision it must have been for my parents to move when they had made the same decision all those years ago. They too, had embarked upon their migration with only a couple of cabin trunks, suitcases, two small children in tow and little money. Our migration was strikingly similar—with two small children of similar ages to what my brother and I were when we left Britain, our suitcases, three packing boxes and very little money.

We arrived in Timaru where we were going to try and sort out some accommodation. Not knowing anyone or how things worked in New Zealand and suddenly having to learn about 'plastic money' (EFTPOS) was a learning curve! Not only that, but coping with bitterly cold weather for which we were ill-equipped was unpleasant. However, with assistance we were soon in a warm house to rent for the first 6 months. John was given a work van to use for work and personal use, but it only had the two front seats. When we went anywhere with the children we got them to lie down in the back in case the police saw them and stopped us, because of course there were no seat belts or child restraints! So there they were, poor kids, usually bundled in with the shopping in the back of their dad's work van!

Fortunately we found a modern well insulated house with electric heaters in the walls and double glazed windows. Just as well, as we had no furniture at all. One of John's work mates gave us some blow up mattresses to use as beds. We had brought a couple of blankets and sheets with us and bought the other basic necessities. Another work mate gave us a small portable TV for the kids to watch and we used cardboard boxes for tables and sat on the floor until such time as we could purchase some furniture.

We had only been in New Zealand for about six weeks when John was hospitalised with a gangrenous appendix. I had no car, but our friends came to my rescue and took me to the hospital to visit Johnny until he came home. Otherwise I walked everywhere; walked the kids to school and to the shops for the groceries and to town to pay our bills and our rent. Luckily for me Timaru is quite small! We made friends with the pharmacist who happened to be South African. I struggled to find work and was continually being told I was overqualified or had no New Zealand experience. Even the Work and Income office said they could not help me because I had qualifications and experience and the people they placed didn't! Eventually I decided I would go back to college and upgrade my computer skills. I had only just finished my course when an advert was placed in the local paper for a temporary position at the college I had been at. I applied for it, and got the job. The job was for 3 weeks, but I ended up staying for 4 months, going from one department to the next as a relief temp. Then a part time job in a law firm was advertised and I applied for it and got the job as a legal word processor. The practice manager was an ex New Zealand Army bloke who had been to Zimbabwe with the monitoring forces during the handover at independence! I stayed with that law firm until we moved to Christchurch four years later. Once I was working, it made a big difference to our lives. We could afford a car and little weekend breaks away and we could buy toys for the kids and start building up our household goods again.

The other thing that had a big impact on us was that John, although a qualified and experienced electrician, had to register to work as a fully-fledged electrician. In order to do that he had to get a breakdown of the exams he sat from City & Guilds so that the electrical workers registration board in New Zealand could assess him for registration. They decided that in order to be able to register he could forego the theory exam but he had to sit the regulations exam, do a practical exam and sit a safe working practices, CPR and First Aid certificate. He passed the practical exam, CPR and first aid with flying colours, but the regulations exams were only done twice a year and involved a huge amount of studying which was almost impossible to complete whilst doing continual standbys. Suffice to say, he finally passed his regulations exams and we decided to move on to somewhere more suited to the kids' growing needs. We moved to Christchurch where there were more schools to choose from, more for the kids to do and the University and Colleges were there, too. Luckily we both had jobs to go to in Christchurch, so we packed up a hired lorry, helped by our Church friends and off we went.

I got involved in a charitable organisation called the ZimCare Trust which was assisting Zimbabweans fleeing the country; mainly farmers being kicked off their lands. I had read an article by a Reuter's reporter in the Press which had incensed me and I had written a letter to the editor who phoned me to say it was too long to publish as a letter but would I mind if they published it as an article. I had no objection and so they did. It resulted in a media frenzy—TV interviews, radio interviews, newspaper articles, liaising with the Immigration minister (who was just wonderful and relaxed some of the rules a little)—It was an endless flurry.

I was helping people in Zimbabwe who were emailing me for advice on immigration and settlement issues in regard to moving to New Zealand—I was probably dealing with about sixty or more emails a night (whilst holding down a full time job). Then ZimCare contacted me and asked if I would be their national co-ordinator. I agreed and the rest is history. It was very rewarding, extremely exhausting and mentally challenging. But I don't regret it. We (John was absolutely invaluable in his support, both physically and mentally, and he did most of the collecting people from the airport, picking up or delivering donated goods etc.) helped so many people to settle in their new country, many of whom had such traumatic and tragic circumstances. After almost four years, John insisted I give it up and pass it on to someone else, as it was beginning to take its toll on me emotionally. One of my best friends picked up the mantle until the need was no longer required when the immigration rules were changed and

Zimbabweans had to meet the same criteria as everyone else. ZimCare was probably the best thing that happened to me as by seeing things through other people's eyes and helping them through the problems I had faced in terms of moving country, I was able to move forward and grow in myself. One piece of advice that I live by now is the one I offered to each and every person I helped. It was, 'You cannot move forward if you are continually looking back. The country that once was—that we remember—is no longer and can never be again. Tuck away the memories safely in your memory banks to be brought out and cherished every now and again and put back again snugly where they belong—in your memory.'

We were well settled in New Zealand and loved our life in Christchurch. We were richly blessed with so many friends and a busy social life and two, now grown up children. We owned our own home and owned two cars . . . ***And then disaster struck!*** The devastating earthquakes of September 2010 and February 2011 put paid to our beautiful lifestyle in Christchurch. It put everything into turmoil and my nerves eventually gave out and I couldn't take it anymore. We made the tough decision to move to Australia, given that we felt moving anywhere else in New Zealand was pointless as the whole country is seismically volatile. It was so hard to leave that country, and everything we had worked so hard to build up. It was particularly hard to leave our children. But they are adults now, and need to make their own decisions and live their own lives. Our oldest child is now planning on moving to Canada for a year and to the UK, and our youngest would like to follow us to Australia when he has completed his studies.

Now I sit here, having immigrated for the fourth time to yet another country and wonder if I have learned anything at all. I guess I have learned not to take things for granted and to appreciate what you have got and how hard you worked for it. We moved to New Zealand with little more than three packing boxes and our cases and seventeen years later we moved to Australia with a twenty foot container, plus our suitcases and a cat! I still don't have a job three months later, but you know what—I know it will happen—it will just take time. It is all about timing and being in the right place at the right time. At the moment the future looks bleak from my perspective and I wonder if I have done the right thing. Did we make a huge mistake, leaving our NZ friends, our family, our children, selling our cars, renting out our home—to come here to be worse off than we were? Or is it just the typical teething problems of the early days of migration? I think the latter. It is early days yet, and in ten years' time when I look back on the experience I will know we made the right move.

Migration—Now . . .
It's all about *Choices* — *Marguerite van Blerk, Oz*

It all started a few years ago when my husband, very carefully introduced the idea of having a "back door". He knew that I was resistant to change and also that I was so close to my Mom and Dad. My stomach flipped and I cried buckets of tears, but I obliged, and so we began our journey. We made our *choice*.

It was only a few months later, after we had attended the 'Opportunities Australia Expo', that I realised that Bruce was serious and that realisation launched an incredible rollercoaster of emotions in me. I cried all the way home and continued to cry the next day. And then came the fear, anger, depression, nerves and a little excitement. We began the process of applying for our Highly Skilled Migrant Visa for Australia, which entitled us to Permanent Residency. We did this because both of us knew, from the beginning, that the move would be permanent, and there would be no looking back. During our application, we were blessed by the arrival of our beautiful little girl, and this only fuelled our urgency to get over to Australia and start our new life—free from fear. And that is where our choices started.

Making the decision to emigrate is certainly not an impulsive one. It takes time, effort and money. You question your decision and face criticism, but we had the support of the people closest to us, and even when it seemed as though we would never get the opportunity to come over, we knew we had made the right decision.

It finally happened when Bruce received an offer from an engineering contracting company, and we had 8 weeks to sort out our lives and make our move. As soon as I arrived in Gladstone, Australia, I knew that in order for us to succeed and achieve our dreams, it was all about *choices*:

The choice to wake up in the morning and embrace the challenges and discoveries of the new day,

The choice to be supportive of my very hard working and committed husband, despite sometimes feeling so isolated and lonely,

The choice to get out every day and meet new people,

The choice to acknowledge my sadness and anger, but also to be positive, despite the negative emotions because I had a family to take care of,

The choice to engage with our daughter positively and enthusiastically so that she too could enjoy our newfound freedom,

The choice to make a big effort to celebrate all the special occasions like birthdays and Christmas, even though, deep down, we missed our families so much,

The choice to celebrate, every day, the new life that Australia has given to us.

I have moved past being angry about the reasons why we left. I choose not to dwell on the negativity I left behind. We chose to leave—we were NEVER forced to do so. I feel that the secret to our success is the fact that we have chosen to be positive, and chosen to make it work. That is not to say that there aren't days where we feel overwhelmed, sad, stressed—but on those days we share our burdens with each other or new friends, take a deep breath, and keep moving forward.

All of this was our *choice*—and it was a good one!

Scatterling Tales

> *If we are always arriving and departing, it is also true that we are eternally anchored. One's destination is never a place but rather a new way of looking at things.*
>
> -Henry Miller

Scatterlings . . . *Karen de Villiers, UK*

I don't think about it now anymore. In the first two years I exhausted myself with the issue of being here and being there. Tripping in no man's land. Exhausting . . .

This patriotic issue increases tenfold when you are taken from the place you simply call home. I cannot remember ever being that patriotic before; not like the Americans, hanging their flags outside the porch. One does not dwell too much on the subject of being a patriot.

There was no angst in being born in a small Free State Town, going to a good government school, university and following the path of marriage, children and being part of a community. Never hung the flag outside the porch.

Fast forward to manic swings of homesickness, angst and depression. I become a patriot of unnerving proportions. The homeland I had left is one perfect advertisement. An untainted idyll of happy people and pretty scenery. I turn into the cliché of wanting what you cannot have. So I bake rusks, trawl the internet for news, sigh at the sound of a South African accent. I find places to buy biltong and Mrs Balls' chutney. I forget the people of the country I live in now, only to compare them most unfairly to all that is better, brighter and smarter back home. At least from a distance, all looks better, brighter and smarter. England has grey skies. I hang onto that to justify my melancholy. I stop short of wearing a Green rugby jersey and crocs in Wimbledon.

I marvel at my ability to romanticise my past . . . I go back often as my family still live there. I make notes of what is better and what has deteriorated too fast in too short a time. The cities gleam like symbols of Liberty and Hope. The rural towns are dust and quite forgotten. Time has turned back for the *Platteland*. People are still living there only no-one seems to pay much attention to those without water and basic sanitation. For the reverting to candles. No one is immune to pain when living conditions fail to keep up with the lives of the ordinary. They do not feature on the tourist brochures.

We play a game when I return. My friends tell me how wonderful life is and I nod in agreement. They speak of hope and progress while I watch the blind man begging on the corner, jostling to find his way amongst the throngs of illegals, selling everything from washing pegs to blow up dolls. They do not ask me how I am and when they do, I am humble in my self-depreciation of a new life cleaning my own home and living well below the plumpness of my previous life. I fear if I say life for me now is challenging, but in a good way: that I am now the common man who can find pockets of happiness on a local bus or train bound for Cambridge. I fear that if I say that, they will think me arrogant or pathetic and I will lose the ties I have. So I tell them jokes about carrying groceries up three flights of stairs and how I need to re-cycle; how I see any doctor at the hospital. It neutralises unsaid thoughts.

I miss so many things. I miss space most of all. I miss the hanging up of cold, newly washed sheets in the hot sunlight. The sound of the Hadeda and the dove in the poplar trees—the voice of the African tongue, curling and clicking at sounds like a crackling twig—long grass that slaps and swishes around your legs. I miss real dried apricots on a mesh in the back yard, an open fire, my friends and family. I could write a tome of the things I miss. Many of them no longer exist in my homeland.

Do I cling to other South Africans in my new country? Cling would be the wrong word. I have ties with those like me, because I need to nourish my roots from time to time. I am making a new stitched blanket of souls like mine who speak of elephants and *safaris* as if we took them every week. We laugh at ourselves. I never made a *braai,* nor danced a Zulu dance. I never ventured into a township. Other than actually being a South African, I had no idea of the unseen hallows of a deeper South Africa. Few South Africans do. Few citizens of a country do.

All we know is our own reality. Venturing into the political spheres of others is for a daring few. I followed the letter of the censored page and never stopped to question anything. When all were given the chance to vote and live as free men, I welcomed it, but few ended up doing so. The majority are still in chains; chains of poverty, guilt, no education and unemployment. Suspicion and blame are destroying any chance the youth have at finding a common path. The media cannot sway the masses any more. There is no euphoria left to cling to.

Am I bitter? A little. Guilty? About things that could have been prevented yes, but not about my choice to feel less worthy or more used because I was once of a privileged society. The lesson for me. I have left South Africa to realise that I am a true South African. I have fallen in love with my homeland, perhaps for the first time. When one can step back and realise that there are such treasures we do not find when we are too busy passing blame.

I am calm now. I have settled in my new land. Living in Europe has brought back the circle of my family ties. My grandfather once stood at the dock in Amsterdam. There was no work for an architect in Holland; for a young man, desperate to make a good living and marry his sweetheart.

There were two ships. One for America and one for South Africa. My grandfather hopped on the latter. His decision defined my destiny. Despite the struggle he built a life for his family. I am the grand-daughter of an immigrant. We all are. When he died, he spoke of his deep love for South Africa. He was passionate about his country. I had to leave to realise, for the first time, just what he meant. You can blame me for leaving. But you can never blame me for loving. I need not your approval, but what I know is that there is blood in the sand, my blood and that ties me forever.

My escapades—UK to SA and then to the land of OZ
Cristina Salva, Oz

I came to South Africa in 1993 after a friend convinced me that SA wasn't just like any other African country. I was working in Angola with the United Nations and I was planning on spending Easter with my mother and siblings in England. That never happened as my friend convinced me to visit SA. Down to South Africa we flew, landed in Johannesburg International, drove to Pretoria and I fell madly in love with the country, then and there. I rang my mother and told her I was moving to South Africa. She thought I had lost my mind (as she explained 'Why on earth would you want to live in the most racist country on earth?'), and being that I was black I was "supposed" to know better ('the history of the country and all'). Well I did, and my heart was stuck on SA . . .

Fast track to 2009. Yes, the love was still there, but having lived so many years in the country, the 'ugly' had started to raise its head. Firstly, as a black female, I was constantly asked why I didn't speak Zulu or Sotho. Secondly, after having been told again and again that I was a coconut. (At first I thought they meant I was stubborn; my beautiful daughter later enlightened me on its true definition). I was by no means amused. I was tired of what was happening around us in the country. I was sick to the stomach of the reverse racism, and was shocked when I encountered bad services, not by people who "knew" their job or had the proper qualifications, but instead had the "skin flavour of the moment". I was growing sick of it. You see I come from a family who are practically the colours of Benetton, so literally I hate racism. I believe if I am to despise a person, no matter their skin colour or nationality, let it be something else, for example that they are absolute idiots and just despicable creatures who the good Lord himself wouldn't' wish to waste his time on. But seeming that's impossible, why bother, so in general I don't waste my precious years on God's good earth hating other people/races etc. Nah, too much of a headache!

Speed forward to 2010, my daughter and I, one morning lazing around on my bed, talking about much or less the events of the century—I asked her what she thought of Jacob Zuma as the president. To my surprise, she told me that her friends and she had found him unfit to govern and that he was an embarrassment to the country. Let me state that this was my 11year old daughter telling me all this and not forgetting that she thought the country was literally going to the dogs and she really wasn't keen on being raped in South Africa. My daughter, who at the time studied at Crawford, Lonehill, Johannesburg, loved her school, LOVED the country, but didn't love what she and her friends saw happening to their beloved country.

That very moment, I decided I could never forgive myself IF something dreadful such as Rape happened to her, and for WHAT; just to live in a huge house, with a swimming pool, beautiful garden, maids, etc. Nope, I decided it wasn't worth my daughter's life, so I talked with her and asked if she'd like to visit Australia with me. Of course it was like, "WHEN are we going . . .?" So visited Oz we did . . . fell in love we did . . . and moved we did. By the time I told my friends and family, half of those friends stopped talking to me, for some reason or other some hated my guts, and others thought that as a black female I had it good in SA (oh boy they were sooooo wrong!!) and I was over-reacting . . . yeah yeah. 'You'll be back within a year; call us, we'll pick you up from the airport when you return crying!'

So we moved to Brisbane, Queensland, Australia. Boy, someone should have warned me it was so HOT, hotter than Durban or Cape Town. Of course my teenage daughter loved it at GO! To be honest, we really didn't like the wooden houses in Queensland, but hey, nowhere is perfect, right?

We had a friend, Veronique, who had a company in Brisbane assisting South African families moving to OZ. She secured us a rental before our arrival, which helped tons. I had already secured my daughter a place at a private all-girls school in Toowoomba, which she LOVES to death.

It's been two years since we left South Africa. It's only now that my daughter opened up and told me that the first three months she wanted to return back to South Africa, but she felt too guilty to share her worries with me, seeing all the tears and money that went into the immigration process. What helped was that at her school there were several 'ex-Saffas', even her class teacher was an 'ex-Zim', and within those three months, she finally found a new home/country. When asked where she's from, she proudly says, 'I'm an Aussie mate'. That's too cute . . . she now even speaks and sounds like an Aussie. At times I have to ask her to speak "Proper British" English to her poor mummy . . . hehehe.

I must say, at times I go through the emotions of missing South Africa (my huge house and our Labrador, which a friend adopted from us) . . . ahhhh . . . I went back last Easter, and oh boy was it an eye opener. Everything seemed more expensive, a lot of people of ALL colours are talking of immigration . . . much to my surprise, and one of my ex-friends apologised for the way she'd acted. I won't say that I would never live in SA again, but I honestly don't know if I want to. I personally feel that if I left OZ, I would prefer to live in NZ, but never SA. *SA feels like an old boyfriend who knows you so well, but who just doesn't "cut" it as boyfriend material.* My mother still wants us to move back to England, but that love affair died way back.

All I can say is that Australia has given my daughter the freedom which I knew as a child in England. She and her friends ride their bikes around freely, go to the mall, movies and parties without me having a semi-heart attack and worrying every single minute, and in general she's in a safe, caring environment and for that I will ALWAYS be grateful to the Australian government.

The green, green grass of home . . .

Morkels.wordpress.com   *Anne Morkel, Canada*
January 4, 2012

How do you feel about moving to Canada? These were the words that greeted me as I raced through the door after a full day of teaching. This question came as a shock as my husband had not been out there looking for job opportunities out of South Africa. We had been living in Gauteng with our family and moving to another country had been the last thing on our minds.

Little did I know then, that MOVING was going to be all-consuming for the next 6 months. I ate, slept and drank moving!

The first thing on the agenda was to sell our beautiful home 'Vista della Collina' that nestled up against the Lonehill nature reserve. I knew that it would be heart-wrenching, as we had come to recognize and grow attached to the local flora and fauna that had set up home there. The *dassies* (rock rabbits) would herald in each morning with their grunts and moans as they fought for the choicest grazing along the fence and the resident eagle owl would always give his final hoot as he settled down to sleep after a long night of catching rodents. He used our chimney as a vantage point and was vigilant at keeping away these any unwanted furry rodents from our garden.

Then there was all the sorting, throwing out and administration that had to be done. I never realized how time consuming it would be to close off household, telephone or bank accounts. My life was filled with the occupation of 'filling in forms.' I approached the whole process like a robot and slowly worked my way through the paper trail. There were numerous 'to do' lists that stared at me from the fridge and I felt like I was not making any headway. All this drained my energy and we had not even begun to pack yet!

Fortunately my sons and good friends kept me focused as my husband had already moved to Toronto to take up his new position. There were many phone calls back and forth with all the logistics that had to be organized. We filled one and a half containers with all our worldly goods. Our precious furry child, Josh, the Jack Russell, was ushered into a wooden crate too, so that he could make his long journey over to his new home. I felt like everything had to fit into a box and was ready to jump into one myself!

The last part and the hardest by far were the goodbyes that had to be said. It was a sad process that took us to different parts of the country to say our farewells. We knew what we were leaving behind and our hearts were heavy. This was not only about being far away from our dear family and friends, but we were also leaving behind our African lifestyle. Fortunately for us there was some respite, as we were not running away from anything. We saw the move as a great new experience for all of us as a family.

These experiences became so overwhelming at times that I was encouraged by my son to write a blog. He wisely suggested that the writing might be therapeutic and it would help me to keep in touch with loved ones back in South Africa. It was not to become a travelogue but was more to be about 'change' and how one perceives a country when you know that you are living there and not just passing through as a tourist. My blog has been a wonderful tool and I still marvel at the way in which technology makes the world a really small place.

A story of loss and love . . . *Lyall Mc Carthy, Oz*

My story starts five years ago, in Amanzimtoti, South Africa. My partner and I were supporting a large family; his parents, going into pension age and struggling financially, his sister had just lost her job, and his brother wanted to study. I had a young daughter, who was in a marriage with a bloke who didn't have a job, and we needed to increase our income to help them all in some way.

I saw an advertisement for mining jobs in Australia, and we sent my partner's resume off. He is a fitter by trade. Some weeks later we received an invitation for an interview with a company who specialises in job recruitment for Australia, from SA. A few months later, and much documentation and money well spent, we found ourselves packing for Australia. We sold our house and stayed with family and friends until the day we left.

This all sounds like plain sailing, but underneath emotions were swirling in little eddies, coming and going. I would be leaving my much loved daughters and grandchildren; he would be leaving his family, with whom he had a love-hate relationship . . . and I found out later, a girlfriend or two that I never knew existed . . .

We left South Africa on a Sunday afternoon. I cried all the way from South Africa to Singapore, where we switched planes in the dead of night, arriving in sunshiny Sydney the next morning, to be met by my brother-in-law, Paul. Spending some time with him was lovely, but we had no sooner shaken off our jet lag when we were on our way to Tasmania, where the employment agency had arranged work for my partner. We were at that time on a work sponsored visa, but had submitted our application for permanent residency.

Our first night in Tasmania was very special for me, but my partner hated it; no smoking in the hotel rooms, he didn't like the food, the bed or the TV channels . . . I lapped it up like a thirsty person in a desert, savouring every minute of it. The next day we met with a lady from the Tasmanian government, as they were sponsoring us. We had lots of paper work to do and then they took us to our new home for the next two years in George Town; a small little town of less than 5000 people, an hour's drive away from anything, right on the beautiful Tamar River.

My partner hated everything; his work, the company house where we stayed, and subsequently the unit we moved to after a few weeks. He hated the food, the weather and the people. He also began to hate me, blaming me for everything, and accused me of forcing him to move to Australia, and we lived a very miserable life together. I had secured employment with a finance company after two weeks of job hunting, and felt myself to be one of the most fortunate people alive. I loved everything, made some awesome friends, and enjoyed my work. I felt like I had come home, or was in heaven, depending on my mood. I totally fell in love with the little island of Tasmania and its inhabitants. I used to tell everyone and everyone on the SA forum about how marvellous Tasmania was.

After two years of miserable living with my partner, I left him and moved in with a friend, whose brother I had met earlier, and subsequently fell in love with, and am now married to. A genuine salt of the earth man. We have everything our hearts' desire, and more, except my family. Deep inside me I have this enormous endless dark pit, and hidden in there is the sadness I have about my children. I sometimes take it out of hiding, cry over it, and push it back in again.

I met Tim, on an internet dating site called 'Plenty of Fish', recommended to me by a friend from Sydney. I'm not sure about the fish; I met plenty of frogs before I met my prince. But I enjoyed it. It was an eye opener and an experience. He had only met one other woman as he's a bit shy and not too forthcoming, until you get to meet him, then you can't shut him up! We have a really good marriage and are currently in training to foster children who come from broken homes, and though we are currently living and working on the Gold Coast, we are hoping to move back to Tasmania later this year, after a much awaited trip to South Africa, where Tim will meet my darling family.

When in Tasmania, my 'then partner' went to an Afrikaans new church that they formed. The group ostracised me for not being part of 'the holy grail'. I followed the beautiful nature of Tasmania, having being disillusioned by Catholicism for some time, and found myself drawn to the forest and rivers as my solace and my guide. The peace and serenity I felt after communing with nature far outweighed the stifled feeling of the groups' religion. 'Then partner' told them I was practicing witch craft. I had a beautiful garden, filled with flowers and fruit trees, and my pride and joy herb garden. I also loved things like candles and incense and I had been given a black cat by a customer from work. If these things made me a witch, well then so be it! Who is to say who is 'good' or 'bad'? Who are we to judge another human being?

My whole point of this addition into my story is how sad it is that we have the same roots, but just can't work together, and I think this is part of the problem in South Africa. No one ever said we had to be best mates just because we left SA and moved to the same country, but I think it's sad that South Africans are such judgmental people, and even without hearing the full story; those judgments were made and put in place.

I try not to let this colour my relationships with other South Africans living in Australia, but I keep away from them and I much prefer the Australian people, and choose my friends from them. Of course this has not changed any of my feelings for my dear friends that I already have, either here or in South Africa.

I received permanent residence eight months after being in Australia, went to Auckland to have it validated, and loved every second of being there. New Zealand is like Tasmania on steroids, bigger and faster paced, but just as beautiful. I loved the place names and the attitude of the people.

The Australian government, mainly the department of immigration, gave me a pretty rough time with my residence application; over fifty years old, no skills that they wanted, and no ties in Australia. I still count myself blessed to be granted the honour of living here, and sometimes think I'm going to wake up from a happy dream. I am so excited because later this year I qualify for citizenship. The day that I get my Australian passport will be one of the most exciting days!

In the beginning, one of the reasons for leaving South Africa was to be able to help my family in South Africa out financially, and I still do that. It's a burden, but one I shoulder with a smile and a light heart, knowing that my grandchildren are getting a good education and are eating well due to me sending money 'home' each fortnight. I still consider South Africa home in an ethereal way. I will never lose my love for the land of Africa, and its people. I can only dream that the people will find peace and harmony, but it remains only a dream, at least in my lifetime. I pray daily that my grandchildren will have good lives in that future country. I still listen to Afrikaans music, and support the rugby and cricket teams. In my heart they will always be 'mine', but I have embraced the Australian way of life, music, sport and its people. I have a very soft spot for the Aboriginal people; I feel a link with them, however tenuous.

My other reason for leaving was a sense of adventure. Even in South Africa I was a bit of a nomad, moving every couple of years. I've got a true understanding of that saying 'Freedom means there's nothing left to lose.' I live and travel light, always wondering just what IS around the next corner. My anchor in life is my husband, Tim, and my grandchildren are my guiding star.

Unintentional Migrant   *Kgomotso Mathabe, USA*

I left SA in 2007 and lived in England until 2009, then went back to South Africa for my son who was then aged 4. I then moved to the USA in 2010. I had no intention to leave SA in the first place. Why did I leave? I did my undergraduate studies at a Technikon which was predominately black. When I wanted to convert to a traditional university to do an Honors Degree, Pretoria University and Witwatersrand University felt that I was not qualified or knowledgeable enough to do an Honors Degree. My field of study then, (Biochemistry) was mainly dominated by white people and the committee felt I did not qualify. I am one of MANY cases. They wanted me to start with a BSc from scratch. So, I applied outside the country where I was admitted for a MASTERS degree at the University of Cambridge (biochemistry). I went back home to try to implement this and I was given crap from the company where I worked. They had a lot of bureaucracy, and being a young black woman worked against me.

I then applied for a Doctorate (Major in Plant Biochemistry and a minor in Politics) here in the USA and again, my qualifications were not questioned. People often think that only WHITE people are discriminated against in academia or in the job market. Trust me, we are too! I am not sure when I will go back home but I will. Like most, I've had my cousin murdered, we have been burgled, I've experienced 'smash and grabs', know of relatives that were raped . . . and I am BLACK.

My Journey

Anonymous

Moving to NZ was not the first time I moved country, but it was the first with my husband, as opposed to with my parents. Having had some experience with selling and packing all the material things, this went off without a hitch. About six months after we decided to immigrate, we were ready to leave—everything was sold and we had a ticket in one hand and a suitcase in the other (we had never been to NZ before). We planned on arriving and getting the "three month visitor visa". After a LONG flight we arrived at Auckland airport and took a taxi to collect the camper that we had hired for five weeks.

Now the fun begins; the two of us, our few possessions and a map book in a camper (the size of an SA taxi). We set off to drive from one job interview to the next all over the country. Five weeks' worth of driving and interviewing later, my husband received a good job offer and we applied for work permits. We received the work permits a couple of weeks later and life in NZ began for real, including looking for a house to rent and a car to buy, etc. Initially we moved into a hostel set-up where we stayed for three weeks while we walked wherever we had to go and waited patiently for our visas to arrive. We had to start from scratch and it was great fun being able to shop for EVERYTHING one needs in a house. We slept on a mattress on the floor for a couple of months and used a cardboard box as a coffee table. What this taught us was to appreciate absolutely everything when we purchased it. A lot of thought went into everything and we were so excited with the smallest things.

It was a great experience, but it was extremely stressful! The huge uncertainty, limited funds and lack of friends didn't make it any easier. For some reason I lost all my confidence once we arrived here. I did not want to drive, was scared to speak to people and was still looking over my shoulder every two seconds like I had been doing in SA. This is not the person I used to be. Back in Africa I had a good job, taught at a college part-time and taught aerobics to fairly large groups. It took me a long time to adjust.

We have been here four years now and have two 'Kiwi' children. The reason we left was that we did not see a future there for our planned family. I was very scared having experienced a couple of crime related episodes. We felt it was time to start somewhere new where we could safely raise our children and where we would be treated fairly and have a good opportunities. We chose NZ because we wanted to move soon and it was the only country where we could do what we did visitor-visa-work permit-residence permit-all in one trip without having to wait for years. We also liked the climate!

We often speak about our move and neither of us wants to go back, as there really is nothing to go back to, apart from friends and family. I do not want to take my children to South Africa, as I would fear for them. I enjoy being able to sleep at night without listening to every little noise and not waking up with my heart racing.

Best things about NZ—I love the weather, being safe, not having to worry about locking doors too much, or holding onto my handbag for dear life. NZ is beautiful. We love the environment, beaches, towns and cities.

What I miss about South Africa are my friends. We have really struggled to make friends in NZ. I don't know what the reason is, but it has not been easy. The smaller things I miss are things like Woolworths and a couple of places we used to eat at. If I had one wish it would be that some of my friends or family would move here too!

Migration to here and there!

Angela Quinn, NZ and Qatar

Our migration journey took seed in 2001 when hubby visited NZ, toured the north Island for over 2 weeks in his cousin's little Honda Civic from Auckland to Wellington and back. He arrived back home after his trip and announced that we were moving! This revelation coincided with the horrific rape of a 9 month old baby in SA and it was like a sign. There was a national man-hunt and the case shocked the nation. It was the proverbial straw that broke the camel's back and cemented our decision.

After lots of research from various friends and family members who had had undertaken the 'big move', we were able to plan ahead, thereby avoiding the pitfalls they had encountered, such as ensuring that we had adequate cash in hand and had budgeted for expenses such as food, transportation, rent and school costs.

We started the actual immigration process in 2005 via an agent and paid for half the cost but did not rush them, which enabled us to pay off most of the costs. While waiting for the residency to come through, Bradley accepted a job in Qatar in 2006, after 18 years in the Cape Town Fire Department. We had already decided that I would remain in SA while our eldest child completed her matric. Our residency came through in Sept 2007. We decided to sell our house, pack up everything and move to NZ instead of joining hubby in Qatar and moving twice (before the 1 year to get into the country from date of residency expired). While all this decision-making was taking place, hubby had to leave to go back to Qatar (but came home every three months). The day after he left in October 2007, my car was broken into and our house was burgled the next day in Cape Town. Despite the ensuing trauma, we put the house on the market the next day, while installing sensors and an alarm system. Two weeks later our house was sold and we started the big pack up (with the help of a moving company, which required more research).

At this point I realised the irony of the actual reason that we had decided to leave was to give our kids a better chance in life, as we knew that the spectre and the aftermath results of apartheid would not be eradicated in our kids' lifetimes. Yet crime had unceremoniously pushed us out and 'waved us away from our homeland'.

Brad came back in January and again two days after he left, we were burgled by the same people (who were obviously watching the house and knew our movements)! The police were quite nonchalant and the insurance brokers quite 'annoyed' by this time . . . clearly all our precautions were useless.

As I need to mentally prepare myself for any big decisions, I was quite calm and composed on the day we eventually left. We survived mentally with lots of love and support from our friends and family. I now realise that my calm and confident manner helped my girls a lot after we landed in NZ. We travelled alone, hubby still in Qatar, and spent 10 days with family in Auckland, before proceeding on to Wellington. My younger sister was in SA at this time, so we were met by her husband and we had a good reunion as my kids had not seen their cousins in four years. Two months later, hubby joined us, as he came down for pre-arranged job interviews and elected to take the job offer in Wellington as opposed to the position in New Plymouth. In the one month he was there, we bought a car and home and went to visit family in Auckland again; *shoo*—tired just thinking about it!

Hubby left again to wait for a contract for a job so he could resign in Qatar and join us. This only happened 4 months later due to delays with the contract and he had to give 2 months' notice. During this time, both girls settled into school and Uni surprisingly well.

I was unaware that we were all suffering from severe anxiety, especially my eldest, which she experienced due to the trauma of the break-ins. She was in a daze and didn't get to say 'good-bye' to friends, family and Cape Town properly. I empathised with her and she only managed to find closure three years later when we went to SA last year. Now they both agree with hubby and me that NZ is our home and they would only go back to SA for a visit.

Funny how I think back to how we tried to raise our kids not seeing colour but having it shoved in their faces while out in public places or school in South Africa—a charming by-product of people who had not moved on after apartheid. We explained how people are bitter about the past and how we had been born into a country on the verge of change. We could go to any school, live in any area, provided we could afford to do so. The boycotts were a turning point for us, even though many did not agree with the methods used to achieve this 'freedom'.

We first experienced the after-effects of apartheid while entering the job market . . . affirmative action was a new anomaly and many companies used it as a tool to turn so-called coloureds down. What was ironic was that 'whites' were still coming up trumps as legislation was not yet in effect, so although outwardly adverts stated 'affirmative action' post (yes, true story); whites were still getting many jobs in Cape Town! Hubby had signed on at the fire dept. and rose in the ranks only by studying hard while working. It was hard with a family but I worked as well, as we both had the same goals. I matched hubby eventually career-wise and excelled, with on-the-job training. This was to stand me in good stead working in NZ, as I had the best working experience while there. Hubby was still working in Qatar at this time but resigned citing immigration purposes to his bosses. He was upfront with them from the start and must have made quite an impression on them as they told him to advise when ready to come back and they wanted him to apply for a new post, as opposed to his current one of fire instructor! Eight months later he was hired as Area Fire Chief of the offshore Fire Dept., quite a coup as once you leave Qatar you have to wait two years before you can work there again.

About a month before we were to leave for Qatar, our daughter Shanelle decided to finish her studies in NZ as opposed to joining us. This was heart-wrenching for me as we had never been separated before hubby worked in Qatar, and the 18 months I spent in SA was hell! She was in her last semester of Tech and was to start Uni the following one. After much discussion on the practicalities and logistics I finally made peace with her decision. Had it not been for my two sisters living in close proximity, I would not have relented. My sisters called every day to check up on her and the day she sounded a bit down they would tell her to pack a bag and pick her up. This was a great comfort to me where safety wasn't really a concern.

The day we arrived in Qatar, we left temperatures of 8-10'c and arrived to 45'c. My husband was terrified we would hate the place and asked us to just give him a year . . . 3 and 1/2 years later we are still here. The culture shock was intense and the weather was the greatest obstacle, living in 'canned air' instead of NZ's fresh mountain air, being surrounded by dust instead of greenery. I suppose I have made it work as I need to mentally prepare myself for change and I believe kids sense the acceptance and follow suit by adapting. We arrived at the start of the summer; one week after the schools closed and missed the mass exodus out of Doha. The driving here is atrocious but I had to bite the bullet or be dependent on taxis or drivers when hubby went offshore for 7 days! I decided to be proactive by researching things to do in Doha. I joined Doha Mums group, went to various coffee groups, even one with ladies who had older kids. When Chelsea started school in Doha, she made two friends on the 1st day and I could not stop smiling, as when your kids are happy, everything just falls into place.

We have since visited SA three times and were fortunate enough to grant Shanelle's wish to have her 21st birthday in SA. Shanelle felt that her visit to SA after 3 years made her understand our reasons for leaving . . . even though we had long discussions with our kids, due to the trauma of the break-ins, she didn't get to process the 'goodbyes' of her birthplace. She can now admit she would never be able to live there again, but CT and SA will forever flow in her veins . . .

Life has been comfortable for us thus far and we plan to move back to NZ by next year, as we would like to work towards our citizenship. After Chelsea is settled in tertiary education, we will probably be back in the Middle East and use it as a tool to travel the world. In conclusion, I firmly believe we are where we are today because we are meant to be here . . . nothing was handed to us, we had to work hard for everything, thereby appreciating the small things and feeling richer for the journey.

Peru—Living the Legend   *Michelle Orsi, Peru & Oz*

' . . . whether a place is a hell or a heaven rests in yourself, and those who go with courage and an open mind may find themselves in Paradise.'

—Eva Ibbotson

December 18th, 2010, the day finally arrived. This was the first day of the rest of our lives . . . This was to be our greatest adventure ever! Filled with conflicting emotions of excitement, fear, sadness and trepidation we embarked on our journey to distant shores; to the land of exquisite sunsets, treacherous mountains, spectacular Andean landscapes, snow-capped mountains and turquoise blue lagoons. Remnants of Ancient Inca civilisations and gorgeous churches beckoned. Okay. STOP! Rewind . . .

Let's start at the beginning. I think that we're a relatively normal, middle class family. We live in the plush suburb of St Andrews in Bedfordview, Johannesburg, in a house we've been renting for the past few months. Dad is an Electrical Engineer, mom (that would be me) an avid photographer and Graphic Designer and our two girls are Daniela (11 years old) and Alessia (10 going on 25). Both girls attend St Andrews school for Girls, a private school not too far from where we live.

A year or so ago, we put our beautiful home in Fourways (Johannesburg) on the market because Raffaele's (that would be my husband) company informed him that in order to grow in the company, an overseas assignment would be required (to 'Globalise' they said). In fact it was not really negotiable, but where to exactly, we did not yet know. Since the company is International with three offices in Canada, one in Australia and even one in Shanghai, we were 'sort of' expecting to be sent to a civilized part of the world (We were secretly hoping it would be Canada). Can you imagine the look of sheer horror on my face when my husband told me to pack up—as we were off to Peru . . . ? Seriously? I don't even know where that is!

The house was eventually sold and we started selling off all our possessions. We decided to travel light, knowing that the company would be furnishing our apartment for us. We also didn't want anything holding us back as we decided as a family that we would use our four year contract in Peru as a stepping stone into Canada. Truth be told, we didn't really want to return to South Africa at all. Rising crime, political instability, high costs of private schooling and an unsure future for our girls made our decision to follow another star easier. Peru it will have to be then!

Okay, so now we can queue . . . December 18, 2010 . . . No-one came to see us off at the airport that day; all our goodbyes were said the night before. My family don't do goodbyes very well . . . This way was just easier for everyone (especially for me), but honestly, although I was sad to say goodbye to my friends and family . . . AND my beautiful homeland, I was so ready for this new chapter in my life . . . in OUR life. *Vamoos!* (That means 'let's go' in Spanish).

We landed at Jorge Chávez International Airport in Lima on the 19th December . . . two tired children and a grumpy husband in tow (no cigarette in 22 hours—can you imagine?) (I don't know which was worse). We were driven to our hotel in stunned silence. The girls had eyes as big as saucers. At one point I remember thinking to myself, OMG, What have we done? Lima was chaos; taxis as far as the eye could see, drivers with little, (or rather, NO) regard for their fellow road users, and the hooting was deafening. Flashing neon signs on just about every street corner read 'Casino' or '*Tragamonedas*' and the smell of burnt meat combined with exhaust fumes hung heavy in the air. Talk about sensory overload! 'Oh my word—is this what hell is like?'

After a few days, however, things started to settle down—a little! Granted, by this time we had hardly left our hotel room at all . . . we were so scared that someone was going to speak to us in Spanish! (Oh, by the way, we didn't speak a word of Spanish.) We were due to move into our apartment by the end of the week . . . We just couldn't wait to be in a place of our own. The novelty of living in a fancy hotel tends to wear off after a while as you can well imagine. True to their word though, we were in our new place 3 days before Christmas . . . Oh crumbs! Christmas—I totally forgot about Christmas! Panic and more stress.

How do I explain to my ten year old that Santa will probably not be able to make it in time this year because of all the confusion with time zones and addresses etc? She's already onto me about his existence as it is, so I hail a taxi (this is the first time that I've ever done something like this in my life) armed with the name of a shopping mall written on a piece of 'hotel issue' paper and a couple of hundred *soles* (that's the currency they use in Peru). I embark on my first solo Peruvian adventure.

Christmas went by without a hitch. Next thing we have to get through is New Year. We have been invited to my husband's colleagues home to celebrate with them since we have absolutely nothing and know no-one else here. New Year is an experience in itself. So many traditions and superstitions with promises of good fortune, loads of money and travel if you follow all the rules which we were to learn soon enough! Everything at New Year is Yellow . . . Yellow is supposedly a colour that symbolises good luck, even your underwear is meant to be yellow, so we rush out to the market to get yellow underwear . . . I'm not taking any chances here—if I didn't have bad luck, I'd have no luck at all! But who wears yellow underwear—Orange maybe, but Yellow? (Okay, my Dutch tendencies are coming through here.)

We begin the evening with traditional Peruvian dancing; Peruvian folk songs accompanied by the beautiful sound of the acoustic guitar and laughter echo around the room. The Peruvians are a warm and friendly people and there is always room for one more guest at the dinner table. Delightful treats and exotic Amazonian fruits are displayed beautifully on the tables . . . The Peruvians are much like the Italians, in that they enjoy eating to live . . . They live to eat! We sing late into the night and drink copious amounts of home-made *Pisco Sour* (That's something like our home-made *Mampoer!*) and then close to midnight the superstitions and traditions start.

I'm rather intrigued as I don't know what to expect, but we've resolved ourselves to the saying 'When in Rome, *yada, yada* . . .' We have to make this work as four years is a long time! My favourite Peruvian superstition is an old one that says that if you run around the block carrying your empty suitcases at midnight, you'll be sure to travel in the upcoming year. So just to be sure, I take two bags and head out the door (far too many *Pisco sours* at this point to even count.)But at this time I miss home so much and anything that will get me back to my parents and three sisters I'll consider doing, even if it means crawling around the block!) Peruvian New Year is also celebrated like they do in Hillbrow (Johannesburg). You know, out with the old, in with the new . . . watching nervously I'm half expecting an old washing machine to come flying out of an apartment window at any time, as I make my way around a strange neighbourhood carrying my empty suitcases, but fortunately nothing but a couple of *centimos* (cents) land on the ground around me . . . (another superstition). In the early hours of the morning, my husband's colleague hails a taxi for us and we clamber into it rather noisily, (still reeling from the *Pisco* . . .) Now if you think the taxis in SA are bad then you know nothing! My husband gets into the front seat and is handed a large metal container contraption 'thingy'. It's the petrol tank . . . We look at each other rather nervously. But the taxi driver gets us home in one piece, although his battered 'krok' looks like it's held together with chewing gum and a frantic prayer. As we get out, my husband says *'Baie Dankie!'* (Thank you) Señor Castillo looks at us blankly, shakes his head and drives off . . . Gringos! Raffaele and I look at each other again. At this point we cannot contain our laughter any longer. Strange how your brain knows that it's in a foreign country (no English) and automatically reverts to another language—Why Afrikaans, we'll never know! Raffaele can't even speak Afrikaans!

Next on our 'Things to do list' . . . a bit of sight seeing is on the cards. We're trying to familiarise ourselves with the place a little, so we decide to embark on a Lima City Tour . . . Mmmmm, pamphlets are all in SPANISH and we end up making a HUGE mistake! Okay, it really wasn't all bad; we saw some amazing sights . . . Ancient Huacas (Inca Ruins right in the city centre), beautiful Spanish Architecture and the Malaccan (beach front), but we also ended up at an old Monastery (Catacombes) where they buried all the Peruvians during the Spanish Inquisition . . . Hundreds of skulls line the walls, femurs lying everywhere and the musty smell of rot hangs in the air . . . The girls are freaked out and are crying hysterically, Raffaele is claustrophobic and needs a cigarette and the tour guide rambles on and on about God knows what . . . It's all Spanish to me, anyway . . . we just really want to get out of there, thinking next time we'll pay that little bit extra for an English speaking tour guide after all. Now where is that exit sign?

February 2011 . . . We've been here just over two months, and so far so good. The apartment is wonderful; I've never lived in an apartment before. We have this elevator 'thing' that opens up into our living room; just like in the movies . . . . it's strange but so cool. Our apartment is huge, so not at all like living in a flat. In fact it's probably a bit bigger than our house that we had back home, but NO garden, eeeeck! We are rather fortunate in that we have private access to a beautiful park from the basement though. We even have a few pet squirrels there and a hawk. The brightly coloured Macaws frequently visit us, too. I still don't have a housekeeper and ironing is the pits . . . In fact I'm sure that there will be dishes and ironing in hell! All our personal belongings arrived safely from South Africa the other day, so unpacking all our boxes was really exciting! Just like Christmas all over again! I can't wait to start making my apartment feel like home . . .

Yay! I've finally found a housekeeper . . . '*Pero, no entiendo ñada Engles*' (But I don't understand ANY English!) Oh crumbs . . . I quickly weigh up my options . . . my ever increasing pile of laundry and 'a slight language technicality' and I quickly realise that it's virtually a 'no brainer' . . . You're hired!! What I also find on the World Wide Web is probably the most fabulous tool and definitely something an expat should not go without . . . GOOGLE TRANSLATE! What an absolute life-saver. I type in an instruction, press the translate button and Isaura (My 'by-now domestic Goddess') understands exactly what I need her to do. Sometimes however, even Google gets it wrong and then she just stares at me, raises her eyebrows and says '*Ke?*' (In other words, WTH). "Oh well" I shrug, "don't worry, it doesn't really need to get done today anyway". I LOVE MY HOUSEKEEPER!

March 2011 . . . The Girls are ready to start school. We have found a wonderful school, San Silvestre, 'A place of eternal belonging' which is an International Catholic School for Girls in the heart of Miraflores, quite lose to where we live. What an amazing place . . . and the people! My worried mama's heart is at ease. Granted, it's right in the middle of a city, so space is severely limited. There are three stories of 'earthquake safe' school with one field in the middle of it. It's a beautifully modern school but still a far cry from the facilities we were accustomed to. We're soon to learn that all sports get done on this patch of grass—concurrently! Softball, Hockey, Athletics and the odd javelin flying overhead all at the same time is the norm, but still it feels strangely like HOME! I know that my girls are going to love it here.

The first day of school is over and I'm so excited to go and fetch my girls . . . I leave the house early only to find them both sitting in the quad in tears . . . I rush over to them thinking that something terrible must have happened . . . "Mommy, I don't understand anybody, I don't have any friends, and I sat alone at lunch time (in the bathroom) . . . and everything is in Spanish!" I sigh . . .! Oh dear, somehow I knew that this would happen . . . They took a few Spanish lessons in South Africa before we came to Peru and a few more before school started, but I don't think anything could've quite prepared them for what they experienced on their first day. I have the Headmistress and all the Academic staff around trying to comfort us, (by now, I'm in tears, too). Everyone *SO* wanted this day to go well, but it didn't . . . In all honesty, the girls' first day at school was probably one of my darkest days in Peru. My heart was broken! *(Although San Silvestre is a British International school, they are also a fully bilingual school and many of their lessons are in fact in Spanish and the majority of the girls that go there only speak Spanish, English being their second language. What we found was that in true human form, the Peruvian girls were too scared to speak to my girls because they didn't want to look and sound silly when they spoke in English . . . (and vice versa) so they just avoided each other altogether.)*

The next two months were hell . . . I packed my bags several times . . . I counted three times in one week alone. Daniela and Alessia struggled to make friends, 'limped' along in their Spanish homework and woke up every morning with anxiety and stomach aches. I was a nervous wreck and my husband was hardly home due to work pressures and the task of having to set up the Lima office. I started self-medicating on anti-depressants (Medicine is freely available over the counter in Peru without a script; very different from SA where you need a script just for paracetamol.) I slept for most of the day and spent the rest of the day watching really old 'Grey's Anatomy' re-runs . . . And then, just as suddenly as the anxiety started, it stopped . . . Soon my children were reading beautiful bilingual books, ordering for us at restaurants (in Spanish) and correcting our very bad 'Taxi Spanish'. A parent at the school even commented on my daughters' beautiful English . . . Um, that's 'cause they are English! She could not believe it. She honestly thought that they were Spanish speaking. And then the words came one night while we were pouring over Spanish book reports that brought a song to my heart . . . 'Mom, this Spanish thing is a whole lot easier than Afrikaans!' . . . Alleluia—We have a breakthrough! We, on the other hand have resorted to charades and sound effects most of the time. Typical Gringos! But, it's a ton of laughs and we get it wrong all the time!

One of our funnier moments in Peru was up in Cusco exploring the wonders of the Inca Ruins (Machu Picchu) when a Llama spat at my daughter. They tend to do this when they are annoyed or threatened.

She was horrified. Large chunks of grass and spit was hanging from her eyelashes! Naturally, we couldn't stop laughing, and this upset her even more!

I remember going to the supermarket with Raffaele one day and we spent about ten minutes looking for the butter. We still couldn't read many of the labels on the products and most of the time we returned home with the wrong item. (We learnt to laugh at ourselves a lot during this time.) But, back to the butter, Raffaele decided to ask a shop attendant for assistance. Incidentally Raffaele is Italian and if he doesn't know a word, whether that word is Spanish or English, he reverts to Italian. So he goes up to this kind looking youngster (Peruvians have beautiful kind looking faces) and asks, '¿Dónde está el . . . burro? ' (Butter in Italian is Burro). But in Spanish what he was actually asking is, 'Where is the donkey?' I'm sure the shop attendant must've thought I'm looking at the Ass right now! Fun times lay ahead!

Another wonderful experience I had in Peru was trying to order pizza over the phone in my very broken Spanish. I must have had the phone put down on me three or four times, and then I discovered how to order Pizza online. Necessity truly is the mother of invention! Ordering Domino's pizza became a regular thing, but this time without the added stress and anxiety of actually having to talk to someone that clearly didn't understand a word of what I was saying. While we're on the subject of food though, I must share what happened one day while I was lovingly preparing my family a meal . . . So, I'm happily cleaning a chicken for a roast dinner and I proceed to open the stomach, like one does, and this chicken's head pops out. I promise you, beak and all . . . glaring right at me. Obviously roast chicken was called off that night and Domino's Pizza received another online order from me. So that was my introduction to Peruvian cuisine. They also eat Guinea pigs in Peru, and I have since become an activist for these furry little creatures.

Back to school, with their new found confidence, the girls started getting more involved at school. Alessia played softball and Dani played hockey and did Gymnastics. Both swam and were involved in the Eco-team. They were flourishing in their schoolwork and soon became popular members in their class. They had made many friends and adored their teachers. Their little worlds were intact, although, Daniela did come home horrified the one day as San Silvestre played an 'away' hockey game at another International school in the area. "Mom, do you know that we actually played in a CAR PARK!" We had to laugh!

Once again, with my girls' 'content', my world slowly started returning to normal, too. There seemed to be a glimmer of hope for me after all. I was told by a close friend (who has seen many International families come and go over the years) that when families migrate internationally, it is always the Mum who carries the weight of smoothing the transition and very often her needs are ignored and forgotten. How true this was in my case . . . the full impact of our move to Peru had finally hit me. I was *LONELY*! Now, although I actually enjoy my own company, I quickly realised that I don't love it that much! And then it happened. My Angels appeared!

The South African Women's Group got in contact with me through the South African Embassy in Peru. I didn't even know that the group existed. All in all, about 20 South African families were currently residing in Lima and I didn't even know. All of them, mainly from mining or infrastructure backgrounds—English, Afrikaans and Zulu speaking. I LOVED THEM ALL! We met once every two weeks for family braais and even a potjie here and there! And then in between, we ladies met for coffee every other week. It was '*Blerrie' Lekker*!' (Bloody nice). Finally people that understood me! Naturally we ALL reverted to speaking in Afrikaans when we were together too, eating vetkoek, koeksusters and MELKTERT! It was such fun, good times!

Everyday things started looking better, more promising and more inviting. I slowly ventured out on my own little Peruvian adventure . . . day by day . . . one step at a time while my daughters were at school. I found little 'Green Grocers' along the way, colourful markets and local food halls, the inviting coffee shops and the delectable pastries . . . soon I realised that my Spanish was not that bad. I quickly learned how to say "Where are the shops?" '¿ *Donde están las tiendas?*' and now I am fluent in Spanish! I even joined a local softball club. My team mates were amazing. They accepted me as one of their own. They must've seen that I could catch a flyball and decided that this 'Gringa' was not so bad after all! The softball field was a sandlot. Old rusted bed posts stood upright against the walls and old paint tins lined the boundary fence. The dugout was literally a hole dug out of the ground, but I was in my element! I was at home!

I started going to a really nice church *(there are only 3 English Churches in Lima)* so my choice was somewhat limited, but it was fine. The church met in the Cinema on a Sunday morning (due to space constraints a lot of buildings double up as other businesses, clubs etc.)

It was rather unconventional with the offering buckets being popcorn boxes! We would get a live feed from the States, so it was like watching those TV Evangelists. It took some getting used to though. The singers were Spanish people trying to sing in English. I will stress the word TRYING! There is so much opportunity here to get involved with mission work due to the dire poverty in some areas. It just broke my heart. Occasionally our church went to build houses for the people in rural villages and teach children's church, which was so meaningful.

The joys of finally belonging, of fitting in and of being a piece to someone else's puzzle was overwhelming and wonderful. I remember standing in the local grocery store one day, looking at the wine rack and debating the differences between Chilean versus Peruvian versus South African wine with my husband when I spotted a lady out of the corner of my eye making a sprint at me. I was slightly taken a back, but then I noticed that she was crying. "What part of South Africa are you from?" She asked . . . and "Can I please hug you?" It turned out that she had been in Lima for a fortnight, knew no-one and she couldn't read the labels on her groceries. These were the things that no-one warned us about when we agreed to our wild adventures in South America, and yet they were big enough to throw one's world into tilt. From that day forth we were great friends. I taught her all the Spanish I knew, showed her all the little markets that I had discovered in my meanderings around Lima, showed her how to hail a taxi off the street and even got her to eat the crazy Peruvian cuisine.

We became inseparable as we limped through life together. Back home in South Africa, we lived in the very same suburb and more than likely shopped at the same Woolies and ate at the same restaurants. Under normal circumstances, would we have become friends; more than likely not? But I thank God every day for the friends I made in Peru, the life lessons that I learnt and the wonderful things that I encountered there. He most certainly knows what he is about.

23 July 2011 was the day when the beautiful, exciting little world that we had created for ourselves came crashing down. Raffaele had accepted a Director position at Hatch, (the company that sent us to Lima to begin with) but it required him to be based in Africa . . . So we got ready to pack our lives into boxes once again and after being in Peru for exactly 10 months (and lots of heartache and frustration later) we were right back to where we started, but this time, minus a house and furniture. Positive though was that we had learnt a new language,

experienced a new culture and experienced a wonderful world. I was devastated to say goodbye to Peru, but I know that I will return someday as there is so much that I did not get to see or imbibe . . .

What a sad, sad day!

OUR coming to Peru, mysteriously, for such a short time, was no mistake—the Divine Potter is tending, shaping and forming every detail of our lives—interior and exterior and at every moment. He knows what He is about! You have no idea how much the stint in Peru has changed my outlook on life and on people. Amongst other things, I've learnt valuable lessons about what is important in life and what is not. I spent the last couple of weeks in Peru working, walking, wandering, wondering, and often I found myself in candlelit churches at twilight as day kissed night—thinking . . . "How wonderful life is!"

Oh God, on my past night my heart was in ruins! I failed dismally at holding back the tears. Peru stole my heart. Indeed heaven on earth. Memories made over the past months were tucked away in my heart forever! On my last day I read one of Alessia's mini assignments and I got Goosebumps . . . "I am South African, but in my heart I am Peruvian." What a change in my child! What a change in us all! I thank God for the amazing opportunities that we were given. But for now, we needed to answer the call of the wild. The next day our hearts would beat to a different drum. We would be going HOME. But honestly, where exactly was HOME? I'm afraid I just didn't know anymore . . .

We were back in South Africa for six months, and what a tough period it was. I didn't recognise my own country anymore . . . I don't recognise my children anymore . . . and more importantly, I no longer recognised myself anymore. Anger, fear, anxiety and depression gripped at us all over again. But this time, we'd all been hit and HARD! The girls were no longer coping at school. They were back to dragging their mattresses into our bedroom at night because they were too scared to sleep alone and I had to schedule an appointment with the educational psychologist. The friends we had all moved on and my girls had somehow been left behind, although they were way ahead in most of their school work and were bored and frustrated. The obvious decline in the country and the schooling system was evident and very disheartening, or had we just set higher standards now? Either way, no-one was happy. The country that we had once pined for was no longer the place we remembered so fondly. We longed for the simplicity of Peru. Its vibrancy and sense of adventure, noise, chaos and colour appealed to us more than we could ever have imagined. Photographs and memories taunted us, cruelly reminding us of what we once had and took for granted . . . But I've come to realise that life's like that. One never knows what one has until one loses it. But then again, it's also far better to have loved and lost, than never to have loved at all.

And then it happened, the call that was going to set out lives in yet another direction. That global mobile phone of my husband's is similar to that of the emergency telephone in the White House. When it rings, you take note and you listen! Secretly my heart pleaded for it to be Peru, but deep down I knew that that chapter of our lives was over for good. The company's request was for us to go to Brisbane, Australia—and immediately if possible! And so we began packing our lives up in boxes yet again. We had done this so often that it came naturally to us like brushing our teeth. We aren't sentimental people so we packed only what we could not get in Australia—a few personal belongings, my beloved books, photographs, original paintings and our Christmas tree. Strangely, this time around there was no anxiety, no fear, just perfect peace. The relocation and paperwork went off without any issues and within 5 weeks we found ourselves in Queensland. What a breath of fresh air. What an amazing place to live in. We felt truly blessed beyond measure.

Post Script: We have all adapted beautifully to life in Brisbane, as was to be expected. The girls are flourishing in every area and my husband is making a name for himself at work. Many people have mentioned that moving children so often is detrimental to their development, but I choose to disagree. As a family unit we have discovered strengths we never knew we had. We are resilient as individuals and a stronger family for it. The girls have experienced new languages, new cultures, and they've got to see the world. How much more have they learnt, than by sitting in a classroom? They have grown in leaps and every day that goes by, I see that they truly are Citizens of the World . . . My heart is at peace! All will be well!

> **'You have made us for yourself, O Lord, and our hearts are restless until they rest in Thee.'**
> **—St Augustine**

I spent the day driving around Queensland looking for that one picture that would make me smile and it was literally in my own backyard all along . . . THE GIRLS ARE HAPPY! How blessed I am to be able to afford them the same childhood memories that I have. Playing out in the street until sunset, riding bicycles with friends and the opportunity to be a child again! Life sure is good at the moment!

Reasons for Leaving Southern Africa . . . Work permitted

Kirsty Poppelstone, UK & Kenya

Travelling had never been one of my priorities. My parents weren't particularly well-off back then, so we didn't see the option of taking a gap year and "travelling". It was something that some schoolmates planned on matriculating. "I'm going to travel," no doubt planning some charitable work to ease their post-Apartheid conscience.

I went to study towards a profession that meant we were paid while studying; always an attractive option for an independent materialist like me. Radiography in SA was a diploma course, which led to some derision from my university-bound peers. I was going to get paid though, and after three years I would be employable, unlike those who did three years' worth of BA or BSc and little to show for it.

On qualifying there were no posts available in the Western Cape, and so I began my career as a nomad, undertaking locums in remote towns like Caledon, Alexander Bay and Oudtshoorn. I didn't know then that I wouldn't live permanently in Cape Town again for at least fifteen years.

Ultimately it seemed that no attractive positions were available in parts of SA that I wanted to live in. My mother had qualified as a physiotherapist in London in the early 70's and was adamant that I should spend some time in the UK. On investigating the possible visas, we discovered that I qualified for an Ancestral Visa: my British-born grandfather (who died while my father was still a child) meant that I qualified for ancestral rights. Essentially I could work and live in the UK for up to four years with the option of residency after that.

It sounded perfect. I could gain experience at prestigious hospitals in England and return home with an edge over others competing for the same positions. My qualification was recognised in the UK and all that was required was the (expensive) process of professional registration . . . I remember it as a time of great excitement and anticipation about my new future but with a little concern at the reputation that the Brits weren't initially welcoming and it would take a long time to make friends . . . And so I flew to England, alone, aged 23, due to be collected from the airport by friends of my mother's that I didn't feel I knew very well.

This is a long-roundabout way of saying "It was never my intention to emigrate". I didn't see myself as leaving South Africa. I hadn't sold up my entire life and set out to make a permanent move to a different country. I had registered with an employment agency, so fortunately I had a locum position lined up within a week. South Africans are generally welcomed to professional positions in the UK. We have a reputation for working hard, not being clock-watchers and we're generally loyal to employers. Even as I write this, I wonder if this is still the case . . .

The promised British coolness was obvious from the outset. It was months before I was invited to join any colleagues in a social setting and those who invited me were South African. It seemed that professional and social circles are kept very much apart. One would never dream of "popping in" uninvited; something I remember my parents and I doing regularly as a child. Or maybe security-consciousness in SA has changed that too.

My own Great Trek

Some cultural aspects took me totally by surprise. The street sweepers, the weekly refuse collectors, the bus drivers: they were all *white*. It took me further by surprise that I should find that unusual. They are roles, however, that in South Africa, until I left at least, would never be filled by a white person.

The class system in England also bothered me. I was offended at the immediate assumption that I was a confirmed racist, while the oppression of those considered to be in a lower class, regardless of their skin colour, was accepted as right.

I acknowledged references to Spitting Image's "I've never met a nice South African" with a fake smile and gritted teeth, thinking all the time "You lot are far more irrational in your dislike of others than most Saffa's".

My mother's family date back to the original Great Trek farmers. My great uncle was one of the Afrikaners who supported the principles of Apartheid. He believed that black and white people were different, but *equal*. Most of the black people I encountered as a child were farm workers, uneducated labourers, who lived in such remote areas that facilities for education had simply not reached them.

You just never learn your lesson

Naturalisation and a British Passport opened a significant door: my own front door. As a foreigner, a first-time buyer would be required to pay at least a 20% deposit in order to secure a mortgage on a house. As a citizen, that deposit commitment was reduced to 10%, but 10% of £200 000 was still a fortune. My parents grudgingly assisted when I fell about £3000 short of the required total, probably knowing it was the top of a slippery slope.

The mortgage lender agreed to a mortgage of five and a half times my salary. I was delighted—I could buy a house! I chose not to see much further than My Own Space. Not many other expats had managed that, especially not on a single income. It took me a little longer to come to terms with the reality. I fooled myself for too long, my budget initially covered my expenses, but I hadn't counted on the little things: the inevitable additional little costs that one never considered.

Nostalgia isn't what it used to be

Visits home on holiday were a mixed blessing. I planned my holidays back to Cape Town for February where possible: the time when the damp and the dark of the winter became too much to bear and Cape Town's Southeaster had calmed enough to prevent bare legs being sandblasted on every trip to the beach. I particularly enjoyed returning to work with a glorious tan, ("You're dirty, go and wash it off," I was often told), but mostly just a feeling of having been Home.

"You sound more South African after you've been home." God forbid! Most South African accents are hardly attractive to international ears.

My school and student acquaintances had moved on; mostly married with children, with their worlds shrinking as much as mine had expanded. I was, exactly as I had been in Surrey, lonely. There was something wrong with the picture. I'd come home to be amongst my people.

I'm 30-something, not twelve any more.

So my holidays were largely spent growing ever more frustrated with my long-suffering parents. "You really need to stop smoking. Don't you think you're drinking too much? How much do you think you drink in a week? You really need to budget."

"But there's nothing else to *do* in winter." "It's what everyone else does in the evenings." "I've got friends at the pub."

Three months at home had been like an extended holiday—the previous holidays where I'd felt nagged, felt I needed to ask permission to go out.

Tourist in my own town

My best mate from the UK came over to Cape Town for a holiday after I'd been back for a few months. In her company, I got the best of both worlds: the gossip, the reminiscing, the feeling of longing for the England without actually wanting to go back there.

I came to see in myself a trait that I had despised in the UK: many South Africans, especially those based in London, would spend all their time with other South Africans, speak Afrikaans as much as possible, criticise SA from a safe distance, reminisce about home, but adamantly vow never to go back there.

And we did the tourist thing as I had never done it before. I suspect few Capetonians would make the time to do the tourist things if they weren't showing others around, assuming of course that they could afford it. Table Mountain, Boulders Beach, The Two Oceans Aquarium, two nights at a private game reserve. I could pretend I was paying in pounds and to hell with the cost.

Karibu Sana (You're very welcome)

On hearing that I was taking on a contract in Kenya, many expressed envy. "Kenya is beautiful, the scenery, the game parks, the mountains . . ." It sounded like the best bits of the Lowveld that I remember from family holidays.

The catch was, and is, that I'm not in Kenya, I'm in Nairobi; in a very third world African city were nothing is familiar, where suddenly the white people (*"mzungu's"* as we're known) are in the far minority. The white people in Nairobi are mostly transient: United Nations workers or diplomats or business people who come to contribute their bit to Africa and then leave again. It's a slightly cynical attitude, but I got spoilt in the UK. I still believe that the adjustment to Nairobi would have been easier if my time in England had never happened.

I feel that I'm African at heart, but I realised just how convenient it is to say that when it suits us. The white people in Kenya are targets for every form of ruthlessness imaginable. It is presumed, probably rightly, that the whites have money and so I am pestered by countless beggars, street hawkers, roadside flower/fruit/curio/puppy-seller. It's no secret that a white person will get charged significantly more for the same item than a Kenyan.

It's an isolating world. I have company at work, but at 5pm everyone goes home to their families and their lives and that is when you realise how important a support network is and to what extent 'Face Book' just doesn't match up.

And so I watch endless reruns of Top Gear and Waking the Dead and Spooks. I *know* that world. I get the innuendoes about Burberry tartan and Skoda's and a curry after a night out. Or perhaps everyone in Southern African gets them now. Perhaps their world now includes Hello and OK! and The Sun (online probably).

I spend fortunes on Mrs Ball's Chutney and Ouma Rusks.

I love—*The* Southern Cross, The RWC final in the White Hart, a *Braai* under a garage door, baked beans for breakfast . . .

All expat Saffas may be strangers, but we have something in common.

I resent colonial expats in SA—it's my country to criticise.

You know your heart is still in SA, when these things make you want to be home:

The Boeing flying over Newlands in 1995

Any David Kramer /VW bus advert

'Jock of the Bushveld' . . . Any fawn Staffie with a white patch on his chest . . .

It's always been about our boys . . .

Jenny Hubbard, NZ

It's always been about our boys. From the minute the first one screamed his way into our lives—it's been only about the boys . . . .

So there we were—a young married couple, successful, owned our own home which we had spent 10 years renovating to exactly how we wanted it with two small boys aged five and a one month old baby when we decided to make a change that would alter our lives forever.

The eldest was about to start school and we were not zoned for a good enough school in our area, so we knew we would have to sell and move to ensure a better education. So, we thought, surely moving around the corner and around the world cannot be too different?! We chose New Zealand . . .

My husband left first in search of a job and I stayed behind, packed up the house and got all our affairs in order. Saying goodbye was probably, no make that definitely, the hardest thing I have ever done. I had to keep thinking of my boys and that seemed to calm the tremors I felt in my heart.

Arriving in NZ was scary, exciting and unnerving. The first thing that struck me was the cleanliness and safety. When we arrived at the house my hubby had painstakingly picked out as our first home, I thought—'where are the burglar guards and fence—is he crazy?!' It didn't take long for the irrational fear of life that I had always assumed was normal to dissipate. Before long the eldest boy was going to the loo alone in the mall and walking to school unaccompanied! I knew that despite the long and hard road behind me and the fear of the unknown ahead of me, it was all worth it when I looked at my sons—flourishing in this new place.

It is not easy. I have always smiled with the knowledge that only someone who has done this can understand when I hear "immigration is not for sissies"! We arrived with very little and had to start again—almost soul destroying when we had achieved so much in SA. The loneliness is heart-breaking. Luckily for us my brother was here and we were later joined by another brother and my Mum. Family is the glue that kept me together when I felt that surely I cannot get up and face another day. There were also many days of pure joy. Every journey was a journey of discovery in this new land, and we grew to love the natural wonders NZ had to offer.

There was no rape, murder, high jacking, burglary that we personally experienced that made us decide to leave SA. Only our two little boys' future, which was too uncertain in SA and not something I could risk. I salute South Africans who have stayed and fought for a brighter new SA. I am grateful to them and proud of that fighting spirit. I know there are those who wish they could have done what we did, but cannot for various reasons—For those I feel their pain.

I have now lived in NZ for six years and can say that I feel settled and happy MOST of the time. I have days when the pain in my heart, that yearning for my home is incredibly strong. That sense of belonging is never quite there; of just being understood, the amazing South African sense of humour. I am about to apply for New Zealand citizenship and I am grateful for the many countless opportunities I have been blessed with here. I will happily pledge allegiance to this country that accepted us and gave us the chance to mould our young boys into men who will fill my heart to bursting with pride. BUT—I will always be South African . . . and proudly so. I will never forget my roots, nor allow the boys to forget theirs. I will always pray for my home country, pray that it rises to the great potential it has. And I will always shout for the Bokke!

As I proof read the book, Jenny had a bonny Kiwi daughter delivered on 1 November 2012.

We're a biracial same-sex couple. Or are we a same-sex biracial couple?
12 November 2012　　　　*Louis de Araujo, Vancouver, Canada*

In South Africa, I was White and he was Coloured, even after the abolition of Apartheid. In Canada, we're a couple, plain and simple. After half a lifetime in a land where labels defined us and were an integral part of our daily existence, it's refreshing to know we'll be spending the rest of our lives in a country where labels are reserved for clothing, groceries and drugs. Canadians have this multicultural unity-through-diversity lark down to a fine art. I guess you could say we're a rainbow nation too, except without the baggage. Which is not to excuse White Canada's well documented history of repressing its Aboriginal citizens, but that's someone else's story to tell, not mine. I'm talking about the country we embraced—and which, in turn, embraced us—when we emigrated from South Africa in 1995.

Life for a Gay White man in the Jo'burg of the Sixties, Seventies and Eighties was a breeze, really, even if you were living on the wrong side of the law as, anyone who ever had a run-in with the SAP back in the bad old days would know. Homosexuals could be law abiding citizens, and still live on the wrong side of the law. From time to time, friends would endure heart stopping encounters with thugs from the dreaded Vice Squad, usually in the form of a surprise visit after dark. I know, from personal experience. If they figured you were gay, that surprise visit could turn into a living nightmare. The worst I experienced, though, was an unscheduled sleepover at John Vorster Square in its glory days (the late Seventies) when the gay club where I was bartending was raided one night. The owners had fallen behind on their 'protection' contributions and the cops wreaked vengeance by shutting them down—but not before confiscating the club's entire stock of liquor and throwing its barmen in jail. Perhaps not so scary in itself, but those were the dark days of detention without trial. If memory serves me, the law allowed for us to be imprisoned for forty eight hours before being charged. We found ourselves in a communal cell alongside some pretty hard-core thugs, including a wife murderer and a card carrying Angolan 'terrorist' who was actually a Cuban mercenary. In the event, palms were greased and we were released without charges the following evening, shaken up but none the worse for wear. Ironically, this caper came back to haunt me almost twenty years later, when I requested a police clearance certificate as part of my application for Canadian citizenship. Thanks to the SAP's nefarious dealings with the gay club owners, all 'transgressions' had gone completely unrecorded. Without a clean police record, I wouldn't have stood a chance.

My partner—a model citizen in every way, I hasten to mention—endured his fair share of police harassment. He was a high school student during the years of the Soweto uprisings which sparked the monumental changes that South Africa experienced in the late Seventies. Coloured teens who dared to take a stand were dealt with severely by the police. I stand to be corrected—I don't know that any of them lost their lives at that time, but they certainly knew what it was like to be pursued by *sjambok* (leather whip) wielding policemen with dogs, and to suffer the ruthless punishment inflicted on them if they had the misfortune to be caught. I understand they were generally allowed to go free after their parents had paid their admission of guilt fines—a luxury not afforded black schoolchildren fighting the same cause. Police stations in Johannesburg's Coloured townships must have made a killing during those times.

Turbulent high school years notwithstanding, he grew up confident and proud, and thanks to his ambition and drive, made a smooth transition from the township to the central business district, where he embarked on a career in finance. He had witnessed many relatives, his brothers included, get the short end of the stick because of their race, and he was determined never to allow the Apartheid laws to stand in his way. Long before the notorious Group Areas Act was repealed, he was living in a Whites only suburb, dining in Whites only restaurants and attending Whites only cinemas. I'm not suggesting he turned his back on his Coloured heritage—far from it, in fact—but he was prepared to risk living his life as he felt he deserved. There were many Coloured people who lived in the same way, and they would have been fully aware of the risks they were taking. If you were renting an apartment in a White suburb and were 'unmasked' by your law abiding landlord, for example, you could expect to come home from work to find all your belongings on the sidewalk. That's exactly what happened to him once, when a canny landlord figured he wasn't actually 'Portuguese'. How we laugh about that now! Around that time, he enjoyed the opportunity of traveling abroad and even lived for a couple of years in New York and Toronto, so there was no way he was going to tolerate life as a second class citizen on his return to his own country.

Our paths first crossed in the late Eighties and we became an item pretty much right away. We were not the first biracial couple in his family (or mine, for that matter), only the first Gay biracial couple. Over the years, a few of his relatives who had taken White partners had been forced to live in Swaziland or Mozambique, safely out of the reach of Apartheid's draconian laws. Our union was greeted favourably by my White relatives and friends, although many members of his family still have issues, even though we've been together twenty four years. Less because I'm White than because we're Gay—it's an Evangelical Christian thing.

From the outset, our relationship has been a stable and conventional one. We share bank accounts and own property together. Like many of our fellow countrymen, we resolved to make the most of our lives in the new South Africa when Apartheid was abolished, although we soon discovered we were not being entirely realistic about our expectations of the opportunities available to qualified presentable, articulate, personable, professional Coloured people. Although he had a successful practice managing a small financial portfolio of wealthy clients, he presented his credentials on a regular basis in the hope of pinning one of the many senior executive positions which were being offered to 'Affirmative Action eligible' applicants. Before long, however, it became clear that being CFO of South African Railways was not in the cards for him. Wouldn't you know it—he was too black for the old South Africa, and in the new South Africa, well, he was never going to be black enough. Fair enough. Moving on.

That was probably our prime motivation for emigration. Having said that, after numerous overseas trips over the years, I had long harboured a desire to live abroad one day. After carefully investigating our options, we shortlisted Canada and Australia as viable destinations. Canada won out because we appreciated the progress the Liberal government of the time was making with issues of paramount importance to us, such as rights for Gay, Lesbian and Transgendered people, specifically with regard to adoption for Gay parents and same sex marriage. *You know; basic human rights.* And our choice has not let us down. We enjoy the full rights afforded all Canadian citizens, including marriage. Not same sex marriage, or biracial marriage, or any other kind of labeled marriage, just marriage, the way Nature intended. As things have turned out, after seventeen years, Australia has yet to legislate in favour of that basic human right, so we're happy things worked out as we planned.

In our immediate neighbourhood, we're surrounded on all sides by heterosexual couples of Spanish, Chinese, American, Thai, Polish, Filipino and 'whitebread' Canadian origin. To the best of our knowledge, they refer to us, not as the South Africans, the Gays, or even the Chequerboard Chaps, but simply as The Boys—one label we could never object to.

Zodwa and Jim's love story   *Zodwa Presley*

I come from a very big political family in South Africa. Some of them are in parliament and some were on Robin Island with Nelson Mandela for years.

I did not move away from home because things were bad; on the contrary, things were very good for me. I was happy due to all the opportunities the new democracy had opened up for us. We fought for our country like many others, and so we enjoyed the earned freedom.

I was exposed to crime all along in SA—having grown up in the township before 1994. I know how violent it was. In many ways it's much better now. I too, experienced violence perpetrated against me, many times, from both the white government and their police, as well as from blacks. But that did not make me wish to leave. It is my country for better or for worse. Twice I moved back for a few years and we plan to move back to retire in SA in the future. I have also experienced crime perpetuated against my family here in the US. But I love America, and most of all I love New Orleans. But I love SA more.

I came to USA to visit friends and met my future husband, Jim Presley in New Orleans in June of that year and decided to get married in August. We married and have been here for the past ten years. New Orleans is very laid back; it's more European, than American, so it was no culture shock for me. My American husband and my cultures are different, but also similar. My family has always been mixed and have always been liberal in our world views.

We got married in a beautiful hotel, The Venetian, in La Vegas. However there was the issue of *Lobola*, as in the Zulu culture, a man must meet the family to ask for the bride's hand in marriage and pay *Lobola*. (A Zulu traditional marriage agreement). Jim agreed to this and so we planned to travel back to KwaZulu Natal, South Africa two years later to 'do the right thing'. We also planned a real big wedding in SA to allow family and friends to participate.

My husband was well prepared to go through this very serious custom and he invited his parents to accompany him, as he was told that he needed to have a team to negotiate with the bride's family as part of the *Lobola* custom. Jim met a family friend, George, who stayed with us during his business travels, who grew up in Durban. Even though he was white, he understood the custom as he worked closely with Zulus. He felt honored to represent my husband as the Chief Negotiator (*UMkhongi*), and did some research about how to conduct this very important task.

We travelled to Durban, where my husband Jim and George met with my husband's parents to discuss the process. He appeared to have learned a lot from his research and so everyone felt comfortable.

The day of *Lobola* arrived and it was a big day for the whole family, mostly for my husband's family, who had never heard of *Lobola* before and felt privileged to be part of the experience.

George commenced by telling my family that they have come from very far and had crossed not only rivers but had crossed oceans . . . That is the usual opening in *Lobola* customs, because it shows how serious the groom's team are and how important it is to make this relationship work. But little did he know that by saying that they have crossed many rivers, and the ocean that it was going to work against him and cost them more money. My Uncle responded by telling him that they appreciated his honesty and because it is very far away where they have come from, it would take them too long and would cost too much money to cross many rivers and the ocean to go to America to visit their daughter/niece if there were any family issues that needed to be resolved!

It blew his mind and became a joke as he did not know what to say after that. But they did not ask for additional money and it was all taken in good spirit. There are many twists to negotiating *Lobola*. It is not straight forward like a business deal. In the end it went well and was a great experience for all of us. The whole city learned about what happened and George was hugely proud to be *UMkhongi,* so much so, that he bragged about it during the wedding ceremony which followed a week later!

Currently I teach half day at a Pre-school and run my ministry in the afternoons and weekends. My counseling ministry is here in New Orleans. It is a healing and holistic ministry through prayer. I also give talks at schools, NGO's, churches and private groups about African spirituality and God. I am also a civil rights movement member and a freedom fighter that fought against apartheid in South Africa. Hopefully you will hear more of Zodwa in years to come because of my involvement in the human rights campaign with US civil rights leaders, which I hope to table in my prospective book.

The Day Our Lives Changed Forever

Shane Bignoux, Oz

Wednesday the 10th of February 1999, the day started out just like any other day; went in to another busy work day as usual in PMB. I had been meaning to phone my Mom that day. They had a pension pay-out day at our family Spar Trading Store near Mapumulo. Pension days were always good for business, but risky because it is all cash business, and we did not like to keep large amounts of cash on hand.

My day had run on, I had got home late and Bronwyn and I had supper and watched a bit of TV. Bronwyn went to bed, while I stayed up till midnight surfing the internet. I never got around to phoning home. I had just fallen asleep when at about 1 a.m. the phone rang—that dreaded call in the middle of the night! It was Denzil, the older of my two younger brothers, calling to tell me that my parents and youngest brother, Brett, had been attacked at the trading store and our family home, and that Mom, Dad and Brett had been shot and Mom was seriously injured, and that he and his fiancé, Megan, were on their way to Dhlakati from Mtunzini. Bronwyn and I hurriedly dressed and jumped into the car to head out the 150km to Dhlakati, Mapumulo. As we headed out the gate I realised two things, one, I had to fill the car up to get there and two, my guns were in my Dad's gun safe in Mapumulo, so here I was taking my wife into a possible deadly situation, unarmed! We had the petrol tank filled and headed out to Mapumulo, bypassing Greytown on the Mispah road and then past Kranskop to Mapumulo, then down the 12km of dirt road to Dhlakati Spar, which is at the confluence of the Hlimbitwa and Umvoti rivers.

On the road we had managed to talk to Brett via cell phone. He had managed to call the Police in Mapumulo and raise the Garnett's who were family friends, who farmed about 20km's away and they were also on their way to help and had called out the Commando unit in Stanger and raised the alarm with all the farmers in the surrounding areas. We also phoned my Mom's sister, Margie and her husband in Umzinto to let them know. It took us just over an hour to get there from PMB—the longest hour of my life, that somehow also went by quite quickly; still don't know how that worked.

In the last 2km down to the store, one comes over a hill and you look down into the valley where my brothers and I grew up. It is a beautiful valley and that night my view of home and so many wonderful family memories changed forever. We could see the lights of Dhlakati along with part of our store on fire. Our lives had changed and we were now on a new path.

As we drove the last few yards over the Dhlakati River that our store is named after, and onto the bottom of the driveway up to the store, we were greeted by the horrific site of a Police van with its doors still open, lights on and the body of Sgt. Andreis Zungu, the driver, lying in a pool of blood next to it. He had been shot in the back of the head. Our friends, Chris, Louise and Craig Garnett, as well as Denzil's fiancé, Megan were there to greet Bron and me. They were all in shock and nobody really wanted to say what I think we already knew in our hearts. We could see by their flashing lights that the ambulances were already up at the house with the paramedics attending to my Dad and Brett. I walked up the steep hill and as I came through the gate I could see my Mom lying strangely in her dressing gown next to the burning building that used to be our tearoom. I knew then for sure that my Mom had passed away. As I walked up to her I could see the Paramedics busy loading my Dad and brother Brett into the waiting ambulances and I knelt down to talk to my Mom. I remember thanking her for all the wonderful things she had done for us all and for all the people that she had helped over the years, and how she was going to help God in his Great Garden. I wondered aloud why such a wonderful Mother's life had been cut short. She was 59 years old and we had recently had a big Family meeting planning out the Family's future and our way forward in the New South Africa. I then said a short prayer and walked up to see my Dad and Brett before they were taken to hospital, first to Stanger to stabilise them and then onto Entabeni in Durban.

The number of Police from all over the surrounding areas, as well as the Stanger Commandos that came in to help try and capture the attackers was amazing and people were wonderful. A special thanks to the Garnett Family for their response and help, true friends no matter what. We covered my Mom and then set about doing what has to be done in these situations. It was now dawn and the Police could begin to look for clues, the Fire brigade had arrived from Stanger to make sure that the fire was not going to spread any further and that all was safe. We arranged for the Priest from St Philomena's Catholic Church to come and do the Last Rites, the painful call to my Mom's sister Margie and her husband Robbie, and to all the other relations.

I had to formally identify my Mom and take custody of her wedding and engagement rings and help load her into the vehicle to be taken to the morgue in Greytown. It was hard for Denzil and me, but somehow we found the strength to carry on and sort things out. Telling our almost 50 Staff what had happened and try to reassure them that they still had their jobs was not easy. The following evening travelling through to visit my Dad in ICU and Brett at Entabeni Hospital was hard, and all the time one is trying to piece together what, how and why things happened. People and customers were amazing. We had numerous cases of local people walking; sometimes from more than 40km away just to offer their condolences. In circumstances such as these one always finds out just who your true friends are.

We could make no funeral arrangements until an autopsy had been done on my Mom. This took about a week. In the interim my brother, Brett and I attended Sgt. Andreis Zungu's funeral, which was near Thrings Post. Being a Policeman who had died in the line of duty, all the stops were pulled out. There were about 20 speakers, of which I was number seven. It was a hard speech, my Zulu is not up to formal speech standard, but I did my best. He was a sole breadwinner for his family and of course we are eternally grateful to him for coming to our family's aid. We made arrangements with my Mom's sister to meet at Doves in Durban to make the funeral arrangements. It was difficult to organise things with my Dad still in hospital. In the end we had two services, one at St Philomena's near the store for the local people to attend and one service in Durban. I remember speaking at the service in Durban. Bronwyn was horrified because I made no notes and just spoke from my heart. I think it was the hardest thing I have ever done, but also easy because I had so many things to tell from my heart about my Mom. I did feel bad because my Aunt Margie had given me a sheet with things to say and I forgot about it in my pocket. One thing that I said was that my Mom was an avid gardener and that almost everyone at the service had something from my Mom's garden growing in their garden to remember her by.

As I write this we recently had the fourteenth anniversary of her passing and not a day goes by without some sort of memory of that tragic night; an event that has had a profound effect, not just on our immediate family, but for many other families, too. We lost a Mother, a Wife, a Sister, a Carer, my brother Denzil's daughter, Emma and my daughter, Caitlyn grew up without a Granny. My Mom would have loved to spoil her Grand Daughters, as she always wanted a daughter of her own. Her sister Margie's children missed out on an Aunt. Both Denzil and Brett never had her at their Weddings. Over a period of some years our Family business went downhill and closed. That meant that over a period of time nearly 50 people, many of them sole breadwinners lost their jobs. A number of people that we know of emigrated as a direct result of this tragic event, because that was the final push factor for them. We now live in Australia, as does my brother, Denzil.

My Dad stubbornly decided to stay on at Dhlakati, despite being 80 years old, and in a really vulnerable position. One good thing though, is that he has remarried to a wonderful lady who seems to put up with his nonsense. The thing that is sad is that no one in the current Government in South Africa has any idea just how vast and far reaching the effects of these sorts of tragedies are.

For many years we all believed in The New South Africa and then we had children, and we asked ourselves, are we giving them the best start in life by staying on in the New South Africa? Is my heart still in South Africa? I ask myself, and I think that the answer is, that for many of us expats our heart is still in South Africa, but our hearts also lie with our children, and after all blood is thicker than water.

In Memory of Marion Dawn Bignoux Davies.

We will always remember you and we miss you! Although your Grand Daughters, Emma and Caitlyn, never got the chance to have and know you as a Gran, we know that you watch over them every day along with your sister Margie and her family. We know that you are always with us and watching over us in God's Great Beautiful Garden. Thank you for all the love you gave us and the wonderful values you taught us all. We love and miss you! Darrell, Shane, Bronwyn and Caitlyn, Denzil and Emma, Brett and Rioma, Margie and Robbie, Rory, Liz, Melize and Robyn, Rhett and Mandy and Tony.

The Great Trek *Anna-Maria de Vries, NZ*

In the 1800's, the Dutch left with their wagons and ventured into the interior of Africa in search of a better life and better prospects. 200 years later, there once again a mass exodus from the land of milk and honey. And this is how we find ourselves in 'The Land of the Long White Cloud.'

Prior to 1994, we were not white enough to share the beaches, restaurants, certain jobs etc. Post 1994, we are not black enough. Suddenly you need to speak a "Black" language, an official, acceptable language other than English and Afrikaans. And, having two sons, it meant that they were eighth in line for any job that would become available. Then we heard that this would apply to applications at universities and schools, too. My husband's job became redundant and that was the final straw. We investigated our options and decided on New Zealand as the culture, language and climate was much the same as Cape Town. We started the process and applied for all the documents we needed. All the documents arrived except my husband's birth certificate. I ended up phoning Pretoria every Monday in search of this document. It didn't matter what time of day I phoned, there was seldom a response. Even phoning senior officials didn't help. I asked the staff what the hold-up was. They didn't know. I asked the staff, "So what is your name then?" Answer: "I don't know." That was the last straw that broke the camel's back. I sent a fax to the Minister of Internal affairs and told them this interesting story. A week later, I had an apology and the official document that I needed. A few weeks later, NZ residency visas were in our passports.

After that everything started in earnest. Setting a departure date first, buying tickets and putting the house on the market. We did this because we wanted a clean break; SARS (SA Revenue Services) clearance and all, and finally packing everything into a container. A psychologist recommended us taking as much as possible with us to make the move less traumatic for the children, especially their bedding and toys. So, container leaves on a Monday, house transfer on Wednesday and flights on Saturday, plus running to the bank with cash money to transfer into travellers' cheques—a risky business in South Africa! Our flight from Cape Town was at seven o'clock. I did this as I thought that people wouldn't come to the airport to see us off as I wanted to prevent a tearful departure . . . But they still came . . .

Arriving in Auckland on a cold, wet, grey day was uninviting, but we were so keen to adjust to the new lifestyle and get on our feet that we lived through this, and it wasn't long before we were acclimatised to the weather.

Before leaving South Arica, we'd decided that we would present ourselves to the church when we got here, as this would help us settle into the new lifestyle. It was even better to meet a Priest who had been to visit Cape Town and also the church we attended and knew people whom we knew. We felt quite at home in this church. We stayed with friends for a few weeks and found suitable accommodation. It was such bliss when our container arrived. It was like Christmas and really a blessing not to go out and buy everything from scratch. We even brought boxes of food and alcohol to tide us over the first few months. Meeting new people and old friends was also a good experience. We settled our kids into school and knew that the childcare was expensive, so we decided that the first one to find a job would work and the other one would stay home to take care of the kids for the first six months.

A year later, my sister followed us and moved to New Zealand, and in 2008 my parents' residency visa was approved and they joined us too. They had been spending 9 months in New Zealand and 9 months in South Africa. So now just a brother and sister are still in Cape Town, plus the in-laws.

In 2010, my sister in NZ was sadly diagnosed with motor neuron disease. The medical staff came to visit her at home including a social worker and hospice support and inexpensive medication was provided. Carers come to look after her, we get support for looking after her and even time off for a holiday from caring for her. My brother in SA said we should send her back to Cape Town. To what? No medical aid and limited medical support from government and no suitable place to take care of her? Here we can send her to a home and the government will still support her. And she gets a disability from the government weekly. Not in South Africa . . . so, better to have a terminal illness here than over there (especially if you are not well off over there). We just find that we have almost too much support, but we are not turning them down. We are thankful for all the help we're receiving. Thank you to the Kiwis for opening their country to us. We are happy to contribute to this country because we know that we are being looked after. Every day I give thanks to God for giving us the courage to make this step and for New Zealand for giving us the opportunities to give our children a better and safer way of life.

We were SA Cops . . . *Janene Magson, NZ*

My husband and I studied hard and were promoted quite early in our lives in the South African Police Services (SAPS)—We both worked at the S A Police Dog Training School in Pretoria where my husband was the National Section Commander of Narcotic Training for dogs and Handlers. We lived a comfortable life in our own house next to the *veld* in Centurion, but we were burgled quite often.

When he was 12, our son didn't want to go to 'After school care' and was as at home in the afternoon on his own. He was so busy playing computer games that he didn't hear the burglars trying to coax the dogs to the gate, and not having success, going around to the *veld* behind our house, where they cut the razor wire and stole the bikes that were standing a mere metre away from where my son was playing games. When he went to the lounge and saw through the window that the wire had been cut, he immediately phoned me. He was so terrified that I had to call the neighbours to go and calm him until I arrived. The break-ins were almost a weekly occurrence; if not during the day then during the night—which meant sleep was minimal. My husband travelled extensively, so I was often alone with the children. I would sleep with the 9mm pistol on the bedside table and drink Redbull to keep awake, and would be so sleep deprived after 2weeks, when he would get home . . .

My daughter was diagnosed with type1 diabetes when she was five years old and this made me leave the Police Force, so that I could find a job closer to home.

In 2007 a friend of ours whom we worked with in the SAPS, came to NZ for an interview at Dept. of Corrections. On his return he showed my husband the photos and he and an old school friend and colleague decided they were going to do the same in April 2008. Richard and his friend, Pieter stayed with friends whom we knew back in South Africa. They arrived in NZ on the Sunday evening and went for the interviews at Rimutaka Prison on the Tuesday. They were so badly jetlagged that they failed their tests (being the 1st of April, we thought they were joking!) Their predicament was discussed with the HR person, which lead to them being permitted to rewrite, passing the test and leading to them being offered jobs.

We then applied for the visas. My husband's visa was approved more or less immediately and he had to start work on the 15th of August 2008. Megan, our diabetic daughter's student visa was a whole other story. It was delayed as we were told in no uncertain terms that if England decided Megan was too much of a risk we would never be able to go to NZ, which put my husband between a rock and a hard place. Does he go and take a chance or not and we stay . . . he left and we followed 7 weeks later. Richard was in training and our friends had to try and keep Richards's spirits high because as time dragged on he was losing hope that we would be able to join him and he wanted to quit and go back to SA.

We finally arrived safe and sound and were met at the airport by Richard and the friends he was staying with. We stayed with them for a few months and Megan and their daughter Liezl, took off where they left off 3years previously.

My husband was a prison guard at Rimutaka Prison and worked shifts (something he had never done before). For the first 3years it was challenging for us. We were like ships passing in the night. (He now works for NZ housing, and is very happy). We had only known how to be policeman/woman—so we're not qualified for anything else. I took the first job that came my way; customer services at a Glass factory. I hated every day. I had unsuccessfully applied for other jobs, so finally went to see my boss to ask if he had anything else for me to which he said 'yes'! I'm now the Health and Safety officer for our factory, so I'm finally doing something that will get me further in this country!

Our eldest (Richard junior) has just finished year 13 and will be going to Victoria Uni and Megan (our diabetic daughter) has two more years, then she is finished school. We've had ups and downs, but we will persevere!

Farewells
Goodbye South Africa—Land of my Birth—*September 2008*   *Carol Champ, NZ*

Getting older and SA is not a place to be, so I'm going over to New Zealand to set up home there, and my family will follow early next year. The reasons are so many I cannot list them all, but what follows is a reminder in the years to come, of why this decision was made.

I'm tired of being stressed about being safe. I'm tired of driving past people that urinate in the street for everyone to see. I'm tired of worrying while driving on the road that if I break down I'll be in danger. I'm tired of seeing no improvement in ANYTHING—and have totally lost faith in my country.

Thousands of Rands leave my pocket each month to pay medical aid and the only reason I do this is in case of an emergency and to ensure I can get into a private hospital as the state hospitals are more of a danger to our health than anything.

I've had two maids admitted to state hospitals for headaches and they never came out alive. I've watched my father die in a state hospital that was so filthy, I could not even touch the doors and equipment myself for fear of contamination.

I'm tired of paying thousands of Rands into a Pension Fund and Retirement Fund that will just not support me when it eventually pays out.

I'm tired of seeing the aged live out their twilight years in a small one-roomed "flatlet" at the back of their children's property, more evidence that the retirement benefits we spend our lives paying for will never be enough.

I'm tired of paying high taxes to a government who has no interest or power in protecting and uplifting its people.

I'm tired of hearing that the crime is being caused by illegal immigrants, yet our Government has absolutely no interest in controlling the flow into this country.

I'm tired of never leaving my home in the evening for fear of criminals.

I'm tired of not being able to walk in the street.

I'm tired of living behind electric gates and owning big vicious dogs for protection.

I'm tired of living behind burglar guards and locked and bolted doors.

I'm tired of checking that my kids have arrived at work safely every day and arrived safely home at night.

I'm tired of hearing about another child being abducted and killed for their body parts to make medicine.

I'm tired of hearing a story about another baby that was raped.

I'm tired of hearing about another young girl being raped and their parents being forced to watch.

I'm tired of hearing that the 50 murders per day are only the reported ones.

I'm tired of constantly checking my front gate when the dogs bark in case it's someone trying to break in to rob, rape, torture or kill us.

I'm tired of hiding my mobile phone in case I get shot for it.

I'm tired of hearing how African students at schools have burned down their school because they were unhappy with a situation and then those that go to University have rioted because they don't want to pay the fees.

I'm tired of the stench and filth that lines the streets with no care.

I'm tired of tipping the car-guard, tipping the grocery packer, tipping the petrol attendant, tipping the waiter. I'm told they have consortiums that will target you if you don't tip.

I'm tired of the faces peering into my car window begging for money at traffic lights.

I'm tired of being scared at traffic lights, watching left and right with my foot ready on the accelerator in case of a hijacking.

I am tired of hearing how corrupt the SA government officials are.

And most of all, I am tired of being scared beyond my wits every minute of every day as I feel vulnerable everywhere I go.

I am not a racist (but possibly rather a culturist)—in fact, I raised my children not to be racist at all, and put them in schools that were mixed. Growing up most of their friends were African. I also had many black friends in business, and love them dearly, but these well-spoken, decent well-mannered friends of mine don't constitute the majority. There is sadly a culture at play here that I just cannot merge with; a culture that has no regard for human life, a culture that has not learnt to live in a clean environment, a culture that believes that sex with a virgin cures Aids, a culture that considers rape of a minor an achievement, a culture that believes killing small boys so that they can cut off their penises and wear them as a dried ornament will cure a sickness, a culture that believes that they can have, take, and own anything they want because they are black, a culture that has an ingrained hatred of white people and takes pleasure out of taunting us, a culture that will take every opportunity to take away from you, everything you have worked hard for.

There are things I see that I just cannot ignore—like . . . I have already had a family member killed in a bomb blast, and the man who killed her is now a minister in government.

-I myself have had a gun in my face when my company was robbed.

-My home city is so filthy that the stench of urine and human excrement is sometimes overwhelming.

-My past hope for a new generation of black people who can live in harmony and cleanliness and decency seems to be waning.

If I stay . . . . I have to accept

-that this place is no longer a westernised country with culture, and that grubby habits, filth, rapes, robberies, torture and death now become a way of life;

-that stealing includes taking bolts out of electricity Pylons which would cause an entire area to be without power for days; in addition to the normal power outages.

-that cars/taxi's no longer regard red traffic lights as something to stop at, but something to edge into to get to the other side, causing traffic problems daily.

-that my body space no longer exists, and standing in queues means putting up with people who literally climb on top of you they're so close, and cough down the back of your neck, or sniff loudly in your ear.

-That you can only jump in the front of a queue if you are a non-white.

-That if you are white you wait for service only after everyone else is done.

-That using a rubbish bin is no longer valid; you can throw anything, anywhere, anytime . . .

-That my culture no longer has any place in this society . . .

-That the current education system will continue to deteriorate further.

-That my family and I will be a target first and foremost of crime . . .

-And that every minute of every waking day will be consumed with fear for our lives.

Again I re-iterate, this is not a racial issue, but a cultural clash and I cannot see it changing into a civilised society in my life time. If a Westernised person decides to stay in South Africa they need to accept the situation. Does one honestly think that a small percentage of people can change the culture and habits of over 30 million people? I think not. I re-iterate—This land no longer accepts us, and judging from the rest of Africa, it never will. If you stay, you accept and live with a culture that is foreign to you, and in years to come hope like hell that we don't follow the path of the rest of the African countries (we are one of the last economically viable countries left in Africa).

—The development and industry that was created in the past no longer belongs to us, and has been literally handed over to people who have limited or possibly unverified qualifications. Hence now issues such as the Eskom saga and not enough electricity to power the nation.

—The Government and their policies no longer will take into account Westernised society—the cultural backgrounds and beliefs that are ingrained by the new regime will be the deciding factors on issues.

—The new Expropriation Bill Amendment Law allows the Government to take away your land/home for any Black empowerment purposes it deems necessary, and at whatever cost they like. This in essence means that our homes we have purchased are at the mercy of whoever decides they need it.

—Jobs will always be given to black persons first and foremost.

—Companies by law have to deal with at least 70% of black empowered companies.

Stay?? I think not. So, sell everything I have ever owned, put my clothes (which are my only material belongings) in a suitcase, and catch a plane to a country that has respect for human life, that provides decent medical care and looks after their citizens. I am prepared, at my middle age, to sacrifice all I have built up and start from scratch, and make a way for my children and grandchildren to experience a life that does not consist of filth, locked doors and fear. I prepare a way in another country with one single vision, to see my grandchildren ride their bikes in the street, to allow them to walk to school with no worry that they will be targeted because they are white.

I give up my birthplace, my home, and release it to those who seem intent on its demise. I am on my way. I pray for the safety of those who are not financially able to find a life elsewhere, or choose to remain. I pray for South Africa, my magnificent country, and that the leaders will somehow see its value and move it towards a better future. And I pray that people, like me, can one day look upon our birthplace with pride.

Updated March 2009

I have arrived. Six Months in a new country, a new people, and a very new perspective on what it's like to emigrate.

To those of you who have told me that I am another one of those South Africans who have run away, may I humbly correct you. Running away denotes getting out of a difficult situation into an easier one. Well, let me enlighten you. This is by far the hardest thing one will ever do in one's life time. The illusion that you can just jump countries and settle is just that—an illusion. I can honestly say that in my experience, emigrating has been far more difficult a journey, than just staying. Staying is the easy way out, as the familiarity of the fear that one lives with seems comfortable compared to this unfamiliar territory.

For most of us, the months leading up to actually leaving South Africa involved dealing with the Department of Home Affairs, getting much needed paperwork together for one's new country. This consisted of endless queues, lost birth certificates, unregistered marriages, incorrect birth dates, more lost documents, and clueless home affairs employees who have absolutely no interest in helping you. Surfing the web about one's new country, figuring out what immigration entails, reading blogs, making decisions on which city one wants to live in, browsing the job market, browsing cost of living, organising banking and transferring money out of the country, rules and more rules. One discovers that one's money does not really belong to one, with limits on what the SA government allows one to take out, and the horrific charges one incurs with transfers, travellers cheques, and merely converting cash adds to the burden. The banks make a fortune out of this exercise. Cancelling Pension Funds and Retirement Annuities (R/A's) were the real shocker. Our R/A's, we discovered were worth nothing, and would not have covered our old age. Now cancelled, years of hundreds of Rands wiped out, and the pension took 7 months of fighting with the fund to pay out, via emails and telephone calls from our new country. Cancelling our TV licence itself shocked me as I had to prove I was leaving the country, otherwise the debt would continue to rise without any proof.

Finding a solution for one's pets, as R40, 000 to relocate a pet and months of isolation in a kennel at a cost of about R3, 000 per month was just not a viable solution. The task of finding a decent home and picking new "parents" for these animals, who became our children, was the most heart-wrenching experience ever. For some the decision to resort to pets being euthanized almost amounts to the legal killing of one's children. Three animals to re-home, three thousand tears.

This, in addition to leaving much loved family and friends behind . . . Yes, there will always be friends and family who do not come with you and your rationalisation for leaving them is that your priority is your family (husband, wife and kids). You continually justify to yourself that your children deserve a decent future, and if you don't make this move, they will one day leave the country anyway, as so many are already doing. Many parents have already been left behind by their kids, and you realise that you will be one of them if you don't make the move now. So, saying goodbye to those who can't come with you is another three thousand tears.

It took years to finally own our own home, and years to get to a stage where it was almost paid for. Selling this part of you in a property market that has all but crashed smashes any security you have left. A lifetime of building this security disappears in an instant and every possession you have, gets either given away, or boxed into a container, awaiting your instruction to ship to the other side of the world.

I need not go into the last day in SA, filled with goodbyes, and not knowing if you will ever see these much loved people again.

Who said the plane ride would be fun? Twenty kgs. each in our suitcase was not enough, and trying to get about 15-20 kg. additional stuff into our hand luggage was an experience, especially trying to swing your hand luggage like a 2 kg handbag up to the baggage counter trying your utmost to make it look light. Two days in a space smaller than a single toilet can almost destroy you and setting foot on land again is a *hallelujah* moment!

The excitement of actually being in a new country takes away a lot of the pain, while the business of trying to organise your new life brings a new kind of stress. It was a night landing in Auckland, and we were collected at the airport by a South African man with whom we had pre-booked a 'home-stay' so we did not see much. Two days on a plane with almost no sleep, and going forward 11 hours in time had taken its toll, and we were asleep before our heads hit the pillow.

We were up early to start our new life, banking being the first priority to transfer our funds and to cash in our travellers' cheques. Our first day consisted of a bus ride to the bank. The banking was a pleasure—open tellers, bank managers that invite you into their office to discuss the best possible solution for your money, and thirty minutes later all was set up. The first thing that struck us was the lack of high fences, gated communities, front gates, and less security. The second was the different cultural mix. Coming out of Africa, it took us time to get used to this—some white people serving in supermarkets, cleaning the streets and doing road works. The third was the relaxed and rush-free environment. The pressure of living in South Africa in general from just driving to work on the mad taxi accident prone no rules roads, then working in an environment trying to do 3 jobs in one due to 'head freezes' and working to 150% capacity to just keep your job as 'black replacements' were standing in line to take it over, causes one to always be alert, fast, tense and vigilant.

Living and working in South Africa felt similar to waking up each morning and running on a treadmill at the fastest speed until you went to bed at night. Now, in this new environment, it immediately felt as if we had jumped off this treadmill, and stepped onto one of those slow casual "travelators" you find at the airports, slowing moving with time to look around at the life that passes you by, a very weird sensation and a shock to the system. People here walk more slowly, cars drive the speed limit (50 km in the city, 40 km in the suburbs and max 100 km on the motorways) and trying to maintain this slow speed is quite a task. Our initial feeling was that we had stepped into a "Stepford wives" kind of environment. The cleanliness of this place still amazes us today with not a scrap of paper or rubbish anywhere but in a bin. The honesty of this country was also a surprise from filling our own petrol tank (a first for us and it was a real hoot!), to "self-check-out tills" at the supermarkets; yes, you heard correctly, self-check-out tills! (You take your own groceries, scan them in yourself, pack it and swipe your bank card to pay . . . . *voila*! all done.) We had to restrain ourselves from whipping out our camera to take photos of it. Imagine what the locals would have thought if we had?

We noticed that people here were very friendly, with many greeting us everywhere, supermarket cashiers asking how our day had been, etc. Initially we would look at each other and wonder what the heck they wanted, but it did not take us long to realise that they were just being nice. Nice people are something we were not used to and if someone spoke to you it was because they wanted something. Onto the subject of people wanting something, we discovered here that there is no such thing as tipping. The minimum wage is adhered to for the most menial of jobs, and is a liveable wage. There are clothing bins at certain places around the city and suburbs that you can put your old clothes in and the poor merely go to these bins and take out what they need. Even the poor here do not take advantage and grab everything just because it's free; they take only what they need. Honesty boxes are everywhere; if someone is selling something, for instance such as a flower seller, they need not be there. They leave bunches of flowers, leave a sign of how much they cost, and all you do it put your money in a box and take a bunch. For us South Africans, this is 'la-la land', like living in a cartoon. In SA we were used to people trying to bribe or pinch from us or generally trying to get what they could, that we had to alter our perceptions and start becoming less suspicious and more trusting.

Having covered just how pleasant our new country is, let me move onto the meat of settling. Upon arrival, we were full of illusions of how easy it would be to find work and settle, and after purchasing a car and a GPS to find our way around, we decided to travel the country, stopping overnight at the closest town to us, and just take in this new environment. The fear that I had been living with for so many years in South Africa disappeared the minute I landed, so the driving through rural country, stopping anywhere and everywhere, was wonderful. Issues such as getting lost, or breaking down, (and the fear that came with this of high-jacking, murder or rape because you were in a remote location), did not exist. I would have been happy to sleep in my car in the middle of no-where. It felt that safe. The untouched beauty of this place moved me to the occasional tear, as I realised that my own country probably had the same beauty, yet so much had been exploited or defiled.

Despite the trauma that preceded the decision to leave, I have discovered here in New Zealand that I am a South African and will always be. I have left my country, only to find it within myself, but realise with much sadness that the country I was born and raised in has evolved into something very different. As I walk in the streets of my new home I can smell the freshness of my youth, and see the life that should have continued. I realise that freedom has been stolen from me in my adult years, but console myself that my offspring will reap the rewards of this new place. They get to grow in freedom, they get to live without fear, and they have the opportunity of living the life that I knew in my childhood. Now, here in New Zealand, while I deal with the trauma of losing the only life I knew, my children get to find theirs.

Our reasons for leaving SA . . . *Chantel Abbott, NZ*

I'm tired of driving with my bag in the boot and all the doors locked all the time, forever fearing RED robots and having to watch everything around me, in case someone tries to break my window, or pull a gun on me for my BB or cell phone, or bag, or whatever they want to get from me. I gave my maid's son a chance to work for us, as they were battling with jobs . . . he was cleaning the windows outside and spotted my daughters' cell phone in the lounge, came into the house while I was over in the cottage and stole it. We did get it back, but I was sickened by the whole thing. My OH (other half) was high-jacked at gun point, car stolen and terrorised. We have been burgled three times; they even took the food out of our fridge.

- Medical aid was costing us an arm and a leg every month. We still had HUGE shortfalls and the hospitals have deteriorated beyond imagination.
- School fees are unreal and the standard sucks. I have to drive my kids to school and fetch them, as there's no freedom for them to come and go as they desire.

221

- We are stuck behind an electric fence with outside beams. *I hate being a prisoner in my own home!*
- I am so sick of being overlooked for a promotion at work, as I am not the 'right colour'. Give me a break—I have to teach them how to do the job and they get paid more than I do!
- Standard of education; terrible and our degrees are not recognised.
- I would love to road run again, but can't, as we are harassed while running and cycling, so have to run on a treadmill in a secure environment like a little rat! I CANNOT wait to try out my brand new Asics on the dedicated paths, in safety :)

I'm dreaming of freedom, safety, cleanliness, happiness, joy and being with my hubs again. He is in love with NZ. He has been there for 6 weeks without us and says that we are NOT making a mistake.

I have to admit, I am nervous and so are my kids, but simply cannot wait to get there. We leave SA on Monday and arrive in Auckland on Wednesday afternoon, so spend a few days with our darling friends before settling in our own place.

Letters from the Edge—Sharing tapestries . . . The 'accidental immigrant'   *Abbi Osbiston, UK*

I lived in South Africa until I was 23. I was born in East London to a South African mother and a Dutch immigrant father. My father, despite being an immigrant, is proudly South African to the point where he's rivalling American patriots. When I was very young we moved to Johannesburg and I grew up in a liberal house free of racism that celebrated an equal, free South Africa with a hope and excitement. I loved and still love being South African. I wasn't living in fear of crime or affirmative action or any of the things that seem to be the basis for most immigration.

In 2004 when I was 23, a group of my girlfriends and I decided we were bored and that it might be a laugh to live in London for six months; after all they were handing out visas like Smarties in those days. I never, ever intended to stay. However exposure to London fundamentally changed who I was within that six month period. I came back and found South Africa small and closed. In London I could explore exciting aspects of music, art, fashion and culture which lead to me exploring parts of myself that I never knew existed. Suddenly I could wear whatever I wanted to and say whatever I wanted to . . . I got my nose pierced. I got big tattoos. Nobody looked at me. Nobody even noticed. It was wonderful.

When I go back to South Africa people stare and they assume things about me because of the way I look. I regularly get asked things like, "Aren't you worried about getting a job?" In SA I would struggle, but here I'm a senior manager in a big corporate company.

Over time I also became used to being able to walk home alone at night and live my life without looking over my shoulder. When you don't know any better you don't realise what you're missing. Now I go back to SA and I'm scared. It's a wonderful place for a holiday. I just don't want to live there anymore.

I have married a British guy, whose family adopted me as if I were their own. That pretty much put the nail in the coffin for me and now almost eight years later, I guess I am officially an immigrant, not a migrant.

I'm not a Saffer—I'm an Afro-Celt! *Beth, UK*

I was born in Zambia (Northern Rhodesia) in 1959 to Scottish parents and have travelled and lived in various parts of Africa. I did live in SA for a good few years and both my sons were born there. Matthew is now 26 and lives in New Zealand with his girlfriend, who is also South African. My younger son, Andrew, aged 17 lives with me here in Surrey, Great Britain.

We left my husband behind as he didn't want to move with us—very much proudly South African! And now he is alone.

On our side—no regrets at all, though I do miss my eldest son who is in NZ. We Skype and Face Book and are making plans to meet in South Africa. Yes, we are Scatterlings, but we've brought things and ideas to this country that perhaps will spread . . . . and we have learnt things here that we will use and keep.

I am happy :) My younger son ? Well he will make his own decision one day and I will have to live with that. As said—no regrets.

Zim Artist   *Kt Grubb, UK*

I have just read about your proposed book in 'The Global South African'—a wonderful idea, which I'm sure will be well received. I have been interested in the same subject for years. I'm a 47 year old Zimbabwean artist. I've been in the UK for 15 years, and the pull 'home' never releases me. For the past five years I have been making art that represents my longing for Africa, and the myriad of issues therein. I've also written two dissertations relating to this topic, and to the journeys we take and how being 'displaced' affects us. It is a subject of endless fascination to me.

The Zimbabwean story differs from the S.A. one, but I believe the core of finding yourself in a different environment from the one you have grown up in is the same. I—like you—had the slow realisation that all was not as it seemed during the Rhodesia /Zimbabwe transition and beyond. Indeed, I did not know about the Matabeleland massacres (Gukurahundi) until I came to the UK and heard about it here! I was probably innocently lying in the sun next to our swimming pool while that was going on. Growing up in Africa is a wonderful experience, albeit a very complex issue when one looks back! I have family and many friends in South Africa and I visit SA and Zim every year if I can, thus keeping in touch with where my heart lies.

Canadian   *Diane Stafford, Toronto Canada*

I think your book will resonate with many of us, as we'll be able to relate to the stories that are told, and the hardships that we've had to go through. I attended a home concert by Jeremy Taylor in Toronto when I had newly arrived, and always remember his words— *"You can take yourself out of Africa, but the flame of Africa never leaves your soul."* That has grounded me through those dark days, until we come to the realisation that you don't have to deny Africa, and where you are now is not bad, it's just different. But, rebuilding a life doesn't happen overnight, and now four years on things are slowly becoming the norm, and friendships being made, and yes, it will be all right.

It will be interesting to see if the same thoughts resonate with people over the globe, and if they experience the same emotional hardships. Living in Canada, I so miss the hot, yellow, African sun! I have often been envious of Australian Saffas who can at least get the sun, if not their friends of old.

Ex Zimbo   *Ian Erasmus, NZ*

Finding myself unable to sleep, I was reading a few on-line papers and came across a write up about your proposed book.

I'm an 'Ex Zimbo', who was displaced into South Africa as a teenager and now live in New Zealand since 2003; a lot of water is under the bridge.

My first reaction is anger . . . anti Afrikaans, anti South Africa. Here in NZ I often get asked if I am South African (our Accents of course). I am very quick to retort to the Kiwi, "Oh you must be Australian?", and when they reply "No way!" (Often in feigned disgust), my reaction then is, "Don't insult me then, I'm not South African!"

Being a Zimbabwean coming to SA as a teenager, wanting to study tertiary education, I was unable to, and was then forced to do two years National Service, because if I didn't I would be unable to get a Student loan from the bank, or even get a job. That started building up the anger . . .

I saw the worst of the Afrikaner in the Army, nothing short of thugs; self-centred bullies who nine out of ten times professed to be God-fearing people. Maybe I was victimised having an Afrikaans surname, but unable to speak the lingo fluently, coming from Zimbabwe. I saw while in the Army resentment of people of colour and how we were brainwashed by apartheid. The aggressiveness of the average Afrikaner in the Army was unbelievable.

I've found it very strange here in New Zealand. Having met many Afrikaners living here or South Africans in general yet none of them supported Apartheid, or will come out in the open admitting it!

I guess I'm angry at having to leave my homeland. I would go back tomorrow if I could go to Zimbabwe to try and help rebuild a once beautiful Nation, but having four children, two born in NZ, means I am unable to, for reasons we're all familiar with.

My disgust is also towards South Africa, who sold the then Rhodesia down the river to try and take away the spotlight from themselves.

South Africans here are known as being aggressive and arrogant, and think that they have a place above all others. They should go home. They made their bed and should lie in it. I guess this is not what you wanted to hear, but a short version of an ex "white Zimbo", who lived in SA for 20 years, now displaced in New Zealand.

From Tracy

Tracy Swift, NZ

I was interested to hear about the book that you are writing and would love to contribute our story. My husband and our then 3 and a half year old moved to NZ in1997. Having had a son here in 2000, we have become part of the fabric of our community. I ran my own business for a few years and worked for three different companies. NZ has been sooo good to us! However, unbeknown to us at the time, when we left, a large chunk of our hearts remained in African soil.

So it's been fascinating to watch a deep (indescribable) yearning for Africa, slowly increase over the years, as most South Africans living here think we have lost the plot! We understand that not everyone's journey is the same, so having raised both our children as Kiwis, we now face the daunting, yet thrilling task of attempting this adventure called immigration all over again! We are currently investigating and planning to move back. Psychologically I can tell you—living in two places at once . . . I love the idea of the book and wish you all the very best in your endeavours!

A Saffa in Calgary

Lesley Delmar, Canada

I read about your proposed book and thought to myself that you are doing a good thing and wondered if you'd be interested in my story?

In a nutshell—my husband and I left on a job opportunity in 1995. We headed for Jersey, Channel Islands on a two year contract (Russ is a civil engineer), where our second child, Andrew was born. We voted in the first free election shortly before leaving and experienced the SA win over The All Blacks in the 1995 Rugby world cup final from afar.

After Jersey, we accepted a position in Toronto, Canada and have been here ever since. We had another child, Nicky in 2001. We did not emigrate, but rather our situation was one of opportunities that arose and we felt that it was a good option. We love SA and have all our family there still. Our first child was born in Bethlehem, OFS in 1993 and she will compete in Montreal in the Canadian Olympic trials for London 2012, where she has a legitimate shot at making the swim team.

All this to say, we have adopted Canada as our home too, and lustily sing the national anthem 'OH Canada!' as we proudly cheer our children on in their pursuits. We have a divided heart at the same time, closely watching the SA situation and remaining in touch with family and friends.

I can relate to your "rebirth" experience in emigration, as I feel I underwent the same. I had a promising teaching career in Stellenbosch at Rhenish Girls High at the time we began our travels, and although I taught briefly in Port Elizabeth, that was the end of my teaching—it was just more fitting that I stay home with the kids in a new country. I'm so glad I did, but sometimes wonder what would have been had we stayed in SA. I was also very involved in sport in SA and represented three provinces in three sports (Athletics/field hockey and biathlon) between 1980 and 1990's and all that hard work and accomplishment died (or became irrelevant) when we emigrated. My identity that had its roots in sport and performance meant nothing to anybody. I became just a 'stay-at-home mom', and so I needed to find myself in another sense. I'm a Christian, and so naturally my search for self took on a spiritual perspective. I can say today (16 years later) that I have learnt who I am and it's a good thing. I've died so much and come alive to so much more! My identity is first and foremost in Christ and how freeing that is. Emigration, for me, was the thing that helped provide the battleground to purge, cleanse and purify through tough times.

I've had the privilege of working on the team for a television production called 'Context' with Lorna Dueck, which broadcasts out of CBC in Toronto—I manage the viewer relations across the country and operate a satellite office out of Calgary where we now live. I have started road running again and I am on a campaign this year to complete 2012km before January 1st 2013. I also recently completed a TESL certificate in teaching English, Second Language and hope to use this to help settle new immigrants to Canada. I felt compelled to reply to you and to say 'Good luck' with your book!

Leaving SA   *Sharlene Striepe, Oz*

We had many burglaries, about 8 or 9 in total. Each time one picks up the pieces, fixes the house, puts in the insurance claim and purchases new stuff. That's the life we simply got used to. It wasn't so bad; we had a lovely home and a child going to a great private school in the northern suburbs.

In 1999, all that no longer seemed important as we had an armed robbery and my little fox terrier was killed. The intruders had attacked us from our back garden; all apparently planned in military style. We never heard them come in. We were sitting in the house, door open on a summer evening in Jo'Burg. We had our daughter, aged 6, niece, aged 7 and our nephew in the house, all having good fun, until the intruders stormed through the door.

My husband had gone outside as he heard the Alsatian barking, but never thought anything of it, as she used to bark at birds, the wind, you name it. I noticed that he was talking to someone and thought it was our gardener, but it was five armed robbers. They hit him with a metal pipe and pushed him. He had always told me to close the door on him if I was alone in the house. I did this, not locking it though. How hard that was to leave him outside, but he told me if ever something like this happened I had to think of my daughter first and this time it was her cousins as well, who were too small to defend themselves. The robbers came in, pushed him and me onto the floor and went and got my daughter and her cousins out the bathroom where I had told them to hide. They pushed them along with a gun to the heads, to come and sit in the family room. We had to sit with a gun pointed at us whilst they grabbed the TV, almost letting the cabinet fall on us and took mobile phones and watches etc. All the time the alarm was going off as I had pushed the panic button. However, ADT Security never arrived. It felt like forever. Then the robbers ran out the door, but not before shooting into the family room, towards the floor, where we were sitting. I was shot in the lower back and buttock area. It was mostly shrapnel that hit me, which later cost me three operations, a month off work, R20 000 and lots of pain. Thankfully our neighbours had heard the alarm and rushed over to help us and called an ambulance.

I never saw my little dog again and only had the Alsatian left. We got a Rottweiler to grow up and be with her for companionship and for extra security, but it never stopped the burglaries. We had three more and another armed attack a month before moving to Australia. Luckily my husband pushed the door so hard on the one guy that tried to push it open and thank God he ran away, otherwise that would have changed things and I could still be in SA as a widow.

The major armed robbery happened in 1999 and we only left as in 2009 . . . why you would ask? It's not easy to leave behind your culture, your friends, family, church, schools and jobs and to start all over again. My husband was looking for a new job and came across the Australian recruitment site; not sure how, but he applied for a job, not thinking he would even get an interview, but he did. He got the job on the skilled basis as he is a civil engineer. At the time he was 49; not easy.

We had 3 months to sell our house, find a new school for our daughter who had loved attending Brescia House in Sandton and was doing so well, and would so miss her school and friends when she arrived in Perth in 2009.

We lost about R500 000 on our house at that time, as it was not a good time to sell. We sold cars, fish tanks, furniture etc., and the saddest thing was to say goodbye to two loved dogs and our birds. Our Rotti found a home 6 months later and our Alsatian got a home with my sister. Sadly she passed away recently, but I managed to see her in 2010 when I visited SA alone. My daughter and husband have no desire to go back, but I have parents and sisters there, who I will always miss, and will try to see every few years. I still love SA, miss it at times, and the people, but now this new country is my home.

My daughter is safer, and has opportunities which she would not have in SA. She did very well at school and is currently studying biomedical science and forensics at Murdoch Uni. We have to pay for it, as we aren't Oz citizens, but it's worth it.

We came on a 457 visa. I would never recommend it; just too scary and costly. We got our residency in November 2009, just eight months after arriving, and we are due to apply for citizenship in January 2013. We have applied to keep our SA citizenship as well, but have heard nothing from SA yet.

The first year was the worst of my life. I was so depressed and home sick—it was unreal, but I soon volunteered in childcare and later was offered a job there. I am still at the same place where I work each day. My husband has suffered stress and depression, so has my daughter, but we will get there in the end and look back one day and say 'Thank you God for getting us out of South Africa'. It breaks my heart to say those words, and when I saw the Springboks playing a month ago here in Perth, and went to the match, wore the green and gold, and sang the anthem, I felt the worst sadness, but I also knew that Perth is my new home and I must embrace all it has to offer and thank them for giving us a home.

Our reason for leaving SA: CRIME, and the fact that my daughter and husband would not get any opportunities due to the colour of their skin. I pray each and every day for things to come right in SA and especially for all our loved ones we left behind. I look forward to your book being published and please keep us posted. By reading everyone's stories I won't feel like we were mad in moving all this way!!

Our Tale *Marijke von Molendorff, NZ*

Mario and I were doing really well until about June 2011 when he lost his job working as a loss adjuster. As he doesn't have any real "skill" as an ex SAPS (SA Police Service) member, he battled to find work. In fact we sent CV's for any and every position available. I don't want to exaggerate but it must've been over 500 in a 3 month time span. I still had my job but things were getting really tight. We had the same expenses but with half the salary to cover them.

In the meantime, we had a few attempted break-ins where the intruders climbed over our walls and helped themselves to our garden furniture and other things. At that stage, whatever savings we had we invested in fitting electric fencing to our property as we had three teenage girls, one granny and me to worry about. To add injury to insult, I was almost hijacked TWICE.

It was there and then that we decided that we needed to make a change. We have family in NZ and we discussed our options with them. At that stage Correctional Services were employing ex SAPS members without residency and my husband came to NZ on a visitors' visa in Feb 2012. He was verbally offered a position but they wouldn't put anything in writing due to his visa status. They said to him to come back with a work visa and they will give him a job.

I resigned to get my pension fund, sold my house in SA and applied to study Accounting (as it is on the short term skills list), in order for my husband to get an open work visa. We landed in NZ at the end of July to find out that Correctional Services have changed their employment criteria and as we don't have residency, my husband would now not qualify for the job.

He has a job offer from a company in Russia that has a contract with UNICEF to combat child trafficking in Moscow and will be away for 3 months at a time, while I am here in NZ with our 3 year old daughter. I am continuing my studies. Fortunately, he will be earning US$ so we will be able to afford the costly international student fees for me. I plan to qualify as an Accountant and get residency.

I must say, this road has not been the easiest! We have left our 3 teenage girls in SA, as well as our mothers and siblings. We have always been a close knit family, but we realise that this is for the benefit of these same girls. They will be able to come to NZ once we have residency and go to Varsity on merit and not be excluded because of their race. That is what gives us strength to persevere—it is for them!

I love New Zealand. It is so clean; almost greener than my beloved Natal where I grew up. The idea of not having to lock my doors and not seeing burglar bars on the windows excites me! What an eye opener for a "fresh off the boat" Saffa!

From Anton in South Africa

Anton Bohmer, South Africa

I noticed your research for your book on immigrants from South Africa. As a fellow psychologist there is an interest on the impact of immigration on identity, sense of self and community (sense of belonging).

What I hope for is that you will also include the voices of those immigrants (like me) who decided to return to South Africa (not to turn your book into a return to SA booklet either) and the psychological journey that we have undertaken. I have never discouraged anyone who wanted to live abroad, but have encouraged others to return (who are exploring that option) after time abroad, as my own homecoming has been such a rich and rewarding experience for our whole family.

You have hinted that you would like to gather a spectrum of voices, but will not tolerate racist opinions. I believe that a real challenge will be the more subtle assumptions that are caught up in language. For example, as you noted "some Saffers simply can't leave" is an opinion that excludes those who choose not to leave or those (my family included) who decided to return. There are obviously psychological journeys involved in these decisions as well, some of which our family and friends (in SA and abroad don't or won't understand).

Another potential pitfall would be to write a book that is essentially "white", excluding the majority of South Africans who are living in SA and those from other backgrounds who might have left for a variety of other reasons (e.g. who are solely working abroad in order to finance their children and families who are living in SA).

Finally, an interesting (smaller) group of people of whom I have over recent times encountered a few of, are those who have left SA "for the sake of their children", but now find themselves isolated in their new countries as their children have grown up and decided to come and study or live in SA again! It just shows what a dynamic process immigration is and how decisions can go full circle.

I am not sure if it will open the boundaries too wide to include all of the above, but I hope that you will be able to present a broad spectrum of viewpoints, experiences and decisions in your book! Best wishes—Anton.

Sharing Thoughts and Reflections— Sober Reflections Before and After Migrating

Before—

I used to love the A. A. Milne stories about Christopher Robin and his buddies, mostly Pooh Bear, but also Tigger, Piglet, Roo, Owl etc. Actually I still love them and find that the story lines and characters provide rich analogies about real life.

I felt as though I was Christopher Robin going on his '*expotition*' to the North Pole, tugging Pooh Bear and the others along, getting hopelessly lost in the snow, while traipsing in square circles. Only my own teddy bear's name was Bally-Hoo. I used to use him as a pillow and I really did want to take him on my *expotition*, although it wasn't to the North Pole and he was just too big.

I kept saying to myself, "For goodness sake, I'm only going south to 'the land of the long white cloud', which is inhabited by many South Africans, anyway . . ." But whenever I reflected on the situation, (which had somehow come about by default), but to which I'd committed myself, I just didn't care a sod about that. I was going to be '*stok alleen*' (totally alone), so I may just as well have been at the South Pole or on a remote unchartered planet. It all felt quite illusionary and surreal. I think I was in a vacuum and was floating in a type of never-land.

I'd been interviewed telephonically in March 2008. It had been 9 p.m. in South Africa and 8 a.m. the following morning in New Zealand. I was donned in my PJs and had a candle burning—just in case the electricity went out, which it was prone to do, due to what was termed 'load shedding'. Whilst I was conversing on a conference call to New Zealand, I was sipping Old Brown Sherry to ease my nerves and clear my throat. I laughed at the sight of myself sipping sherry by candlelight in faded PJs and violent pink slippers . . . how ludicrous it all was!

When I heard a week later that I was the successful incumbent, I tried to convince myself that this was the opportunity of a lifetime as a psychologist in New Zealand. I reassured my shattered self that this was my 'mature rite of passage', but the feeling inside was only imaginable to anyone who had gone off to the North or South Pole at the age of 50-something, sans their precious ensemble. How could I justify this? I kept asking myself. Somehow I felt that it wasn't about justification. It felt more that I was following a preordained destiny for the future of all my children and grandchildren. I convinced myself and believed it, because it had happened not by my individual choice, but as though it was a universe-directed *journey*. A sacrifice greater than I ever imagined that I was capable of undertaking. Reminding myself that it was a sacrifice made out of love made it easier for me to bear the pain then. In hindsight I'd have preferred to lose my left arm or to be confined to a wheelchair for us to all remain together; but somewhere safer than South Africa.

People, it seemed, gravitated somewhere along the optimism-pessimism trajectory correlating with their own life-views. There were the Tiggers that bounced up and down patting me on the back till I was winded, bellowing enthusiastically, "Wow, well done. It's fan-*bloody*-tastic that you're going off on an adventure and I'm soooo jealous/proud of you . . . bla bla" and then there were the Eeyores who interrogated me in a bleakly monotone drone: "Do you actually think you'll survive?" Or even worse, they acerbically insinuated that I was abandoning the great ship of Africa which truly pissed me off, while the Piglet's cushioned in their cotton-wool niches whispered that it was an unqualified *skande* (scandal).

Globetrotting may be a walk-in-the-park for some or a total no-no for others. Whatever it was, I felt that it was a deeply personal odyssey. I wanted to shout to the world that I, too, have Africa in my soul and that I would miss myriad things.

In life we're told to 'seize the moment' and yet so many of us are too fearful to. Maybe I had never had the opportunity to seize such an opportunity before. But I so wished that it had happened at a different time in our lives—not when it could sever our family. I kept reminding myself again and again—'It is also for the children's futures that we are doing this . . .'

I spent a great amount of time creating justifications while I was packing up odds and ends, selling pieces and shopping for items to take. Time seemed to march loudly in my ears those months. Dust seemed to clog my throat. Tears jabbed at my eyes. A heavy anger shouted in my chest. My eyes screamed and flames of burning hurt tarnished my every breath. *I wanted Africa to hurry and implode so that everyone I ever cared for could leave with me, or to get better in a flash, so that we could all stay. I wanted an instant miracle, nothing less, nothing more!*

A major paradigm shift brings with it excitement, challenge and massive trepidation I told myself. I was already aware that it would be horrendously painful having to shed the gut-naked stuff wedged within my soul. It was neither about hedonistic pleasure nor gratification. It was about making immense sacrifices, which I believed would existentially grow us and those whom we were closest to. It is now five years since those feelings. It is still too soon to tell . . .

One goes through peculiar sensations when one's about to depart. I'd lived on a farm in the Freestate as a child and lived much of my adult life in the Pietermaritzburg, Kwa-Zulu Natal area. The terrain was so absurdly familiar, as though I could draw the roads, their names and landmarks in my head. Yet on departing I suddenly saw it all through different eyes.

When I drove to work those last three months from the late March 2008 telephone call confirming that I had been offered the post, till my departure, I spent the time trying to assimilate every minutia in graphic detail. There was the winding route down from Winterskloof along the Sweetwaters Road. Each day I saw a bedraggled man walking up the hill barefoot and I thought that before I left I must give him some shoes. I momentarily lost the thought as I navigated a different vista.

There was the effervescent man donned in his red overcoat. When he spotted my car he did a jovial dance to wend his way through treacherous traffic to sell me The Witness newspaper. And I thought 'I must give him a shirt' before I leave. I would find myself counting how many trees were on the verge before Victoria Road. Finally in Retief Street, the laden cabbage truck was there and a flock of birds flying overhead. Always the same familiar scene. And around the next corner was my school, and I'd immediately be thrown into another precious almost last day as the Principal of 'my school' of amazing staff and very dear, special needs' kiddies.

I came to the realisation what a personal choice it was to go anywhere and that there'd always be two sides to every story. There'd be people who were adamant that they would stay in their land come hell or high water. And there'd be those who felt dissatisfied with their lot and were envious, wishing that they, too, had a job offer someplace else. There were those who were incensed and disparaging, those who were overwhelmingly supportive and those who were avoidant.

Possibly, it is only those, with families shredded by vast oceans, who can truly conceptualise the pain and courage required to head off into the unknown . . . in the hopes of establishing foundations for future family security in a less vulnerable environment.

1780 poem by Goethe:

> *There is a stillness*
> *On the tops of the hills.*
> *In the tree tops*
> *You feel*
> *Hardly a breath of air.*
> *The small birds fall silent in the trees.*
> *Simply wait: soon*
> *You too will be silent.*

After—

When I close my eyes or reflect with eyes stationary, not seeing, merely fixed, I'm aware that there is another entire world in my head. I see it as being lodged quite high up in my right cerebrum. I can touch the place with my hand. In it is housed my entire fifty eight years of existence in Africa. It is a vast place, untamed, wild, free, glowing in ochre's, olive greens and delicious textured red earth hues of dust and rain and dramatic storms. It has a world of odours, of sounds, of vistas. My greatest joy is that while I'm alive, this colossal part of my memory bank can't be extinguished. Parts may fade to stone-washed less pronounced hues, to a dusty collection of cameos, each cobbled together and interconnected, spanning over fifty years in time and space.

It takes time to make an unbiased judgment about the impact that moving country makes on one's life. And one needs to be mindful of the fact that one uses one's homeland as one's yardstick, which contaminates one's data, as one is comparing something new and alien, sans family and infrastructure, with all that is old and familiar, well worn, well-trodden and comfortably used. It's like dandy new shoes that pinch one's toes instead of good old worn out *pantoffels* (slippers).

My friends back home wanted to know how it truly feels. They want the *'snot en trane'* (mucous and tears) embellishments; not only the euphoric delights. When I had been in New Zealand for six months, I was still trying to create an overview of the experience for the benefit of the curious, sanguine and Eeyore "I told you so's."

Moving country, I knew, was one of the top stressors in life, preceded only by the death of a loved one, or an acrimonious separation. Through migration one lost one's identity, one's deeply entrenched roots and home, and became severed from family, friends, work environment, colleagues and hometown.

Everything on the other side of the *'grens'* (border) is new. One has to start by adjusting one's watch on arrival, which becomes symbolic of every conceivable adjustment that follows-

Unfamiliar roads to drive on with different rules, a new city, new places to shop, new flavours, new brand names, new vistas, new work environment, colleagues, rules and protocols . . . different accents, different norms, rituals and celebrations. Different politics. Beyond the initial raw pain of those searing airport farewells, the side effects after several flights in transit, and the adrenaline-charged reactions to all that is new and strange, means that one is in immense shock. One's sleep patterns disintegrate for several weeks and one's body feels heavy and dizzy. A few months later, adaptation starts to creep in, shock subsides and reality kicks in. Only then does one feel an indescribable heartache and the "melt-downs" start, due to only then internalising the deep grief and sense of bereavement of all that one has lost. It starts to hit home that it isn't a dream, but reality!

As mentioned, I played my 'metaphorical death' and 'after-life' game with myself as my way of mustering up the strength and courage to pursue what seemed like an unscheduled preordained scenario. The game unequivocally helped me. Texting, Skype and e-mails also bridged the gap between this "afterlife" and my former life. But that was and still is painful in itself. Hearing beloved grandchildren's voices is sometimes the last straw. One aches to hold, to touch, to kiss their heads and cradle them against one.

After a mere six months I found that friends 'back home' were bored of my news, my pictures, my life. Their lives went on perfectly merrily without me, and so inevitably I started to feel redundant. I came across South Africans wherever I went in NZ and still do. There's an obvious profusion of them and it's a topical joke that New Zealand is another province of South Africa. Those I've met are idyllically happy, else bravely trying to adapt, acculturise or acclimatise. Some have come with their children and families, which is obviously easier. I have met a few disgruntled South Africans, who have battled to eat humble pie and to be short poppies. Others I've met have inspired me with their courage and philosophical adaptation, as well as the way in which some have spiritually evolved, once removed from their previously well-feathered lives. Other South Africans return home, maybe broken by grief or due to the global recession and having arrived with just a wing, a prayer and a suitcase. And others' marriages collapse due to the strain. For Ant and me the journey has strengthened our bond.

Sacrifice is part of the deal. One balances the scale with the positives—sleeping without one's ear cocked to every creak; the bedroom door open to the outside elements, no burglar bars or electronic fences, no paranoia if one breaks down on the road at night or in a remote place. And if one drives home alone on a rural road at midnight it won't be deemed bloody foolish.

One learns that one will always be a "foreigner". It's exhilarating starting life all over again at this age. But it's also '*eina*' (sore) and not for the faint hearted . . . .

Before and After—both first published in The Witness 2008

Responses in the media to my pre and post migration articles in 'The Witness'.

Posted by Anonymous on 24 Dec 2008

Hello Eve, I have read your story with much interest (including pre your departure), and I have to say that my family are considering the same; i.e., the slightly older parent/grandparent generation leaving first and creating a pathway for the younger generation. I, like you, have given it lots of thought. (We are thinking of Europe as opposed to NZ). I am of the older path making generation like you, and I realised that if we go ahead with it, it is us, our generation that would be making the most emotional sacrifice, for the very reason that you have given, that of being the first ones, the alone ones, the ones who'd have to crack the ice in the new country for those in the family who follow, and perhaps also make the largest financial sacrifice too. I, like you, feel it's a worthwhile sacrifice to make for the long term health and happiness of these and future generations of the family—especially the young grandchildren's generation. But it is a very knife-edge decision that could go either way—it's like being pressed tightly between two walls—whichever way you turn it's gonna hurt like hell. The lure to stay in SA is HUGE. It's the hardest thing in the world to contemplate. The longer you stay, the more you notice the signs that you're not welcome here anymore, and in a previously unheard of way, that you just maybe don't fit in here anymore, and overriding the crime and corruption and all the drivers that are pushing many people to foreign countries, is the sheer LOVE you have for your own home country and all its people; for the land of your birth. I think, having made your choice, it's that you really have to get behind your decision and work really hard to create your spot in your new country, pray like hell that the rest of your family catches up with you eventually. I also think maybe a sort of 3 year time frame is an idea—so if by the end of the 3rd year you don't feel a whole lot more settled and happy, that you are brave enough to say, 'what the heck, let's go home!'

Posted by Dave Allen on 24 Dec 2008

I have always said that if you're born in Africa, then Africa is in your veins. There is a real difference between South Africans in particular and other nationalities that I have noticed many times. The climate is hot here, and I think maybe that makes us warmer human beings. We have lived through huge national stressors over a very prolonged period of time, and I think that makes us strong. In many ways, too numerous to mention, we're utterly different to people from other lands—and I think we take that 'differentness' with us wherever we go. We are the type of people that work hard because we've had to. We have never had huge government social support. We are laughing people; we find humour in just about everything and we can laugh at ourselves and with others and at others. We have a "can do" attitude, and I think we have a certain brand of inner strength BECAUSE we are South Africans. It is BECAUSE we are South Africans that we shouldn't feel we need to leave South Africa. But many of us do, and in many ways it's a state sponsored exodus.

Posted by Aussie Reader on 26 Dec 2008

Don't listen to the gainsayers, Eve. Emigration is not for everyone and it is a personal thing. There will always be those who think you made the wrong choice because they would not have made it themselves or could not have made it themselves. A friend who had emigrated once said it is like being in mourning. And like a bereavement the pain goes, though memories and nostalgia remain. But opportunities and adventures await you that you would never have had, had you remained in South Africa. In five years you will look around and be a little astonished at how many new friends you have made and how much your life has been enriched. The effort and discomfort is worth it. So as they say here "You go girl!" Have a blessed Christmas and a wonderful 2009. PS. My wife Lindy sends her best wishes. She taught with you at Bisley back in the 1970's!

Migrant ex SA

Regarding the article by Hemming and one of the responses, I would like to comment that Anon is painting a rather rosy picture of South Africans. On the other side of the coin, they are often opinionated and arrogant in their new country and love to talk loudly about how superior everything in South Africa is and be sneering about the shortcomings of the country to which they have immigrated! Sometimes we wonder why they ever left . . . They are not the most popular nationality in the multicultural society on the other side of the world.

Posted by Eve Hemming on 28 Dec 2008

I'm responding to Anon & to Dave Allen. I think Anonymous, you've summed it up well re being stuck between 2 tightly pressed walls. I wish you well with your decision and it may be easier if one makes a 3year plan. One shouldn't make a rushed decision to leave or return. It's a process that needs to slowly distil and unfold. But that doesn't ease the pain. I'm relieved to be here in this new chapter, but seeing in the crystal ball would make it loads easier! Yes, Africa is in the bones, but sadly the legacy of Apartheid still lurks, leading to feeling unwelcome. And Dave, I'm going to 'go girl' as I'm doing with head held up, and do say hi to Lindy re our teaching together 40 years ago! Life's an adventure and we need to be grateful for our past lives, present lives and whatever the future holds for us all. And, as long as we embrace it with the fullness of being and honour our feelings of joy and sadness.

Posted by Anonymous on 29 Dec 2008
RE: Aussie Reader

I know in a lot of countries with large immigrant groups, the local people often tend to box up the immigrants and label them, and have slightly xenophobic attitudes to those groups of foreigners who take up jobs etc., (which really makes it hard for the newcomers to adapt), but to be honest, I didn't think it happened in Australia! How many South Africans in your country have you honestly befriended, or what do you base your opinions on? I challenge you to extend the hand of friendship to some of those brave South African souls who dared to dream of a better life in your country!

Expats' Memorabilia Magic, Emotions and Snippets

My life in a box!! A special box came into our house this evening!! So many years, so many places, so many experiences, so many people . . . all treasured and loved. All our history, heritage and beautiful memories came tumbling out of a box from Africa. These photos breathed life back into our past. Thank you, thank you to the folks who took care of these precious photos and things for us and to Hennie and Leonie who brought them to us in their container. Words simply cannot express how I feel today. Totally overwhelmed, super emotional, but deliriously happy! Treasure your photographs guys. Even if you come with just your suitcases of clothes, make sure you arrange to have your photographs and special goodies shipped out to you. I have waited three long years for these photographs to get to me. I have so missed them. My past is whole again.

Janet Musto, Auckland, NZ

How often we miss the small stuff—little things, that when you take the time to notice, have the potential to make your heart sing with joy—even if only momentarily!

Mandi Crawford, NZ

We only received our stuff on New Year's Day, 1988, with much joy and excitement, especially for the children, to see all their belongings again! During the years without, the people here that we knew helped us out generously with odds and ends.

Glyn Macaskill, USA

I think we were under so much stress in SA, plus the stress of moving country, obtaining residency etc. It's like we come off the adrenalin/ stress high and it hits us with a '*doosh*' and puts us off kilter. We wouldn't be normal if we didn't have a reaction to it all.

Louise Werth, NZ

My partner of 21 years arrived here on a work permit on 3 January 1999. His company were retrenching whole sections and there was no work. But we were lucky as NZ were looking for qualified technicians. He did a telephone interview from Durban, SA and got the job and came over. I followed him on the 13 Nov 2000. It took me a while to settle down as I was home-sick and then later discovered that I have Crohn's Disease. But we love it here, and the sense of freedom, safety, family and friends, who I now think of as my extended family. We all shared the ups and downs, the heart ache and the sad moments of immigrating and of leaving family behind. But most of them have, over the years, come over and are living a better quality of life than what they did in SA. My resolution for this coming year is to just "BE ME" . . . love, laugh and peace.

Vanessa Ritter, NZ

We came to NZ in 2006 on 'holiday' for ten days to scout out the Uni for my daughter and to look at housing and jobs, and of course the life style. By the second day we knew this was our life to be. By February 2007 we had immigrated. Many ups and down, but no regrets. My daughter and her husband have made a huge success of their lives here and earn more than they would in SA. They have everything they need. One cannot put a price on freedom. My hubby and I sleep better at night knowing they are safe and happy no matter where we are in the world, and how much money it took and the sacrifices to get our kids a good life . . . it was worth every penny, and we would do it again. None of it would have been possible without GOD's grace and love in our lives. He opened doors and made the impossible possible for us. We will always be grateful. It has been life-changing for us all, spiritually and mentally.

Leigh Dalton, Saudi Arabia

In 2003 we decided to give our young kids an 'overseas experience'—the idea was for a few years. Well, that changed and it became permanent; eight-nine years later. The kids are grown up; my daughter has moved to Perth this year and my son is now more of a Kiwi than a South African. I went back home twice . . . Yes, I always refer to SA as 'home'. But I realise no more for me. NZ is now home and I have achieved far more here than in SA, given the great opportunities.

Gesan Naidoo, NZ

There was a reason that we decided to start the search. It was when a little 3 year old Nigerian girl was shot in the head by armed robbers, who stole a video machine from her parents in SA in March 2007. She woke up and started crying from fear and the robbers panicked. After hearing that on the news, I said to Elmarie that my children need decency and safety growing up. That was also after my stepfather was stabbed and died because the air-ambulance from Beaufort West had no fuel to fly him to hospital in George! And the murderer is still free even after admitting the stabbing to the

242

police. Then my father-in-law was high jacked at gunpoint for his 1year old Jetta which the hijackers sold for R5000. Fortunately the tracker helped to recover the vehicle, but enough was enough!

Andreas Senger, NZ

I still lock my car (26 years later) and make sure the windows are all shut when I go away for the day. And I never leave stuff on the back seat of my car—always lock it in the boot. We had groceries on the back seat of my friend's car a few weeks ago and I was terrified someone would steal them. My friend thought I was crazy but I have never been able to forget the SA way of life.

Sheena Hayes, NZ

NZ is such an amazing country. I can walk around with my friends at midnight and not be scared. But sometimes I wish (like most probably all of us do) that SA didn't turn out the way it is now.

Alandre Allie Venter (17), NZ

My hubby and I love it here. We have been here a year and won't go back; no matter how different things are here, or how badly I miss my parents. There is no way I will raise our 5 year old son in fear. He loves it here but still has night terrors from SA about 'bad people'. We had two break ins, and one was someone who was busy removing his bedroom window when he was two. He was terrified and can't sleep without nightmares. There is no way, what with all that immigration takes out of you, to make me go back. Things may seem hard here but I believe one must 'suck it up' and have a future. There are hundreds of South Africans who would give their front teeth to come and live in NZ, but they aren't on the skills list. We are truly blessed. I don't want my bread buttered both sides. We just want a brighter future and safety for our son. SA can't offer that, but NZ can.

Leonie Havenga, NZ

It is hard to adjust because you long for your friends, family and familiarity. You go to the shops and don't see people that you know. But it does get better. Eventually you get to know and meet people you know. I had a lot of adjustment, tears, heartbreak and longing but I love New Zealand and I would do it all again.

D.P NZ

We may not be able to control our circumstances, but we can control how we deal with them. I might have had to leave my beloved home and country behind but there is no way I am going to let what is past have a negative effect on my future. The one thing I realised when I left was how much I had taken for granted. I try to be grateful for the opportunity to have lived the lifestyle I had in SA and use that as a goal post to improve my situation here. Things are different here and we have to learn to appreciate things in a different way. Move away from the 'WHEN we' . . . and into your future. It's what YOU will be living in tomorrow.

Louise McLaren Werth, NZ

What Saffa expats love about NZ

At 11:35pm tonight it will be 11 years since my sister and I landed in NZ (parents came 3 months later, while we stayed with our relatives). Moving here brought the biggest of life's challenges along with it, and for a long time I couldn't understand why my parents wanted to uproot us and bring us to the other side of the world. Now, at 25, with my own house, a good job, just starting my own business, with the ability of driving around alone with my doors unlocked, being able to stop at a red light at night, having windows with no bars across them, not holding onto my handbag when I'm out, not fearing for my life, knowing that one day my children will be safe, and having an incredible future full of all of life's possibilities, I realise why they made this choice . . . this is really LIVING! I count my blessings every day and thank my wonderful parents for the sacrifices they made for our future!

Parents—take heart that your children will thank you one day for what you have done for them (when they realise, if they haven't already.)

Children—the tough times will get better, so thank your parents for what they have done for you.

Everyone—missing family and friends is tough, adjusting is tough, fitting into a new culture is tough, but look at what a magical place we live in, appreciate it every day and know that we are lucky to have the opportunity to live here. There are many that would do anything to have half a shot at what we have!

Candice Baker

New Zealand, especially the East Coast Bays, is a dangerous place to live. When I leave my ranch slider door open at night, the *mozzies* come inside to BITE me and the stray cat of the neighbourhood invades the house under the cover of darkness to eat my cats' food! I can't live with all these dangers. Maybe I should consider another country where life is safer without *mozzies* or stray cats!

Dewald Kritzinger

Safety would be my number 1 reason for loving NZ. Knowing my kids actually have a decent future would be right up there, too. Service delivery that works is also high on my list. And it amazes me how clean it is when I walk round.

Janice Le Roux

Cleanliness, diversity, green unique scenery, crystal clear water, friendly people, awesome dining, cultural experiences and a lot more.

Michelle De Wet

I love the freedom, to drive alone, day or night with the window open and not in fear. Not having a security guard at the entrance to a walled estate. Not checking over my shoulder for possible danger and sitting outside without barbed wire obscuring the view. I love the absolute lack of fear which to me translates to freedom—and the fact that many of my family and friends are here too.

Tracy Levey

I love the safety, freedom, organised emergency services, no high fences, can drink tap water where we live (Christchurch has the best water here!), food, scenery and good service. When my kids were younger—the fact that they could walk/bike to school by themselves and to friends, sports and activities. Also the school premises' are open over weekends so kids can go and play on the playground equipment, tennis courts, netball fields etc. I also like the way you can leave parcels etc. in people's letterboxes or at the front door and they won't vanish!

Ozzie Forsyth

I love the amazing freedom and sense of 'belonging'. My kids have a chance to be what they want to be and know they will be rewarded for their efforts.

Angela Quinn

I think what I love about NZ is the fact that we have family time always, no matter where we go. This beautiful place—so much is free and we can spend loads of fun time with our kids in a safe environment; beaches, parks, botanical gardens, swimming pools etc. I can go on forever!

Theo Oosthuizen

I love it that if one loses something, it gets handed in at the police station! Police stations are closed over weekends because often there is no need to have them open where we live! I love not having to look over my shoulder all the time, not getting that jittery feeling when a group of people are walking towards you and you're on your own. Forgetting the doors open at night. Forgetting to push the button to close the garage door and its left open all day, facing the road and its chocka with a boat, fishing and camping equipment bicycles, tools etc. and you come home and it's all there! Having parcels delivered and you're not at home, so they're left at the front door and they are still there (and if they're not, the neighbour has taken them home to keep dry because it looked like rain was coming) And all this and no fence, wall or gate, no burglar bars or security door in sight. Should I go on? I can get started on the wonderful education, the roads, the people, the shops, the amazing country and facilities etc. etc.!!

Claire Gifford

We have been in NZ for nine years and never looked back. I will always love my country, but here my son can walk home from school or take the bus, taxi or train with no problems. I can leave him home alone and no problem. I can go to the shop at night alone. I have even done my shopping at 3 a.m. after my night shift at Countdown. Little to complain about except missing my family a lot!

Sonita Louw

My two wonderful Kiwi born children and Kiwi wife make my happiness complete, combined with having the opportunity to run a business and travel the world unimpeded when I go through customs. I still have SA in my heart and this is as close as it gets to my children growing up the way I did in a carefree environment without fear. There is crime in NZ, but nowhere as much as in SA.

Gavin Nel

It is easy and affordable to go on a holiday to a little slice of paradise like Raratonga Island— we would not have been able to afford that in SA.

Jeanne Herringer

I want to share one of my favourite experiences since living in NZ. For me it really sums up the kindness of people here and the kind of place we now call home: When I had my first child, I was really stressed; didn't help that he was a screamer either. I got SO stressed in shops when he would scream continuously. On one occasion I was at Countdown doing my grocery shopping and as usual he was screaming . . . I was trying to carry him and push a trolley at the same time, while trying to calm him down. A VERY kind lady saw that I was obviously having a hard time and offered to push the trolley through the supermarket, while I finished my shopping. She stood in the queue with me while I paid and then took the trolley to my car and unloaded my bags for me; just because she was kind, not because she expected anything! I LOVE NEW ZEALAND!

Franda Zondach

Viva New Zealand! You've hosted me for 15 years, I still hate your soggy, wet, damp, rainy, mouldy Winters, but hey, I'll take it in my stride!!

Dewald Kritzinger

Freedom, a job that I love and where I don't feel pressure from situations in SA.

Glynis Longhurst

Finally being able to call it home!

Rees Lewis

Fifty shades of green, and in NZ I'm not a colour, I'm just unique!

Patty Govender

It's great to go to bed with no burglar bars and not have to worry about crime. Sure, we got broken into when we lived in Gisborne once. They didn't harm us and only stole our camera and some DVDs. The cops caught them and returned the camera. The thieves currently reside at Hawkes Bay Prison! No further incidence since we have lived in this beautiful country.

Roxanne Bam

I feel so blessed after leaving SA ten years ago when our son was 17 and our daughter 23. Both have done extremely well in their careers, as has my (ex) husband. I have a disability from a stroke in SA in 1998. The NZ government has been fantastic to me. I have a mobility scooter!! NZ is the country we call home. It's an amazing country!!

Renate Engelbrecht Koning

I am married to a Kiwi and have lived here for 27 years. I enjoy being able to go on bushwalks and fish along the rivers in safety (no snakes or crocodiles!) and camping in the middle of nowhere, too. We enjoy wild pork, venison, wild duck and the lack of people (South Island)

Sheena Hayes

I have renewed appreciation for this country we live in!! We are truly blessed! My heart will always beat to an African drum, but this is home now . . .

Celeste Selby

I am thankful today—seeing 3 small kids unattended, riding their bikes and having the time of their life; such freedom. So in the midst of emotional heartache and yearning for my African Skies, I say 'Thank you'. I am grateful, and I am truly lucky to be in this Blessed Country that I now call my home.

Carol Champ

So we woke up this morning to the front door wide open—all still here—all still alive, only Willow went for a walk—Love living in NZ!

Vicky Oliver

Best things! Watching my two boys grow up safely, having the freedom to walk the streets and not having to look over your shoulder every five seconds, my kids being able to walk to school and back and not living behind closed doors and six foot walls and burglar bars . . . just to name a few!

Diane Schipper Thompson

I love the way I don't have to give my ID book, signature, fingerprints, husband's permission and a DNA sample at the bank before they will do anything for me!!

Beverley Smit

I love the freedom to explore this country without watching your back and love the honesty boxes.

Gesan Naidoo

I like the fact that we are equals and it doesn't depend on your skin tone . . .

Debbie Shanahan

When you park your car in a parking garage, you are not confronted and harassed and there are no car attendants that will 'look after your car' while you go shopping.

Ozzie Forsyth

Definitely for me I love being able to drive solo at night without feeling anxious . . . even being able to stop at a red light.

Sandy Benson

Amazing what I have seen . . . women leaving their purses/handbags unattended in their trolleys when shopping . . . so much freedom. Love to be myself and not having to worry about theft as much.

Debbie Shanahan

Knowing that I would be giving my kids a passport to anywhere and everything. This is what we have given our children! I LOVE NZ ~!

Neila Schroeder

I just regret that we didn't come earlier when my kids were smaller. I also love the fact that you don't have to drive a brand new label car or have to live at the right address. Everyone is just happy with what they can afford and just get on with it. No pressure!

Lindy Van Der Merwe.

Waking up in the morning and realising I'm still living that life I only saw in the movies. I never knew such a wonderful existence was possible. But to sum it up—no fear! It is also awesome to be able to appreciate the small things. If we were Kiwis we wouldn't know the difference.

Carol Champ.

Twenty years ago I'd walk around in Auckland and just hear Kiwi accents. Over the years at a shopping mall I would get so excited on hearing the DISTINCT South African accent. Auckland has such a diverse amount of accents now; not colour-coded, it's music to my ears. In the past I just couldn't help myself by approaching anyone with a South African accent—just to say hello.

Geeta Singh

I'm excited about what the future holds for my children in NZ. I feel that they can be and do almost anything That's what we came here for. God Bless NZ!

Jenny Hubbard

Love going to a park or a beach and not being harassed to buy something by vendors; the freedom, no taxis hooting or pushing you off the road.

Dawn Ellis

I enjoy the freedom, safety and cleanliness. It's a green environmentally conscious country. I get great first class medical service, with my medication subsidised and so very affordable. There's no road rage or cars falling apart, and the country has stunning scenery. I love that there can be houses, farms and a factory all in the same block. We can leave the car doors open and find everything still there when we go to fill up with petrol and go indoors to pay. People are honest and will even run after you to hand you your packet of groceries or wallet that you left behind and all your money is still there. Kids get wonderful opportunities that we never had, like sailing, rock climbing, driver education, lifesaving etc. The air isn't polluted and there are lovely forest walks that are close to the city. Being able to go to a public toilet anywhere and they are clean and there is toilet paper is a treat. Customer service is great most of the time . . . and so much more!

Vanessa Ritter

I love the wide open door! *Eve Hemming*

When we're home, the door is often left wide open, unless there's a chill breeze blowing the polar bears and penguins in.

Paddywag seems to attract some interesting friends who cruise in without knocking. Last week it was the local ducks that waddled in and then did a route march out again in single file. The previous week it was the Rhode Island Reds—3 local chooks, (though I, for some absurd reason, allude to them as the 'the boys'), ascended up the stairs, through the open doorway, down the passage to make a beeline for Paddywag's doggy pellets. On respectful request, they refused to leave and proceeded to sun themselves on our veranda all the while making exultant clucks. Husband finally got the illegal tenants to evacuate using some persuasive primeval 'soosh' sounds. They didn't even bother to pay rental in the form of depositing a golden egg. The lads are generally affable, conversationally cluck away and walk the cul de sac silly. They also enjoy demolishing our garden.

Then there are the dogs; Henry the West Highland Terrier, who is the neighbourhood vagabond, cruises in and makes himself at home, as though he's a long term member of our clan. Then there's the fox terrier. I asked Husband what Foxy's name is. He replied, 'He often pops in, but hasn't had the courtesy to tell me yet.' He's a high octane bloke that enjoys bouncing on our bed! The other pooches come and enjoy Paddywag's chew toys, too.

The neighbours on both sides of our home have 'massive vicious cats', (in Paddywag's words)—the types that have those eyes that out stare you. They haven't quite been indoors yet, as they and Paddywag are arch enemies. But they do come and peer in through the window, which means that Paddywag gets anxious and makes pathetic 'Help me' whimpering noises.

That's not all. When it's Halloween, we have 'Trick or Treat'. We need to have loads of biscuits, sweets, apples, raisins, popcorn etc. stocked up. The kids aged about 2 to 15 pour in from about 5 pm—9 pm donned in witch, dragon, weir wolf, fairy, angel, goblin and whatever else costumes with big smiles and funny tricks. They're so adorable, but now the novelty has worn off!

Emotions about 'Home'

I live in a foreign country . . . at times I feel so lonely . . . so vulnerable . . . so foreign! Yet . . . when I look at pics of Saffers on all different websites . . . I belong again! My heart jumps a leap whenever I see the pic with the tree in front of the sunset or sunrise in Africa. I guess . . . my heart still belongs to Africa . . . and always will . . . I now only hold on to all the special times and memories of my country called Africa. I have moved on . . . trying not to look back. It is hard, as it is in your blood! But . . . I will always be proud to say . . . I lived in Africa . . . I was born in Africa . . . I experienced Africa . . . . I am South-African!

Jacqueline Henzer, NZ

There are moments where I'm so home sick and sad and miss my friends so much and then I have one of those ugly sobs? Just one word in a sentence will just bring a nauseous reminder to me and that sadness is unbearable . . .

Zelda Ivens-Ferraz, NZ

Home is where your heart is. Everything in life is a mind-set. Every one of us has his/her own opinion and we are "taught" to respect those opinions, but not necessarily agree with them. I do believe not to burn one's bridges and all importantly to be true and honest with one's self. We cannot dwell or go back in the past but we can start a whole new beginning and strive for a brighter, better future in our own lives. Whatever the choices or direction, just try to trust that it was all meant to be and keep focusing on your goals.

Pieter Koekemoer, NZ

I'm back from a trip to SA. We stayed with my dad in St. Francis Bay, and drove up to KZN to see my sister. We had a wonderful time and the drive to KZN was a highlight. We were last in SA three years ago and this time the Transkei looked amazing, so very clean. I think the Soccer World Cup put so much pride back into everyone and they are making an effort. It was totally heart-breaking to say goodbye to my folks, my baby sisters and brother and all the nieces and nephews. I found it extremely difficult and now we are back in NZ it is like starting all over again.

On the 2nd December we had our residency for two years and have been in NZ for five years in 2012. I thought I was over the pangs for 'home' but this trip made me realise how important family is. I keep thinking to myself 'being safe in NZ is so important for my children BUT the bond of a close family is so important too'. I'm so confused. But I am and always have been a very positive person so I am forcing myself to get up and carry on with our wonderful life in NZ. I started a Diploma in Digital Photography in 2012, so I'm trying to focus all my energy into that. I think having goals is very important. My little girl started school on Monday. All I can say is I am blessed, heartbroken, confused all at the same time. Is that possible? Thank you again for the cyber support. It means so much to me.

Samantha Milne, NZ

To live with the statistics is not easy. A serious crime is committed every 17 seconds in South Africa and Johannesburg is the epicentre of the crisis. The reality behind the statistics means that I lived behind a high brick wall, topped with an electric fence in Johannesburg: At the epicentre of the crime crisis. I cannot see the street outside: I cannot see the horizon. My house is alarmed day and night, so is my garage. I pull in and out of it fast; most armed carjackings take place in people's own driveways.

They are often serious in the extreme. They are fatal. I've worked across this African continent for years on the basis that I'm happy to call an aggressive man with a gun "Sir" and to give him what he wants.

So far I have survived the ill-disciplined rebel fighters, militiamen and soldiers. But in South Africa it is different—the armed men don't always give you the chance to hand the car over. They just shoot. Of course, sometimes they don't shoot. But it is the fear of what may happen which is paralysing, which restricts your life, which is a daily exhausting stress. It's also an extreme irritant—for some South Africans, crime and how in their view the country has gone to the dogs since a black government took over five years ago is a wear me down.

Hector Forbes, NZ

I LOVE the fact that I know my kids are safe in their beds and I don't have to live in a prison anymore. If you think of how you had to live in SA in fear each day, especially on the farms, where people get held at gun point and get murdered and the fact that our kids won't ever get work in SA. I am sorry; I miss my family in SA, but not SA!!! And it is true, all of us here in NZ made the right choice for ourselves and our kids when we moved, because the Crime is too much in SA. Yes "daar is baie mooi nog in SA al die natuur soos die kruger wiltuin ensovoorts en mens kan dit deel, maar ek kan nie anders om ook die negatief te se nie want ek is deur baie hartseer in SA. NZ is ons huis."

Thea Oosthuizen, NZ

I have just recently come back from Cape Town, having just finished studying. And now I am in Pretoria visiting my mom before I leave for NZ. My mom is ill with a lung disease and doesn't have much longer to live. And yet, I want to leave SA! I've lived in SA my entire life and consider myself a *"Boertjie"* (Farm girl). I am moving to NZ in a month's time. I am writing this lying in my bed, knowing my mom is terminally ill and I am sad for her and scared for my life and for my little niece who is 4 months old. She is sleeping in a cot next to me. I lie in bed, knowing I have burglar guards, an alarm, dogs and a security at our gate—and yet—I am scared! This is not the way to live!! At all!! I can't wait to be in NZ. I'm going there all by myself—no family. I'm only 22. And I'm going to sacrifice all I know—for safety and freedom. I am prepared to give up absolutely EVERYTHING in SA—which shows how desperate I am to leave. My mom is practically on her death bed. It sounds harsh. But I am not going to sugar coat it. This is reality. And reality is real.

Camille-Claudel Nortje, SA

After an absence of 18 years, it was a complete head spin to see the changes in Cape Town. I come home with conflicting feelings that my experience of such a breathtakingly beautiful city was marred by a constant sense of feeling unsafe. While I refused to believe the rumours and did not once witness a crime, I just couldn't shake that 'looking over my shoulder' feeling off the entire time I was there. I leave my folks there with a gut wrenching feeling of unease.

TM, USA

As a press photographer in Durban from '84, I was as close to the transition of SA as anyone can be and would never ever have dreamed that it would turn out the way it did . . . even after my brother and his family left in '99, I never thought there was ever a reason to go,. but after seeing the change of the people in power and their minions, after being chased out of places where before we were welcomed, after my son having a few terrible mugging experiences and my partner being hijacked, I decided enough was enough. In 2010 I left with my suitcase!!!!

Sherelee Clarke, NZ

I was looking at pictures of family at my SA house; started crying when I saw the burglar bars on the windows (It's amazing how quickly you forget things). I'm so thankful to be here in NZ.

Penelope Stewart, NZ

SA robbed us from our family. We had to choose, our safety or our blood spilled over mother Africa. My husband was hijacked and held hostage at gunpoint, my ouma's sister was raped at the age of 70. We were robbed 3 times in 2 weeks; one time they were right next to our beds. Three men harassed me for R50 and our daughter and her friends were targeted on the beach. SA is a beautiful place . . . The hardest thing I ever did was to pack up and leave, but I could not stand the worry anymore. All of this happened between 2008 and 2010—not so long ago.

Alaire Engelbrecht, NZ

The thing is that people still living in SA know no other way of life and accept the lifestyle there. Only once you have experienced the life that all human beings are entitled to (i.e. personal safety and security, freedom and honesty), do you truly see what a 3rd rate life we had in SA and accepted it. I wouldn't say to anyone 'drive without a safety belt and see what happens' so would I encourage anyone to move to SA and hope for the best?

We all have our reasons! Bad stuff happened to me in SA too. I came here to be with the person I love and have known for 23 yrs. Only after arriving here did I come to understand why there were such a lot of South Africans that came here and are still coming; only then it all made sense. Life here is just so freeeee! No fear! Freedom is such a great feeling. My sister and I live here and our eldest sister and 82 year old mom are still in SA. Nothing bad had really happened to my family back in SA until two months ago when my eldest sister had a cocked gun put to her head in broad daylight and they tried to smother her 92 year old father-in-law living with them, forcing her to look! By the grace of God they stopped, as my sister started praying out loud, but she has immense emotional scars! I pray for their safety every day as I feel so privileged to be here and inhale the fresh, beautiful NZ air! (I used to live in Gauteng's filthy air.) I feel blessed.

Anita Du Plessis Dutton, NZ

I've just got awful message from my best friend in SA—'Last night my uncle, aged 90, was murdered in his home in Eshowe. A few years ago, while out walking his dogs on his farm in Ntumeni, he survived being attacked when he was thrown down a ravine and left for dead. Family moved him into town where they thought he'd live out his life safely and peacefully. What and why do these cowards!!!(%@%$) do this to a helpless defenceless frail old man?!!'

Sheena Hayes, NZ

Ok this is it—no more fighting about which country is the best or worst!. If you choose to live in crime, so be it, but hell I won't go back to SA. My husband was held at gun point and I was mugged twice. Everybody that thinks SA is not "SO BAD" then go back and let the people that want a better life for their family stay in NZ!! We have been in NZ for 4 years and are loving it!

Tatanja Janse Van Rensburg, NZ

Another senseless murder . . . it's almost too much to bear. It's killing us all on the inside—we're probably all suffering from post-traumatic stress to some degree. And I wish the police would get it right: This was a MURDER, not a robbery—the stealing bit is opportunist, a bonus for these 'scum'.

Anon, SA, 2012

My family and I had moved to NZ, lived here 2 years, decided to go back to SA for family and emotional ties. We were back 6 months and knew that what we had wanted and missed in SA was no longer there. The country, yes, but not the spirit of what we had missed so much. It took us going back to SA to realise. Sometimes choices are not about wealth or where you live or luxuries but rather about whether you can put your head down tonight and fall asleep with a full tummy and a smile of peace to your soul. We left SA again after 2 years and have been back in NZ for over 5 years. We will visit, but we do know home is where you make it—heart and soul and spirit. For me, acceptance led to NZ becoming my SA. I embrace it with thankfulness and a sense of wonder each day when I wake up.

Lynn Andrews, NZ

Living in SA is like being in an abusive relationship. Every day you tell yourself it will be better; tomorrow will be good, but the next bit of abuse is just around the corner. The hardest part for any person in an abusive relationship is admitting and accepting that it will never change, which is why people will stay in it for years. But one day you get slapped the last time, and you pack your bags . . . And I know one of the main arguments for living in SA is that it is beautiful and that is absolutely true. But the Democratic Republic of Congo is just as breathtakingly beautiful, yet nobody will see that as a good enough reason to move there.

Zelda Strydom, NZ

A woman is raped almost EVERY 17 SECONDS in SA. One person is murdered almost EVERY HALF HOUR. I'm sure you folk didn't take your visitors through the "*Kasie*" (Umlazi, Khayalitsha) during the day. I lived and grew up in the real South Africa that a lot of you didn't and I hope will never see. It is a beautiful place, but I wasn't about to let my wife and kids stay to become another statistic. It is this same "rose tinted" view that is shattered only too soon when you wake up to shouting and find an AXE buried in your front door. That view is EXACTLY the same as saying one would remain in an ABUSIVE relationship.

Malik Canham, NZ

Sadly in SA, as beautiful as it may be, you stand more chance of being in the wrong place at the wrong time than elsewhere! It's senseless crime there, where killing you for your mobile phone is not a problem. Thank God when we come home here at night, we don't have to sweat that there may be someone unexpectedly waiting to attack us.

Erica Clyde, NZ

I am in no way a religious man, those who know me know that. But at some stage I had someone watching over me. It wasn't my time . . . My dad had a contracting company installing telephone lines for Telkom. I was working with him on a job in Cato Manor installing lines of the RDP programme for that area. We had ten or so locals to work with us and everything was going well. A group of guys walked past with a wheel barrow and asked for a smoke. No problem, as there was plenty of work going on, so we thought nothing of it. Next thing I heard the crank of the shotgun in my ear. That ice cold shiver and draining of blood is something I will never forget to this day and it happened over 15 years ago. My dad had a 9mm shoved into his face and we were pulled from our vehicle and forced to sit on our haunches leaning against the wheel arches on either side of the car. The worst part of the whole ordeal was not being able to see my dad. They robbed us whilst looking for guns: "*Umlungu*" (white man) must have a gun working in Cato Manor". We didn't. This frustrated them and things got a little ugly.

As they were finished with us they walked away and as they were doing so, the leader of the gang holding the 9mm gun turned around and with a farewell "bye bye *umlungu*" shot at me from about twenty metres away. The tyre next to me popped and for me that was the most beautiful sound I can remember of the day. I drove out on the rim of that tyre and couldn't believe he had missed me. It didn't take long to decide on moving and I am truly thankful that we did. This is a beautiful place and reminds me a lot of where I grew up in my youth. I am also thankful that we could afford our kids this pleasure and safety for them too

Jassen Elliott, NZ

At the moment I feel mad . . . Mad 'coz everything we Had was taken from us . . . Mad 'coz we had to live in fear . . . Mad 'coz I'm in New Zealand, not 'coz I WANT to, but 'coz I HAVE to . . . Mad 'coz I miss my family and my dad in SA, but there is nothing I can do about it. But then I remember how I can walk alone home from a party at 11:30 at night here . . . We have so much freedom. We are SAFE and don't have to live in fear. I'll never go back to South Africa 'coz that's not my home anymore, New Zealand is my home now . . . SA will always be in my heart . . . I'll always be a *"boere meisie"* with a twist of kiwi:):) I don't miss South Africa, I just miss my people a lot today.

Alandre Allie Venter, NZ (17)

I have suffered and am still suffering with a lot of depression here in NZ. I think I never fully processed the traumatic experience back in SA. About 5 years ago I was a victim of an armed robbery at my work. Eight men with guns came into my work and held a gun to my head, hit me around and at one stage I was taken alone to an isolated office and I really thought I was going to be gang raped. I did everything they told me to do and yet they were still violent. Whether the guns were ever loaded or not I will never know. They stole my freedom from me and my family, and I was not prepared to wait for this to happen to my family. It's because of them that my kids will not be around their families and that my youngest child born in NZ will never know his family, be held or touched by them. That gets to me so much. My family is safe here but I feel as though I'm paying the price.

Anonymous, NZ

There are a huge amount of emotional issues rolling around in my mind, which are hard for me to make sense of. I grew up in Zimbabwe surrounded by firearms, and the armed forces. I knew how to use, strip, reassemble, load and unload a gun before I was ten years old. My father and my friend's fathers were involved in the 'bush war'. We knew the drill in case we were attacked or ambushed. We were fortunate to have never been attacked, although violence sometimes came very close to home—personal friends/family. Despite all of this, I had a happy early childhood . . . We left Zim and moved to SA when I was 10. I spent the next 25 years in SA. Some Zim experiences I don't want to elaborate on, and to this day I still grapple with the incredibly overwhelming feeling that had we not left the farm, it could have been our small children and me that were involved in one of the attacks. In 2008 we decided we were coming to NZ. We arrived here a few months later—Masses to organise in such a short space of time.

Anonymous, NZ

My husband was held at gunpoint twice for his cell phone and money and the third time they assaulted him badly, took the car keys and drove off! Thank God my husband survived, but enough was enough.

DP, NZ

I left South Africa to follow my boyfriend, and my parents secretly breathed a sigh of relief. A few years ago, my mom said as much as they miss us and especially the grandkids, that if we ever decided to move back to S.A she would be at the airport with a shotgun and force us to get back onto the plane! Many times I catch my breath and think to myself "It's been 48 hours since I've last spoken to them. I hope they are Okay!" Then when it's a decent time in the morning I text to ask how they are, as they are 'soft targets'. I would sponsor my folks in a heartbeat but they're 'old school' and do not want big changes in their lives . . .

Tania Van der Merwe Levy, USA

I'm sorry but I can't and won't feel romantic about SA, not after my experiences there over the last 10 years. Obviously if one has not been abducted and tortured for one's pin code to your bank account, or your family members shot in front of you, one my not see SA as I do. I don't know of anybody in Johannesburg not affected by crime; I mean a crime involving violence with weapons with serious consequences. I grew up in the south of Johannesburg and it was a rough area, but nothing like the last 10 years while living in Bryanston and Sandton.

Robin Christie, NZ

Reliving some of my SA experiences brought on a few flashbacks of the sleepless nights, the endless worry over safety of my wife and children while they were at work or school. I remember when our neighbour adjoining our property at the back was killed in his garden on his 60th birthday at 8:30pm; my children heard everything over the wall, the screaming and gunshots etc. My children would not go out the house for months afterwards; in fact they never really played outside again. My son became very quiet and my daughter slept very badly. Only about 6 months to a year after landing in NZ did both children begin trusting life again and venturing out into life. Now 3 years on they are totally adapted and at 10 and 17 are well adjusted, level headed (even the 17 year old) and happy to be in NZ. I thank God every day that we managed to get out and are living here. Thank you NZ for taking us in. We'll always be South African, but will make NZ a happy prosperous place to live.

There were many more criminal events, but that was the last straw. It is wonderful here. I am still often moved to tears (can you believe it); real tears on occasion when I see the freedom of movement my children have and how fantastic it is here.

Robin Christie, NZ

In South Africa we lived in constant fear of being robbed or hijacked. We lived behind 6 foot walls, with trellidoors, burglar alarms and armed response. We knew to always put our bags and parcels in the boot in case you are a victim of having your window smashed and your things grabbed out of the car. I never drove without my car doors locked and never allowed my children in the streets alone in fear of them being kidnapped. When I had to fetch my grandchildren I was in constant fear of getting hijacked and them driving away with the children, so from the age of 5, my grandson was taught if a man stops us and starts shouting, to get out he has to unlock his chair and get out quickly.

We were robbed in our house and my husband caught 2 people on different occasions trying to enter our homes. When we first got here I could not sleep with the door open because in SA our door was locked to our bed room, even though we had an alarm and armed response but still never felt safe. My husband used to say we are safe now but it took me many weeks to feel confident enough to leave our bed room door open at night, and the constantly listening for noises at night is still with me after 5 years of being here.

A controversial thought . . . The SA Diaspora is not unlike the Jewish Diaspora, post WW2. We want to move forward, but our anger and frustration at having to move on because of the actions (and inactions) of others, has generated a desire for vengeance, or retribution against who we perceive as the prosecutor of evil against us. A shame really, because one of the outcomes is likely to be the continued divisiveness, and perpetuation of the anger as well, as whether we like it or not, we are likely to be perpetrators of similar attitudes against those whom we perceive are against us. See the case with children who are abused—they often become the abuser in later life.

Don Marney, Oz

South Africa will always be in my heart and if I had the money I would go back tomorrow. I don't live in the fantasy of the old South Africa and am happy to say that evolution should take place—I know many good people there and if we all just keep to positive communication then things will change for the better—what comes around goes around. We should not fight with each other about our point of views—we are all different and look at things differently and we all have the right to do so. We will never truly know and understand what the next person's life experiences were like back in South Africa and therefore should not be allowed to judge. We all have different life lessons to learn. This time around whether it is in New Zealand, South Africa, Europe or America—Your decision determines your destiny. Love and Blessings to you all!

Karen de Vos, NZ

Adaptation
As Quirky as Kiwi . . .   *Eve Hemming*

Four-something years later and I'm still alive, well and living in New Zealand. (The Maori name is *Aotearoa*). Auckland, where I live, is a sprawling city where almost half the entire country's population reside. Auckie's a 'global village' in its own right, with inhabitants from many cultural backgrounds calling it 'home'.

This gives one the latitude to express one's own identity, with the full spectrum from conservative and conventional through to unreservedly 'off the wall'. Anything goes regarding hair length. It can be regular through to dreadlocks and ponytails or bald with a long beard for blokes. Women wear layers, especially in cold weather. Kids, too, are permitted some imaginative latitude. The 'pants off the ground' adolescent boys' style does not cut it for this gran! It takes some getting used to, after living a large part of my life in the vicinity of 'Maritzburg, fondly dubbed 'Sleepy Hollow.' One learns not to stare while bumping into lamp posts.

NZ is bound by The Treaty of Waitangi, which makes it a unique country, with a Bi-cultural society which is defined by Maori and everyone else; referred to as 'The Crown'; the majority being *Pākehā*, (New Zealanders of European decent), *Pasifikas* (People who hail from the Pacific Islands), as well as other Europeans and Asians. One soon learns to assimilate Maori words, phrases and customs into one's repertoire. One has a *powhiri* when inducted into an organisation and meetings commence and end with a *karakia* or a *waita* (prayer or song). We greet with *Kia Ora* or *Morena*.

In the same way that others can't understand how we South Africans tick; one can't always fathom the Kiwi headspace. Kiwis seem to have paradoxical personas—some seem quite reserved, and others have an outrageous sense of humour. One area where we can all take a leaf from the Kiwi's book is their lack of judgement about disability or anything unusual from the norm. Kiwis are PC, big hearted and compassionate. There're always exceptions to the rule, but these are the Kiwis I've seen and worked with. This also applies to the education system, where children with disabilities are accommodated in mainstream inclusive schools. We can also take a leaf out their book about equity and egalitarianism. Women drive buses and operate forklifts and the 'postie' could well be married to a neurosurgeon.

Ensuring that a country of only 4.5 million functions, every *i* has to be dotted, every *t* crossed and every $ accounted for. Kiwis are strict on safety regulations—one can't staple together a parcel, as it could hurt the 'postie's' fingers, and tough blokes wear earmuffs when operating anything from a lawnmower to massive machinery. (I do laugh sometimes!)

The lingo delights and baffles me. You 'shout' a mate a coffee and you 'gift' someone. If you're comical, you're called a 'dag'. 'Naff off' is get lost, 'flash' is good and a 'hissy fit' is a tantrum, while 'get off the grass' means stop pulling my leg! If you're happy, you're 'a box of birds', an idiot fast driver is a 'hoon' and anything awesome is 'sweet as'. You never say goodbye; just 'see ya later'—even to strangers. And best not to 'root' for anyone. It has sexual connotations in NZ which I discovered the other day.

Kiwis love tattoos, motorbikes, wine and beer, extreme cars with immense engines and exhaust pipes, rugby, netball and coffee. There's a 'coffee to go' on every corner. They're self-confessed coffee gourmets with a vast array to choose from in small to giant soup-bowl sized. They're animal mad. Dogs trail along to every park, beach or outdoor function, the owner taking a 'poop bag' along to scoop up any evidence. And they're also animal lovers. Last year they had a state funeral for Mocha, the amiable dolphin from Gisborne, who used to frolic in the ocean with the locals. And recently they rescued 'Happy Feet' the King Penguin, who was operated on and returned to the Antarctic once he had rehabilitated.

It's astounding the way Kiwis go through winter; some in sandals and T shirts, while I'm donned in jacket, boots and a scarf. They're fitness fanatics (Aside from the hefty ones and smokers). You see parents jogging, pushing their toddlers in rain protected pushchairs though the drizzle. Come Summer, Kiwis go even wilder; embracing the elements, swimming, sharing supper on the beach, sailing, and just celebrating in a hundred 'crazy as' Kiwi ways. Part of my adaption is learning about Kiwi ways, their culture, lingo and charm . . .

Adapting to a New Land   *Ian Macaskill, USA*

Emigrating from the land of one's birth to a new country is metaphorically much like a tree being transplanted, be it a spindly sapling or a mature tree with growth rings already in place. The roots are there, bound to the earth and providing nutrition and anchoring. Sunlight, wind and the seasons become embedded in the psyche and play a vital part in growth and development. After being transplanted, the tree can be stunted in growth or even wither and die, if it is not well anchored or is unable to adapt to the soil and the ecology of a new environment. The transplanted tree does leave behind in the place it came from, fragments—shed leaves, pollen, seedlings and some roots.

After immigrating to a new land, now with 28 years of "growth rings", I am able to reflect upon the adaptation that has been necessary, in order to continue to grow, to have stability, to mature and be comfortable in the garden, or the grove or in the forest. Anchoring is the most essential of the means of adapting, with new and deeper roots required.

What are some of the other challenges in this process of adaption? Resettling in a country with at least the language of one's native tongue does help, but the hurdles of dealing with accent, manner of speech and pronunciation, can be daunting. Subtleties and nuances in cultural, ideological, religious and educational background all have an impact on adapting and in being accepted within a community, where one is "the stranger". And of course age and the time spent in the land of one's birth, greatly affect how easily and effectively one makes the transition.

For me and my family putting down the roots and being anchored, has been possible through education, previous but also new and challenging careers, new friendships, interest in the sports of our adopted land and most of all, in building a new and very personal home—a true haven for me, my wife Glyn, our children, our grandchildren and our pets. Transplantation to a new land as a family and being able to lean on one another in stormy times, grow together and after time become an extended family, have been the source of the new roots, the anchoring and the nutrition necessary to successfully adapt and to flourish.

Adapting to another country is a learning process *Glyn Macaskill, Louisiana, USA*

Our family flew out of South Africa on August the 30th 1984 for Ian to teach at Louisiana Tech University, in Ruston, for one year as one of the Professors took his sabbatical. We had been discussing the possibility of looking into alternative plans for the future of our children, so took the opportunity and left with our 5 children, ranging between 15 and 4 years of age, plus 3 cats and a bicycle! We were excited at the prospect of experiencing America and all it had to offer. Now here we are 28 years later, very much settled in the USA; all citizens, with 5 beautiful American Grandchildren.

Ian, at that time was earning a small income and I was unable to work, not having a green card. But we managed to buy a dream-come—true little wooden house on 2 acres, out in the country with our travelling money! Unfortunately after 18 months we had to sell, as we couldn't afford to pay the monthly down payment. Then we found our family home on Maple Street, where we were very happy for 20 years.

A lot has happened over the years but obviously having all our family here has been a huge advantage. I have been fortunate enough to visit SA 7 times and find each time easier than the last. The hardest was in 1987, after spending three months there, because by then it was obvious that we would not be returning permanently.

Having grown up in Pietermaritzburg, I closely relate to brookie laced homes, of which there is an abundance here in the States, even in Ruston. The Azaleas bloom profusely, Wisteria grows everywhere and we love all the wild birds, the Cardinals, Hummingbirds and Blue Jays that frequent our natural yard.

Cape Town will always be a part of me and I am eternally grateful for having those years to reflect upon, all sixteen of them. Moving to Jo'burg was gut-wrenching for me, but proved to be an advantage, as being close to my sisters and their children was so special, of course, and it enabled me to care for my ailing Mother, during her battle with cancer. It is hard sometimes to realize that we only lived there for 3 years.

In 1996 we attended the Summer Olympics, in Atlanta, with our two sons and actually stayed with a recently immigrated SA family. We proudly displayed the SA flag and wore SA clobber. But we find ourselves no longer following the news in SA. We haven't for a long, long time.

The simple life here in this small, but quaint town has something very appealing. We cherish our wonderful memories of growing up in SA, but now look forward to seeing our Grandchildren develop to fulfil their dreams, in a place we call home.

Acculturation as an African-American

Colleen Webb, Florida, USA

I sit next to my pool in the cool of the morning sipping coffee and watching Blue Jays vie with squirrels for the bounty in the bird feeder. The muted roar of a lawn mower several houses down signals the start of summer, and a soft breeze nudges bright pink Bougainvillea blooms into the aqua still of the pool. I tuck my feet underneath me and hold my cup firmly with both hands. This is one of my favorite times of day. Some things never change.

I have heard it said that the only thing certain in life is uncertainty and change. I am an African from Africa, with an English heritage, living in the United States of America, home to immigrant settlers from around the world. I come from a land south of the 'smoking thunder.' A place of ululation and blood, overcrowded cities scarred with poverty and sumptuously luxurious nature reserves; a place where prehistoric Hadedas wander with guinea fowl, wild oceans swarm with sardine and sharks, and people *braai* meat and drink *rooibos*.

The bougainvillea and soft grey doves that float to the ground beneath the feeder in my garden could have been transplanted from my South Africa, but the Blue Jays and squirrels are pure south Florida to me. And the fact that we are slipping into summer in June, when all South Africans know June is the beginning of winter, is clear indication I must be either speaking nonsense or living in a completely different world!

Quite literally my world has gone topsy-turvy. I used to live on the bottom half of the globe, where people drive on the left side of the road, in cars with steering wheels on the left side of the car, fill up with petrol, put their groceries in the boot, stop at robots and be home in time for tea. Now I am perched on top of the globe where people drive on the right hand side of the road, in cars with steering wheels on the right side, fill up with gas, put groceries in their trunks, stop at traffic lights and grab a drive-through meal on the way home!

When I moved to Florida more than a decade ago I was horrified at driving on the wrong side of the road with four lanes of traffic racing along in the wrong direction. But the single thing that amazed me most about living here was how much stuff people seem to have. Garages so packed with stuff that cars must park outside are pretty standard. And when the garage is too full, people rent storage facilities and fill them up with even more stuff. And people throw away so much stuff too. Every month a 'bulk pick-up' is scheduled by the city in addition to the bi-weekly garbage, or rubbish collection. Bulk pick-up is for throwing away things that are too big to fit in your rubbish bins! This includes furniture, sometimes only slightly used! I furnished my entire house through bulk pick-up when we first arrived here! Sofas, chairs, dining table, chests of drawers, you name it! Funny thing is that I think we have bulk pick-up in South Africa too. Only it gets picked up from inside your home before we've decided we need to get rid of it!

Learning to live in a new country, a new culture, a new context, strips you of landmarks of knowledge of yourself and the world around you. The initial culture shock you feel no matter whether you move countries or continents, or both, is pretty standard. It is part of an acculturization process I studied briefly as part of my Masters in Counseling Psychology. According to the textbooks, acculturization begins with a honeymoon phase of euphoria and excitement, and is followed by the 'culture shock' of the dawning realization of the differences of your new reality and the grief of loss. This sounds familiar, if incredibly abbreviated. The books go on to say this 'culture shock' may last months but at some point will be followed by a gradual recovery of equilibrium and a slow movement into either assimilation or acculturization.

Assimilation is the term used to describe the process of those who become swallowed up by their new culture and lose their own. Acculturization is the term that fits me, and so many ex-pats I know. This is when you adopt new things from your new home, but still retain and value things from your former culture.

In my acculturization process I have become truly African-American. I will always be a Durban girl. Cut me and I bleed Africa. But I have embraced the things I value in my new American home. I love my freedom here. There are no burglar bars on any of my windows and I don't have a gun, guard dogs, or a panic button. The front of my property is not even fenced. Sure I watch over my kids as protective as any mom, but I don't live with the level of fear for our personal safety as I did in South Africa. I don't live looking over my shoulder all the time.

My new life is not perfect and it certainly has not been easy. I have gone through a divorce and a period of unemployment and financial stress. But I have also experienced great joys and have a deep appreciation for what I have and what I have learned along the way.

I left South Africa about 15 years ago headed for a life of adventure on a small island in the Caribbean. I was not sorry to leave behind the crime and violence-saturated culture of my home. However, I was sad to leave behind my family and I deeply missed my friends and my life, my beaches, mountains and game parks. After a few years in the Caribbean I came to a crossroads: either return to South Africa or begin immigration proceedings to the United States. My daughter was only a year old at the time. The thought of raising her in a country with one of the highest crime levels in the world drove my decision. I feel that all the things I love and treasure about South Africa are tainted by violence. The beaches and mountains I love are unsafe for the isolated walks that fragrance my dreams! For my daughter's safety I chose to make my new home here—at great cost. My parents and many other family members are still in South Africa. I have some great friends, but no family here. This is a real void in my life.

Thank God for Skype! Thank God the days of counting minutes on long distance calls are over and I can sit and chat with my parents for hours on Skype each week, sharing cups of tea on opposite sides of the globe. But as comforting as this is, my longing for time together is a constant dull ache in my heart. I sit on one side of the world with my children, their only grandchildren, and they sit on the other behind razor wire fences. I worry for their safety. I worry for them aging without me there to care for them. My heart breaks for the absence of their grandchildren! And my children only see their grandparents for a few months every couple of years. These are the high costs of immigration for me.

Then there is the fact that quite simply Africa is in my blood. The ocean in the Caribbean and south Florida where I now live is beautiful. But I miss the wild crashing seas of the South Coast where I grew up, the salty tang in the breeze, surfing on powerful waves, violent waves crashing and booming on the rocks below my parents' home. I miss the smell of sugarcane burning, the open *veld* and the smell of rain. The crunch of dry grass beneath my feet, smoky fires and aromatic *braais* on our camping trips to Sodwana, holding my breath, watching elephants cross the road in front of my car in Hluhluwe-Umfolozi. So many things I miss, sounds, aromas, sights. A blurred symphony of memories I finger in my mind—my security blanket; the context of my past that partly defines who I am today.

Yet even while I miss these things with a longing as deep as my DNA, I savor my new home, my new life, the new memories I am making. I sip the coffee from the mug gripped firmly in my hands and breath in the jasmine scented new morning as dragonflies skim the surface of my pool. A pair of squirrels skip sure-footed along the wooden fence of my garden and a Mockingbird bursts into clear warbling torrents of sweet sound from the tree above me. The pages of my journal flick over in a short burst of breeze. It is symbolic of time sweeping inexorably by; new chapters of my life. The book is indelibly African flavored but I am the writer who gets to design the new chapters. And I am writing them sweet, with a new American flavor!

Colleen Webb is a Counselor and Life Coach—www.lifecoachforpurpose.com

Saudi Arabia—A Saffa Migrant in Transit—
SA to NZ to Saudi and then to OZ . . .
Leigh Dalton, Saudi Arabia 2006-2011

Leaving SA was the hardest and most profound thing we have ever done as a family. We had it all in SA. It had taken ten years of us both working, trying to save, and paying for Hubby's varsity degree, as well as raising our daughter and son, to eventually buying our very own first house and vehicles.

We spent seven amazing happy years in that home, with our two children, five dogs, and two horses and had wonderful domestic staff. We pumped all our money into the house and the children's education and sport and activities. We scuba dived, skydived, holidayed, went to the movies, ate take-outs, visited the family and had *lekker braai's*, (nice barbeques). The kids' friends would sleep over and at some point we had about five kids a weekend staying with us. LIFE WAS GOOD!!

The only problem was that while doing all this "stuff" we never really relaxed! There was always that underlying tension; of watching our backs. If the dogs barked we'd always look out the window to see why. Even the dogs in SA were conditioned to be "on guard". High walls, security lights, alarms, Five Rottweilers, and we still did not fall into a deep sleep at night.

We had been chatting to friends and many were leaving SA to immigrate. NZ and Canada were popular choices at the time, as in the 80's and 90's Australia was the "place to be". It was easier to get into Canada and NZ . . . SO WE HAD A "FAMILY CONFERENCE" and decided that it would be good for our children's futures. Our daughter would be able to pursue further studies and a career. Our son was still very young at the time, but we knew that in ten years' time he could struggle to find work in SA as a white male. We got started on the immigration papers for NZ, and within nine months we were ready to get on a plane as Permanent Residents! Our house went on the market the Wednesday, and Friday morning it sold. WE WERE NOT PREPARED FOR THAT! We thought it would take months, so we rented out a house down the road from our sold home and began to pack frantically. Magna arrived, put our life in to two containers and shipped them off. Our home and possessions were sold and our dogs given to amazing homes. We said all our goodbyes to loved ones we left behind, and waited to leave for the airport. After many tears and laughter we said our goodbyes. Only once the plane had lifted its wheels off the South African runway did I REALISE THERE WAS NO TURNING BACK!

We were fortunate to get our NZ home via internet. Yip, we took a gamble looking for a rented place that way, but it was our only option at the time. We arrived, very fresh off the boat, in this case plane, and immediately fell in love with Auckland's beauty and friendly people. We bought a car at an auction, so we had a house and a car, but no furniture . . . it was still on its way! We had ticked all the boxes except for ONE! Hubby had no job; we took a leap of faith by doing this! Long story short, Hubby did get a job but was retrenched during the recession, leading to a stint back in SA to recoup our losses.

We cannot explain the feeling of landing in SA with just our bags, and nowhere to go "home to", although our whole family and network of friends were there and all our past memories. We felt like strangers in our own home town and country. We just wanted to get back on a plane and go HOME to NZ. It was the toughest 13 months of my life, after having given up so much in SA, HERE WE WERE BACK AT ALMOST SQUARE 1, but we had achieved one thing and that was to give our daughter a better chance at life. She had an excellent job and income in NZ and a great apartment with all the appliances provided.

Finally the time was over and we returned to Auckland, beaming! This time round we were not making the same mistakes, or so we thought. The economy had picked up slightly, and we had enough money to last us a year. But disaster struck; the worst dip in the market ever to be known in the world and in NZ, too. So, the next chapter was in Saudi Arabia!

When we look back, there are things we don't regret as we grew in leaps and bounds and found out that we are strong. We persevere, are hard workers and never give up. It's NOT easy, not always fun and not all peaches and cream! It is tough, and painful. It is scary and lonely and there is doubt . . . BUT YES, IT IS WORTH IT!

It's good to be honest—to tell people who want to emigrate that it will be the hardest thing they will ever do in their lives, but also rewarding, combined with the wonderful release from one's chains. I was a routine person and organised and planned everything to the last minute. Who knew I would have moved so many times; kicking and screaming, but doing it anyway. It's tough on your family and on your marriage, but if you look at the glass half full, there's nothing stopping you. We look forward to returning home to NZ and to see where life takes us from there . . .

For now we are living in Saudi Arabia so that we can make up the financial losses we had experienced from migrating during the recession. It's just a two year stint. Compared to NZ, one can pick up a car here for next to nothing and of course petrol is only 18 NZ cents as compared with NZ $2.70! It's just crazy when I think about it. The people are very friendly here. We have many expats here and our local vet is a New Zealander! Life is interesting to say the least. The sunsets are breath-taking reds and gold's in the desert. It reminds me of the bush walks we had in SA as kids!

IT MAKES YOU LONG FOR NZ'S GREEN MOUNTAINS, ICECAP PEAKS, AND CLEAN FRESH WATER AND AIR, and of course the sea all around you all the time. The desert is a great experience. The Saudi people have shown us that a good life can be obtained here, even if you are only surrounded by sand! It is such a contrast of old and new, as they cling to their beliefs and traditions of mud houses, women wearing *Abayas* and not being permitted to drive, but at the same time building huge sky rises from glass and men driving huge American cars, such as Hummers and Yukon's. They have ELABORATE MALLS, with all American take-outs, like BURGER KING. THEIR FOODS ARE GREAT TO TRY AT LEAST ONCE, and the little *souques* (markets) are delightful and not expensive at all. Food prices are really good here.

When I am here I long for NZ; for the things we take for granted like women driving. Oh, I miss driving my car, but mostly having the car window rolled down and smelling the sea air. It's too dusty here to have the car windows open at all, and also too hot! I miss being able to shop quietly in a mall and sit with a friend or family member sipping coffee. Here they have prayers five times a day, so shops are closed five times a day. It is so frustrating and inconvenient, as you have to rush! Most Saudis shop at night from 8 p.m. to 1 a.m. We westerners love to shop and swim in the day. It has been ten months where all we have seen is blue skies, hardly a cloud here as rain is not big here! We are going into winter here which is about 19-25 or 30'—'good summer weather'! But our summers are from 40-57 degrees, so we enjoy the cooler weather. It took a while to get used to it after NZ. We became *'whoosie'* about hot weather after having a cooler summer and winter in New Zealand, but now we're used to it. We mostly miss walks on the beach and the trails and certain foods like Tim Tam biscuits. And of course roast Pork!! And the SA shops back home in NZ and *rooibos* tea.

It has been a humbling experience as a woman living here, and at the same time liberating, as you don't see women behind the counters in the malls and the supermarkets. It took a while for me to get used to it, like a man selling bags and shoes and underwear for women seemed all wrong . . . after all this time I still haven't been comfortable to shop there, and instead buy what I need on Amazon. They have women doctors, nurses and pathologists, teachers and beauticians, but that is where it ends. I am a landscaper and a window dresser by trade, so there is no work for me as a woman here. My hubby is bringing home 'the bacon' and I am being a house executive and home schooling our son, so it is a very different life indeed. So to all of you and mostly to you ladies whenever in a traffic jam or who have to go to the dairy to buy milk or bread whenever you feel like it, or moan about four seasons in a day . . . please remember that your life is good! You are free to choose what you want to do every day and to go where you want to go, too. Please think of me when you are on a ferry or in your car on the motorway, with your windows rolled down and music on and you're on the open road! The only thing that keeps us from going insane here is to get through the next 18 months knowing that we can leave and never have to endure this again. Most people don't have that choice!

Addendum The Daltons now reside in Oz, where Larry was offered a great position.

Onam Festival   *Angelique Goldsworthy, Abu Dhabi*

As a South African expat family, living in Abu Dhabi, we are often invited to events hosted by people of different cultures. Recently we journeyed to Dubai to attend an *Onam* (Harvest festival) hosted by the Kerala community of my husband's company. I borrowed a sari from an Indian friend in my church and went round to her house to see how to drape and fold it. We were chatting so much I probably never paid enough attention because the following morning when I tried to put it on, I became entangled in miles of cream and gold fabric and got into a complete state! I ran across the road (in the petticoat and tiny little bare-midriff top) to find the Indian maid who works for my neighbour. Well, it turned out that she is actually Sri Lankan and completely refused to help me. I think I committed some sort of Middle Eastern faux pas. Don't they also wear saris? I felt like a complete idiot!

So we set off for the event (me still in my undergarments). As we neared the venue, my husband phoned an Indian colleague of his who sent out two ladies to help me into my sari when I arrived. I was ushered into a little dressing room where all the Indian dancers and traditional drummers were getting ready to perform. The kind ladies wrapped and folded and pinned and tucked and adorned my hair with sweet-smelling jasmine flowers. I felt like a Bollywood princess and even got applause when I entered the auditorium! The festivities included traditional dancing and singing, a re-enactment of the return of King Mahabali and a meal of delicious vegetarian dishes served on banana leaves. We had a fabulous day full of dancing and feasting.

Out the Mouth of Babes
Children have an inimitable way of saying it as it is . . . !

I remember being horrified when I was at our little shopping centre in Hilton, KZN, SA. It was early 2008. I was ambling along the walkway when a young mother screamed at her small child. He must have been close to 3 years old . . . "Hurry hurry . . . it's the money lorry. It's the money lorry!" In a croaky voice he ran holding her hand saying, "We must hide" . . . I glanced over my shoulder to see the ATM coin truck approaching. There had been a heist there some months previously. I thought, "Is this the way we have to bring up wee children?"

Shortly before I left for New Zealand, we had breakfast at Yellowwood Café in Howick, South Africa. My grandson who was then aged four could see the Howick Falls from the veranda. He delightedly bellowed: "Look, I can see New Zealand"—having seen a New Zealand calendar with photographs of waterfalls and mountains. I thought—"I wish it was so close."

My eldest grand child, who then aged 7, asked me if she could fly over for a sleep-over once I arrived. When I confessed that it was a tad far for that, she asked if there were any vegetables in New Zealand and, if not, could she post me some; also some chocolate cake from her next birthday party.

Those types of scenarios made me experience massive wobbles, questioning myself and they shredded my heart. But then the untenable or a monstrous event smacked me square-on to remind me why it all happened in the first place . . . ultimately to pave the way for these precious people—if they ever made that their choice . . .

I still had the naïve belief that in some or other way all our children and grandchildren would have their own epiphanies and move to higher ground if the allegorical floods of atrocious happenings continued to immerse the country. Of course I am angry at myself for not believing otherwise, but when one tries to remove oneself from one's denial and draws a line in the sand it feels as though the courageous finger in the dyke simply cannot stop the floodgates from opening . . .

When my eldest grandchild was going into Grade 2, I gazed at her petite frame, the delicate outline of her perfect features and her slender hands. I observed her intensity. At our last family Christmas dinner in South Africa at the 'Funky Table,' she said grace and added, "And dear God please see that the poor children get food today and a happy birthday to baby Jesus". At that stage I did not know that we were leaving, that a thunderbolt would hit us and change the direction of our lives forever. It is moments like that which I galvanise and hold in my heart—at the table with all of our treasured children, children in law and grandchildren.

My 8 year old grandson said that he was unable to get rid of his old toys, even if broken and replaced with new toys "Because of the memories . . ." He moved to New Zealand when he was six. My ten year old granddaughter, who moved to NZ aged 8 said, "I don't want to say anything in your book because I don't want to upset anybody's feelings . . ." (Why, I muse have I not learnt her sage discretion?)

An Oz Gran's Zoo tale   *Lyall McCarthy, Australia*

I left South Africa for Australia the week after my granddaughter's fourth birthday. We've always been close, and she is my reason for living, as I'm devoted to her, as she is to me. Now she's almost eight, and I've missed so much of her life. Her mother is my youngest daughter. I have four daughters and seven grandchildren, all of whom I miss totally, but little Rileigh is the one that my story is about.

When I left SA, I explained to the grandchildren how I was going to live in a nice safe place, where everything is clean and no one goes hungry . . . that sort of thing. I used to send them postcards over every month, (I stopped a while back for no apparent reason, which is pretty bad of me and will post one again tomorrow!), and for some reason I only ever sent pictures of animals . . . kangaroos, possums etc.

When Rileigh started school, they had a 'show and tell' morning. She took all the goodies she needed, because she was going to talk about her granny in Australia. That afternoon the headmistress phoned my daughter and said they hadn't known whether to laugh or cry . . .

Rileigh had stood up and put her photographs of me up on the wall, plus some of the post cards I had sent, along with a toy kangaroo . . . and her speech went like this . . .

"My granny lives in a zoo, she lives with all these animals, and she's very safe. She's looked after carefully and she's well fed . . . The zoo's name is Australia. My granny doesn't want to come back here, because she lives with the kangaroos . . ." (I'd sent her a photo of the kangaroos that came into the garden . . .) The teacher had videoed it and showed it at the Parents' evening the end of that year.

Snippets from Kids

My son said "The children here are not kind". He was 9 at the time & we had just moved to Adelaide. It was upsetting, but I knew he would soon settle.

Bronwyn Hale, Adelaide, Australia

On our recent hols to SA, my nearly two year old kept on pointing to litter and saying "oh dear" or "*mors*" (mess). He gave up after a few days as he could not keep up with all the rubbish. He does not see much of it in Sydney.

Anon, Australia

My youngest child, aged 7 went into third term, grade 1, when we got to Oz. On her second day, she asked her teacher "Where are all the brown children?"

Beryllu Zwaanenburg, West Australia

My brother, Carl, who was three at the time, didn't understand what Australia was. He called it 'Our Stralia' as if it was something that belonged to us or we owned! "We are going to Our Stralia"!

R.W. Adelaide, Australia

My son aged 15 showed how resilient he was and had a great sense of humour. He could not let the chance go by when he was asked about the Wilderness he had come from, when asked by his Oz friend. He said that they had lions and panthers for pets. Needless to say he was most popular from then on!

K.C., Adelaide, Australia

We came over to New Zealand in October 2008. At that time my son was 20 months old. At first we did not realise what he was doing, but every time he got to an open window he would be sticking his head in and out the open window. Then we realised he noticed that there were no burglar bars in front on the windows. It looked so funny, but it made us realise that we made the right choice to bring our kids here to give them a safe, upbringing, and lots of freedom.

Noalene van Loggerenberg, NZ

Our sons were born in NZ. When we returned to SA on a visit, our son, Peter, aged 4 asked us why all the people lived in cages.

Sonja Goedeke, Auckland, NZ

Our youngest son wasn't yet 2 when we came over to NZ. Three years later we went on a holiday in Cape Town and driving through Muizenberg he commented that the people must have been very naughty as they were all living in jails. (Burglar bars were something he was not familiar with at all!) Our eldest son was 6 when we moved to NZ. He commented that it was nice that he could have the car window open when it was hot, when we stopped at traffic lights!

Tracy du Plessés, NZ

After about two months our son stopped telling me to lock the doors in my car and to keep my bag under my seat. When we moved into our first house in NZ we had very low walls and a corner house, and my son was not able to sleep at night, as he was scared someone was going to climb over our wall. It really affects them at all ages! We did the right thing leaving SA.

Leigh Dalton, Saudi Arabia

My youngest son Liam is 5 years old. He was nearly two when we arrived here! He is bug, insect, spider and animal crazy!! He can't wait to go back to SA to see all the '*noo-noos*' that they have there! I don't think that he has ever seen a live snake! He is going to be in his element when we go back to visit. I wonder if I am going to be able to drag him back to the airport without a fight!

Megan Van Zyl, NZ

I told my son Tristan (9 years old), to please stop asking me to buy him 'this and that' all the time because we are trying to save to go home to SA for a visit for the first time since being here in NZ. This is our fourth year now. I said that we need to save as much as possible so that we have enough to go home. He must have given it some serious thought because he came to me and said, "Mom, I want to give you all the money I have saved up so far to put towards our plane tickets home at the end of the year." (I felt so bad). He said that he really wants to go home to visit all our family and friends and the family animals we left behind. He misses them all so much. Makes my heart sore!

Megan Van Zyl, NZ

I thought I would like to share this as it goes to show that our kids get homesick too. My 5 year old asked me, "Mom how long are we going to be staying in New Zealand?" I said "Forever" and he said, "Do we have to, because I miss my *MA* (that's my mom) so much. I really want to go back to South Africa to see her." It brought tears to my eyes. I can't wait for her to be here one day . . .

Eloise Du Toit, NZ

My daughter was 16 at the time and started school at Howick College in Auckland. One of the children asked her if she went to school on elephant back when she was in SA. She replied "Yes we did and in our back garden we have Lions as our pets" These kids believed her and also asked her if she can speak South African, so she asked "Well there are 11 languages, which one would you like to know about?"

Cathy Schwartz, NZ

Today our son, Greg (20) asked us how long it had taken for us to become residents and get our citizenship. Andrea, our daughter, almost 18, overheard the conversation. My husband added his bit and said to Andy "You never even went to school there, that's how long ago." Her reply "Oh yes we did. Mine was that one in a cage!" Those are their

SA memories. Andrea was referring to a little pre-school class that was attached to Greg's junior school at the time. A gate locked the two classes in and the entire play area was surrounded by a high fence and some walls and they had the obligatory barbed wire on top.

Claire Gifford, NZ

My son was 9 when we moved to NZ. We'd been chatting to some Kiwis, and as we said our goodbyes, my son asked me, "Do they speak English in this country?" I said, "Yes of course". He replied, "Then why didn't they speak English to you now?" I looked at him and said, "They just did. It just takes time to hear them correctly." That answer sufficed and off he went to play!

Leigh Dalton, NZ

The first time my 3 year old saw a Maori with tattoos on his face he said (luckily in Afrikaans) "*Kyk Mamma, 'n seerower!*" (Look Mommy, a pirate!) *Die ou het ons so snaaks gekyk* (The guy looked at us oddly.) So I said, "He was just admiring your tattoos". My husband got a tattoo just weeks after we came over because it's the trend here!

Nikki Van Heerden, NZ

My eldest was 12 when we arrived, now 15 and loving every minute of it but he misses family. We're Afrikaans so I was worried about schooling in English, but he's doing great! The younger ones are losing Afrikaans, even though we speak it at home. When my youngest was 4 we asked them to tell us the name of a lion in Afrikaans. They had no idea, so my husband told them the answer '*Leeu*'. The 4 year old remarked: "That's disgusting!" My husband asked, "Why?" and he replied "Loo. is a toilet!" It was hilarious!

Nikki Van Heerden, NZ

It took my girls about two years to stop asking permission to go and play outside. (They were so used to me telling them that they can't play outside without supervision due to danger in SA.)

DG, NZ

My husband reminded me that when we came 'down under' our eldest, then aged 12, asked why we didn't have a '*kaya*' (staff quarters) on our property.

Beryllu Zwaanenburg, Australia

We worked in the Police Force in SA, so we always went to investigate when we heard or saw movement outside—(we had *veld* {field} behind us) and we always went with loaded guns. My children told me recently that they were so scared when we told them to stay in the house when we went to check outside—things we never knew—Very sad, but that is behind us now.

Janene Ferreira Magson, NZ

Oh my word, our daughter who just turned 5, has just come up to me out of the blue and said, and I quote "Mom, I love it here. I don't want to go back to South Africa". I'm speechless. She was only 3 when we got here! It just shows how we have no idea what goes on in their innocent little minds.

Janice le Roux, NZ

My 7 year old grandchild heard a news report the other day about a shooting somewhere in SA and said "We need to leave this country mommy. We are going to get shot." It breaks my heart, this perfect little soul, who I love so very much has no choice but to stay with her stubborn, money crazy parents! What will it do to shift their mind sets . . . when is it too late?

AW, SA

A Teen's Perspective *Meryka Potgieter, Invercargill, NZ*

When I first heard that my family would be moving to New Zealand I was ecstatic. The thought of finally being able to go on a plane was amazing. Being only eleven at the time, my excitement got the better of me. But even though I couldn't sit still or stop squeaking, the plane trip was a great adventure. Of course beyond my obvious excitement and happiness I was worried as well. I didn't know what to expect when we landed here in NZ. I didn't know how the kids would treat me or how different school would be, or even how much the transition from speaking Afrikaans most of the time to speaking English almost all of the time would affect my understanding and my bond with my heritage, culture and my native tongue. The move was hard and we had our ups and downs but there were also great things about our little adventure.

When my parents told my brother, sister and myself that we would be moving to New Zealand I couldn't contain my glee. Our grandparents had moved to NZ two years earlier I couldn't wait to be able to see them again. As the days drew close and our departure date loomed in front of us like a massive impassive mountain range, we sorted out all our things and sold the furniture and extra possessions we wouldn't be able to take over to NZ with us. But we made the sacrifice with open hearts because we knew that the little bit of sacrifice we were about to make would lead us to a better life. When it came to our departure day, I was scared and happy all at the same time. My heart was beating like a drum and my feet wouldn't keep still. Saying goodbye to our family was one of the hardest things that I ever had to do, so far anyway, there was an ache in my heart and a river of tears streaming down my cheeks. Saying goodbye to the people who had helped me grow and learn since I was a tiny baby was painful, but when we walked through the terminal and arrived into the boarding area, I knew everything would be fine because I knew that saying goodbye didn't mean it would be forever. Our goodbyes also meant 'see you later'. The trip on the plane was fantastic, but still a bit scary.

When we landed in NZ, the first thing I noticed was how extremely cold it was. I was dead tired when we landed, and the cold wasn't helping. When we arrived at my grandparents' home, the first thing I did was climb into bed and snuggle under warm blankets. I fell asleep immediately and woke up hours later at six in the morning. The one thing that I loved more than anything else was the peace and quiet.

When my mom enrolled my sister and me into the primary school I was scared witless. It's one thing moving in SA and starting at a new school but moving to a different country and starting a new school and not in one's mother tongue is another! *Eish*, it takes that first day "will I fit in" panic to a whole new level. I was lucky though as when I met with the principal he told me that everything would be fine and if anything bad happened I could come and speak to him immediately. The teachers were all just as welcoming and the students were even better. On my first day I made a whole bunch of friends, and funnily enough one of the girls I befriended was a South African. She showed me the ropes and explained some of the rather stranger kiwi sayings that some of the kids used.

The one thing about school that bothered me was that I would have to speak English the whole time. It was challenging at first and the curriculum was hectic. The things that the other kids in my grade were learning and already knew were things that I would have started to do in a year or two if we had stayed in SA. It was hard fitting in, and still is. The kiwi kids are almost nothing like the South African friends I had when we still lived there. Even today kiwis still continue to shock me, and we've been here for four years. I don't really fit in with them though. I was brought up to believe that drinking and smoking is bad for you and you should avoid it. But most kiwi teens nowadays do those types of things on a daily basis. Some kiwi teens have this thing where every fourth word they say has to be a swear word. It is utterly disgusting, but even though a lot of them lack proper grammar and use foul language most of the people I've met have been sweet and helped me fit in with my surroundings. I've never been part of the whole "let's get drunk" scene, even though loads of my friends are. They accept that swearing, smoking and drinking aren't part of who I am. They have never tried to pressure me into trying things that I didn't want to do. They have been very understanding and supportive. It just depends on who you hang out with.

Since I started high school here in NZ I've learnt so much and I discovered that I had a secret passion for writing. The schools here give students millions of great opportunities. The curriculum is one of the best in the world, and the classes and equipment we use are all 'state of the art' and help to enhance our learning. In the two years I've been going to high school I've learnt so much, and I've gotten smarter. When I was in year 9, I was in the middle to average classes a.k.a B band. But now in year eleven I'm in the high intelligence classes a.k.a A band. All my teachers have helped me to learn and grow in the areas I struggled with. The teachers here want to help. They want to make sure you achieve with the highest possible grades. Because NZ schools don't offer Afrikaans as an elective I have sort of lost touch with my heritage, but thanks to my parents I have learnt so much about what it is to be Afrikaans. The most important part that helped me stay in touch with my roots was that my parents and my other family and friends always talk about the things that they did in SA, or the beautiful places they had been to.

New Zealand is an amazing country. I think that if you're looking for a fresh start or for a better shot at living a good life you should come on over. At first it will be tough. Yes it will take a while to get on your feet, but there is a whole network of South Africans willing to help you and let you lean on them. Here in NZ we all have to band together. It's a wonderful place to live. Give it a go, you will love it.

Refugees

What is a Refugee?—*It's about having no choice!*

Refugees differ vastly from migrants. They have no choice, but to flee empty handed due to a life threatening crisis. Migrants choose to leave and to settle elsewhere, and are able to relocate their possessions. Because of the urgency of departure for a refugee, they have not had time to assimilate what is happening and are emotionally ill prepared. Conversely, migrants generally have a few months to farewell family and to have some emotional preparedness for their journey.

Refugees arrive in a new home traumatised, ill-equipped, with no financial resources, debilitated by feelings of deep grief, fear and guilt. Invariably their own and the host countries' cultures and languages differ vastly. Migrants are generally better equipped to acculturate and may have done some research into schooling, employment and housing prospects. They also have some financial resources.

Refugees probably can never return home, whereas migrants can return to visit family and friends in their homeland, and can return home permanently if they do not settle. The sense of finality and displacement for the refugee is thus far greater.

Who is a Refugee?

'A refugee is: any person who, owing to a well-founded fear of being persecuted for reasons of race, religion, nationality, membership of a particular social group or political opinion, is outside the country of his/her nationality and is unable, or owing to fear, is unwilling to avail himself/herself of the protection of that country.'

United Nations Convention Relating to the Status of Refugees Geneva, 1951.

Refugees are referred to as 'the human causalities that stream from the world's trouble spots. They are driven from their homelands by major crises such as war, religious and political persecution, brutal regimes, ethnic cleansing, military uprisings and anarchy.' (Refugee Health Care: A handbook for health professionals. New Zealand Government.)

Most refugees experience physical or emotional trauma. The physical and psychological sequelae are common aspects of being a refugee. It is reported that as many as 40 % of refugees have witnessed violence such as killings, often of a family member. Some may have survived detention, physical violence, or rape, before finally getting to an overcrowded camp where provisions are limited.

The frightening statistics are that there are currently as many as 42 million refugees and displaced people in the world. (as at 2012). Most refugees remain unsettled and only 2% per annum are resettled.

Reportedly women and children are primarily vulnerable, exposed to the rigours of a long journey into hiding and repeated sexual abuse. They suffer from forced impregnation and abortion, trafficking and sexual slavery, leading to sexually transmitted diseases and HIV/AIDS.

'The danger is the same. Near or far, but there's no wood nearby. When we are there getting the wood, local people sometimes take the girls' clothes off and do bad things. The people wear green uniforms. Some have camels, some have horses. At the place where we get the firewood they tell us 'line up one by one'. They say, 'Stand two by two', and they take us off like that and then rape us . . . Sometimes this happens until evening. We have told the police, but the police say, 'stay in your tent and nothing will happen.' (African refugee woman—Women's Commission for Refugee Women and Children 2006).

My Long Journey From Suffering to Life

Santino Atem Deng

One of the "lost boys" from Sudan recounts his story of trauma and resilience.
When I was nine years old, I fled from the civil war in my home country of southern Sudan. This war has been raging as long as I can

recall. My long journey began when random shooting was followed by the burning down of our pre-school and houses in our small village. At that time, everybody was running away to the forest for safety and, in the process, I was separated from my parents. I joined a group of adults who were able to take care of me and other young people as we made our way to Ethiopia. Since I was so young, I had many questions, but most were unanswered. When I wondered where my parents were, no one seemed to know. When I asked who was shooting at us and burning down our houses and school, they told me it was the Sudanese government. Not being satisfied with their answers, I asked, "Why do they want to kill us?" They might say, "Because they hate us," or they did not know, and there were no more answers. I often asked where we were going and whether we would ever meet my parents. They were sceptical and said, "Maybe or maybe not, because we don't know where they are at the moment." But they assured me that we were going to a safe place. In Dinka culture, children are not always told everything or may be given indirect answers about something bad that might have happened. For instance, if a parent has died, young children cannot be told straight away because they are too vulnerable; they would be shocked by the news of death and might lose hope. Therefore, I was not given any specific information until we reached Ethiopia two months later.

I realized some years later that my father and other relatives were among the casualties. Our travel to Ethiopia was difficult. We ate wild fruit, leaves, and wild animals, when they were available, but we spent many days and nights without food and water. We often went without sleep as well, as we were travelling day and night. We also were in danger as lions, hyenas, and other wild animals had developed a taste for human flesh. Although I had seen most of my friends die in front of me, I was not able to cry anymore. I had cried all day and night, missing my parents since our journey first began.

After we arrived in Ethiopia, we were resettled by the UNHCR to Payiudo, a refugee camp not far from the Sudan border. Since there were no hospitals or clinics and no good food or shelter, many died in that camp from diseases. We slept outside in the rain because there were no houses. After some months, I was determined to get military training so that I would be given a gun to fight those who had burned our town. Although my size and age would not allow me to carry a gun, let alone complete the military training, after witnessing so much violence, anger prevailed and I felt life was not worth anything anymore. I was prepared to die trying to do something to save the lives of others. My strongest desire was to go back and search for my parents, whether they were dead or alive. I was not able to see very far into the future, since I thought it was the end of my world. Fortunately, the Sudan Peoples' Liberation Movement (SPLM) recognized this flawed thinking and young people my age were singled out and sent to school in the camp. We were told that we were too young to join military training. In fact, they warned us that those who had escaped and joined the military training were now either dead or disabled, reclaiming children and youth. Most of them did not have a chance to go to school. Their anger drove them to fight in defence of their loved ones. We were given training in self-defence, which later helped me to survive, but I was angry that I was not allowed to have a gun, so I could go and search for my parents.

We were trained to manage and look after ourselves and were told that those in our group were our brothers. We learned how to support each other when we began thinking about our parents and other loved ones who had been left behind, unsure whether they were dead or alive. When I returned to Sudan as a young adolescent, I thought that things might be different, but our journey back to Sudan was even worse than our earlier journey to Ethiopia. We travelled for ninety days by foot during the rainy season when almost all the roads were flooded. The traumatic memories of seeing many of my friends killed along the way by crocodile, snakes, and hippopotamus are difficult to forget. Although many of my friends from previous camps were here, I learned that many had died in their long journey.

For the first time in the refugee camp, primary and secondary schools were opened. I began to realize how important education was for my future. I finished primary grades and began secondary school. When I resettled to New Zealand, I finished secondary school and started at the University of Auckland. Presently, I am doing extramural studies at Massey University, while working for the Ministry of Education and the Ministry of Health. I am a registered public health interpreter for those who speak Dinka, Sudanese, Arabic, Swahili, and other languages. Working with young people as a Behaviour Support Worker with Special Education has given direction to my future. When I enrolled at the University I did not have a clear vision of a career. Therefore, I studied International Relations and

Foreign Policy. Later I began to work in special education and was inspired to work with kids with behaviour problems who lack social skills. Young people often have issues due to family background; many of our clients are children of refugees who had to flee. Now I am completing an undergraduate degree in psychology. Through support from our team at the Ministry of Education, I have been able to stay focused on my studies. Working with people who are traumatised is not easy because one often experiences trauma as well. But I now realize that an encouraging environment is important for success for anyone.

While I was a student in secondary school in Kenya, I volunteered to work with young children and taught at the primary level. My experience in youth leadership in both Kenya and New Zealand has contributed to my decision to work in this area. Training in mediation, arbitration, and litigation has helped me to assist young people when they are in conflict. On our team, I am able to give cultural advice on behalf of the Sudanese and other African clients. Different types of sports at school help youth who have very challenging behaviours and social skill problems, for example, not knowing how to share with other kids or not coping in their new surroundings. Last year, a soccer programme was developed in one of the schools for kids who were exhibiting challenging behaviour at their school. They had lived with their families at refugee camps where the kids did not attend school and did not learn social skills. They were extremely traumatised from the suffering they endured at the camp, including family violence. Now faced with a new culture and a new country, not to mention a new language, they were having a difficult time adjusting. Southern Sudan has lost three generations in the civil war, and southern Sudanese are scattered around the world today.

Before I came to New Zealand, I was planning to go to the United States, because I had never heard of New Zealand. I only knew then of the US, Canada, where my brother is, and Australia, where my cousins are. In New Zealand, I have had many opportunities. Many of my friends, who are often referred to as the 'Lost Boys of Sudan', are now in the United States and have stories like mine. We are no longer lost, for our long journey has led us from suffering to life.

Santino Atem Deng has enrolled for his Doctoral Studies at The University of Victoria in Melbourne, Australia. He is concerned about children around the world who are victimised, especially those who suffer because of civil war in their homeland. He can be contacted by e-mail: atem_deng@yahoo.com.au

Rootless—It hurts not to have roots
(From an African-American) *Anonymity requested—RR*

I find it frustrating in my feeble attempts to paint pictures using words where only stark white canvass stands. Gibran once said, "Thoughts are like a bird of space, that when placed in a cage of words can indeed unfold its wings but can no longer fly". My thoughts, like Gibran's, find themselves perched upon a precipice seeking the winds of life that may one day raise them to the heavens.

I have for many years embraced who I am and the thoughts that are uniquely a part of my psyche. I grew up in a house with my parents and grandparents. For a little while my father stayed with the family, but in time he abandoned us to search for whatever he thought he needed. I wondered on many occasion how my life might have been different had my father decided to be a man and remain with us. I suppose I sound a little bitter, but I think I have long since reconciled the notion of being bitter. The way I see it is by being bitter I only hurt me and in my estimation, that is no way to live.

Although I grew up in a large family, I felt as though I didn't fit in. The older siblings never really had time for me or wanted me to be around them and their friends. I have always been the type to be able to find my path alone and with little or no guidance. I have from the time I was seven years old, and I cannot remember ever not working, one way or another. My first real paying job was at a store cleaning and mopping the floors and cleaning the counter. The pay wasn't good but the benefits were enormous to me at that time; I could read all of the books in the display case that I wanted without being run off. Books taught me how to read and lit my imagination afire.

I believe in reincarnation of a sort, not like some of the eastern religious philosophies, but a philosophy I have come to understand in my own way. What I know for certain is the inner spark which ignites my being is unlike the frailty of the body and will never fade. I believe we all transcend this life and at some point in time we return; we return, because we are still learning to be citizens of the universe-, learning to love unconditionally, learning to accept each person for the light found within, and not the materials of their wealth, learning to recognize we all carry our imperfections and as such are not able to elevate ourselves to the level of omnipotence.

I believe that at some point in time after we have learned the lessons necessary to make us more understanding of our responsibilities as citizens of the universe we are allowed to move on to a higher plane of existence. I believe I am intensely spiritual and have a connection with something that goes beyond our measured comprehension. I find the "mental noise" of organized religion to be too pervasive for me. But, I know there is a God each time an unseen hand bows the head of the mighty oak, or a flower blooms, or a child's laughter fills the air, or a baby is born.

I have come to the realization that we humans are fragile beings capable of many things, but most of all capable of being just that. I am aware of my weaknesses and embrace them as innate qualities heaped upon me at the moment of my creation and as I plod through life, the steps I make are graced with a certain understanding of my small place in the universe. I accept my frailties, knowing full well I will make mistakes in life and not fool myself into thinking I have qualities that may at some point in time elevate me to the level of being Godlike. I love inhaling all of the passion that one greater than I has bestowed upon me and I will not deny that.

I suppose in the quiet of the night my imaginings take flight and I allow myself to wander and wonder of the world I have not the capacity to yet understand. I wonder how this life will end and if this tiny spark that set my soul in motion will somehow find its way to another plane of existence and understanding. Somehow I know deep within, this energy that animates me from day to day, that gives me emotion, thoughts and awareness beyond me will continue for eternity. I consider myself a spiritual but have always been baffled by how man in the name of a loving God can perpetuate such hate and discontent. I sense there is a power greater than I and am cognizant enough to know I have not been given the capacity as of yet to grasp its understanding.

There are times when instinctively I feel most assured life is indeed on the wheel, (where there is no beginning, and no end) and we all must travel its circumference in gaining ultimate knowledge and eventually take our rightful place as fully aware sentient beings. At times I grow impatient but I have come to realize all of my experiences on our little blue marble are lessons written upon a universal slate that can never be erased or rewritten. So I embrace the day and each lesson transcribed upon the wall. I know if I listen to the sounds of the universe my song of life will emerge like a new world symphony. My new world symphony consists of the many and varied notes formed by the music that rare individuals bring to my life. I will listen most attentively to the notes others strike, hoping against hope I have the capacity to replay their riffs and syncopations and in the process bring to the fore a symphony of jazz yet unheard.

My day has been at a leisurely pace in preparation for work tomorrow. The weather has been rainy and overcast, which always has an effect on me. I find gray days seem to cover me in a cloak of warmth and I find myself carried back to childhood days; days when the rain fell on tin roofs and the rolling of the thunder either lulled all to sleep, or the adults quietly talked and my siblings sat on the floor and listened in wrapped fascination at the stories they brought to life. Funny isn't it, how memories are triggered by a sound, a smell, a word or a glance. In my humble estimation, memories are the only things in life that are truly ours; all else is transient, but memories are a unique experience no matter if the instance that became a memory is viewed simultaneously with another, each carries his/her own sense of that moment and at times they even become palpable.

Earlier this morning, I went to pick up coffee and as I approached a highway I must cross, I didn't see a car or another human being as far as the eye could see and just for an instance as I looked each way I felt as If I was the only person on earth. I suppose at times we all feel alone on a mountain top or adrift in the ocean of life. It would seem life always asks the questions and we constantly seek the answers . . .

I have given a great deal of thought regarding my ancestors. It is most humbling to realize ones past comes to an abrupt halt after a couple of generations. I suppose people like my family are among the lost souls of immigration, where we find ourselves locked in an Auschwitz of the mind where the ghosts of our past have no faces and the only echoes we hear are silent wails of so many from the past.

It hurts not to have "roots"; to be able to know where one comes from must be an indescribable feeling. I do so envy those who have and know their past. I would describe the feeling I have as walking into a room for something and then realizing you can't remember what you came for, (it's right there, but you just can't quite touch it). It's a feeling of Déjà Vu of an amnesiac.

I wonder what it would have felt like to be a true immigrant, looking forward to the start of a new life, new adventures with the only thing holding one back is the will, (or lack thereof) to succeed. To demonize a person because of the color of his skin is one of the cruellest irony's perpetrated against human kind. Why are we so committed to destroying ourselves? I must apologize for seeming so forlorn but some thoughts really . . . well you get the picture . . .

I would like to share a poem I wrote, which I feel captures some of who I am-

"The Path"

Drops of thought, like rain borne by gravity
seeking the path of least resistance-
Slide down my mellow mind, caressing ever changing
truths-

A catalyst to ignite word or action—perhaps, only a
circle of thought-
Never ending echoes muffled by the muck of infinity
locked in an embrace of confusion-
Truth but a perception, changing within the parameters
of its confinement
What is the substance of it? Glorious, reprehensible,
stagnant?

Within the eye that is my mind, substance stands
inconsequential
And burdens fall on weary shoulders, heap upon heap
for no good reason

The path of least resistance grows worn and deep—
difficult to escape
Until the flow of everyday toil would seem the
universe

So my soul, like thought, seeks a path of least
resistance and I follow and I follow and I follow . . .
But a fathomless desire exists . . . freedom it seeks
A chance to blow through the walls of this spiral
maze-

Around and around sprawled against forces yet unseen
knowing full well control lies not within my hands. RR

Uprooted

Don Marney, Oz

(As told through the eyes of a 48 year old 'cape coloured' male,
who left South Africa at the age of 12–13.)

Where does one start with something so raw that it hurts to the
core? The logical scenario is to provide some background about 'our
community'. We are the 'Uprooted people'; the ones that are too dark
or too light . . . We are the people who were severed by the archaic
Apartheid laws which defined some of us as white and some of us as
'non white'. We are the people whose families were shredded apart.
We are the people who were uprooted, some forcibly removed from
living in white areas and others permitted to remain there. My family
was confined to living in a demarcated area with others of colour,
irrespective of our different stations in life. My light skinned father
chose to be 'classified' as coloured, so as to marry my 'coloured' mother.
This was against his father's wishes, which were to re-classify him as
'white', (noting that a number of his siblings are classified as 'white').
We are the 'classified' people, shredded by callous laws.

How did we come about? We are a delightfully heterogeneous
group of people with a fascinating ancestry. We have African,
European, Indian, Indonesian, Khoisan and Malaysian roots, to name
a few. I am finally learning to embrace and feel a pride in my cultural
mix of European, Indian and African within me, and yet the skewed
South African mindset still evident from the old legacy obliterated my
capacity to value myself, which ubiquitously impacted my life and my
life world.

I am the eldest of 3 boys born to Julia (nee Davids) and Owen
Marney. We left Cape Town, South Africa in January 1978, by chartered
airplane as we had literally missed the last ship, and someone had

organised tickets on this plane which travelled via Mauritius which included a 4 day stopover in Bangkok, Thailand, on its way to Sydney, Australia, where we changed planes to travel to our eventual home town of Melbourne. My father was a Carpenter and Joiner and mum was a stay-at-home mum. We had never been in an aeroplane before, and never been tourists before either, so the experience was quite novel for us.

My feelings and thoughts prior to migration were filled with excitement at the prospect of getting out of the country, because even at the tender age of 10, I could see that my people and I were not permitted a fair go at life, in that education for my parents and other adults around me was limited because of their skin colour. In addition, work opportunities were limited because of the lack of education, and the preservation of many jobs / positions of leadership and authority were safeguarded for those 'blessed' with a fair skin, or with access to wealth.

My experience of SA was about being told 'we cannot go to that beach' or 'we cannot use that toilet' or 'we cannot enter through that door', or 'we cannot sit in that seat'. The harsh reality of why we were leaving SA was brought home to me during our last days in the country, when our church minister who was a 'white' man took us into his family home for a few days after my parents had sold the home (to pay for the airfare), prior to us boarding the plane to leave. The minister and his family lived in the white area of Plumstead, and when one of his neighbours saw us staying there, they complained to the authorities, who promptly had us evicted from this home. Needless to say that another member of the church congregation put us up after this episode.

As I started to read and take in the world around me as a youngster, I could not help but notice the relative poverty of my people compared to those who were white skinned; as well as the relative wealth of my people compared to those who were more dark skinned than us; i.e. black Africans. This sense of inequality was foremost in my mind as I migrated, with the hope that we would not be treated in this way. It was blatantly obvious to me as a youngster that my country was one which was based on slavery, and I sought out literature that validated this as much as possible. This was not always possible, because of the high degree of censorship practiced by the white regime.

Upon arrival in Australia, we stayed with friends for a few days, while our parents looked for a rental property with suitable schools in the vicinity. They settled on a property in Cheltenham, and found schools for us to attend. Since I was starting high school, I had to catch a bus, while my younger siblings attended the primary school which was within walking distance of home. The bus experience was challenging because I was incredibly uncomfortable sitting next to 'white' people; bearing in mind that less than 2 weeks prior to this, I was not allowed to be in a 'white' area or sit in the same section of the train or bus as them! And to top it off, I had wavy hair, and in SA as a coloured, we were made to feel ugly if we did not have straight hair—straight hair is what the 'whites' had, and all our models of beauty in SA were based on a 'white' model, so I felt ugly.

At school the feeling of loss and isolation was stronger still, because I was sitting in an entire class of white only children. They talked to me as they did to each other, which was difficult for me to comprehend and accept. Again, I could not believe the absurdity of all of this. Luckily the teacher was a Sri Lankan lady who helped settle me in over those first traumatic weeks. The trauma was perceived and felt on my part, and it may not have been real, however, I felt displaced and like a fish out of water. I went from being a confident extrovert child to one who was shy and an introvert overnight. The school was great, because when I experienced racist comments by a fellow student, he was expelled, after being reported by my classmates.

The twice daily bus journey was uncomfortable because sometimes I would have to sit next to someone and I often preferred to save them the embarrassment of sitting next to a 'non-white' person by standing. This is why I pleaded with my dad to buy me a bicycle, which he did during my second year of school. I discovered that although I spoke great English, my accent was problematic and often led to me being misunderstood. This led me to hating English and being drawn to the science and maths subjects which did not require the same level of linguistics.

My discomfort in the presence of white kids led me to be introverted to avoid being conspicuous. My one joy was playing soccer, at which I excelled. However, I often found myself electing to come off the field at half time, because I didn't feel worthy of taking a white kid's place for the entire match. This became such an issue, that the coach yelled at me on the field in front of everyone, saying that I was as good as anyone else, and that I was not coming off the field. This changed the way I progressed from then on and I went on to play state league soccer.

As a result of watching my parents struggle on account of their colour and always saying that 'If you get an education, no one can take it away from you', I became determined to get the best qualification (regardless of whether I liked it or not), and although I did not love science/engineering, preferring economics, history and social sciences, I chose to pursue a career in these areas because in this way I could acquire financial stability and hence feel safe from white people in my laboratory—yes I know it was incredibly naive! And when I got the first degree, it was logical to pursue subsequent degrees because that was 'doing well' or doing 'better' for a coloured boy. I was very much still operating in a South African mode of thinking, being aware that my parents' future had been deprived because of lack of inherited wealth and not having a white skin. If the latter had not been a factor, they would not have had to tolerate unqualified white people telling them what to do, and getting favoured jobs in all sectors of the economy. Being white enabled you to be a boss irrespective of if you had the necessary experience or qualifications, and enabled you to the best education and a more favourable economic future. I thus figured that I would strive to get the best education I could get in Australia because it was free; ironically so that I could become the boss of white people! This is crazy because white people are no different from non-white people anyway; it's just the distortion of reality that was created by South Africa.

Now in my midlife, I find that I am earning a reasonable income and 'doing well' as a scientist in the safe scientific zone I established for myself. I am not necessarily doing what I would possibly have opted to do, due to the negative way in which I perceived myself. To a degree I locked my options, although I believe that this is not entirely true; if I'm prepared to take some risks in life, continue exploring, actualising and reaching that place of total acceptance . . . and dare I say forgiveness?

Shaky Roots—Home isn't where it used to be
5th November 2011   *Sharon Gill*

Home used to be the place where your family was safe, or the country you chose to live in . . . But things have changed. Do I feel safe in my own home? No. Do I think of this country as home? Not anymore. Home, for me, is going to be somewhere else.

Violent crime has become so commonplace that South Africans have lost the capacity to be shocked by it. It doesn't make front page news anymore. Hell, it rarely gets a mention on page four of the community knock-and-drop. If somebody gets stabbed or shot in England, Sky News runs the story repeatedly for days. If they covered every stabbing, rape, shooting or mutilation that happens in South Africa, they'd need a dozen channels and no 15-minute loops.

Another woman hijacked at gunpoint and then shot in the head as the thugs drove off in her car. Another man savagely beaten, robbed and left for dead in his own home. Another family robbed, with the man held at knifepoint by one thug while another rapes his wife.

When they've stolen what they came for, why don't they just leave? It's almost as if it's not crime anymore—it's entertainment. Something to do on a Friday night. And then the after-event disinterest.

You could die of old age waiting for someone to even answer the Flying Squad's 10111 number, let alone actually dispatch someone to the scene of the crime. And if they do bother to show up, it's a rare police officer who accurately records the event. Even rarer for any effective action to take place, that might lead to an arrest, unless you're a local reggae star, or a tourist from a civilised country.

My dad had the crap beaten out of him by four savages when they discovered that the 87-year-old pensioner had nothing of value for them to steal. When the police finally put in an appearance, they didn't even go into the house to inspect the mess, the damage, the pool of my dad's blood on the floor. They didn't venture further than the driveway gate.

For the record, residents suspect it's the same group of four youths that has been robbing houses in my dad's street for the past five or six years—sometimes three or four houses in the same week, and some people have been robbed three times or more in the past couple of years. I have their names, phone numbers and robbery details; which, I suspect, is more than the police have, since it's often too much trouble for them to open a docket.

The first time the police contacted me after my father's incident was almost a year later, when they phoned to ask me to retract a comment I'd made to The Citizen newspaper about police incompetence which got them into trouble. I said I'd retract it when they start making an effort to do their job properly.

This country has bred a generation of criminals who think it's acceptable to get whatever they want by stealing it from someone else. And they get away with it because nobody cares.

The police don't seem to care otherwise they'd have nailed the bunch that's been terrorising my dad's street for more than five years.

The insurance companies don't care. If they can't wangle their way out of settling claims, they recoup their losses by hiking everybody's premiums.

The hospitals don't care. If you have medical aid, they'll get paid. If you don't, they refuse to even look at you. So you go to a government hospital where you'll be lucky not to die of something filth related while you're ignored until the staff tea break is over or the admissions clerk finishes picking her nose.

And we put up with it because we've grown accustomed to being treated like we don't matter. To add insult to injury, we get bombarded with accusations and insulting platitudes.

The police say you were careless for not locking yourself in your house. Well, in order to get into and out of the house, you generally need to open the security gate. If you have a garden, you should be able to use it without having armed guards on standby. And when you return home, you should be able to drive into your own property without first sending in a 'SWAT' team to check for armed thugs hiding in the shrubbery.

And if you survive a violent crime with most of your body parts still intact, your friends tell you how lucky you are. *Bullshit!* I resent the expectation that I must be grateful they didn't kill me. What I'd be grateful for is if they didn't rob me at gunpoint in the first place.

Violent crime is chasing law abiding people out of the country. Those of us who want to stay in this country rethink our security measures. We reinforce the burglar guards on our windows. We put tamper-proof locks on security gates. We decorate our boundary walls with electric fences and razor wire. We install motion sensor lights and elaborate alarm systems hooked up to armed response security companies. And we wonder if it's possible to buy a bazooka on eBay.

But too many people have had enough. A lot of my friends and most of my family, all of whom had more brains, more guts or more money than me, left South Africa a few years ago. The country's crime levels and lack of career opportunities drove my own daughter overseas in search of a better and safer life.

And now I'm sick of living like a prisoner in my own home and sick of being a neurotic wreck every time I go out. Sick of driving around with my car doors locked and windows closed and timing my arrival at intersections to coincide with green lights.

I loved what this beautiful country used to be, but I hate what I believe it's become—a crime infested, AIDS-riddled, lawless shit hole run by corrupt, greedy, mentally defective fools who are too busy feathering their own nests, being 'pally' with unsavoury characters like Bob Mugabe and Muammar Gaddafi, and making exhibitions of themselves at media briefings, to realise that a large percentage of the people who voted for them will probably starve to death before the next election.

I want to live in a place where I don't have to live behind bars and gates, where I can sit in my own garden without hearing the neighbours' ceremonial slaughtering of a goat for the weekend festivities, where my kids can walk to the shop without getting stabbed for their cell phones, where I can get out of my car without having a gun shoved in my ear, and where my dogs can be pets instead of guard dogs.

I want to live in a place where rape is a serious crime, where politicians don't encourage racism by singing hate songs. Where protesters don't brandish placards telling HIV+ criminals: "Don't shoot to kill, do sex to kill".

And the hand-wringing bleeding hearts can shut up with the excuse that people steal because they're hungry or they can't find a job. A lot of my friends and I are battling to find work—not least because of "affirmative action", and we haven't gone on any thieving sprees.

The writing isn't just on the wall. It jumps out and screams at me in my dreams: *'Get out before it's too late!'*

At my age, it's frightening to start over in a strange country, but that pales in comparison to the fear I live with every day in the country I used to call "home".

Advice to Wannabes

On Reason and Passion—*Kahlil Gibran*

"Your soul is sometimes a battlefield, upon which your reason and your judgement wages war against your passion and your appetite.

Would that I could be the peacemaker in your soul, that I might turn the discord and the rivalry of your

Elements into oneness and melody
But how shall I, unless you yourselves be the peacemakers,
nay, the lovers of all elements? . . ."

Time for that evaluation *Eve Hemming*

What would my advice be to my family, friends and colleagues? People frequently want me to forward their CV to some or other NZ destination and to ask myriad questions about immigration . . .

My answer is this—*no one can give one a definitive answer or make a choice for you.* For those who left SA due to a family member being ravaged by violence and their inner sanctum being violated, the choice may first and foremost be to seek refuge and a place to heal; whether at home or elsewhere. For some they may wish to leave as soon as possible, whilst for others they may not have the emotional or financial resources to leave, and will more than anything else desire to be close to family roots and a familiar infrastructure.

For those who leave as political activists, or in an endeavour to avoid a heinous occurrence, which could splinter the core of their psyche, the choice may be more complex. Either way one lacks totality. If abroad, one will forever experience the pangs of desire for one's loved ones at home, and the essence and imagery of Africa. Else remaining 'at home', one will never know how it would feel to taste a new life and never know when the bad could rear its head. There's good, bad and ugly everywhere. It boils down to quantity, random occurrences and dare I say, luck?

There are days when I do regret taking the plunge and there are days when I wish we'd done it sooner. It's taught my husband and me a great deal of reflection and has provided fodder for inner growth. But I continue to wish that my husband and I could find 'the perfect place' near all our treasured children and grand children . . .

One needs have to be patient with one's loved ones. Immigration is a process. Ten years ago we would never have dreamed of leaving SA. Now we can't wait to get out. The reason we stayed so long was that we held on to hope that things would eventually get better and finally we gave up hope. So many others we know just aren't in that place *yet*. One has to be patient, as friends and family have to work it out for themselves. My cousin has lived in the States for about twenty years now. On one of his visits to SA about ten years ago, he commented how uncomfortable he felt visiting us; how unsafe he felt walking down the street. At the time I didn't really understand his point of view and was irritated by his comments. A few years later on my first trip to Europe I experienced a sense of freedom and peace of mind and have never looked at SA in the same way since. There are things that happen in my suburb that people a few kilometres away are oblivious of. It's due to many crimes not being reported. What's the point, anyway? The chances are that they won't get caught or the legal system will let us down. The other reason is that I get the feeling that the Government is trying to suppress/hide the statistics here in SA. That is why social media is so cool, as it is ahead of the Govt. and their propaganda. Recent stats say that violent crime has decreased. Is that truth or concealment? Living here with a gradual steady decline means that so many locals can't see the wood for the trees. With all that goes on, I still can't believe why some people are questioning us about why we want to leave, or worse are trying to get us to change our minds! We in SA are like the frog in the pot on the stove. We are warming up so slowly that we barely notice. But after years of this, we are almost at boiling point. *Jean Reah, SA*

I don't believe that you ever break the roots. I am very proud of my heritage and one day I will make it clear to my children what their roots are (even though they will be born and raised in NZ.) The hardest lesson to learn (for me as a white middle class girl) when moving to NZ, was that even though people look "similar", for some reason we assume the culture will be similar, but it really isn't. It makes your mind struggle, but once you have come to terms with it, you can appreciate the differences in culture and be more accepting that things are different, and people become more accepting of you and your differences (in work ethic, in traditions, in tastes etc.) Your expectations need to be different when you think about the Kiwi culture versus the South African culture—even something as simple as a SA barbeque versus a *braai*, it's just not the same, but when you don't expect it to be, you won't struggle as much and feel continuously disappointed. PS. Sorry for making people emotional, but it shows we go through the same challenges, so that we are able to stick together and support each other through the transition. There was no Face book 11 years ago—it would have been awesome to have this support network then. *Candice Baker, NZ*

After 27 years abroad I still call South Africa home

Barry Levy, Oz

I still feel it pump and bloat, bubble and swagger in my heart . . . What South Africans have to realise, and get out of the old 'Cold War-Apartheid' mentality is that because they don't like Zuma or his predecessor Mbeki or BEE or whatever, is that this doesn't mean they have to hate the country, or for many, the old country. The government of the day, yes, maybe. Hate them. But not the country! That is our soul. A part of our flesh and blood, a part of the oxygen we breathed when we first burst into this world . . . And what a wonderful part of the world it is—so wonderful that our country, once a pariah nation of the world, eventually conquered the biggest scourge of the planet, Apartheid.

Not only that, South Africa is known today as one of the most democratic countries in the world. People in the country, and some abroad these days even, freak out when they see the government tampering with that freedom—and I am very proud of that. To this Nobel Peace Prize winning accomplishment, I say cheers, as in well *bladdy* done; this is the way to remember our country, not ever to say goodbye! In the end what I miss above all else about South Africa, above everything physical and tasty and creative, is the greatest thing anyone can have from any country: the emotional anchor of home.

Home away from Home—*Musings of an Immigration Junkie*

Culture Shock—It's Real!   *Di Russell, Canada*

I previously touched on culture shock in my post about pre-immigration syndrome, but I'd like to explore it here in a bit more detail.

Most people have heard of culture shock and quite naturally associate the term with the challenges involved with adapting to a new culture, whether during travel, living as an expat or as a result of immigration. We generally think of differences in language, food, religion, tradition and interpersonal behavior as triggers of feelings of discomfort and frustration when living away from home.

But what exactly happens in culture shock, when does it happen, and why does it happen?

Obviously, culture shock affects people in different ways, but there is a widely accepted pattern of 'symptoms' that tends to present itself in a predictable order.

Essentially, one can expect culture shock to mimic the typical progression of a romantic relationship:

Stage One: In the beginning, the newcomer is mesmerized by EVERYTHING!

The sights, sounds, tastes, and energy of the new location produce a 'high' of note by providing constant stimulation and appealing to our human need for new experience and variety. Much like the rush of emotion one feels in a 'love at first sight' moment, the intense excitement, fascination, and need for MORE make Stage One an incredibly positive time in one's life. New surroundings bring out latent aspects of one's personality, and the newcomer feels like she/he is undergoing a personal/spiritual growth spurt. Family and friends can expect to be bombarded by emails and postcards full of adventures, Facebook pages full of new photo albums, and probably a stream of never-ending blog posts about how this new home is the most incredible place EVER. New friendships are forged, very often with other people who are experiencing the same thing, and there is a sense of urgency as one wants to do, see and try everything the country has to offer.

Stage Two: After the shine rubs off and the endorphins leave one's system, the newcomer quickly realizes that his/her initial impressions may not have been all that accurate, and the 'uglies' of the place start revealing themselves. A degree of embarrassment/shame usually accompanies this discovery, given the landslide of glowing emails, Facebook photos and blog posts they had just been spamming their people with back home. The niggling feeling that one might have been WRONG about first impressions is too difficult for some to accept, so Stage Two may be temporarily avoided as the newcomer frantically attempts to maintain the fantasy of Stage One. Inevitably, the illusion does slip away, and the frustration and anger of Stage Two rears its ugly head.

In Stage Two, newcomers may feel disillusioned, disappointed, disgusted and/or disapproving of their new culture. The inner critic takes over, projecting one's personal struggle with change onto the new culture, turning their new home into enemy number one. What was initially 'cool' and 'exotic' becomes ridiculous, sub-standard and irritating. The food is too spicy, the people are rude, nothing works properly, the shopping is crappy, etc. Just as a man might initially fall in love with a woman's voice but after a few months of daily nagging that once beautiful voice becomes the cackle of an evil shrew, the novelties of the new culture can suddenly become burdensome and annoying beyond measure. People in Stage Two are awful to be around—they moan, complain, compare, demand and generally act like self-entitled brats.

Stage Three: If a newcomer survives Stage Two, he/she can expect to be faced with Stage Three, which I prefer to call the 'paralysis stage'.

After the anger passes, one is left with a feeling of emptiness or despondency. There is a sense of being stuck or unable to affect any change in one's life. Homesickness may really set in at this point, and a feeling of lethargy underlies everything one undertakes. I suspect that this downtime is part of the integration process whereby your previous identity (ego) stops fighting the new influences and becomes more receptive to the unconscious changes that are taking place deep in one's psyche. Like any long-term relationship in which the partners have periods of withdrawal, depression and apathy, newcomers can also feel helplessly lost and alone during this phase of integration. Right now, I think I'm transitioning out of Stage Three. I've been in an incubator for the last number of months, waiting for a new, integrated identity to hatch so I can re-engage the world. It's been a difficult time particularly because I'm also an introvert, but I see the light at the end of the tunnel and feel optimistic that I will land smoothly in Stage Four when the time is right.

Stage Four: Although many people will never understand their new culture on a deeper level, hopefully they will be able to reconcile the differences, work through the internal changes that the move has triggered, and finally accept their new home and new identity with an air of grace and wisdom. Stage Four is about truly 'living' in one's new home, participating as a member of society and becoming part of the local social fabric. Of course there will always be frustrations, but a person who reaches Stage Four is able to make them liveable, the same way he/she lived with frustrations in the country of origin. Internally, people in Stage Four have managed to incorporate aspects of their new culture into their identity, which results in a new sense of self and an expanded way of perceiving the world. Like a couple who have been married for a number of years and who have grown comfortable with each other's differences and quirks, people in Stage Four are settled and feel very much at home in their new world. *http://dirussellimmigration.com/*

Advice from an Oz Saffer   *Peter Niemandt, Oz*

As an expat living in Australia, I can vouch for 99% of the same thoughts and experiences that this person describes.

1. **You can't live on 2 continents at the same time**
   Africa is now a place where I used to live. It is a place that has changed in as much as I have changed as a result of the choices I have made. One of these choices now finds me and my family in this Great South Land where barbies, and beaches, my daughters singing lessons and my son's tennis lessons form the edges of my weekend. And because I live here I choose not to live in South Africa at the same time. Sure I keep in touch with family, but I am here and now, in Melbourne. I live on this continent. This is where I live. Not in Sefrika, as you can't live on two continents at one time!

2. **Integrate, don't separate**
   We, like you, came from Africa to start a new life in Oz. One of our reasons for coming was that we wanted to be part of this amazing society where rule of law counts for something and people are appreciated. Seven years on we are now naturalized, settled and feel Australian. This doesn't mean forgetting our heritage, but rather focussing our efforts on integrating. Has it been easy? Not always. Though what has helped has been us reaching out. How did we do it? Simply, by volunteering. From barbequing sausages at our church, to getting involved with our children's school; with the sole purpose of making connections helped us kick start our integration. It has had the added benefit of helping us 'Ozzify' our language, like "barracking for our footie team" and not "rooting for them", which we soon discovered has a totally different meaning over here . . .

3. Keep your 'Why?' on the fridge

Things were unusually tough in the beginning for us, (Did anyone reading this nearly burn down their brand new rental apartment within 6 months of immigrating?) At these times it made us question whether we had done the right thing bringing our family over here. Most immigrants have felt the same way at one time or another. In searching for answers, we found two things helpful:

Remembering why we had made the decision to leave Africa in the first place. For us it was the violent robberies, living behind electric fencing and owning dogs that ate bags of Epol weekly and people, if we wanted them to.

Always remembering when things got tough here in Oz, to count our blessings. To remember that our house windows don't lock and that is was not critical. That our small dog is fun to have around, and, the deep comfort of knowing that our daughter is safe as she travels to and from school on the train.

4. Go back to school

Both my wife and I had very successful careers back in South Africa. I ran my own business, and she was a high flying corporate executive. Coming to Oz was like starting all over again. We had to be prepared to do the kind of work that we last did in the early 90's. Yes, it was difficult and humbling . . . But we agreed that when my wife got a one month HR contract, that we would see it as going back to school and learning how things are done in Oz. Within a year she was on her way. Now she is back on top of her game! So for us the lesson learnt was to observe how business was conducted, see everything as an opportunity, see how decisions are made and earn our Ozzie stripes.

5. Relax Mate

In the beginning we found it is exhausting living as 'Two-Sefrikin-Parents-Giving-it-a-go-Show' in Oz. Dropping off and picking up kids, doing the ironing, the gardening and vacuuming, all on top of a full week at the office. Week after week after week . . . What aggravated the situation was the Sefrikin trait in us, to strive and achieve and get things done. Perfectly! Every time! *Onmiddlelik!* (immediately.)

The turning point for us was to change our approach to living in Oz, like cutting ourselves some slack by not having a perfect home, with a mowed lawn all the time. It meant moving from living to work, to working to live. Immigrating for us was more of a big thing. We had to learn to be a bit gentler on ourselves and to focus on what was really important as the keys for our psychological survival. As for everything else, well, that is discussed around the 'barbie', while holding a Bitterly Cold One . . .

6. Breathe. This too will pass

Kak (shit) happens. No matter where you live, in Oz or in Afrodisneyland. That is life. Psychologists say that one of the tricks to keeping sane is to keep things in perspective. A bit like getting on a balcony and watching yourself in action. So, remember as you go through the down times, that they will pass. Also resist the urge to look back to Africa in a romanticized way, and justify all with a "Yes but . . ." The lesson for us as a family was to keep perspective (and sanity) through reframing "challenges" through two lenses:

Would the issue, really be that important in two years' time? And if you really think so, then what is the lesson you are supposed to learn that can help me later on?

Don't dwell on things, get up and move on. Life is going to continue, with or without you, so you might as well go along for the ride.

7. The Great Australian Adventure

What is still critical for us on an on-going basis is to accept that even with the best intentions we are going to sometimes mess things up living here. On a smaller scale I still upset people with my "quirky" humour, or not understanding how sensitive certain topics of conversation are.

After one particularly difficult day my wife coined the phrase around the dinner table, "This is all part of our Great Aussie Adventure." That was a turning point for us. We began to view all experiences as part of our adventure and so gave ourselves permission to make mistakes and sometimes get things wrong without beating ourselves up.

Picture the scene, us in a coffee shop, trying to order a coffee . . .
Me: "two wik flet whites pleez" Coffee
Bloke: "What yer say mate"?
Me: "Ah sed, two flet whites pleez . . ."
Coffee Bloke: "Sorry mate, we only do coffees yeh" . . .

Enter my wife to save the situation The lesson: Laugh much. Don't take yourself too seriously. Learn as you grow.

8. **Take care of your money**
   In Africa we had a sense of who the Good and the Bad guys were. They stood out for us. A deep intuition guided us through most of the pitfalls when it came to financial dealings, from buying helicopters to clothes, from hiring builders or choosing clients. BUT we soon discovered that things are different here. For us the Good and Bad guys all sounded and behaved the same. However it is amazing how quickly one learns when large amounts of hard earned cash are taken from you because you've misjudged people. So to minimize this happening two lessons would have helped us:
   Find people who have been referred to you and who have a history and reputation of integrity and competence. If these people have a South African connection all the better as there is likely to be empathy for your situation.
   If the deal sounds too good to be true, it invariably is. *Quo vadis.*
   And lastly:

9. **Have you done your daily check up from the neck up?**
   Let me get right to the heart of it! Are you your own worst enemy? Are you expecting terrible things to happen to you tomorrow, or are you generally positive? No matter where you live, you take yourself with you. That means your attitudes, your beliefs, your views and the way you react to what you see as threatening and negative.
   Here is a thought: Maybe, just maybe, your mind-set needs a renovation, or at least a paint job. In other words, it may not be where you are living, but more a case of how you live between your ears and in this Dry Brown Land we now call home, that is, for us,

a daily challenge. If you are up to the task, I challenge you to do the same and live life to the fullest in Australia.

The Niemandts arrived in Melbourne in 2001.

Advice about Attitude

As far as advice to people wanting to come across, I would say: 'Come with as few expectations as is humanly possible!' (That is not being said in a negative light; there is just a huge divide, despite New Zealand being a 1ˢᵗ world country, and an English speaking nation).

Mandi Crawford, NZ

We may not be able to control our circumstances but we can control how we deal with them. I might have had to leave my beloved home and country behind, but there is no way I am going to let what is past have a negative effect on my future. The one thing I realised when I left was how much I had taken for granted. I try to be grateful for the opportunity to have lived the lifestyle I had in SA and use that as a goal post to improve my situation here. Things are different here and we have to learn to appreciate things in a different way. Move away from the 'WHEN we' . . . and into your future. It's what YOU will be living in tomorrow.

Louise Werth, NZ

We found that we became less materialistic in our outlook and focused more on what is available in abundance here in NZ; Family Time.

Andreas Senger, NZ

Immigration is not for the faint-hearted but I recommend that you do your research, keep a positive attitude and remember why you want to leave SA, and you won't look back. As for those who have gone back with negativity, they either expected too much or they are using negative comments to justify their going back, and not wanting it to look as if they couldn't make it. We love NZ, promote and support it, and are grateful that this beautiful country is still taking us in, as it probably won't much longer as the immigration rules are becoming stricter.

Tracy du Plessis, NZ

Saffers come here thinking that it is going to be so wonderful and can be arrogant and loud and believe that the world owes one something but when one gets here, one finds that status and money mean nothing and it is a big adjustment. We have settled well and our children have followed us and we are all in agreement that we made the right move. It is like a breath of fresh air to not have status and money hanging over our heads, and to be able to walk in the streets and allow the children to play in parks and ride their bikes in the street.

Anon

Advice on what to bring

It is for the psychological adaptation that I recommend that one should be surrounded in one's sanctuary by things inherited from your mum, gran etc., and gifts from loved ones, plus memorabilia and Africana artefacts. It is your legacy and identity and is heart-warming to be surrounded by one's familiar goodies.

EH

If you can afford it, bring everything—when you walk into your home, it will feel like home!

CG

I left my beautiful Cyprus wooden furniture which I had specially made and although I get sad about it, I realise it's only material stuff . . . people are what makes life great in paradise.

SC

When we arrived, we had no history here and we had to create a history for ourselves and introduce our children to furniture/paintings/artefacts/foods etc. that meant so much to us and our family when we were young. These are the memories that are so valuable to all of us and no-one can take them away from us.

OF

We brought some of our stuff over, and it was sooo nice when it arrived two days before Christmas. It felt like Christmas unpacking all our belongings. This feels like home now. NZ is a wonderful country. We couldn't be happier.

ADP

We only came over with suitcases, and it was so exciting every time we got something new. I think it's pretty easy starting over here.

PDLH

It's different for everybody. When we moved to the States, it was just a few suitcases. But then we didn't have kids. When we moved from the States to NZ, we had kids. They didn't seem to settle down until we had our stuff.

CK

Hubs and I came over with just suitcases (just the 2 of us, no children). We had some boxes of photographs, special treasured bits and bobs and sentimental goodies back in SA which we arranged to send over. Those boxes meant more to me than any pieces of furniture as they contained our heritage and SA history and treasured memories. We loved the joy of setting up our Kiwi home from scratch. It kept us busy amongst all the stress of the immigration paperwork. And in the great scheme of things, it did not cost us the earth. We have mostly new furniture and I love our new home here. I don't miss our SA furniture. But it is a personal decision.

JM

Who cares where we all live, eat, drive, wear, do, and more. Coming to NZ has been a humbling experience . . . Not just did NZ give us a new meaningful life, but it has brought me joy and understanding that possessions and the clothes you wear are not what define you as a person. I wasted so much time not knowing that before. Being safer in a country that is beautiful and one can embrace without people trying to squeeze every dime out of you is priceless.

GR

A good idea to bring stuff if you can. We just came with a suitcase, a toddler and a baby, but survived . . .

MFV

We only brought a little bit of stuff—if I had my way again I'd bring my entire household with me. It's been really tough starting over from scratch!

GM

Sobering Reflections

Reflecting back on Africa—how I felt before I left in 2008 . . .

Eve Hemming

If Willie Shakespeare was around he'd be bemoaning the state of South Africa, as he did the state of Denmark in 'Hamlet'. I'm reasonably intelligent, but as I see it none of us has a solution.

A friend asked me what my hypothesis as a psychologist is in terms of this state of affairs and what the solution is. I replied, "If I knew, you'd be the first to know. Maybe it's something like 'Exponential Catastrophic Reactions'."

"What do you mean by that?" she asked. I expounded about survival, competition for resources, power and control, and about collective loss of control. "That's when the process unhinges, gaining uncontrollable momentum. There are generally watchdog mechanisms, which curb society when it loses control. I think that the South African syndrome is about being in the loss-of-control loop. It needs more than a watchdog. We talk about the democracy of the rainbow nation. I think it's gone past democracy to laissez faire . . ."

Recently, I heard something interesting on the radio. It was about an experiment conducted on male drivers. When men listen to an advertisement about lipstick or romance they drive sensibly, whereas if the advertisement is about macho stuff, they drive aggressively and competitively. This sent little messages pulsating across synapses in my brain. I saw my theory taking shape . . . There is a positive correlation between witnessing something and acting it out. When people watch a violent film they walk out adrenalised with a need to express anger. A passive film evokes serenity. One floats out of the film with a feeling of enchantment.

There have been massive drives and petitions, marches and letters in the press against violence, to no avail. The violence, criminality and disregard for human life for now, seems ubiquitous as well as exponential. That's what I mean by "exponential catastrophic reactions", I said.

With a collective exponential state of catastrophic reactions, it's like a blood-curdling scream of violence—a bit like Edvard Munch's famous Expressionist painting 'The Scream'; it's like an illness that permeates and spreads like lava. If everyone remains fearful and angry it fuels the volcano . . . That's what the psychopathic mentality desires. It gives it more impetus, a blood thirsty craving to disempower and demoralise the fibre of society.

I don't think that the media help by their outpourings of negativity. Does it become seen as the norm? Does it desensitise the perpetrators to the point that they can only obtain gratification from increasing acts of violence? Does it create mass levels of fear in a society that lives behind barbed wire?

Obviously poverty alleviation will assist people who become caught up in the machinations of crime. But I see the pandemic as larger than poverty related. There's worldwide poverty and not all people affected by it suffer from this malady. It's more like a lawless runaway mind-set.

Those that "have" exist behind massive walls with techno gadgets, fearing Robin Hood et al, while the "have nots" standing in queues waiting for their meagre pensions are also robbed. Violence is rife in impoverished areas, where drug lords and gangs are challenged by community police groups who patrol the streets at night to voluntarily protect their families . . . Having a thousand more policemen won't cure the disease. It rests in the heart and soul of the individual and a colossal paradigm shift in the country's meta-consciousness as a whole. We do require punitive aspects such as prisons. But we need to focus more on positive reinforcement and rewards. Respect for humanity and the perpetuation of positive values begins with discipline, security, affirmation, incentives and nurturing in the home and at schools. (*First published in The Witness*)

Reflections— *Tani du Toit—11 January 2012*

The South Africa.com

After 11 years in Australia I have my moments; I struggle to feel at home. I've made some wonderful friends along the way—more so in the past few years—but I still have those times where I realise I am a fish out of water, and that I don't really belong, because people simply don't 'get' me.

And how are the similarities over here? It looks so much like South Africa, that the faintest whiff of a bush fire sends your mind back there so fast, it leaves you breathless. That sun mixing that orange haze into that thick blanket of smoke coming from those townships across that country. Bliss.

Oh, and when the pot of *mieliepap* (maize porridge) simmers away, it's not the taste, but the smell of the thick crust it leaves behind in the bottom of the pot that reminds me most of my mother's kitchen.

Salominah Mahlangu, our soft-spoken domestic worker/mother/ friend who was with my family for almost 20 years, had ways of cooking pap and *sheba* (tomato relish) that made your mouth water at the front door. The history of South Africa's domestic employment has been criticised by a lot of people, but few actually have an insight into where they fit into our lives, and few have bothered to ask. Many don't realise how much we loved them as they loved us. Over and above her being an employee, my parents helped Salominah build a family home, for example.

Those women came and went in and out of our lives. They cared for us, cried with us, and loved us like we were their own. All the while their babies were left with others—their grandmothers, aunties, strangers, and women like Salominah saw her own children perhaps twice a month. We grew and grew with their care and love, fed food from her hand and cuddles from her bosom.

As a child I was *abba'd* (strapped onto the back with a blanket in a sling-like fashion) to and from the corner shop by my grandmother's domestic worker and on the way back, she would produce a lollipop or some such to me over her shoulder, making the rhythmic trip back all the more memorable. It's only later I realised every time she bent over in the shop to tighten the grip on the sling she was actually stashing something sweet in her bra strap for me.

Such is the big heart of the African woman, forever finding ways to give, accepting you like her own and hardly turning her back on you, no matter how much pain she was caused by whatever the regime of the day had to say. It's the big smiles waiting at the bus stop and the tender hands cutting doorstop slices of bread for peanut butter sandwiches that guided us home after an afternoon of play outdoors. It's the pride in their eyes when we would pass them as they sat under their afternoon trees discussing things and pointing to us, nudging their friend saying 'that's one of mine'.

And they passed on their generosity of heart and hand to me and others like me, and to us those values are as common as beach sand is to Australians and as easy to give as the sun that keeps shining here. Intimidating as this big love can be to those who aren't used to us and our affection . . . we often surprise non-South Africans with our touchy-feely ways. So much so that I'm sad to say I've had to kerb my displays of warmth a long time ago.

As a teenager, I would sneak into Salominah's room some nights to chat about her 'other' life. Sitting at her doily-covered table, she sat exposed without her cap and overall, her chocolate skin gleaming with the oils she rubbed in every night, her soft chuckles at the game show on the tiny TV interrupting our discussion from time to time. Watching her I wished I'd shown more interest in my *Sotho* lessons at school but it was always the dots of grey hair framing her face that tinged my visit with guilt that I didn't do more for her. She was, after all, older than my parents.

Looking at her trinkets and things, her bed on bricks to fend off the *Tokoloshe* (a mythical gremlin-like creature that gets you at night), her photos and posters of her favourite musicians, she unknowingly taught me no matter how close or far you lived to your kin, what mattered was being bigger than the distance: never to shut our love off because the longing for those who aren't close enough to touch, actually does have the ability to stop you from feeling anything.

She taught me to open my big African heart and to keep it open just as you'd keep your front door open to good friends, because sooner or later they will sit at your table too, see you exposed, and also ask to see your special things from your 'other' life.

Africa will always be in my heart and soul . . .

Jeanita Orton

From the stillness of the bush, the smell of a Highveld thunderstorm rolling over the *veld*, brewing a cup of steaming *rooibos* tea with its unmistakable flavour or the distinct smell of the African bush . . . I am still in awe today by the beautiful wildlife, of the privilege of seeing elephant, rhino, giraffe, lion, buffalo, hippo etc. in their natural environment and the bountiful fauna and flora in the Cape; the Africa with all its nationalities, languages, cultures and customs living in a melting pot of chaos, noise, poverty and corruption. Africa is the land where roots take hold and don't let go, solid as the Baobab tree that has always been and will always be there, standing steady and solid against the menaces of time.

The real Africa is the one they never show you. It is hidden beneath poverty and hunger and death. The real Africa is submerged beneath shanty towns rife with dirt and disease, where children are forced to grow up much too quickly to survive. The real Africa is concealed under a no man's land of desert, bare and dry.

No, that's not the real Africa . . . the Africa I know; the Africa that is reflected in the warm sunshine that you can feel burning inside you. The Africa that shines from a warm spontaneous smile. The Africa that is at the heart of sky high mountains and tropical jungles, of golden sand dunes, beautiful beaches and lush green grassland. The Africa that is at the heart of different peoples, different languages, different cultures, different identities all who call this land home.

My Africa is where my heart resides even when I am long gone and far away, where my mind drifts across the distance of a never ending ocean. The real Africa can be smelt the minute you step off the plane onto African soil and you feel the air calling you, beckoning you home. The real Africa is the chaos and the calm that exist side by side as honking cars zoom past in streets that run parallel to cows grazing peacefully in a field.

This is the real Africa, the one they never show. This is the place I call home.

Arriving "home" triggered overwhelming emotions *Eve Hemming*

After 17 hours of flying from Auckland via Sydney, I peered down to catch my first glimpse of Africa, from the height of 34, 000 feet. It was a poignant moment, where I felt sucked into the magnetic pull of this continent. I felt as though I'd been away a lifetime. I surveyed a fleeting vista of a meandering chocolate-hued river with ox-bow lakes, midget African homesteads and vast expanses of rugged landscape. I wanted to dance down the aisle and parachute downwards there and then!

Arriving back in South Africa at O.R. Tambo Airport was a revelation. The airport's transformation was impressive, as it has undergone expansions and wonderful cosmetic surgery in preparation for the 2010 World Soccer Cup, compared with my departure, when one walked alongside an endless expanse of seemingly chaotic and shoddy barricades.

Being reunited with my SA family was immeasurably profound. Over and above my state of constant euphoria, I had managed to notice numerous positives from new structures and developments, to more occupancy in some of the malls. Of course it wasn't all a bed of roses. I had to attend a court case as a witness at the 'Maritzburg Magistrate's Court. The first set of loos was locked and out of order, as was the second lot. The third option yielded more success; one functioning loo, sans a seat or loo paper. "Same old, same old," I confess I mused.

But when in SA, I realised how easy it is to be lulled back into the charmed life experienced by the more privileged sectors of the country—the endless balmy days, a robust unique energy, an infectious optimism and the ravages of the global recession not being too conspicuous. Contrasted against this was still an element of gloom and anger voiced by some. As one acquaintance I bumped into commented: "South Africa is a place we both love and hate."

One of my days on my SA visit was spent in the Tugela Valley where I had the privilege of touching base with the raw part of Africa, where we had to stop the cab repeatedly and circumnavigate past a long-horned stalwart ox, a summit meeting of mangy donkeys and some dust-rolling goats. I felt immense pride as I shared the day with my older son, a hydro engineer bringing water to the rural inhabitants of an isolated and almost inaccessible region, where huts and thorn scrub cling precariously to steep outcrops.

Too soon it was time to go back to my home in Kiwiland. Saying goodbye to family was unquantifiably heart-rending. On my departure, I took a moment to reflect. Maybe I had been harsh in my judgment; too lacking in conviction. None of us can accurately predict the future. To date, some astounding developments and amelioration's have materialised since Madiba's long walk to freedom. I was returning to New Zealand and my life, my work, as well as to a place with its own startling beauty and different challenges.

As I departed through my tears, I saluted the South Africans who were optimistically fortifying the nation. However, with the knowledge of on-going unacceptable levels of crime and corruption, I knew in my heart that our painful choice had a reason behind it as pathfinders for whatever eventuated. South Africans are robust people. My continued hope was that wherever we were, we could make a positive impact—like a stone thrown into static water, to create ripples outwards at home or beyond. (*Original version first Published in The Witness*)

A month since we flew back from our trip to S.A.!

Eve Hemming

It's hard to believe that it's almost a month since we flew back to New Zealand . . . . in some ways it's as crystal clear as yesterday that we were there . . . I can still hear the sounds . . . and can smell the smell of African rain on red dust, the smell of freshly cut grass, the smell of a *veld* fire. I can still hear the 'Piet my Vrou' calling, and I can hear dogs barking and our son's neighbour's wretched car as he maniacally revved it to a clanging crescendo each morning while we stayed there. *And now we are back.*

I'm back at work as though I'd never been away. My office walls are decorated with pictures of my NZ and SA 'cherubs'—all six of them. In New Zealand Maori, a grandchild is called a '*mokopuna*'. My 'moko's' pics smile at me and get me through each day. How I long to hold and kiss them all. Sometimes Skype just 'doesn't do it.' But hell, it's loads better than no Skype.

One has to look forwards and not perpetually 'in the rear view mirror'. It's about living in the here and now and enjoying local people and places without discounting that that part of one's life in Africa is still palpably part of one and always will be. So yes, my next trip back to Africa is planned. But for now we have some exciting ideas swirling around in the ether, are engaged in interesting things, meeting people, going places and sharing quality time with our NZ family, plus local mates.

Going back does, without a doubt, unsettle one. When there, one easily gets seduced into the lifestyle and so easily puts on the blinkers and shuts out some of the uncomfortable truths. One becomes seduced. It was so good for the soul . . .

One's soul gets kissed . . . it has it's top up!

We made those special connections with family and friends again, and for me, my connection with my grandchildren was profound. We still dream of our loved ones coming, but then I remember Kahlil Gibran's '*The Prophet*' . . . 'Your children are not your children . . .' and I try to be patient . . . it could take forever, or never or soon . . . and it's their lives, not ours . . . but we love them all boundlessly; those close and those far. And so I try to rest my silly heart a while . . .

My thoughts today on emigrating   *Carol Champ*

Looking back after four years away from SA, I have realised that the emotional turmoil (apart from leaving family etc.) is the fact that in SA we lived "on guard" ALL the time. It is a very harsh environment that requires both partners to work their A*%sses off all day, while living in a constant state of fear and awareness of the environment around you. I personally never had a good night's sleep for years till I landed in my new country. Then, when you do land and start your new life, the fear and constant 'on guard' state disappears and there seems a void of nothingness to a point of just wandering aimlessly in the new environment trying to figure out what to do. It's like having spare time in your brain and it's confusing. It took me two years to adapt to what is a "normal" life, with loads of tears and heartache in-between. The reality and well known fact is that Saffer's live off acquiring wealth and status and pride and relocating shoves you very quickly to the bottom of the barrel, and particularly in NZ, where status is nothing and everyone is equal, no matter what you own and what you drive. This is a massive culture shock which sends you spinning into loads of closed doors and brick walls until you realise you have to throw off pride and become humble and slowly work at earning the respect of your new nation's people. The best advice I ever had was from an ex-Saffer in a powerful position here in NZ who told me to "pretend" I knew nothing, don't talk about SA too much as they just won't understand and are not particularly interested, and work on gaining trust. Being naturally loud and outspoken it was a bit hard, but I still work at it and it is the best attitude I can advise anyone to take. Being humble and trustworthy will lift you into a position of respect and with this comes the rewards.

Trafalgar Square, London—July 2012—*From a dear friend*

As our friends and family started to leave our beautiful country, we wondered if we were not heeding the signs that the winds of change were blowing hard. Following the murders of two close family members, the hijacking of others and numerous other unpleasant incidents, we came to the conclusion that if we were looking for signs, the only one left would be to receive a Handwritten Note from God.

We left and tried to make a new life and to some extent we have. But never a day passes when I don't yearn for an African sunset, to see those miles and miles of bush, to hear the crash of our ocean, to be back home.

I thought our many tragedies were unusual, but it seems not. Perhaps we misinterpreted the Note? Now we wait for the sign that peace will prevail, that each man will be valued on his own merit, regardless of his race or creed. We wait to hear we will be safe, as we sit in gloomy rain and longing. And then we remember each one of those "incidents" happened on a beautiful sunny day. We wait and we long and we remember . . .

Coming and Going!

"Life" she wrote, "is just too short to spend in one place."
Anne Townsend

SA—to the world—to SA—and can't wait to get out again!

James Basson

I'm in SA for business and in the process of moving a company from SA to NZ. It's a long and frustrating process, especially when dealing with SA. The problem is that South Africa's issues now have issues from a business point of view, unless you are attached to the mining industry or servicing one of the major corporations it is very difficult to do business here. I can also no longer find the right skills here and in my industry South Africa has become very uncompetitive. I am also tired of the corruption and politics in SA. It is part of everyday life here now.

My impressions of South Africa might be a little different to most South Africans as I have spent less than half my life here. I spent a large part of my childhood in America and most of my working life in Europe. So always felt like a foreigner in SA. But I loved the bush and the wildlife and thought of South Africa as a spiritual home. I came back to SA three years ago . . . the single biggest mistake of my life. I have found SA a dreadful place to live in and I live better than most people do. People here are literally prisoners in their own homes.

Doing business with South Africans in SA is extremely exasperating. Things that came easily in Europe and most developed countries are a nightmare here. Also unless you have known someone here since a baby and went to the same kindergarten or are in some way financially beneficial to them it is a very difficult place to make real friends. "Backstabbing" seems to be a national sport in this country. In short every positive view I once had of SA has been totally destroyed. There are some places or things that are still holding out or are "Islands of Excellence" e.g. The Kruger National Park or parts of Cape Town, which are wonderful places to visit. But if I look at what is happening around these 'islands' I have to wonder how long they will survive. I no longer see South Africa as a spiritual home or a place of possibilities, but one of the most soul destroying places that I've been to. These are my impressions and I can't wait to get back to my favourite corner of earth; a little place called New Zealand.

My Scatterlings Story—SA—2 NZ—2 SA

Tracy Swift

I spent 18 years in the small farming town of Queenstown, Eastern Cape, SA where my husband and I met. Moving to PE was the first leap towards forging a life of our own. We spent seven years there before moving to Pretoria, when my husband took a promotion to work at his company's head office in Midrand.

Life in Gauteng was certainly different, but very exciting. Initially we loved the fast pace, but soon found that we had very little family life. Working as a manager of the Midrand Branch of a large recruitment company, commuting each day and leaving our 2 year old in day care until 6.30pm, broke my heart. We needed change.

In January 1997 my parents returned from a six month holiday in New Zealand. My uncle had moved to the coastal town of Tauranga a few years earlier and my parents had spent time touring both islands and attending a family wedding. On their return, they could not speak highly enough of the lifestyle and beauty of this country that reminded them of life in South Africa twenty years ago.

Homes without burglar proofing, children walking to school and shops that displayed goods without "supervision" were all reminiscent of a bygone day in South Africa. We were "romanced" by the idea of leaving all the hustle and bustle behind, and could see ourselves settling into this blissful lifestyle . . . envisioning a green meadow with a pony and some "chooks" (chickens), we were sold!

Not one to take time on decisions, I forged ahead with great gusto! At the time of deciding we would attempt residency, we had no documentation; no passports, birth certificates or marriage licenses. Considering my husband was born in Harare, Zimbabwe, it was nothing short of a miracle that we arrived in New Zealand on the 23rd April 1997, met our consultant and got our residency permits the same day!

We returned to South Africa two weeks later to sell our home and pack up. A few weeks before leaving I was offered a role as a Recruitment Consultant with a company who interviewed me in April. Saying goodbye to family and friends was unbelievably painful. Some were very encouraging, whilst others felt angry and betrayed. To top it all my husband got cold feet at the very last minute and it took every ounce of strength to convince him that we needed to "give it a go!" After all, I said, "It's not a prison sentence we can return after three years if we don't like it!"

Fourteen and half years later, here I am recalling this great adventure. Those early days in a new country seem like light years away. New Zealand opened her arms and heart to us. We were overwhelmed by the warmth and generosity of strangers, trying to help this young family settle in.

My husband's journey was probably more difficult. From my experience in recruitment and my close relationships with other migrant families from all over the world (India, Philippines, Australia, Zimbabwe, Ghana, Fiji, UK, USA) it has been the husbands who have taken the most strain. I am not sure why this is, but I believe that it has to do with the fact that their identity is strongly tied to "what they do" instead of "who they are".

Moving to NZ we had made a decision that whoever got the first job offer, the other parent would see the year out looking after our then three and a half year old daughter. So my husband who had a senior marketing role within a large corporate, with all the added benefits of working in a prestigious company, was now a "stay at home Dad". I, on the other hand started working ten days after arriving in NZ. I was given the keys to my company car, a map book of Auckland, a client list and I was on my way. So my transition was much easier, more like just changing jobs, as opposed to moving countries.

There were many challenges in those early days, but my biggest was relationships. I longed for friends, as my only relative was a three hour drive away. In early January 1998 we visited a local church and everything changed for us at that moment. We met and befriended an entire congregation made up of migrant families from the USA, India, Philippines, South Africa, Malaysia, Zimbabwe, Hong Kong, Korea, Ireland, Holland and more places. I would eventually realise that this represented a microcosm of Auckland's population. How wonderful to be a part of this cultural melting pot!

It was surrounded by these amazing people that we were able to settle into life in our new country. We were all in the same boat, trying to make a life in a foreign country. Many were trying to get jobs, residency and homes. Everyone helped out, whether you needed a lounge suite, an entire household moved or just a meal. A sense of community was fostered and out of this we began to feel whole again. Friends became family. My husband was offered a really good job in February 1998 and we were on our way to rebuilding our lives. I changed to working part time to be at home with our daughter in the afternoons and things were looking rosy!

Early 1999 my husband was in a deep depression, longing for Africa and feeling completely "out of place". His role had him working away from home three weeks out of every six. This separation from us just deepened the wound he felt in his heart for his beloved Africa. I was devastated and disappointed that he could not see things the way I saw them. Africa was our past, this was our future. Why could he just not look forward, and stop looking back?

After he changed jobs, things improved and in May of 2000 we welcomed our first "kiwi" into the family; our son was born. I started a recruitment company from home and enjoyed being able to walk our daughter to school every day and run a business.

Many glorious years have passed enjoying everything this wonderful country has to offer, from a gentle unassuming people, who accept you at face value and never ask, "Where do you live or what you drive?" to qualify your social status—to riding in your car without your doors locked. I have appreciated every moment as a gift.

Our daughter has gone to the same college from new entrants to year 13 and grown into a beautiful, caring young woman who values people, not by the colour of their skin, but by the beauty of their hearts. Our son has excelled on the sports field and is an avid supporter and player of our national sport. We support two teams on the field to the dismay of many . . . I explain it like this; "If you give birth to twins, who do you love more?" It's how I feel about both countries—each has a place in my heart and I cannot choose!

In 2005 I had a huge shift in my heart. It was like an awakening and longing in me for the people of Africa in such a deep and profound way that it cannot be explained in words. I remember crying and crying as a huge floodgate opened up within me and I realised that this was where I was meant to be. A future without the sounds, smells and people of Africa felt unimaginable. I no longer wanted to exist in what felt like it had become a "safe bubble"—but I wanted to "live" to really feel alive, even if it meant facing and embracing the challenges and realities of life in South Africa.

Two years ago we sat both our children down and explained that at some time in the near future we would be moving back to South Africa. You see, every nation has challenges, immigrating just means exchanging one set for another! It is a privilege to have a choice (not everyone has one) so we must steward it well, by remaining true to the voice that is within. I cannot let other people's fears govern who I am, or other people's desires steer my course. I am responsible for what has been placed in my heart and finding an expression for it. To my husband's delight, his dream is coming true. A square peg in a round hole will be "home" soon. For some unexplained reason our son has always longed for and loved Africa (he's the only true Kiwi amongst us.) Our daughter is a Kiwi through and through (she was born in SA). So nationality is a matter of the heart. Who can dictate what lies there? . . . So, here we stand perched on the precarious edge of another adventure. Are we scared? You bet! Do we worry we are doing the right thing? Hell yes! Are we gonna do it anyway? Absolutely!

"Life is either a daring adventure or nothing. To keep our faces toward change and behave like free spirits in the presence of fate is strength undefeatable."

Helen Keller

SA—2 UK—2 SA   *Rosalie Paver Howard, SA*

When I left SA to go to the UK, it was when the recession hit us hard in our little business, resulting in my decision to sell up absolutely everything I owned and move (out of the proverbial gold fish bowl, into the big ocean), and of course I had the support of two of my three children that side, so took the risk and left with my only possessions—a bag full of clothing and some photographs!

I thought it would be easy to find some sort of job over there which would fix everything for me . . . initially I had planned to leave for ever . . . Never say forever!! By the time I left, I had decided that I would give it a year at a time. I was heartbroken to leave SA because I left a son and grandson here and my sister who means so much to me. However, I had a wonderful time in many respects in the UK because I spent special time with my daughter and my son and their families and they were so good to me. The job situation was no better over there than here. I only eventually got reasonably paid work on a very temporary basis in the last 4 months of my two year stint over there! By this time I had decided that I was returning to SA and only worked to gather together enough to leave and carry me over for a few months. The main reason I left is because the weather in the UK is disgusting, the lifestyle so very foreign to me and the people just as foreign, (especially in the North West!). Despite that, I did make some lovely friends. That in a nutshell is why I came back, to what is familiar, to the climate, also to SA family and by then my daughter had left the UK for NZ, though my one son is still there in the UK.

However . . . there was always this gut feel from my heart that I NEEDED to be back here. I was unable to put my finger on it; even once I initially returned. My greatest urge was to be here in Gonubie, close to old roots and where I now am. I realised that one needs to listen to one's gut feelings, even though one can't always define precisely why. I think that the point I am making is that one should follow one's heart even if there is no clear explanation why . . .

All I can say is that I am glad I am back in SA, which is home and always will be to me, warts and all, while I am torn between here and everywhere else, with my two other children so far away from where I am! I will get back to KZN where my SA son lives and WILL live with more financial support, at some point, before I am too much older—I have to trust in that as well! My intention is 'out there' and the Universe shall handle the details of how and when!!

I have now been back on SA soil 8 months and despite the many warnings I had from expats about the enormous increase in violent crime . . . this has not been my experience. I will not deny that what is going on here right now is barbaric and unacceptable and the country threatens to crumble as the ANC falls apart and God knows who will be our next leader, but it is still great to be home, broke but happier than I was in the UK because of that country's short comings. I miss the family who are there, however. I can't be everywhere at the same time so have chosen to come home. I'm what some would call an 'old bok' and have also developed some gypsy tendencies . . . It's very different for young people who have their children's futures to consider. In those circumstances, I would also leave and I might well do again! My next port-o-call could well be NZ—tomorrow is another day and might also never arrive! So, I am making the best of each moment . . . moment by moment.

To Kaapstad from the UK

Veronica Baxter, Cape Town, SA

So finally you're back to where the skin shines with a cross between sun-produced oils and sweat, slick droplets run down your sides from the edges of your bra to your pants. You wonder if there is anyone who has even sweat marks under their armpits, or if everyone is doing Vic falls under the right. And water takes on new meaning, as you see it gush out a tap, frozen in the ice trays or mist from those incredible new fans they have in outdoor restaurants now—special Comrades Marathon technology for the eating public.

You're become more used to seeing water run down pavements, gutters, melted into the mud of the field, spattering on the bellies of the shorter dogs, and coating the terriers' legs up to the armpits. Water gushing down the windscreen every morning on the way to work, sluicing off the windows of the library, the bus, the classroom. Evaporating off the jungle of clothes drying in the lounge, splashing through your thin socks and shoes made for a different summer.

But you're home now, and everywhere people are code-switching their way through their day. With an "*aish*" and an "*eish*" and a "serious", perhaps an old-fashioned "*aikona*", the old languages gain hold. Tight smiles relax into broad "*molo*" and "*hoesit*", and that big blue sky makes way for an epic day. Because every day is epic under the African sky blue. There are no Shirley Valentine 'little lives' here. It's all lived out on a grand scale, even when it is small. It's a *tour de force*, a force to be reckoned with. Takes no prisoners. But that's not true, because it makes us all prisoners—of the heart and mind. We are captured and enraptured. All its *kak* and *drek*, it is our heartbeat, this bloody *plek*.

From Fawzia—SA to NZ to Cape Town 2012

Someone once told me that it's not the quantity of your presence or love that counts, but the quality. Eve, you are so surrounded by love, and when you do come to SA it seems that it becomes focussed love. This can only be, when one is away for periods of time. My experience has been that living in close proximity to family brings about mundaneness to the relationships, though the love is still there. The pain and intense missing always passes as family are always energetically connected, wherever one is.

I recently joined a programme called 'food addicts'. I lost weight and feel amazing. But the main part of this programme is the spiritual tools that it provides. One of the things it states is "Do Your 1% for the day one day at a time and God takes care of the rest." Longing, generally is in one's head—but unconditional love is in one's heart. So back to your question of "How-when-no solution" seems to me that things are as they should be.

You know Joseph Campbell's story of the Hero's journey? Do you not find similarities between that and your own journey? Sometimes one is in the belly of the whale . . . eventually ending in the *Heiros-gamos* or sacred marriage within oneself and finding spirit, non-duality and centeredness in the self. So be well, and I take my hat off to you on your amazing journey. With love, Fawzia.

South African Time Line—
Represented by my thoughts and odyssey and a selection of articles, works and open letters

*I*never intended to write a political book, but rather a book which *supported migrants on their complex journey.* But . . . somehow South Africa and politics are synonymous and deeply intertwined. It's literally impossible to separate the two. The entire history of the land has been a political and a cultural maelstrom which continues today. The irony is that everyone remains passionate about the country, but for some it became/or may become an intolerable place to live, due to political mismanagement—past and present—due to inequity—past and present—and due to the ubiquitous levels of never ending violence . . .

I reiterate that I do not support all the views in this book, and feel as though I am merely a conduit for the words written by many others. In fact I see myself as a rather useful conduit because of my political naiveté! I have felt that by offering some others' insights into the country's historical journey, that it could be beneficial and even an eye opener for many of us. I am a person who loves people and have had the privilege of working closely with many cultural groups and language groups in South Africa. I believe that people cannot be blamed for the sins of their fathers and that each person is ultimately accountable for his or her own actions, and cannot be labelled by the actions of others. I also believe in forgiveness and *ubunthu*.

This chapter of the book is not intended to create antagonism. The last thing I wish for is that this chapter opens old wounds for any of us; for none of us can throw the first stone. Instead it's about history, human frailty, of humanity making mistakes and about optimism; that regardless of the country's history, life continues to exist; that the heartbeat of Africa continues, and that resilience and unexpected twists and turns lie before us. *I would recommend that one reads snippets of this chapter, takes from it what resonates for one, discovers some facts at one's disposal and then goes on to enjoy the recipes, poetry and the book's conclusion.*

Alexandra Fuller aptly sums Africa up in her book *Cocktail Hour Under the Tree of Forgetfulness*; "War is Africa's perpetual ripe fruit. There is so much injustice to resolve, such desire for revenge in the blood of the people, such crippling corruption of power, such unseemly scramble for the natural resources. The wind of power shifts and there go the fruit again, tumbling towards the ground, each war more intensively terrible than the last."

Preamble

South Africa (Tiger Books International) sums up the country's antiquity and diversity . . . . ". . . here one finds the oldest rocks on the planet and the earliest traces of life on Earth. Further east are the savannahs of the great beasts: lions, leopards, and cheetahs still inhabit game reserves and natural parks, along with elephants, giraffes, antelopes, and the entire natural paradise of Africa. The coastlines feature beaches and jagged cliffs, flowering dunes as in Namaqualand, and the coral reefs and lagoons of Saint Lucia. Nothing is monotonous in South Africa, even though part of its territory is occupied by deserts. In this 'separate world', where thousands of years ago the evolution of the human race began, (more than) forty million people now live; the remarkable variety of physical and cultural types of these people make South Africa a veritable anthropological laboratory, as well as a challenge for peaceful coexistence, beyond the difference."

An insert from Lonely Planet's *Southern Africa* offers additional insight into early South Africa. "The pre-colonial history of Southern Africa is a compelling, interwoven web of peoples on the move throughout this vast region—the original travellers on our planet.

It's also a story of technology and its impact on our early ancestors. Although Southern Africa's history stretches far back into the mists of time, the only records today are intriguing fossil remains and an extraordinary human diary of Stone Age rock art . . . It's generally agreed among scientists that the first 'hominids' became established in the savannas of East and Southern Africa nearly four million years ago . . ."

Archaeological sites in South Africa hold evidence of very early human settlements, invalidating the notion of 'terra nulliu', so believed by the European colonial settlers who considered themselves to be the first human inhabitants. In 1995, geologist Dave Roberts discovered a set of fossilised footprints 117,000 years old in the sandy slopes of Langebaan Lagoon, on the East coast of South Africa, dating back to the period when the first anatomically modern humans emerged.

For the past 100,000 years, southern African has been home to the San—nomadic groups of hunter-gatherers living in nuclear families. They created a delicate ecological balance with their environment. The San are famous for their astonishing, mystical and spiritual rock art, which can be found in mountain side caves, including the Drakensberg. Their rock art is the gift they have left the world. Most of the San people moved further north to the Kalahari Desert largely due to the habitation of other cultural groups which lead to disputes, as the San were nomadic and became threatened by the ownership of land. Some of you may be familiar with the popular film, *The Gods must be crazy*, which is a humorous allegory, based on a Coca Cola bottle being thrown from a light aircraft, which lands in the Kalahari Desert, and is perceived by the San people as an odd gift from the Gods. The rhetoric presents a powerful allegory depicting the purity of lack of ownership or of possessions and how objectification can lead to conflict and to territorialism.

Some 2,000 years ago a group of agro-pastoralists known as the Khoi Khoi, also settled in the region. About 1,500 years ago, the iSintu-speaking people, who had migrated from the Great Lakes region of Africa, began to cultivate the soil in river valleys of the south-eastern part of Africa. There they introduced edible crops, such as millet and domesticated cattle approximately 1,000 years ago.

South Africa holds a prominent place on the global map, positioned at the southern tip of the African continent. The country measures 1.2 million square kilometres and is flanked by Namibia, Botswana, and

Zimbabwe to the north and Mozambique to the north east. South Africa has the Indian Ocean to its south east and the Atlantic Ocean to its south west. In its north-eastern region South Africa almost entirely encircles Swaziland and in its central eastern region it surrounds Lesotho. The climate is semi-arid, except for the east coast, which is subtropical. (Tiger Books International.)

Historically speaking, we're all aware that South Africa is a land that has been dominated by cultural conflict. Some of us have, over the years, learnt some of the history of the land and its people. Note: Indisputable Historians need to be patient and mindful that this is a mere fragment and by no means a history book. There are gaps and more gaps, as well as human perceptions, which are always flawed by subjectivity and bias. However, for those with a limited concept, I felt that a chapter with a time line of some events, interspersed with some accessible articles or book reviews could be insightful.

The people currently living in South Africa's ancestors emigrated from further north in Africa or from across the oceans. The indigenous Africans' ancestors hailed from further north in Africa, whilst the first Europeans to settle were the Dutch. The Portuguese were the first to navigate the most southern tip of Africa, but opted to settle in Mozambique where the coastline was less treacherous. Jan van Riebeeck arrived in Cape Town on 6th April 1652.

The objective was to build a station and plant vegetables to prevent the sailors on the epic spice routes from Holland to the East from getting scurvy. Other nationalities who arrived were Germans and Scandinavians, as well as the French Huguenots who were escaping from the tyranny of King Louis XIV. The first British Settlers arrived in 1820.

Part of South Africa's rich cultural mix is made up of a fusion of various cultures then inhabiting Southern Africa, including the Africans, Europeans and the slaves from Madagascar and Indonesia; people who were referred to as Cape Malays. The Indians in South Africa are descendants of the first Indian labourers who arrived in the 19th century to work on the sugar plantations in Natal. (KwaZulu Natal).

We have this amazing potpourri of cultures melded together in the never-ending proverbial melting pot—a flamboyant cultural interwoven tapestry. Only South Africans can truly identify with our strange and wonderful world of anomalies. No small wonder that South Africa has been dubbed 'The Rainbow Nation'—being comprised of Africans who speak several indigenous languages, who hail from various northern and eastern tribes, combined with Europeans of Dutch, British, French, Scandinavian, Portuguese, Greek, German and Jewish, amongst other heritages, and Asians, including Indonesians, Malaysians, Indians and Chinese.

The South African journey is documented in the history books, which never captivated me; partly as it was presented in a rote fashion way back in the 50's but more so as my head was more interested in learning about World War 1 and 11, and about hearing my dad's stories about almost dying of malaria in Egypt during WW11. It personally felt more relevant to my own heritage, as my ancestors of Scottish and Prussian decent arrived in the late 1800's and the 1900's and were adventurers, farmers, entrepreneurs and missionaries, related to neither the Great Trek nor the Anglo-Boer War.

The Union of South Africa existed from 1910 and continued until 1948. The official system of Apartheid and the National government's control of South Africa commenced in 1948, two years before my birth in 1950. This atrocious system of segregation and minority rule, which many of us of all cultures were innocently born into, continued until April 1994, when the African National Congress (ANC) became the ruling party, creating what was *intended* to be the most democratic constitution, combined with more cultural equity through African empowerment for the previously marginalised and disadvantaged, plus providing more equity for women. Eleven official languages were introduced; a new flag was designed, as well as a new anthem which combines Xhosa, Zulu, Afrikaans and English . . .

These were adrenalising and epic times in which we all *hoped* for greater unity and for the majority, a sense of pride in belonging. I no longer felt the same degree of shame of having lived in a land where most people were not permitted to vote or be counted or to have opportunities and freedom.

These are the years of history which for me are first hazy; blurred by childhood, followed by ignorance and naivety, and then censorship, leading to confusion and of fear, when a slow distilling awareness of living in a dictatorship state trickled into my consciousness. Our brothers were sent to a Methodist Boys' boarding school and my twin and I to the Methodist girls' boarding school, our Dad being a staunch Methodist of deep faith. We had a History teacher, Miss Kay Neale, who had an expressive elasticised lip-sticked mouth that articulated in expressive swirling motions. She would whisper to us, finger at her lips, "Sshhh . . . we are living in a totalitarian state . . . ." Did we truly comprehend? I'm not sure, but we were vaguely aware that *'all was not right'* and that we had to go to a school for white girls and that we had African peers at a Methodist school for black girls, called Inanda Seminary. Our schools were permitted to visit one another, but had to be issued a licence to achieve this monumental feat. That was in the 1960's. George Orwell's *1984* was published in 1949 . . . Miss Neale alluded to books such as *1984* and Orwell's 1945 allegorical satire, *Animal Farm.* How much did I assimilate? Was I too much in love with my ideological teenage life and a boy called William, and too escapist to deal with reality and grief; my juvenile life impacted upon with an ailing disintegrating father whom I adored, confined to a wheelchair with motor neurone disease.

Those were the days when we thought it was exciting to have Indian friends whom we acquired incense from. My twin and I aged 16, would burn the incense and listen to 'LM Radio' on the garage roof during 'school hols' from boarding school, flowers in our hair, bare footed. That was about as close as we would ever get to anything remotely Woodstock!

Shortly after leaving school (the end of 1968), our wonderful and courageous dad died in the April of 1969, bringing with it a new awareness in my life—about life's transience and fragility. I was a student at a white only teachers' training college (other cultures had to enrol in other colleges). My mail was opened and I was spied on for belonging to a multi-cultured youth group. (One of the alleged spies dated a friend of mine at college and I met him. His Varsity studies were reportedly paid for by the Governments' secret agency and of this we were oblivious. He stayed in students' digs with Victorian red brick walls, covered with a sprawling Ivy creeper in Coronation Street. In checking out his current profile on the Internet, he ironically talks about his anti-apartheid work as a student at the University of Natal!)

Those were the days when my Indian friends, the Hoosens', were stopped by the police for chatting to me. Those were the days when the police shone a light into my boyfriend's car to see if I was kissing a black or a white man; the days when as a lass of 19, I fell in love and married a wonderful man, which changed my direction from being a student, and refocused my attention on a home and mothering.

Those were the days when I wish I had had the time and the knowledge to be more militant, less fearful and less immature. Those days and years were followed by days of mothering our three small children, including a desperately ill child who spent many months in the ICU at The Red Cross Children's Hospital in Cape Town, and which consumed our energy and focus to keep him alive; so much so, that our lives became introspective and microcosmic, as opposed to national or global.

Those were the days of hearing far away gunshots, of maybe burying my head in suburbia, whilst facing the challenges of my own existential existence as an ignorant young woman, wife and mother, while friends my age were gapping it on their rights of passage abroad . . .

I have heard that there were people who were coerced into voting for the Nationalist Government and hence for the apartheid regime. If they did not support the ruling party they were deemed as outcasts and their lives were in jeopardy. I am relieved that my family was never coerced and that we never supported Apartheid, because it's philosophy lacked respect and dignity for all human beings. And yet I remain guilty for being ignorant; for not having done enough and for being fearful and engrossed in my family. I think many of us feel that way.

Michael Ignatieff in *The Lesser Evil* refers to the fact that "civilian complicity makes civilian immunity a complex affair." Regarding South Africa, he states that "Many whites, after all, opposed apartheid and it is doubtful that the system would have fallen when it did, had the regime not lost its own basis support." He asserts that it is thus wrong to generalise when condemning people—and that they should be judged according to their own merits, not as a group in which some are active perpetrators, whilst others may be fearful of threats, and thus seem to be complicit.

I implicitly believe that now hundreds of years later, that the majority of South Africans, regardless of creed or colour are innocent victims, and that as long as the perpetrators, who masterminded slavery, land usurping, apartheid and/or any atrocities in the past or present, are brought to book and pay their penance, 'life' for many can heal and move forward. I likewise believe that in the current regime, many innocent people should be able to live in peace and safety, and that the criminal elements and the fraudulent, corrupt and inept non-functioning sectors of Government need to be rooted out, so that a fresh attempt can be made to find solutions, uplift the impoverished and ameliorate and restore a potentially wonderful country. South Africa deserves to have another shot at it—with a new Government that is non-prejudiced and where people are treated with equity and respect, regardless of creed, gender or colour.

Cultural Background & History
(Data and quotes from Tiger Books International)

"The arrival of Europeans in southern Africa was by far the most traumatic experience the indigenous communities had ever experienced by the 1600s." In 1652 the Dutch set up a base in the territory of the Khoi Khoi for their East India Company (VOC). The Khoi Khoi realised that the Dutch intended to stay. This led to what were called the Wars of Dispossession (known then as the "Kaffir Wars") in the 1770s, which lasted 100 years in the region.

The Dutch settlers overwhelmed the indigenous Africans. The Khoi Khoi became farm labourers, assimilated into their militia, which thus destroyed their political economy. Huguenots, escaping religious persecution in Europe arrived followed by slaves brought in by the Dutch from their Asian colonies (from Malaysia, and from eastern and western Africa, who became the nucleus of the subsequent "coloured" community.)

The British occupied the Cape of Good Hope in 1795. This was during the French revolutionary wars and the goal was to prevent the southern tip of Africa being usurped by the French. It was once again Dutch territory from 1803 to 1806. In 1820 British settlers came to live mainly in the Eastern Cape. With the expansion of European settlements, the Europeans and indigenous populations came into conflict over land rights and livestock. The wars led to the defeat of the indigenous people, due to the Europeans possessing more effective weapons.

The Dutch and British shared a goal to dispossess the indigenous peoples of land. But they had their own tensions. In 1836, this lead to the Dutch *Voortrekkers* (forward movers) embarking on a massive journey—'The Great Trek'—to avoid British colonialism. By moving northwards from the Cape, the Dutch settlers came into contact with areas already inhabited by Africans, who had been moving southwards. At this time the Dutch established the Republics of the Transvaal and the Orange Free State and the British took possession of the Cape Colony and Natal.

The discovery of diamonds in 1867 and of gold in the 1870s brought the arrival of European prospectors, mainly from Britain. This led to the Anglo-Boer War (1899 to 1902). In 1909 an agreement between the British and the Boers was reached which lead to The Union of South Africa in 1910, the year my father was born in The Orange Free State to a Scottish farmer father and a Prussian mother of missionary decent.

Racial differentiation and discrimination in education occurred from the commencement of European colonisation. The education system was designed to elevate Europeans. Other cultures were educated to have more subordinate roles in what was a European dominated colonised society. Many of the initial schools established for Africans were established by missionary institutions. An objective was to assimilate Africans into Western culture, including Christian values of obedience. By 1945, there were in the region of 4,400 church-related African schools, compared with only 230 government schools. The curriculum in these schools was more limited than in the schools which provided for the European children.

To challenge European domination, the Africans established the South African Native National Conference (later to become the African National Congress) in 1912. This was to be the first tribal organisation on the continent and its goal was to gain their country back politically. African poets and authors of the period, such as Citashe and W. B. Rubusana, voiced their aspirations in their slogan, *Zemk' iinkomo magwalandini* ("Your cattle are gone, you cowardly countrymen"). Their objective was to fight with words rather than with spears.

The difficult coalition between the British and the Boers continued into the twentieth century. The *Boers* (Afrikaners) formed the National Party, which came into power in 1948, heralding the era known as Apartheid. Apartheid's policy was "complete separation between Europeans and all others . . . which began the most intensive period of anti-African legislation South Africa had ever experienced." "Homelands" were established as a way to relegate ethnic groups to separate parts of the country. A 'pass system' was set up which was to control people's movements and thus enforce the segregation, developed by the racist ideology of the National Party. By 1961 the National Party had withdrawn South Africa from the British Commonwealth.

This lead to South Africa being excluded from world bodies such as the United Nations, due to its intentional and resolute insistence on an inexorable course of racism, combined with the abuse of the majority of people's human rights.

Resistance to Apartheid among Africans lead to a process of reactivity. Initially the ANC attempted to petition the British crown against African exclusion from power by sending delegations to Britain to lobby their government. Internally, they sent the South African government similar pleas and took part in Native Representative Councils (as advisory councils to the South African government.)

Petitions and delegations to amend the exploitative conditions were ignored. This led to a group, including Nelson Mandela, Walter Sisulu, and Robert Sobukwe forming the ANC Youth League in 1944. "Calling for a Program of Action to challenge European state control directly through protest, they launched the Defiance Campaign Against Unjust Laws in 1951-1952 and employed passive resistance to make their mark on the government and history of education in South Africa."

In 1960 the Government outlawed the ANC, which lead to the liberation movement going underground and embarking on guerrilla warfare. "The government had hoped that it had completely fragmented resistance from the disadvantaged and oppressed and that it had separated these downtrodden groups from their white liberal sympathisers, especially those from the "open universities" which were fertile grounds to plant the seed for revolution. "Black Consciousness" which arose in the late 1960s lead to the emergence of the South African Students' Organization in 1968, (a group under the leadership of Steve Biko). It was forces such as this which would eventually bring Apartheid down to its knees. Students at the 'segregated universities and schools' became a potent challenge to white domination in South Africa."

African resistance was fortified by the Black Consciousness Movement, mobilised to rise against Apartheid. An example of this was the uprisings in Soweto in 1976. This lead to the Apartheid regime outlawing Black Consciousness, as it had already done to the ANC and the PAC. Steve Biko was allegedly murdered in police detention, which further galvanised the fissure between Africans and the Government, due to the oppression and control being enforced by the state.

Despite the brutal repression created under a 'State of Emergency', declared by the government in 1985, the strategy failed with resistance growing stronger. This was supported by international economic sanctions, which led to the defeat of the Apartheid regime. "In February 1990 President F. W. De Klerk, South Africa's last non-indigenous head of state, removed the ban on the ANC and the PAC and announced the release of all political prisoners, including Nelson Mandela, as well as an amnesty on exiles associated with the liberation movement. This set the stage for a negotiated settlement finally reached in 1994."

With the new Government and end of Apartheid, the Homelands system was abolished and Nelson Mandela elected as president. *"However, the social and economic disruptions caused by the Homelands Act and the brutality of South Africa's official structures during the years of National Party rule—not to mention the resultant fragmentation of African families and communities—are likely to take generations to overcome."*

The Truth and Reconciliation Commission from the 1990s onwards has focused on mending some of the far-reaching damage done; for the integrity of South Africans and to help mend the South African soul as a way to " . . . help heal the trauma caused by years of torture, murder, and abuse at the hands of a racist state that previously would not permit individuals of different 'races' even to legally marry."

The Republic of South Africa was a constitutional parliamentary government for many years. It was dramatically transformed in 1994 when the Apartheid system was abolished. It is an amazing phenomenon experiencing this major paradigm shift in one's own life time; being able to be a witness and a spectator to profound change.

With its exceptionally ethnically varied population, South Africa has 11 official languages (Afrikaans, English, Ndebele, Pedi, Sotho, Swazi, Tsonga, Tswana, Venda, Xhosa, and Zulu.) Of the original African peoples who lived in the southern African tip, a few members of the San and Khoi Khoi communities have survived. Anthropologists describe the majority of South Africa's indigenous people as Bantu-speaking people. Many "Coloureds," along with the Afrikaners (descendants of mainly Dutch, French Huguenot, and German settlers), speak Afrikaans, a language reportedly developed from Dutch by Khoi Khoi and Malaysian slaves as a 'pidgin language'. South Africans of British and other European descent (notably Jews from the Baltic States) identify themselves as English-speaking South Africans, while the Indian South African population mainly spoke Tamil, Hindi, and Gujarati, but many are fluent in English.

Social Conditions South Africa has undergone swift changes in its population due to the HIV/AIDS pandemic. "With the spread of this disease magnified by relative government inaction until the turn of the millennium, harsh discrimination and mistreatment often meted out by society to those infected with the disease, and certain dangerously mistaken beliefs and abusive practices concerning protection from the disease, the scale of infection and deaths in South Africa from HIV/AIDS exceeds that in most other countries, including those in the developing world."

Economic Status South Africa has a profusion of natural resources—this is a blessing as it can sustain a large population, "but cursed because the wealth endemic to the land attracted European invaders who subjugated the indigenous population for centuries, creating wide economic disparities and vast suffering for most of the country's population."

The country's natural resources include platinum, gold and chromium, diamonds, and energy sources such as coal and natural gas. Despite the countries mineral wealth, the unemployment rate in South Africa is high and disputes about mine ownership have led to recent fierce strikes (2012) and a high fatality rate.

The History of Apartheid in South Africa

I believe that the perpetrators of Apartheid were caught up in the machinations of the mind-set of that time in the 1940's with Hitler's hideous eugenics' philosophy, in which he attempted to orchestrate the creation of his 'supreme race'. However this is small excuse. It is wretched that humanity becomes easily swayed by the mind-set of a particular era, regardless of how ruinous it is. After writing the above, I fortuitously found some data in '*The Nazi Influence in the formation of apartheid in South Africa.*' (By Elizabeth Lee Jemison, USA.)

"South African apartheid was a system developed to protect the supremacy of Afrikaans-speaking whites and to repress non-white groups through a policy of almost complete separation. The Afrikaner people, the descendants of the first Dutch settlers in southern Africa, were the dominant white minority and, once unified behind the cause of apartheid, formed a majority of the all-white electorate. Apartheid, the Afrikaans word for separateness, began as a governmental system after the elections of 1948 when the Afrikaner Nationalist Party, became the majority Party, and this system lasted until 1994. The Afrikaner white population developed the apartheid system in 1948 in part as an outgrowth of the ideology of Nazi Germany, an ideology the Afrikaners readily accepted because of the affinity they felt towards Germans, and because they feared being dominated by the English minority who had previously controlled the country. The desire of the Afrikaners for complete power in South Africa began when the British took over the Cape area in 1806, in an effort to prevent Napoleon from gaining control of the region. The introduction of another European group vying for power served to awaken Afrikaner nationalism. The British who settled in the Cape area in the early 19th century brought with them concepts of the 18th century Enlightenment and the pro-business liberalism of the 19th century. These ideas conflicted sharply with the conservative Calvinist ideology of the Dutch who had settled in South Africa in the mid-17th century. As the result of the anti-slavery lobby in Britain and of the efforts of Christian missionaries to end racial prejudice, the British advocated a lessening of segregation to allow some non-whites to participate at least partially in the white-dominated society . . ." To be independent from British domination, many Dutch Boers set off northwest of Cape 1835. "These Afrikaners or Voortrekkers conquered the land of native African tribes and established autonomous Boer republics." In the final analysis, the sad and ironic truth is that the Afrikaners and the British were "two self-proclaimed Christian nations going to war against each other when both nations believed in the same God and both were certain that God justified all their actions."

"South Africa was colonized by the English and Dutch in the seventeenth century. English domination of the Dutch descendants (known as Boers or Afrikaners) resulted in the Dutch establishing the new colonies of Orange Free State and Transvaal. The discovery of diamonds in these lands around 1900 resulted in an English invasion which sparked the Boer War. Following independence from England, an uneasy power-sharing between the two groups held sway until the 1940's, when the Afrikaner National Party was able to gain a strong majority. Strategists in the National Party created apartheid as a means to cement their control over the economic and social system. Initially, the aim of the apartheid was to maintain white domination while extending racial separation. Starting in the 60's, a plan of "Grand Apartheid" was executed, emphasizing territorial separation and police repression.

With the enactment of apartheid laws in 1948, racial discrimination was institutionalised. Race laws touched every aspect of social life, including a prohibition of marriage between non-whites and whites, and the sanctioning of "white-only" jobs. In 1950, the Population Registration Act required that all South Africans be racially classified into one of three categories: white, black (African), or coloured (of mixed decent). The coloured category included major subgroups of Indians and Asians. Classification into these categories was based on appearance, social acceptance, and descent. For example, a white person was defined as "in appearance obviously a white person or generally accepted as a white person." A person could not be considered white if one of his or her parents were non-white. The determination that a person was "obviously white" would take into account "his habits, education, and speech and deportment and demeanor." A black person would be of or accepted as a member of an African tribe or race, and a coloured person is one that is not black or white. The Department of Home Affairs (a government bureau) was responsible for the classification of the citizenry. Non-compliance with the race laws were dealt with harshly. All blacks were required to carry "pass books" containing fingerprints, photo and information on access to non-black areas.

In 1951, the Bantu Authorities Act established a basis for ethnic government in African reserves, known as "homelands." These homelands were independent states to which each African was assigned by the government according to the record of origin (which was frequently inaccurate). All political rights, including voting, held by an African were restricted to the designated homeland. The idea was that they would be citizens of the homeland, losing their citizenship in South Africa and any right of involvement with the South African Parliament which held complete hegemony over the homelands. From 1976 to 1981, four of these homelands were created, denationalizing nine million South Africans. The homeland administrations refused the nominal independence, maintaining pressure for political rights within the country as a whole. Nevertheless, Africans living in the homelands needed passports to enter South Africa: aliens in their own country.

In 1953, the Public Safety Act and the Criminal Law Amendment Act were passed, which empowered the government to declare stringent states of emergency and increased penalties for protesting against or supporting the repeal of a law. The penalties included fines, imprisonment and whippings. In 1960, a large group of blacks in Sharpeville refused to carry their passes; the government declared a state of emergency. The emergency lasted for 156 days, leaving 69 people dead and 187 people wounded. Wielding the Public Safety Act and the Criminal Law Amendment Act, the white regime had no intention of changing the unjust laws of apartheid.

The penalties imposed on political protest, even non-violent protest, were severe. During the states of emergency which continued intermittently until 1989, anyone could be detained without a hearing by a low-level police official for up to six months. Thousands of individuals died in custody, frequently after gruesome acts of torture. Those who were tried were sentenced to death, banished, or imprisoned for life, like Nelson Mandela" *http://www-cs-Students.stanford.edu/~cale/cs201/apartheid.hist.html*

Discussing and Identifying with Gordimer's "What being a White South African Means to Me"

On Gordimer's Address at The University of Cape Town, South Africa, 1977

Gordimer asks "What does it mean to be a South African? " She questions who decides and whether she in fact qualifies. Gordimer felt that only white people in South Africa felt the need to ask these questions and that living in Africa did not seem enough to qualify to be a South African.

Being born in Africa holds great significance for Gordimer. She states that one's formative years essentially mould one and that the "early years of a child's life are carried within that child . . . always". Gordimer remarks that "the first landscape you open your eyes on, the first piece of earth you stagger to your feet on, the first faces that bend over you, although they pass beyond conscious recall, put a certain stamp on your perception and interpretation of the world." Thus being born in Africa became part of her blueprint.

When abroad in Europe or America, Gordimer encapsulates a cameo of Africa in her mind; "in that half-waking state when time and distance don't exist—is burned *veld* around mine-dumps and coal mine slag hills." She acknowledges that there is little romance in her vision but that this is what presents for her, her earliest memories.

Gordimer refers to the development of one's consciousness of being a South African—that realisation that one discovers that there is a facade—a lie as it were, that one conscientises through an increasing sense of awareness of one's reality . . . she describes it as "The great South African lie." Her awareness of the lie comes as a revelation. I like what Gordimer says—how can one feel guilty if one has been conned? Reality has been concealed; and then the revelation is an insult to one's sensibility and integrity . . .

This is what Gordimer alludes to as the opportunity to develop one's identity—"working one's way through the central, definitive experience of black and white as people, with undifferentiated claims on life . . ." and in South Africa defined by one's skin colour, language and culture. She adds that this is a simplistic explanation, yet for her she sought ideological and political explanations to conceptualise this.

She adds that long before she had assimilated any understanding of others being exploited or oppressed, one has already lived this in one's life, going to school, ignorant that others may be herding cattle, oblivious of the concept of an education. This is part of the farce that one grows up in.

Gordimer recalls that she began to understand that she was a white South African. But what was paramount to her was her "contact with blacks as people and equals, sometimes very close and personal contact". This shaped her consciousness about their opinions of whites and of herself. Gordimer kept processing between theory and reality, and attempted to aspire towards justice. Through this processing she became "beguiled" by the concept of a "free society".

Gordimer retorts that Jean Paul Sartre's greatest regret was that he was not more radical. She concurs. She feels that she was not brave enough and questions how much one can blame the circumstances of history and the challenges we encounter. She feels that it's not easy to be a South African. It brings with it demands due to the constant changes of the country; as though the metamorphic flow of South Africa expects one to be malleable and changeable at the flick of a switch. She adds that as a South African she does not have the same secure sense of identity as some of her American or English friends have. They will not have to alter the concept of their identity in relation to their country. Gordimer argues that white South Africans were questioning. "Morally our government is illegal." (Quote—Andrew Young—"The South African Government of the time was illegal.")

"Mongane Serote once wrote a little poem: *'White people are white people, they must learn to listen; black people are black people, they must learn to talk.'* It has happened." adds Gordimer. She feels that whites will need to disassemble their thoughts and recreate them with new ideas about self if they wish to identify fully with the struggle for a universal South African consciousness.

Gordimer argues that 'white people' will need to acknowledge "the black premise that the entire standpoint of being white will have to shift", regardless of whether one loathes and has opposed racialism one's entire life, or if one is racially discriminatory. Gordimer concludes that "liberation cannot be gained on one's behalf, by others." *Nadine Gordimer, 1977*

Don't Panic! *Alan Knott-Craig, 2008*

The publisher, Louise Grantham, commences the preface of the book with an explanation behind the book;—It " developed at a time in South Africa when we all needed the positives about our great country to be brought into focus, a time when many of us found ourselves weighed down by overwhelming negative sentiment" she states. The book was triggered by a positive email which Knott-Craig, MD of iBurst sent to his staff. His email:-

'2008 has certainly started with a bang! The future was rosy on31 December 2007, but suddenly everyone is buying candles and researching property in Perth! A combination of recession in the USA, global equity Market negativity, high interest rates, the National Credit Act and power outages have combined to create the perfect storm.

But don't panic!

This is not the first time there's been doom and gloom. Every few years the same thing happens. We experience massive economic growth, everyone is optimistic and buying Nescafe Gold, and holiday homes and Merc's. The positivity gets ahead of itself and the economy overheats, and then panic sets in because the economy seems to be collapsing when in actual fact it's simply making an adjustment back to a reasonable level.

It happened in 1989, when SA defaulted on its international loans and the stock market and the Rand crashed, it happened in 1994 when the ANC took power and everyone thought war would break out, it happened in 1998 when interest rates hit 25% and you couldn't give away your house, and it happened in 2001 when a fairly unstable guy by the name of Osama arranged for 2 Boeings to fly into the tallest buildings in New York!

On each of those occasions everyone thought it was the end of the world and that there was no light in sight. And on each occasion, believe it or not, the world did not actually end, it recovered and in fact things continued to get better.

I think 2008 will be a tough year, but I also see it as a great opportunity to seize the day whilst everyone else is whinging and get a front-seat on the inevitable boom that we'll experience in 2009, 2010 and beyond.

Make sure you make a mental note of everything that is happening now, because it will happen again and again, and if you don't recognize the symptoms you'll be suckered into the same negativity, and forget to look for the opportunities.

It's easy to be negative. Subconsciously, you WANT to be negative! Whenever you open the papers they tell you about the goriest hi-jacking and the most corrupt politicians. Why don't they dedicate more pages to the fact that Jo'burg is the world's biggest man-made forest, or to the corruption-free achievements of the vast majority of public officials? Because bad news sells. Good news is boring.

SA still has the best weather in the world! We're lucky enough to possess a huge chunk of the world's resources, i.e.: gold, platinum, coal, iron. The growth in India and China will continue to accelerate (India and China sign 10million new mobile customers every month), and so will their demand for our resources. The government has already embarked on massive infrastructure projects (some of them a tad late, i.e.: electricity), and this will pump money into the economy.

We are all lucky enough to be a part of the birth of a massive and all-encompassing industry. The Internet has and will continue to change the world. The enormity of its impact is up there with the wheel, electricity, TV, telephones, and possibly man's greatest ever invention, coffee. Not only does it open up an entirely untapped world of commerce, but it is also the ultimate disseminator of information and news. Apartheid would not have lasted 40 years if the Internet had existed! And you're part of it!

I'm looking forward to another year of ASA complaints, IR issues, Plug & Wireless parties, BTS roll-outs, billing runs, irate customers, happy customers, orange bubbles, faulty elevators, etc., etc. The nice stuff makes me feel good, and the challenges remind me why we can beat the competition. Most importantly I'm looking forward to having fun and making memories.

So ignore the doomsayers, install a timer on your geyser, and buy Ricoffee for a couple of months.

Cheers, Alan'

The book has a collection of articles to inspire South Africans to stay and not pack their bags for Perth. The back cover gives an overview as follows—"Don't pack for Perth—stay and put your energy into creating the South Africa we all want to live in. Be part of our drive to turn a challenging year into a year of opportunity. During the midst of the power cuts in January, Alan Knott-Craig, MD of iBurst, wrote an inspirational email; to his staff about turning 2008 into a year of opportunity.

Alan's message inspired hundreds of South African's to change their attitudes in a viral wave that started with a conversation with Zoe, a disillusioned employee, developed into an email to iBurst staff, was picked up by the media and ended with a deluge of support from around South Africa—via blog, email, sms and letter. The positive message was welcomed by countless South Africans looking for a silver lining in the storm of 2008. This book is the result of South Africans wanting to share their positive messages."

Alan Knott-Craig's December 2008 email

From: Alan Knott-Craig
Sent: 04 December 2008 06:42
To: All Users
Subject: Closing out 2008

Hi guys,

Why am I writing this email? Because I'm getting the impression there are some depressed people walking around. Now there are a couple of potential reasons for this phenomenon: 1. Festive season hangovers. Solution: Convert to Islam. 2. Moving offices. Solution: Resign and work from a trailer park. 3. Manic depressive personality. Solution: Prozac or alcohol (see point 1 for solution to hangover). 4. You read newspapers. Solution: Rather work.

It's been just over 10 months since I sent that damn 'Don't Panic' email. Quite a bit has happened since then, some of it good (i.e.: Ricoffee sales have sky-rocketed), some of it bad (i.e.: Ricoffee sales have sky-rocketed).

So let's recap: At the beginning of the year people were panicking about the oil price, inflation, electricity and economic recession. Of those big 4 concerns, 3 have taken care of themselves. Oil is now below $50 a barrel, inflation is not such a big deal because oil is cheap nowadays, and we haven't had any crazy power outages since February (the Eskom saga is a complete mystery to me). What about the recession? Well, as it turns out, that was something that deserved a bit of panic. Especially if your name is Dick and you run a New York investment bank. Fortunately we don't have any Dick's at iBurst.

After the merry-go-round of bad news at the beginning of the year, capped by the xenophobic attacks (note to attackers: neck-lacing innocent foreigners is not a great advert for our country), it's been quite surreal to watch the U-turn executed by those heading for the exit door. It's a bit like watching naïve tourists run into the sea off Camp's Bay, scream in pain, and then race back onto the beach. The water looks so nice, but don't go in there unless you're an Eskimo. Suddenly foreign shores aren't as attractive when there are no jobs, no credit, and no sunshine.

Just to put a couple of things in perspective, here is some info on the year-to-date performance of world stock markets (as of 10 Nov):

Iceland—89%
China—64%
Russia—64%
India—48%
Hong Kong—46%
Brazil—40%
Japan—40%
USA—36%
Australia—35%
UK—32%
New Zealand—29%
South Africa—26%

SA is not so bad, is it? I'd rather be here than in Iceland.

Sunny SA is certainly not immune to the global economic crisis. Our companies are suffering too, which means fewer bonuses and more retrenchments (always a winning recipe for unhappiness). How long will it last? Who knows, but brace yourselves for a tough 2009. The good news is that after every tough time comes good times, so at least we all have something to look forward to!

What is the silver lining for SA? Our interest rates are still high, but at least there is the possibility of a decrease in rates to ease the burden on your back pocket. The UK and USA do not have that luxury, their interests rates are already too low to cut further!

What else? Mad Bob can't last forever. When he heads off into the sunset there will be an absolute bonanza of investment and aid flooding into Zimbabwe, and a large chunk of that windfall will be via sunny SA . . . oh happy days. Who said there were no plusses to having a failed state as a neighbour?

What else? Anyone noticed the cranes everywhere you look? Seen the Gautrain progress? I went down to CT 2 weeks ago, and virtually the entire highway is under construction. The unintended consequence of the government procrastination on infrastructure investment over the past 10 years is that now that it's finally underway just in time to prop up our economy! Gotta love those bureaucrats.

What else? The Soccer World Cup is coming. If we get it right, i.e.: 10,000 tourists are not hi-jacked, we'll be the hottest spot on the planet, and we'll have a shout for hosting the Olympics.

But don't crack open the champagne just yet; we still have our fair share of challenges. Your average Yank may be swapping his house for a trailer, but at least he's not worried about being shot in the head on the way to his next job interview. If any of you have a relative or friend in the government, please pass on this message, "Crime is out of control and most of our schools and hospitals are in disarray." Don't for a second fool yourself that we can ignore these structural problems and live the rest of our lives in blissful ignorance. We must constantly remind the politicians to do their jobs, but we cannot absolve ourselves of our responsibility to make individual contributions. It is our business to make this land a success. Report crime, pick up litter, give to the needy, create jobs, look after the children, practice safe sex, drink filter coffee. We've all got a responsibility to make the magic happen, otherwise you'll just end up lying in bed in 50 years' time, looking back and saying "What if?"

The time of opportunity is upon us, now it's up to us to seize the day. I've said it before, I'll say it again: Life is not about waiting for storms to pass, it's about learning to dance in the rain.

Looking forward to dancing in 2009! Cheers, Alan w*ww.marcforrest.com*

Excerpts from **South Africa: Detailed Analysis: 2010: Collapsing into a Failed State'.**
41% unemployment—The Super AIDS disaster for Black people . . .

Jan Lamprecht, author of 'Government by deception' responds to Dr Jan Du Plessis's 2010 analysis.   Sunday 12 Sept 2010

Dr Jan Du Plessis specialises in producing detailed analyses for corporate businesses.

Some analysts, like him, predicted that South Africa would be heading towards a failed state by 2010. They based their data on analytical tools. Lamprecht states that when producing a statistical report, it is not about propagating any political paradigm, but rather about attempting to present an overview based on tangible data. Data presented here is obtainable from Intersearch.

The article reports that "Between the end of the Second World War in 1945 and 1993 some 50 African countries became independent. The process of decolonisation led to political elections of one-man, one-vote and the subsequent formation of sovereign states. Decolonisation provided an easy mechanism for the transfer of political power from colonial power to the "new democratic government"—very often a different name for the new "clan" or "tribe" in power . . ."

The article states that "from 1945 to 1993 Africa produced a new sovereign state almost every year. Then in 1992 a new word entered the political vocabulary—the formation of a failed state. Somalia disintegrated into war making factions; law and order collapsed and the country and capital were divided among war lords. Since then, the country has not regained its former status as sovereign entity. From 2000 the external community has wearily accepted the fact that more failed states could follow as governing capabilities declined and in some cases basically collapsed . . .".

The article added that by 2010 it was clear that the ANC government was in "severe crisis."

The article reports that dysfunctional trends can be identified on three levels.

- Government in crisis;
- Population in crisis; and
- Environment in crisis.

1. *Government Crisis*—"Over the past decade, the essence of good governance—the relationship between Government and the governed—has been eroded."
   The writer adds that "The ANC won political control of the country, but it lost out on the governing capability. By 2010 the ANC just does not have the governing capital to attend to all the needs of society. As a result, large areas of society have become void of any governing capabilities—in technical terms society has become governmentally empty. The ANC commands a sound political majority, but signifies no governing presence within the key functions of Government. With this, the broad outlines of the failed state have also come to South Africa as the structures for good governance have become destabilised. When Government is in crisis, the whole of society will reflect the nature of the crisis".

2. *Population crisis.* "The 20/20 syndrome explains a situation where society has been losing its human capital over a very short period of time. This, in essence, prevents society from regenerating itself. The impact of HIV/AIDS on the population has been devastating. Twenty years ago the average life span of the population was a healthy 60 years plus. By 2010 the trend is down to 40 years. About one basic fact all the reports and analysts agree: the wrong people are dying in society (19–49 year olds) Society has been deprived of its human capital over the last twenty years."
   "The population crisis is not about too many people, but about too little human capital.

   - The number of people who are poor, is just too high (25.7 million people from a population of 49.3 million);

- The number of people who depend on a state grant for their daily survival is not sustainable (13 million with the possibility of an additional 7 million);·
- The number of people who are illiterate has become unmanageable (24% of adults over 15 years);
- *There is no solution for the number of jobless people. The most recent statistics indicate an official jobless rate of 25,3%. The real rate, according to the Bureau for Market Research at Unisa, has reached 41%. The figure used in the advertising industry for marketing stands on 63%.*
- The number of people with HIV/AIDS is terrifying, as it sucks the human capital from the middle sector of society (5.7 million people);
- The large number of people who are going to die from HIV/AIDS may destabilize society eventually as it impacts on the productive middle sector of society (estimated deaths: 1 000 per day is the most recent figure available);
- The number of Aids orphans is beyond the reach of Government and society (by 2015 some 5.7 million or 32% of all children will have lost one or both parents) and this fact in itself has the potential to disrupt the educational process;
- *The terrifying reality is that the number of people with the necessary human capital—the expertise and skills to support society and capability to pay taxes—is too few to carry the burden of the numbers in need. (5.3 million tax payers, with 1.2 million of them paying 75% of all personal and company tax)".*

3. *Environment in crisis*—"The environment is one of the factors that determine the quality of life of the population. Of direct relevance are issues such as clean water, the effective disposal of sewage, roads, etc.
    - In January 2010 the Democratic Alliance disclosed in a statement that only 32 of the 970 sewage plants in the country are still functioning properly.
    - In a report to Parliament in February 2010 it was revealed that "when it comes to fresh water", only 30 municipalities out of 283 have the capability to supply clean water to the inhabitants."

- Parliament's water affairs portfolio committee was told in July 2010 that "millions of litres of highly acidic mine water is rising up under Johannesburg and, if left unchecked, could spill out into its streets some 18 months from now. The acid water is currently about 600m below the city's surface, but is rising at a rate of between 0.6 and 0,9m a day."

Context of the crisis—"South Africa has a problem with a variety of issues such as law and order, potholes, sewage, bad education—the list is almost endless. These are all problems, but the crisis lies on a different level. The crisis is embodied in the structures of society which are supposed to carry society at large, but have become dysfunctional. When Government is subjected to functional decay, the population is in a process of distortion and the environment is increasingly being contaminated—then the essence of the crisis is really showing.

The country reflects a crisis on three different levels. This makes the country rather unique in the world. In addition, the crisis has been exacerbated by the fact that the three various levels of functional decay, has now started interacting with one another. Very few South Africans really understand what is happening to their own society. The real problem is not the pothole or the burglar, but the internal functional collapse of Government and society."

The writer poses the question—"What kind of Future?" He reports that one can mend a pothole, but how easily can one deal with "functional decay"? Much of the decay is reportedly due to a corrupt society in which people with expertise are ousted in favour of people who vote for the correct political party, leading to rife nepotism at the expense of calibre. The results are glaringly conspicuous, with a dramatic deterioration in service delivery in every sector; from basics such as sewerage, water and electricity, to welfare, health and education.

"What paralysed the government of President Jacob Zuma was that it all happened at the same time . . . The constitution promised a better quality of life, but Government left the people out in the sewage."

"The most unthinkable result of the domino effect will appear when local government becomes so dysfunctional that citizens are compelled to take over services on a large scale and in this process government authority is pushed back to a few urban areas. This will signal the start of a new political system . . .".

Analytical report by Dr. J.A. Du Plessis at Intersearch, Url: http://www.intersearch.co.za/AfricanCrisis Data reported by Jan Lamprecht Webmaster Author of: Government by Deception **"Political language is designed to make lies sound truthful and murder respectable and to give an appearance of solidity to pure wind."**

http://macua.blogs.com/mozambique_para_todos/2010/09/safrica-detailed-analysis-2010-collapsing-into-a-failed-state-41-.html

Alex Matthews on emigration from South Africa

12 September 2010   *Alex Matthews*

To leave or not to leave: that is the question

Have you ever thought about leaving South Africa? Do you feel like spitting on someone who would even consider it? Or have you already left?

At one point or another, I've been all three. So perhaps that's why I've found "Should I stay or should I go", a collection of writing about leaving South Africa (or, in some cases, returning or staying put), has a special resonance.

The stories are always riveting, always compelling, sometimes infuriating. Andre Brink's piece was written after the brutal murder of his nephew. He wrote why he chose, in the aftermath of such a tragedy, to stay in South Africa. Brink harbours no illusions about this country—and he captures, with brutal precision, the corrosive decline of our young democracy, weakened by corruption and its leaders' contempt for the rule of law. But his decision to stay is because of his love for South Africa—a love that even this most seasoned of scribes struggles to define or explain, but which so many of its citizens, myself included, have experienced.

I relished Ways of Staying author Kevin Bloom's appreciation that South Africa is the best possible place to map out his own identity. It is in this place of bewildering complexity and excitement, that the writer can determine his own place in the world.

Journalist Gillian Tucker's grappling with homesickness is understandable, but the conclusions drawn from her visit back to South Africa after living for 14 years in Canada, were not. She contrasts the opulence of her accommodation with the shoddy service she received. To her, this somehow embodies what South Africa has become. I found that strange—poor service is an issue in many parts of the world. Her bad luck to experience it both in Johannesburg and Cape Town is more indicative of insufficient research on Trip Advisor than a meaningful truth about the country.

I wondered whether this was merely the excuse she found for finding the country she had longed for no longer "worthy" of that longing. South Africa has changed hugely in the years since she left. In some ways it is a different country—one that she may simply no longer have an affinity to.

Another excruciating piece was by Barry Levy, who dedicates much of his article on establishing his anti-apartheid credentials and undoubtedly genuine love for South Africa. One wonders why he hadn't bolted back to Mzansi ages ago. He devotes merely a cryptic line to answer that—claiming "life had conspired against me". That doesn't wash.

I wonder whether, like Tucker, he can't quite come to terms with today's South Africa. Despite him loving it and wanting it to do well, perhaps there's a subconscious impulse to remain anchored in Australia's safe, if staid harbour, far from the storms and raging uncertainty that can beset his homeland.

Only one contributor (to my knowledge) was black—the indispensable Jacob Dlamini, whose eloquent musings in Business Day every week are a must read. The ensemble's lack of ethnic diversity amongst its contributors is my main gripe about the book. In some ways this is understandable. Emigrants tend to be from the middle class (those who can afford to leave if they want to), and because of our tragic history, that middle class is overwhelmingly white.

Nevertheless, there are many of a darker hue who have left South Africa. Some went during apartheid—apparently Golders Green in London is a haven for exiled ANC apparatchiks lacking the stomach to return home. Others went later: lured away to Perth and other pastures when the democracy dividend didn't quite deliver what had been hoped for—or because opportunities arose overseas that weren't available back home. It would have been nice to hear these voices.

Angst and political tones tend to shade South African emigration, regardless of why people have left. Perhaps this is because some of those that have left are embittered racists that can't bear blacks attaining political power after centuries of oppression. Then there are those who have gone because they've lost faith in the new South Africa—or in its capacity to provide a safe and secure environment for their families. Others (like me) have departed for more prosaic reasons—I moved because I was offered a job here in London.

Regardless of the reasons for people leaving, South Africans—of all races—face huge uncertainties. They live, after all, in a country where crime is rampant, corruption has become endemic, law enforcement is toothless and basic services often remain inadequate or continue to deteriorate. Meanwhile, ruling party demagogues get away with murder (or at least urging it—"I'll kill for Zuma" springs to mind). If certain factions in the ANC have their way, then nationalism is on the cards, agricultural property rights are threatened, and media freedom is on the verge of being neutered.

Against this backdrop, staying or leaving is a valid conundrum for anyone with the means to consider it. But it is a conundrum made all the more complicated by the kind of place South Africa is. It is a nation of warmth and colour, vibrancy and breathtaking beauty. It also has superb quality of life (the space, the food, the weather!) for those privileged enough to afford it.

We easily forget that emigration—and migration generally—is a global phenomenon. As contributor Daniel Ford points out, most people don't have the same hang-ups about it—and leaving one's country is not interpreted as a sign of betrayal. Perhaps South Africans should attempt to be a little more liberated about this vexed issue. No one should feel forced to stay or go; it's up to them, and their own circumstances.

My favourite philosophical approach to emigration was summed up in the piece by peripatetic English teacher Anne Townsend. "Life," she wrote, "is just too short to spend it all in one place."

Alex Matthews was born in Cape Town. He is currently based in London.

Letter from Gareth Cliff to the SA Government

12th October 2010
Dear Government

OK, I get it, the President isn't the only one in charge. The ANC believes in "collective responsibility" (So that nobody has to get blamed when things get screwed up), so I address this to everyone in government—the whole lot of you—good, bad and ugly (That's you, Blade).

We were all so pleased with your renewed promises to deliver services (we'll forgive the fact that in some places people are worse off than in 1994); to root out corruption (so far your record is worse than under Mbeki, Mandela or the Apartheid regime—what with family members becoming overnight millionaires); and build infrastructure (State tenders going disgustingly awry and pretty stadia standing empty notwithstanding)—and with the good job you did when FIFA were telling you what to do for a few months this year. Give yourselves half a pat on the back. Since President Sepp went off with his billions I'm afraid we have less to be proud of—Public Servants Strikes, more Presidential bastard children, increasing unemployment and a lack of leadership that allowed the Unions to make the elected government its bitch. You should be more than a little worried—but you're not. Hence my letter. Here are some things that might have passed you by:

1. **You have to stop corruption**. Don't stop it because rich people moan about it and because it makes poor people feel that you are self-enriching parasites of state resources, but because it is a disease that will kill us all. It's simple—there is only so much money left to be plundered. When that money runs out, the plunderers will raise taxes, chase and drain all the remaining cash out of the country and be left with nothing but the rotting remains of what could have been the greatest success story of post-colonial Africa. It's called corruption because it decomposes the fabric of society. When someone is found guilty of corruption, don't go near them—it's catchy. Making yourself rich at the country's expense is what colonialists do.

2. **Stop complaining about the media**. You're only complaining about them because they show you up for how little you really do or care. If you were trying really hard, and you didn't drive the most expensive car in the land, or have a nephew who suddenly went from modesty to ostentatious opulence, we'd have only positive things to report. Think of Jay Naidoo, Geraldine Fraser-Moleketi and Zwelinzima Vavi—they come under a lot of fire, but it's never embarrassing—always about their ideas, their positions, and is perfectly acceptable criticism for people in power to put up with. When the media go after Blade Nzimande, Siphiwe Nyanda and the President, they say we need a new piece of legislation to "make the media responsible". That's because they're being humiliated

by the facts we uncover about them daily, not because there is an agenda in some newsroom. If there had been a free press during the reigns of Henry VIII, Idi Amin or Hitler, their regimes might just have been kept a little less destructive, and certainly would have been less brazen and unchecked.

3. **Education is a disaster**. We're the least literate and numerate country in Africa. Zimbabwe produces better school results and turns out smarter kids than we do. Our youth aren't unemployed, they're unemployable. Outcomes-based-education, Teachers' Unions and an attitude of mediocrity that discourages excellence have reduced us to a laughing stock. Our learners can't spell, read, add or subtract. What are all these people going to do? Become President? There's only one job like that. We need clever people, not average or stupid ones. The failure of the Education Department happened under your watch. Someone who writes Matric now hadn't even started school under the Apartheid regime, so you cannot blame anyone but yourselves for this colossal cock-up. Fix it before three-quarters of our matrics end up begging on Oxford Road. Reward schools and teachers who deliver great pass rates and clever students into the system. Fire the teachers who march and neglect their classrooms.

4. **Give up on BEE**. It isn't working. Free shares for new black partnerships in old white companies has made everyone poorer except for Tokyo Sexwale. Giving people control of existing business won't make more jobs either. In fact, big companies aren't growing; they're reducing staff and costs. The key is entrepreneurship. People with initiative, creative ideas and small companies must be given tax breaks and assistance. Young black professionals must be encouraged to start their own businesses rather than join a big corporation's board as their token black shareholder or director. Government must also stop thinking that state employment is a way to decrease unemployment—it isn't—it's a tax burden. India and China are churning out new, brilliant, qualified people at a rate that makes us look like losers. South Africa has a proud history of innovation, pioneering and genius. This is the only way we can advance our society and economy beyond merely coping.

5. **Stop squabbling over power**. Offices are not there for you to occupy (or be deployed to) and aggrandize yourself. Offices in government are there to provide a service. If you think outrageous

salaries, big German cars, first-class travel and state housing are the reasons to aspire to leadership, you're in the wrong business—you should be working for a dysfunctional, tumbledown parastatal (or Glenn Agliotti). We don't care who the Chairperson of the National Council of Provinces is if we don't have running water, electricity, schools and clean streets. *You work for us. Do your job, don't imagine you ARE your job.*

6. **Stop renaming things**. Build new things to name. If I live in a street down which the sewage runs, I don't care if it's called Hans Strijdom or Malibongwe. Calling it something nice and new won't make it smell nice and new. Re-branding is something Cell C do with Trevor Noah, not something you can whitewash your lack of delivery with.

7. **Don't think you'll be in power forever**. People aren't as stupid as you think we are. We know you sit around laughing about how much you get away with. We'll take you down, either at the polls—or if it comes down to the wire—by revolution (Yes, Julius, the real kind, not the one you imagine happened in 2008). Careless, wasteful and wanton government is a thing of the past. The days of thin propaganda and idealized struggle are over. The people put you in power—they will take you out of it. *Africa is tired of tin-pot dictators, one-party states and banana republics. We know who we are now, we care about our future—and so should you.*

Gareth Cliff *Belowthelion.co.za*

From frying pan to fire? *Sharon Gill*
28 November 2011

Relocating from one side of the planet to the other in order to reunite with family is one thing, but if you're looking for a better life, it might be prudent to put a few things into perspective.

Sharon Gill looks at some of the factors that prompt South Africans to pack up their lives and move to a foreign country, and those that inspire them to come back.

Unemployment, unacceptable crime levels, widespread corruption, rising fuel costs and increasing prices for deteriorating public services are just a few of the factors inspiring so many skilled South Africans to leave the country in search of greener pastures. But while many have settled overseas quite happily, others return to South Africa for all sorts of reasons: they miss the lifestyle, the weather, friends or family, or they were better off financially in South Africa.

Unemployment

Back in April 2011, when I first wrote this article, South Africa's unemployment rate was around 24%, second only to Rwanda (30%), and slightly above Spain (20.33%)

In comparison, the unemployment rate in the USA was around 8.8%, in the UK 7.8%, and in the Euro Zone 9.9%.

Crime

This is something of a can of worms, with some countries imposing a moratorium on their crime statistics, and political unrest in other countries skewing the total "murder" numbers.

Five or six years ago, South Africa ranked second only to Colombia on the "murders per capita" listings, with the USA at No. 24 on the list, the UK at 46, and Australia and New Zealand at 43 and 52 respectively.

But according to the UN's latest stats, which are for 2008, South Africa and Colombia have moved down the list to 9th and 7th place respectively, behind Venezuela and Honduras in Central America and Jamaica in the Caribbean.

In comparison, the USA appears at No. 52 on the list, with the UK, New Zealand and Australia not even featuring in the top 100.

Corruption

In 2010, South Africa was rated 4.5 on the Corruptions Perception Index—which measures the perceived levels of public sector corruption in 178 countries around the world.

This puts South Africa midway between "highly corrupt" (0) and "very clean" (10).

Clear leaders in the corruption stakes were lawless Somalia (1.1), and war-torn Afghanistan (1.4) and Iraq (1.5). The Nordic countries of Sweden and Finland (9.2) and Denmark (9.3) were beyond reproach.

But let's compare South Africa's 4.5 rating with the countries that are most often considered in the search for greener pastures: the USA (7.1) and UK (7.6) are hardly exemplary. Much better are Australia (8.7) and squeaky clean New Zealand (9.3).

Inflation

The inflation rate in South Africa was reported as 4.1% in March 2011.

Inflation in Australia and Canada was 3.3% in March 2011, compared with New Zealand (4.5%) and the USA (2.7%).

In the Euro zone—despite bailouts for Greece, Ireland, Portugal and possibly Spain, as well as much speculation over the financial stability of Italy, inflation was 2.7% in March.

Inflation in the UK—a country that retains its own currency despite being an EU Member State—was 4% in March, just 0.1% lower than South Africa.

*Interesting trivia: Zimbabwe's inflation rate of 13.2 billion percent hit the headlines in November 2009, beating the previous world record set by Hungary in July 1946 when it had a **daily** inflation rate of 207%.*

Fuel prices

It's impossible to compare fuel prices by converting foreign currencies to SA Rands. The only way to produce any meaningful comparison is to use some kind of "universal currency", so for the purposes of this exercise, we will use the Big Mac Index—a method devised by The Economist to measure the purchasing power parity of different currencies.

Today, South Africans at the coast pay around R10.47 per litre of unleaded petrol, which is equal to roughly 58% of one Big Mac, or 1.73 litres per Big Mac.

Americans get nearly twice as much petrol for their Big Mac: 29% of a Big Mac per litre, or 3.4 litres per Big Mac.

Petrol in the UK, Australia and New Zealand are pretty similar—roughly 44% of a Big Mac, or 2.25 litres per Big Mac.

However . . .

Property: If you sell a bog-standard 3-bedroom 2-bathroom house in South Africa, good luck trying to find anything habitable in the UK when you convert the proceeds to pounds.

You'll have a similar problem in the USA, Australia and New Zealand, although there are bargains to be had if you're prepared to clock up some home-hunting mileage.

Property prices in Europe are much more reasonable, especially some of the older houses in France and Portugal, although sellers tend to remove anything not cemented into the basic structure. I've seen places with bare wires hanging from the ceilings after the sellers took all the light fittings with them, and kitchen sinks propped up on bricks because they took the built-in cupboards.

There are bargains to be had in Spain, but beware: the Spanish property market is staggering in the aftermath of a property boom that saw unscrupulous developers building houses without permits, leaving thousands of illegal homes on the government's demolition list with no compensation for the home owners.

In January 2012, the UK will drop the 6-month pet quarantine requirement

Pets: The UK has always had strict quarantine laws, which means pets entering the UK from South Africa spent six months in quarantine kennels. This was not negotiable. A friend of mine who is blind was unable to take her guide dog with her when she went to England for a few weeks' holiday. Australia and New Zealand also insist on six months in quarantine.

While the quarantine period itself might not be too much of an issue, the cost of kennelling is.

However, come January 2012, the UK is bringing its pet import policy in line with those of the EU and USA, which have always been more pet-friendly. Provided you comply with the pet import regulations, there is no need to quarantine domestic pets arriving from South Africa.

And those same pets will be able to travel between the UK, EU and USA under the "Pet Passport" scheme.

It remains to be seen whether Australia and New Zealand will follow suit, although considering that every item of wooden furniture has to be fumigated on arrival, and they want to arrest you if they find so much as an apple in your handbag when you get off the plane—even if it was given to you on the flight, I can't see them relaxing their quarantine regulations.

Climate: Durban gets an average of 320 days of sunshine per year, the same as Marbella in Spain.

San Francisco (USA), Barcelona (Spain), Lisbon (Portugal), Athens (Greece) and Perth (Australia) all get 300 sunny days per year.

Sydney gets 240 days of sunshine; New York is slightly behind with 234.

Paris only gets 75 sunny days year, but Londoners count their annual sunshine in hours—1,500, as do New Zealanders in Auckland—2,000 hours a year.

The overall picture

While southern Europe does appear to offer a similar lifestyle to South Africa, it might not be easy to find work if you don't speak the language.

In a lot of countries where English is the primary language spoken, unemployment is rising and housing is expensive.

In the USA the cost of healthcare could kill you, and in the UK the first winter might.

South Africa might not be utopia, and some suggest it might be a case of "better the devil you know".

When this article was first published in *The Crest Online*, one reader who left South Africa a few years ago to live first in China, then Vietnam and now Thailand, offered a simple checklist to use when comparing your current reality with the alternative you have under consideration:

1. Will my children be better educated if I go or if I stay? (Go = 1, N/A = 2, Stay = 0)
2. Are my chances of excellent healthcare better if I go or if I stay? (Go = 1, N/A = 2, Stay = 0)
3. Will I feel less discriminated against if I go or if I stay? (Go = 1, N/A = 2, Stay = 0)
4. Can I prepare better or worse for a secure retirement if I go or if I stay? (Go = 1, N/A = 2, Stay = 0)
5. Will the security of my family, as measured by the fear of violent attack on a family member, be better or worse at my proposed destination than it is currently? (Better = 1, N/A = 2, Worse =0)
6. How easy will it be for me to turn my education and experience into an appropriately paid job once my skin colour is revealed to my potential employer? (Better = 1, N/A = 2, Worse = 0)

7. Will my proposed new country be more vibrant, beautiful or energizing than South Africa? (Yes = 0, N/A = 1, No = 1)
8. Will my proposed destination offer the diversity of cultures that makes South Africa such an interesting place to live? (Yes = 1, N/A = 1, No = 0)

   The answers to the first six questions will determine your long-term happiness.

   Question 7 is the main reason we ask ourselves the first six. If you choose to leave South Africa, get used to the fact that you will always yearn for home. It is beautiful beyond compare. It cannot and will not be replaced.

   Question 8 is only relevant if EVERY culture is prepared to live alongside EVERY other culture without significant prejudice. Otherwise such diversity is a recipe for disaster. Ask the NP.
9. The overriding question . . .

   Can I secure the long-term future of my family better if I leave or if I stay (as far as I can determine, based on the policies of the ruling Party and/or the likelihood of regime change in the next 10 years)? (Yes = Go, No = Stay)

   Note: The answer to question 9 depends a great deal on your ability to pay for the cost of solving the problems posed by questions 1-7, so please consider how fortunate you are compared to others facing the same dilemma before you throw any stones at those leaving. This is particularly so if you were able to answer N/A to any question.

The way things are . . . in Africa
The Namibia Sun, 24 March 2011   *Pashu Shuudi*

ALTHOUGH hard to swallow, us black people despise everything that looks like us. To prove my point, not so long ago fellow blacks who ran away from atrocities in their African countries were beaten, burned and some even killed by fellow blacks in South Africa. In Namibia, black supporters of the ruling party SWAPO and the opposition parties clashed in 2009 and we are still hearing of such quarrels or violence just in the name of politics.

Through history, I have come to learn that we actually disliked one another before colonialism, hence fierce tribal fights during those years.

Colonialism united us all in the fight against a common enemy. After colonialism, we saw the rebirth of what we thought was buried long time ago; tribalism, regionalism, favouritism, etc. Although we do not like others from other tribes, we all love things that we do not produce. We love fine branded clothes, (Polo, Paris Hilton, Luis Vuiton, Nike, Adidas, Lacoste, Timberland) from Europe. We love American and German-made cars, we love expensive wine, we like Jameson whisky, Jack Daniels, Johnny Walker, Red Label, Bell's, Scottish brandy, the beer. Yet no African person brews any of them.

All we own, unfortunately, are thousands of *Shebeens* where we drink ourselves to death, stab each other with knives/bottles, infect each other with the HIV virus, make lots of unwanted babies and then blame others for our miseries. We love all sorts of expensive foreign made items and show them off. Yet we look down at our indigenous products that we fail to commercialise.

As blacks, we know very little about investments, whether in stocks, or in properties. All we know is how to invest our money in things that depreciate or evaporate the fastest—like clothes, cars, alcohol, and when we are at it, we want the whole world to see us. I know some brothers driving BMWs, yet they sleep on the floors, no beds because nobody will see them, anyway. This is what we love doing and this is the black life, a life of showing off for those who have. A black millionaire 'tenderpreneur' living in Ludwig's Dorf, Kleine Kuppe, Olympias, in Windhoek will drive to the notorious Eveline Street in Katutura for a beer where he will show off his expensive car and look down on others. We sell our natural resources to Europe for processing, and then buy them back in finished products.

What makes us so inferior in our thinking that we only pride ourselves when we have something made by others?

What compels us to show off things that we don't manufacture?

Is it the poverty that we allow ourselves to be in? Is it our navigated consciousness, our culture or just a low self-esteem possessing us?

For how long are we going to be consumers or users of things we do not produce?

Do we like the easy way out, such that we only use and consume things made by others? Do designer clothes, expensive wine or changing our names to sound more European make us more confident in ourselves? Our leaders scream at us how bad the Europeans are, yet they steal our public money and hide it in European banks. We know how Europeans ransacked Africa but we are scandalously quiet when our own leaders loot our countries and run with briefcases under their arms full of our riches to Europe.

The Europeans took our riches to Europe but our African leaders are again taking our riches to Europe. Mubarak of Egypt, Gadaffi of Libya, Mobutu Sese Seko of the then Zaire, all had their assets allegedly frozen in Europe. Why do our African leaders who claim to love us run to invest 'their' money in Europe?

Again, when they get sick they are quick to be flown to Europe for treatment yet our relatives die in hospital queues. Don't our leaders trust the health systems they have created for us all? Why are we so subservient, so obedient to corruption when committed by our very own people?

Nobody can disagree with me in this country that we are like pets trained to obey the instructions of their masters. I am sure we look down when we think of our broken lives, but what do we see when our thoughts are down? I wonder if we realise how we sell our dreams to our leaders for corruption, miseries, poverty, unemployment, underdevelopment and all other social evils affecting us. How long are we going to let our manipulated minds mislead us, from womb to tomb?

The sickening smell of 'revolution'
News 24, 06 July 2011 *Max du Preez*

South Africa hasn't had its revolution yet. It is coming, a newspaper editor declared on Twitter this week, echoing the earlier stark warning by writer Peter Godwin.

I'm beginning to smell revolution too. Just a whiff, for now, but still. But it isn't the exciting, promising smell of the 1980s. The smell of freedom and possibility.

It's the sickening smell of hatred, greed and revenge. The smell of rot.

Revolution fomented by greed

Look, I think there are ample reasons for a lot of people in this country to want to revolt. I would too if I lived in a shack and had no hope of finding a job and improving my miserable life and those of my children.

But the revolution I fear is not one driven by a genuine desire for a decent life and dignity. I fear the revolution fomented by greedy, fat cat demagogues lusting for more power, with insecure little men clinging to their coattails.

I don't fear an uprising aimed at correcting imbalances and bringing justice. I fear an uprising that will dump our constitution in the rubbish bin, rob us of our freedom, destroy our economy and put a nasty, super-wealthy bunch of despots in power.

Sense of unease

My sense of unease was not triggered when Julius Malema called a whole section of the nation a bunch of criminals. It was triggered when he said it in front of our president, who said nothing to distance himself from such hate speech, and the ruling party praised Malema by its faint condemnation.

Malema's unchallenged insults were a signal that it was open season. Columnists like Andile Mngxitama and Eric Myeni, Youth League leaders like Floyd Shivambu, writers of letters to newspapers and callers to radio talk shows started spewing racism like we last saw coming from the AWB.

The staid British magazine *The Economist* remarked, "It is becoming more acceptable for black South Africans to scorn and abuse whites openly as a racial group."

Turn your head away from corruption, bad governance and abuse of power; it is time to find a new common enemy to divert the attention. It worked for Robert Mugabe, didn't it?

Supporting economic freedom

The new populist madness dominating our political culture saw Malema's demands for nationalisation of mines and banks and grabbing of land become mainstream thinking in the Tripartite Alliance within weeks, with Cosatu and the SACP backtracking on earlier reservations.

There is nothing wrong with a campaign for "economic freedom in our lifetime". In fact, I support it. But then fight for real solutions to poverty and unemployment, not for a system that can only lead to more misery, suffering and hunger.

I'm not sure about many things, but I'm very sure large-scale nationalisation and expropriation of agricultural land will not in the end benefit the poor at all. The economic cake will simply shrink drastically and you will only be certain of a slice if you're already very wealthy or you are an ANC insider.

I listen when a movement such as Abahlali debase Mjondolo champions as the cause of the destitute, not to the Johnny Walker Blue drinkers who wax on with their racist threats and over-simplifications.

There is no quick way to kill poverty and create millions of jobs, but there has to be a quicker way than the way we're doing it right now. We have to find that way, "we" meaning government, the business sector, the labour movement and the citizenry.

In need of a wake-up call

Mind you, I sometimes think white South Africans deserve a revolution. Too many of them live in complete denial, as if nothing had changed since the comfortable days when they were what Malema and Co now want to become.

Too many whites fooled themselves into thinking putting black faces in government and parliament would be the extent of their "sacrifice" after apartheid. Their racism, although mostly uttered privately or anonymously, matches that of the new breed of black racists. They need a rude wake-up call, or there will be a revolution and they will be its first victims.

As I said, it was just a whiff of revolution that I got. But a whiff that should jolt us all into action. Don't go stockpiling tinned food and bottled water yet. Rather help stop the madness.

Apartheid: The new and improved version—Growthpoint Organisation—Extraordinary People doing Exceptional things.

Saturday, 29 October 2011   *Vusi Mabaso*

I was 4 years old when I saw my Grandfather for the first time. He had been in exile in the UK for 22 years. I can remember him crying when he held me, but I was too small to understand why he was crying.

It is only now that I fully understand what it must have felt like for him reading my Father's letters telling him about my birth, and not knowing if, or when he would be able to hold me. He showed me a tear stained picture of my Grandmother and my Father when he was little. He said he would, every time the sacrifice would become too much, close his eyes and dream of seeing my Father graduating at a university. While he fought for our freedom, my Grandmother would scrub the toilets at a department store. She too just closed her eyes dreaming of my Father's graduation.

From the time my Grandfather had returned he has spent countless hours telling me about the struggle to the so called "freedom" I have today and the atrocities of the past. But the past wasn't something that defines me today being of this current young generation, and neither was it my Grandfather's ideals for me to grow up once again in a society where the colour of my skin is the defining factor.

From my Father's side I have been taught that no matter what the government throws at one, nothing and nobody should stand in your way to achieve your dreams. Even during those Apartheid years he managed to obtain his first degree. I remember waiting up for him when he got back from night classes at Wits doing his Honours. When I wanted to kick a ball with him, he would explain to me that he has to study because he needs to send me to university one day.

But neither of my forebears wanted a repeat of Apartheid. They wanted me to grow up in a colour blind world. So off I went in Grade 1 to a private school, mostly white at the time. I had 6 best friends, all white, and we became blood brothers. We walked the path my parents had dreamed about.

We were too young to pay attention to what was happening to the country my forebears had fought for. It would only be in Grade 12 that the new atrocities of the new Apartheid would hit us. Three of my friends applied to do medicine here and were rejected. They have now left the country and are studying abroad, probably never to return; this—while scores of sub-standard, ill English speaking Cuban doctors are being imported. The other three are here with me at university, but they are all leaving after graduation because they have very little hope of actually being employed, and if they do get employment, they will always have some Affirmative placement above them.

So how is this different from Apartheid? Is this freedom? My friends were born here, they belong here at university with me, so WE collectively can build this country one day when we are older. We are the future of this country, no matter what the current corrupt leaders and uneducated-media-attention-hungry youth league might tell you. You don't need to be a brain surgeon to know that you can't grab land or corporations from its owners unless you equip the new owner with the necessary knowledge and tools to farm this land or run these corporations productively.

Too many of us Africans are still enjoying a revolution that no longer has any relevance in a new and changed world. This continent has been free for the last 17 years, with us being the last to become a full democracy (excluding the ones that chose to crown a dictator instead). What is it that my people still want to fight about? Shouldn't they ask themselves what they have done with their freedom?

My parents told me about the Broederbond of the 60's that favoured certain whites. How is, what is going on with this country's finances any different from the Broederbond? Only certain blacks are driving around in black Range Rovers while the other 99% are still crammed into overloaded unsafe taxis like sardines. Freedom? This is a sad disillusioned freedom.

But the saddest of all for me personally is the fact that my new rulers with all their New Apartheid rules have ruined my sporting career. Like every rugby crazy boy out there I wanted to run on that rugby field for my country. I went to bed every night dreaming of being the black Morne Steyn of this country. My coaches and teachers were behind me and said my boot was worth gold for this country. That was until my father sat me down and painted the realities of our new South Africa for me. He said he won't stand in my way and will support any decision I make, but do I want to be branded a player that made a national team simply because they have to make up a quota? He said every pass I might mess up would be blown up by everybody as the useless quota player. He said I should rather focus on my studies and become something in my own right.

Heart-breaking as it was at the time, I had to listen to him and pack my boots away and get my nose into my books. Maybe when I incarnate into my next life, I will know what it feels like hearing the wind rushing past my ears as I dive through the air scoring a try for my country, but this life has more pressing issues to attend to. My people, of all races, will be starving if someone doesn't stand up for all of us.

When this government reversed Apartheid, they didn't only crush the dreams of many white South Africans, but they shot themselves in the foot and closed the doors internationally to many black South Africans.

If I would ever apply for a position abroad, the international market will cast a question mark over how I got where I did educationally. So every hour of slogging away at these books will be useless unless I do a post graduate degree abroad to prove my own worth.

Please don't give the lame excuse that Africans didn't have the opportunities Whites had back in the dark years and now they need to be advantaged. My Father is living proof of a man that made it big, irrespective of his circumstances. The only benefit he had since 1994, was that my brother and I have been allowed to be schooled in a "white" school and we can live in a respectable suburb today. My forebears dreamed of education, not a free ride in a shiny black luxury German car. But there are Millions that don't have my Father's vision. Millions of blind people who need to see a light.

I have been blasted and criticised by many people of all races as a child not having a clue what the freedom fighting was all about. My burning question to all my opponents out there is the following. Please explain to me how the current political structures are making anybody free, but the few that are on the gravy train?

My question to the government is—Do you have a roadmap forward? You have been spending 17 years at the Mercedes dealership. When are you actually going to get travelling to OUR final destination?

My fight isn't about which race rules this country. My fight is about a country of equal opportunity because Africans don't come in one shade of dark, but some are lighter than others and shout as loud as I do for OUR *Bokke*, Bafana or Proteas when they score!

The Tokoloshe   *Vusi Mabaso*

News 24, 13 November 2011

Four hundred years ago Africa might as well have been another planet in our solar system. We were living in peace in our thatch huts. The 10 piece of cattle were grazing under the African sky. The head of the family sat in the shade of a tree drinking beer, the wives were working the land and the kids were making clay oxen to play with. Every man's dream; even to this day, no matter where on this planet you might come from. It sounds like the African version of the Playboy mansion. You sit in the shade and your multiple wives work for you.

Then the Europeans arrived and laughed at our people who had no education and thought our way of life was savagery. We had to fight them with spears to survive and ultimately lost the battle. They took our land and made us their slaves. They sold us to America and we became a trading commodity.

That is, what it is. We can't change the past. So now 400 years later; what now? We had to learn through bloodshed that we were not a planet of another solar system. We are part of this world and in this world there are certain rules that can't be broken if you want to have food. Whether we like these rules or not, they are a reality. We can fight them like Mugabe does but it would only result in hunger. Too many Africans are yearning for life as we knew it back then . . . but they just love the white man's BMW and Lear Jet. The donkey cart is way too primitive for their liking and the cow hides that once covered our loins are not as "cool" as a Hugo Boss suit. We are a race that conveniently wants to fall back on our traditions when it suits us.

Not everybody has the ability to be as black and white as I am, and I mean that in more than one sense. I accept and acknowledge that. But I had to ask myself where do I fit in? Do I want to go back to my ancestral land in Dundee and demand this land be given back to me, so I can acquire a few wives and create my own Playboy Mansion, or do I like it here in Sandton with a Blackberry?

You would be horrified if you read all the messages I get on Facebook of people swearing at me, calling me a traitor, a disgrace to all black people in South Africa and that whites are paying me to blog my views.

What they don't know is that I have been very blessed to come from a long line of fighters that have fought from the days of the spear right up to the AK47. They fought for my freedom and as sure as this sun is going to come up tomorrow, I am not going to mess up all they have fought for. I have to address this cultural jail that stands between my people and true freedom.

Let us look at the *Tokoloshe* first. (*A dwarf-like water sprite that is believed to be a mischievous evil spirit . . .*) You slept with your bed raised up on a few bricks so that when the Tokoloshe comes at night, he could move freely around your room without knocking his head against any object. For those that know this superstition will know it is a small mystical hairy thing that looks like a psychotic angry little bear and catches you at night. But if he knocks his head against your bed, you are going to get this menace all over you and he has a temper like no other on earth. Stop laughing, I'm dead serious!

I haven't seen him yet. I badly wanted to see him when I was small because while others feared him, I thought he sounded cool and wanted to befriend him. My grandmother would look at me in absolute horror when I wanted to see the Tokoloshe. She would tell my mother "*Eish*, this child scares me!"

When my Grandfather returned from exile, he brought me a Teddy Bear from London. I looked at the Teddy and instantly knew this was the Tokoloshe I always wanted to meet. So my bear got named Tokoloshe. I got smacked a few times because I would jump on my Grandmother when she takes her afternoon nap and scare her with Tokoloshe.

But the modern new reborn *Tokoloshes* sit in Parliament.

Parliament . . . hmmmm . . . let us discuss running this country, being an example to the citizens and our traditions.

In a new African landscape how practical is it having multiple wives? Nice idea, being a man. Come on you guys reading this, admit it! But 20 children? Not so good because if I see what my university education and all the sundry trimmings are costing my father I would hate to think he had to make 20 of us. He would need to join the bank robbers to keep us at university. My mother didn't come cheap either, so he would have had to start stealing cattle from the white farmers if he wanted more wives. She cost him 40 head of cattle back in the 80's. (*lobola*). But wow, she was worth every cow! You should see her today in her Chanel dress . . . but five of them?

That is the humorous side of our tradition, but the more serious side is the following reality. There are only two of us and not twenty. So from my first breath my father has been there every step of my way thus far. We are his life and the reason he works this hard. He has spent every moment available guiding me into manhood (without sending me to a bush so some traditional butcher can slaughter my 'stuff' beyond repair). How, as a father will you possibly find the time to devout this kind of attention to 20 kids? I don't even want to think what life would have been like without my father. Unthinkable.

But what would I have been, if my father happily cavorted around claiming it is his culture and tradition? I probably would have been marching with Malema on the road to nowhere and my father would have been dead by now. I would be visiting a graveyard and trying to find life's answers from a stone. Back in the 80's when he married my mother us blacks hadn't heard of HIV/Aids and those 'enlightened ones' that did know about it, thought it was a homosexual disease.

So unbeknown to us we were killing ourselves. Merrily living out the principles of our tradition, not knowing we were committing suicide and resulting in 2 million orphans just in South Africa alone, let alone the rest of Africa. Wouldn't this be a far more worthy cause to march about than march to get stuff you deliriously think should be given to you for free?

Imagine what must be going through the mind of a 4 year old kid, who is left all alone tonight, with nobody to take care of him or her? None of these orphaned kids asked to be here, so imagine how a child has to try and make sense of all of this? So why do I still have my parents? Because my father knew he can't run around making babies that he can't provide for. He had to think soberly about life with a new millennium looming. He had us because he wanted us. We were to become his legacy. We weren't conceived in a moment of uncontrolled lust or in the name of an outdated tradition.

We won't discuss the merits of the social grant for mothers with kids and absent fathers but alarmingly condoms are still very unpopular accessories amongst the population of Africa. Until recently we had that scary old Bat as a minister of health. Tokoloshe personified. Beetroot juice and cabbage leaves will cure the disease, while the Chief would shower after a bit of *inyama.*

What did my father do 7 years ago when I reached puberty? He sat me down and told me the facts and how it all happens. Every time I leave the house he jokingly says he will draw blood when I return and have me tested. He jokes, but it has sunk in so deep now, I think about the consequences every time I see a gorgeous girl. What do my people do? Until recently it was better swept under the table than discuss the matter. It became unlawful to state a person has died of AIDS on his death certificate. How big is this denial?

Please don't make a comment after you have read this and tell me this disease was invented by the Apartheid rulers to wipe us out. I'm not even going to discuss that old stale story! And speaking about Apartheid, get over it. It has no relevance in 2011. Dead, gone, born 31-05-1961 and was executed on 27-04-1994. Our ultimate justification for everything that we do wrong can't come back so we can stone it.

The most bizarre superstition was invented to "cure" the disease. Rape a girl and it goes away. By girl, I mean little ones that had to helplessly have their lives taken from them without their consent. Grown men believing in rubbish like this. How in the name of God can you possibly justify this, no matter what your traditions or beliefs are?

We have now for far too long shrugged our shoulders and hidden behind our traditions on the one hand, and on the other we want to sit at the UN and pretend we have the wisdom to help decide the fate of other countries. In this world we need to merge with, but you have:

1. One wife. You sleep around, you die.
2. You have more kids than you can provide for; they starve and when they grow up they will steal to survive because you didn't have enough money to send them to a decent school. The government schools are a complete waste of time because the teachers are never in class.
3. You can't sell or trade with your daughters. They are not consumer goods.
4. You study or qualify as an artisan so you can earn your own keep and build your own house. There isn't enough money going around building 40 million free houses. You can wait until the sun burns itself out. It is not going to happen. So live with it.
5. Forget the white man's wealth. It has long gone been transferred to Sydney. There isn't any left here. Create your own. Forget about redistribution. Use your logic. The wealth of 5 million whites was never going to send 45 million blacks into a blissful retirement. The white wealth Malema cries about daily, was only in the hands of a few whites.

So until we move ourselves forward and merge ourselves with the world, we will remain primitive. 17 Years after independence you don't dance from Beyers Naude to the stock exchange and have foreign journalists film your insanity in the name of freedom. We were freed 17 years ago, embrace it and use your freedom to trade with the world, not crash your own stock market.

We can march up to the Union Buildings until the cows come home. We are not going to move ourselves forward until we free ourselves from ourselves!

'Thirty-three out of one hundred'

The Witness, 11 January 2012   *Michael Worsnip*

I JOINED the African National Congress in 1979. It was in Lesotho. I had left South Africa as a war resister. That was all I had done. Soweto 1976 came and went. I read the headlines with rising alarm. I was a student at a very right-wing university, at the time—Rhodes University. We were all white students. There were a couple among us mad enough (or brave enough) to join the National Union of South African Students (Nusas). But not me.

Steve Biko was killed. The news was told to me by a black stranger on the streets of Grahamstown. He was in shock—that was clear. He said what I thought was "Steve Peacock is dead!" I tried to look sympathetic, but had no idea what he might be talking about. I only later found out that it was Biko as all the headlines screamed at me—and still I was none the wiser. Who was Biko? I had never heard of him. I remember that some of us were captured by Biko's death. It was horrific—that was clear. We were students. Students protest. So we protested. The Minister of Police at the time tried to tell everyone that Biko had killed himself by not eating for eight days. So we fasted. We would meet once a day at lunch time in the office of the philosophy professor, an enigmatic ex-Methodist minister by the name of James Moulder. We fasted for eight days. And that was it. There was the occasional student protest about stuff I knew nothing about. But that was it. That was my entire experience of the struggle.

Well, not entirely. Up the road from me had lived Eli and Violet Weinberg—communists under house arrest. The Security Police would sit all night long in a car across from our house, watching the Weinberg house. My mother used to chat sometimes with Eli, over the garden fence. She found it odd that a communist would, on a yearly basis, send us a Christmas card.

Just up the road from us in Fanny Avenue, lived a woman called Helen Joseph. My mother had a strange fear of and fascination with her. She was clearly bad news, because she consorted with the natives, but at the same time, my mother admired her principles and the fact that she stood up for them.

It was only when I was a student at Cambridge that I read some of the speeches from the Treason Trial. I read the Freedom Charter.

They were a revelation. They determined for me that, no matter what, I would not allow myself to be conscripted. I was lucky enough to have a wife then, who agreed with me and supported me. Together, we decided to leave the country. It was a big thing for us. But that is all it was.

So we encountered a very suspicious ANC in Lesotho. Our first contact was with someone whose name we had been given while inside the country. The reception was chilly. We decided not to push the issue. And so we were watched. Background checks, presumably, were done on us. And, eventually, it became clear that we were to be regarded as comrades, rather than spies. That realisation does not give any sense of the dramatic and dynamic change that was happening inside us. For the first time in our lives we were living among black people as equals. For the first time in our lives we were interacting with black people at an eyeball-to-eyeball level. For the first time in our lives we were not the *baas*. Lesotho provided all of us with a foretaste of what liberation might be like. What it might be like to live side by equal side. Cheek by equal jowl.

For many of us, when we found ourselves elsewhere in the world down the years, it was Lesotho that we pined for. Because it was there that we experienced what we could never experience inside South Africa itself. We experienced a unity of purpose. We experienced and we started to live a progressive, revolutionary and life-changing ideal. And once you have crossed over that bridge, you can never go back. It was black ANC members and the people of Lesotho who gave us back the humanity that apartheid had robbed us of. And this is something I, for one, cannot ever forget. Jacob Zuma held underground meetings in our back bedroom. Tito Mboweni learnt to drive in our Volkswagen Beetle. Ngoako Ramatlhodi ironed his shirts in our living room. Others, with equally big names, bathed in our bath, made tea from our kettle and spent the night on the lounge sofa. And then there were those people, whose real names one never knew until they were killed in one of the two raids which the *boers* (and I use that term knowingly) executed with such extraordinary cruelty in Lesotho.

I wish, passionately, I wish with every fibre of my being, that every white person in the country could have experienced what we experienced. I wish they could have learnt, as we did, that white people could not lead the struggle. I wish they could have eaten from that same pot. I wish they could have drunk from that same river. Alas, it is impossible.

But you ask me today why I am still a member of the ANC and I will say that it is the ANC that has led this country to a peaceful and successful democratic reality. It has done so with the utmost generosity and grace to the former oppressors. It has done so in a way which has ensured that, against all odds, the country still functions and the economy continues to grow. It has done so without violence. It has done so in a way which has been respectful of culture and heritage and origin. It has never faltered from its commitment to non-racism and non-sexism.

You and I may criticise the ANC. That, in itself, is an amazing achievement. You and I may stare in disbelief at some of the antics of some of its members, but you cannot suggest, if you are in any way honest, that the ANC has failed. That would be not only churlish, it would be fantastically ill-informed.

The ANC has gone through some difficult times of late, but when I compare policy with policy, position with position, principle with principle, I have no doubt where my loyalties lie. And I would suggest that everyone who has come to love and honour that former "terrorist", who made the difficult decision to opt for armed struggle—Nelson Mandela—should look beyond him to the movement that gave him life and breath and to which he still owes allegiance. Look to the principles of the Freedom Charter. And once you have done that, take courage in the Constitution of the country, which is our joint crowning achievement.

I have been a member of the ANC for 33 of its 100 years. I have had my doubts. I have had my worries. I have had my moments of anger and even rage. But I look back on the 100 years of struggle which this movement has led and I know, beyond any doubt, that I made the right decision way back then. I look at where we are now, and where we could have been, and I know it. I look at the tremendous achievements we have made, and I know it. I look at the peace we enjoy, and I know it. I look at the greed and the gluttony and the shenanigans and the unsupportable nonsense, and I know, beyond any moment of doubt, that the spirit of the Charter and the will of the people will survive it all. We just need to make it so. *A luta continua*!

Michael Worsnip is the land claims commissioner for the Eastern Cape. He writes in his personal capacity.

Live without fear and help to make our land a better place

02 February 2012   *Bobby Godsell*

Bobby Godsell is Chairman of Business Leadership South Africa and a member of the National Planning Commission.

Every generation has the opportunity to engage and change the society they inherited. It is easy for South Africans today to be swayed by claims of uncertainty and fear but it is short-sighted and wrong to think of the world and our future as predetermined and final.

Recently, *The Economist* magazine, a leading voice in global economic opinion, led its front page with a foreboding graphic about an uncertain future and the words, "Be Afraid". This message is misleading and represents a world view of historical western political economic and social dominance that is having great difficulty dealing with its own decline, and with the emergence of another world stepping forward boldly into a future of exciting change and great opportunity. This change is also reflected in SA. We, too, are in an interregnum between the dying of the old and the birth of the new.

In a lecture to honour Tiyo Sogo, the 19th-century Scottish-trained South African priest, theologian and musical composer, Rev Bongani Finca summed up this interregnum rather well. South Africans today, he said, lived in "a time between times" and a "land between lands".

There is *"An SA from which we have departed . . . . But there is a new SA into which we have not yet entered."*

I agree with this analysis. I would go further and caution against the deep anxiety about the present and the idea that we have to be afraid about the future. We should not allow our own powers of prediction, or those of others, staring at their own decline, to deter us from grasping the chance to make a difference, to seize the opportunities and challenges that change brings. There is no need to be afraid; we need to embrace these changes in the world and at home. This is our time.

There is a shift of power and influence away from the European world, and we in SA and people across Africa are starting to take advantage of that shift.

For at least two decades, most developed countries have been living beyond their means and spending money they have yet to earn. Consumers have been drowning in a sea of debt. Further, a combination of ageing societies in the west, and in China to some extent, and underfunded social welfare policies means that the next generation in these societies will be less well off than the present. In many of these countries, social progress may be reversed, which will inevitably place enormous strain on those societies with democratic political systems.

In the coming years, more than half of all economic growth will take place in developing rather than developed societies. Part of this relative decline of the European world is a growth and spread of diverse voices. Around the world, people are expecting not only to be heard but to be listened to; the influence of the Islamic world is increasing, as is that of China and India.

Africa's role in this new world is an intriguing one. The continent has already achieved the highest levels of economic growth measured by continent for at least the past 15 years. A number of key African countries have dramatically improved their economic effectiveness of government institutions. Africa, with its 1-billion people, has a rapidly growing middle class that is demanding expanded and improved infrastructure in transport, power and communication. From a market growth point of view, Africa is the place to be. These are exciting times.

The greatest excitement of my life right now is my work on SA's first ever National Planning Commission. This body, which is similar to those driving growth and expansion in India and China, was established with the task to produce a vision of what our country should look like 20 or 30 years from now. In June last year, the commission produced its first document, a diagnostic report in which we identified nine areas in which we can move from the old SA to that shining city on the hill where all the country's people want to live.

In November, the commission presented the first draft proposals of a set of actions to address the challenges we face. The commissioners are aware that the job of effectively meeting these challenges will rest mainly on the shoulders of the young men and women of our country.

We live in a very young country. The new SA is just 17 years old. The young people of this country have the chance to shape the character of, and determine our collective destiny. Young graduates will experience the surprises and shocks that the real world delivers to all people in all times. They will need to find the resilience and the determination to build and rebuild, to change course, yet reach their destination.

My hope is that they will be real wealth creators. This means taking the available resources and combining them in exciting and new ways that make them increasingly useful and available to society as a whole. That is what real wealth is about. The adjustment under way, particularly in the developed world, is precisely the realisation that the facade of wealth, a sort of house of cards of debt-rich and value-poor economics, needs to be replaced with a solid house that real people can actually live in. So whatever new graduates and school-leavers do, they should endeavour to combine resources and create wealth.

Successful societies in this 21st century will be those that can combine rapid and sustained economic growth with effective social cohesion. Strong economies need equally strong societies. In the Anglo-Saxon world of the second half of the 20th century, success was very often about being clever and being right. Today, in our much more socially diverse world, leadership resides in those who can get people to agree and move in the same direction. The big changes under way in the west will require shared sacrifice. The processes of development in other parts of the world will also require societies to prioritise challenges.

Nowhere will any group (and even less any individual) be able to have it all on its own terms. The ability to define common goals and manage competing interests will be what separates successful leaders from those who fail. And the search for this consensus begins at home. Both developed, as well as the developing societies are creating new ways for people to be in society. A new kind of marriage and a new kind of family.

Waiting for the government to deliver a better life is a fool's choice. Most of our own destiny is in our own hands. Democracy is about the government of the people by the people. We should start, then, by governing ourselves, our families, our communities and our workplaces. On that basis, our youth will become empowered to set demands for a government that serves its interests and that is capable of winning and keeping their loyalty.

This and the next generation of South Africans, from all walks of life, have nothing to be afraid of. We are in a country, in a region and in a world in the midst of significant change, and we have the opportunity to be part of and, indeed, to help steer that change. The challenge for our young people, is to graduate from schools, colleges, universities and academies and go forth to new fields of conquest and dare themselves, and our society, to see a new and better time and make our land a new and better land.

Every generation wants to believe theirs is the best of times or the worst of times. I urge our youth to live boldly. They have nothing to lose, except fear. *www.leader.co.za*

Grasping the nettle—responding to the State of the Nation address

Wednesday, 15 February 2012   *Steuart Pennington*

"Good one Mr President, but when will you grasp the global competitiveness nettle?"

"Tender-handed stroke a nettle
And it stings you for your pains
Grasp it like a man of mettle
And it soft as silk remains"

Aaron Hill 1750

Most commentators have lauded the State of the Nation address. Mondli Makhanya of the Sunday Times said, "this was by far the best performance of his tenure . . . but it failed to properly deal with the biggest catastrophe facing this nation, an education system that is still producing ill-equipped citizens." I agree.

Lindiwe Mazibuko of the DA, more critical, said, "the government has extensive programmes, the nation faces many trials, and our people have boundless potential—it is difficult to outline all of this in one evening as part of a consolidated vision . . . but what our country needed was an honest assessment and a plan of action to address it." I agree.

But both Makhanya and Mazibuko themselves don't grasp the nettle of the importance of South Africa's challenge in improving its Global Competitiveness ranking out of 142 countries. Neither of them mentioned it.

We know that the President's speech focused on infrastructure improvement and the re-industrialisation of South Africa to facilitate economic activity, skills development and job creation, and that the majority of his critics focussed on what he left out or how he was preparing for Mangaung.

No mention was made by any commentator that I have read of the importance of improving our global competitiveness. Why not?

Global Ratings

It is common knowledge that the rating agencies; Standard and Poor's, Fitch and Moody's rely heavily on this data as part of their 'rating' process. They look at the 'whole' country, not just various components.

Our economy is the 30th largest in the world and yet South Africa is ranked 50th on the global competitiveness table of nations. Were it not for some *very* poor ratings in the area of health, education and labour relations we would be placed in the top 30. Were this the case the ratings agencies would move us out of BBB (moderately susceptible) into A (somewhat susceptible) or even AA (very strong). The impact on this 'move' for investment is inestimable.

Anecdotally, those of us who attended "Siswe Banzi is Dead" will remember the riveting scene in the Ford assembly plant where the 'Big Boss' from America "just walked in and walked out and didn't greet us" (said John Kani) "I knew then that my contribution meant nothing, that I had to resign".

If the metaphor of SA's progress post '94 is like a new car being assembled, it is akin to a post-apartheid model with which we have made rapid progress: we have a much better economic engine; we have a constitutionally designed steering wheel; we have an independently powered gearbox and suspension; we are spending big money on the chassis and the electronics; we have upholstery that is more accessible; but—we still have two pre '94 wheels, that of education and labour relations. They both have a slow puncture that no-one wants to repair. Somehow, we think these old pre '94 wheels will do for the meantime, that our post '94 car will go just fine, and compete with the other models out there. And just in case you didn't notice we still have the old pre-'94 'health' spare wheel in the boot that is *'pap'*.

Given the ambitious infrastructure improvement plans it should be noted that in the Global Competitiveness Report we fare better than most would expect.

- Quality of overall infrastructure (60)
- Quality of roads (43)
- Quality of railroad infrastructure (46)

- Quality of port infrastructure (50)
- Quality of air transport infrastructure (17)
- Available airline seat kms./week (24)
- Quality of electricity supply (97)

Nevertheless an ambitious infrastructure development programme is something we need. It will be beneficial in many respects.

We also have 10 measures which rank in the top ten in the world. As can be seen most of these measures reflect on the competence of the private sector—and they show what we are capable of.

	SA Global Competitiveness Ranking (142 countries)
Strength of Auditing and Reporting	1
Regulation of the Securities Exchange	1
Budget Transparency	1
Soundness of Banks	2
Board Efficacy	2
Availability of financial services	3
Protection of minority shareholders	4
Finance through local equity market	4
Effectiveness of anti-monopoly policy	7

But we have a significant number of measures where we rank in the bottom ten in the world—and all of them are critical contributors to improved global competitiveness (and essential components on our national assembly line), and, if I dare say, are the responsibility of government. They are our pre—'94 wheels that should be re-engineered as a matter of urgency if our post '94 car is to compete in the global environment.

	SA Global Competitiveness Ranking (142 countries)
Business costs of crime and violence	136
Business impact of TB	135
Business impact of HIV	136
Life expectancy	130

And we have challenges with some of our lighting and dashboard components:

Favouritism in decisions of government officials (114);
Wastefulness of government spending (69);
Burden of government regulation (112)
Public trust of politicians (88)

So, if we are to re-industrialise competitively then surely we need to pay as much attention to education, government competence, health and labour relations as we have on infrastructure.

Re-industrialisation must mean that our global competitiveness improves across the board. Therefore:

I was surprised that no reference was made to our Global Competitiveness.

I wanted our President to be tougher on teacher unions.

I expected a clear statement on what the performance standards are for every school in the country and what is expected from every principal regarding improved pass rates.

I was hoping that further special attention would be given to modernising our education system to adapt to our re-industrialisation needs.

I wondered why little attention was given to health and our declining life expectancy.

I was astounded that no reference was made to the inflexibility of our labour relations dispensation.

I anticipated that more attention be given to government performance and ministerial accountability.

I thought that corruption, graft, and tenderpreneurship would be dealt with in detail, particularly because much of the infrastructure plans will be the responsibility of government and will, in many instances, fall foul of these curses upon our nation.

The emphasis on infrastructure and re-industrialisation is good for all of us, but there are other aspects of the assembly line that need proper attention. If we don't re-engineer these as a matter of urgency our new post '94 car won't make it through rating agency '*quality control*' without numerous '*re-work*' requests; it won't be that popular with our investment '*customers*' as they look at all the other better value for money models coming out of Africa; and the passionate and committed workers on the assembly line may just start blaming the management—who hopefully will be in their offices, ready to listen—and grasp the nettle.

Post Script

Helen Zille says "There is a growing consensus in the centre of SA politics that sustainable job-creating growth is driven by the private sector, especially small, medium and micro enterprises. The job of the state is to create an environment that will attract and retain investment, entrepreneurship and skills. In a globalised economy, the state must ensure that the conditions exist for SA businesses to be internationally competitive. A key component of this is the provision of excellent infrastructure, including water, energy, technology, transport and roads, sewage systems etc. It is one of the key roles of the state to lead in the development of infrastructure that creates a platform for growth.

We welcome the fact that the President focused on this aspect of the state's role in increasing South Africa's competitiveness. Without this we cannot attract investment, grow the economy and create jobs. But infrastructure is only one aspect of the state's role in increasing a country's economic competitiveness. There are many other roles the state must play, and this is where the President's speech fell short this week."

I could not agree more. *Steuart Pennington*

Source: by Steuart Pennington of South Africa—The Good News (pty) Ltd. www.sagoodnews.co.za

South Africa 2012—OSAC* Crime and Safety Report—Peace or war: It's your call 20 June 2012 *Clem Sunter*

With the report on the News24 website that ANCYL's Deputy President, Ronald Lamola, stated in Durban yesterday that an act *as forceful as war* was needed to bring the land back to Africans, I would like to repeat the comment I made two weeks ago in an article on the latest *South African scenarios*:

"The fourth flag [for a 'Failed State' scenario] is the most lethal one: land grabs which will immediately divide the nation and possibly cause a civil war. We will literally hit the wall and be off everybody's investment agenda. The whole point of identifying a red flag like this is to ask how it can be kept down. We [Chantell Ilbury and I] believe that the country needs an Agridesa of all the major players in the agricultural game to negotiate a land transformation programme with a reasonable chance of success. In other words, land grabs should be pre-empted."

What more can Chantell Ilbury and I say as futurists desperately wanting our country to stay in the "Premier League" of nations and maintain its status as the leading and most advanced economy in Africa? We currently assign a 10% probability to the "Failed State" scenario which is up from the zero probability we were giving it 18 months ago. Quite a few commentators and companies attach a much higher probability, with the latter actively seeking ways of extending their geographical footprint into other African countries where they have a greater trust in a peaceful future. I am not kidding when I say that the CEOs doing this are probably giving 50:50 odds to a future of peace or war in South Africa.

In other words, the fear is that we turn into an old version of Liberia and Sierra Leone, where child soldiers with newly acquired AK47s are driven around on Toyota pick-ups and atrocities become a daily occurrence. The infrastructure of the country is completely degraded, the economy goes into a precipitous dive and the only issues are starvation and lack of medical facilities to treat the dying and wounded. The critical variable then becomes whether the war is purely a black-versus-white affair or whether it descends into ethnic strife with shifting allegiances and all the chaos that entails.

We have to face up to one fact. While we have a free and fair political system, we do not have a free and fair economy. Citizens of South Africa certainly have political freedom, but not economic freedom. The economy is far too centralised and lop-sided to be anything like one which can be called inclusive. For all those critics who talk about an absence of work ethic among the citizenry, I would totally disagree. Entrepreneurs in South Africa are in chains because of their shoddy treatment by government, parastatals and big business that seem to have formed an unholy alliance to keep the economy in as few hands as possible. The unions don't help by pursuing a very narrow definition of decent work which means either unionised employment or no employment at all. The informal sector instead of being supported is frowned upon and ignored. So I will end with the conclusion Chantell Ilbury and I put forward in the article two weeks ago:

> *"We therefore call this moment a second tipping point as the first tipping point occurred in the early 1990s when we could have tipped into civil war, but were saved from doing so by Codesa 1 and 2 which resulted in a new constitution and an open, democratic election. We now need a Codesa 3 or Economic Codesa in which the government, the top 100 CEOs in the private sector, the unions and other significant players in civil society participate to create an inclusive economy driven by a new generation of entrepreneurs and industrialists."*

Zuma's 'Giant Leap'—Off the cliff   *Helen Zille*

SA Today, Helen Zille's weekly newsletter, 1 July 2012

The ANC's policy conference in Midrand this week has dispelled any lingering hope that the ANC can still rescue South Africa from the consequences of 18 years of ANC rule. If the conference resolutions (couched in tired, old Marxist jargon) are ever implemented, they will undoubtedly worsen the crisis of poverty, unemployment and inequality the ANC claims it wants to address. The ANC acknowledges in its own discussion documents, prepared for the conference, that the state is "impotent". It acknowledges that there is a "crisis of outcomes" (otherwise known as delivery failure). But its plan to fix this is—more state control!

Despite the acknowledged failure of almost every state-driven intervention—from land reform to education renewal—President Zuma's opening speech blamed the familiar scapegoat: "white men" and the inherited disparities of apartheid. Instead of the "giant leap" forward Zuma promised, the conference ended in a tenuous "holding operation" endorsing the re-hashed policy proposals adopted at Polokwane almost five years ago.

To be sure, it could have been worse. A large number of delegates were pushing for more radical forms of state-led populism, such as the wholesale nationalisation of the mining industry (which reportedly led to a fist fight between delegates behind closed doors) and the confiscation of land without compensation. If this lobby had triumphed, it would have been the death knell for further investment and economic growth. It is important that these calls were resisted (even if only by a narrow margin, in the case of the "land-grab" protagonists).

But this does not represent progress. It means that President Zuma will be even more compromised than he was before the conference. Policy paralysis is the inevitable outcome. Talk of the "developmental state" leading the "second phase of South Africa's transition" is hollow rhetoric, bereft of content.

Even if some of the policy proposals are implemented, they will make matters worse rather than better. Take the resolutions on mining: they are designed to make conditions more difficult for the mining industry, at a time when many mines are battling to survive. The proposed 50% resource rent tax on mining will inevitably lead to mine closures. The increased revenue government is trying to gain will be minimal compared to the economic and social impact of thousands more unemployed people.

Instead, we should grow mining output by working to reduce costs associated with poor transport infrastructure, inadequate export facilities and rising electricity prices. To grow jobs we need more down-stream industries in mining and to achieve this we should focus on improving the business and regulatory environment so that these industries are attractive to investors. State coercion to force mines to diversify by undertaking "beneficiation" will have the opposite effect.

Then there is the issue of land reform. The conference resolved that land should not be confiscated without compensation unless it had been acquired illegally. And while the concept of "willing-buyer, willing-seller" was rejected, the conference accepted that constitutional change was not needed. So the legal "status quo" remains: if the state and a private owner cannot reach agreement on compensation for land, a court must determine a reasonable price.

But the state's own central role in the failure of land reform remained unexamined. Eighteen years into democracy, an "audit" of land ownership in South Africa is still incomplete. If there was any serious intent to drive land reform and improve agricultural output, the ANC would start by focusing on South Africa's most fertile land along the country's eastern sea-board which is largely unproductive and held in various forms of "traditional" communal ownership. The state also owns vast tracts of land. But instead of using this land to broaden ownership and enhance agricultural production, the focus remains on punishing productive farmers. This is incomprehensible, given that, according to the government's own statistics, over 80% of land reform ventures country-wide have failed.

Then there is the all-important area of investment, economic growth and job creation. It is clear from the discussion papers that the ANC still believes State Owned Enterprises (SOEs) should be the core drivers of "economic transformation" with a mandate to "advance the socio-economic and political agenda of the developmental state".

This jargon is pure satire, given the combined records of Transnet, Telkom, Eskom, South African Airways and the SABC. Between 2008 and 2010, state-owned enterprises had to be rescued by taxpayers to the tune of R243-billion. And to add insult to injury, when their CEOs and senior staff were "relieved" of their positions, it cost taxpayers R262-million to let them go.

As if this is not enough, there are now plans for a new state-owned mining company, a state-owned bank, a state-owned construction company, and a state-controlled "human resource planning entity". Each one of these is destined for failure. If a state is so inept that it cannot even deliver textbooks to schools, its attempt to control the supply and demand of human resources throughout the economy will certainly result in a "giant leap"—over the cliff and into an abyss.

While seeking state intervention everywhere it shouldn't, the ANC continues to resist it where it should. In 2011, R5-billion was budgeted to implement a Youth Wage Subsidy in order to encourage employers to offer "first-time" jobs to enable young work seekers to get a foothold on the first rung of the economic ladder. It remains unspent. Under pressure from COSATU, the ANC has shied away from implementing one of the few interventions by the state that would really boost productivity and opportunity, and broaden the participation of young people in the economy.

Instead, the ANC has opted for precisely the opposite. Although details are still sketchy, the conference mooted an ill-defined "job-seekers grant" offering young people an "allowance" while they look for work. This misdiagnoses the failure in our labour market, where job search costs are a limited contributor to unemployment. Accordingly, a grant with such a narrow focus will be relatively ineffective, increase dependence on the state, and do nothing to encourage more job creation.

One of the defining features of South Africa's unsustainable-socio economic order is that grant recipients outnumber personal taxpayers by more than 3:1. This new "grant" will merely skew this situation further. It will not enable more people to move into the productive economy and up the ladder, eventually growing the number of taxpayers. In fact, it will do precisely the opposite.

To really create jobs in South Africa the Youth Wage Subsidy (that supports the demand-side of the labour market) should be matched by a supply-side "Opportunity Voucher" to give young people the choice of subsidised further education or seed capital or business loan guarantees, according to their individual needs. As the ANC delegates argued (and came to blows) behind closed doors, it was fitting that external developments overshadowed their deliberations. These events, that grabbed the headlines, told us much more about the "real ANC" than the resolutions emanating from its own commissions.

As if to symbolise the discrepancy between the ANC's words and its deeds, the rhetoric of Midrand was obliterated in the metaphorical pall of smoke that rose from the state-sponsored burning and shredding of undelivered textbooks a few hundred kilometres further north (appropriately near Polokwane). Towards the end of the conference, another story took centre stage: the news that the state is finalising a R2-billion deal to purchase a new private jet for Jacob Zuma—that is bigger and better than Angela Merkel's. That tells you all you need to know about the ANC's "developmental state" and the farce that passed itself off as a "pro-poor policy conference" in Midrand last week.

Sincerely yours, Helen Zille

Understand the cancer of crime if you want to eradicate it.

My Tuesday Column, 2 October 2012   *Max du Preez*

South Africa is a very dangerous place. South Africa is also a very safe place. It depends on who you are and where you are . . . I will never be sceptical about the outrage and pain of a victim or the family and friends of a victim of crime. Murder, rape, hijacking and robbery rip people's life apart and deeply traumatise communities.

But I do get annoyed when certain communities turn the crime epidemic into a political tool to vent their anger about other things in our society they dislike. In conservative and right wing white circles, for instance, the high number of attacks on farmers is labelled as white genocide. This campaign is even waged internationally, as we saw last week when Archbishop Desmond Tutu was shouted down and insulted at a public occasion in the Netherlands.

The internet is overflowing with racist propaganda from South Africa and from South African expats that South Africa is a murderous, anarchic place where whites are targeted by violent criminals.

There is no white genocide. Whites are not specifically targeted by criminals. The only time they appear to be the preferred target of criminals, is when criminals assume that they would have more material possessions than the average black person.

Farm murders are a particularly emotive issue and needs to be talked about with great sensitivity. But it is imperative that we counter the propaganda around it. There are two fallacies around farm murders. The first is that they are primarily politically motivated and fuelled by racial hatred and the desire to drive whites off the land. The second is that most farmers who get attacked were cruel to their workers and that these are mostly revenge attacks.

Two decades of research into farm attacks have failed to deliver any evidence that the attackers had a political motive. Farmers are simply more vulnerable because they live isolated without any immediate neighbours and far from police stations. Evidence also shows that the belief that most farmers have firearms contributes to making them targets—firearms are sought after because they supply criminals with the tools to commit more crime.

Black commercial farmers are attacked in equal measure, but because there are so few of them, we don't see news of these attacks in our newspapers on a regular basis. Research has shown that farm attackers would not hesitate to kill black farm workers if they get in the way or if there is a possibility that they could identify the attackers afterwards.

Similarly, the large volume of research into farm attacks has shown that the overwhelming majority of these attacks are perpetrated by criminals not associated with the specific farms. There are very few recorded cases where disgruntled workers have attacked their employers.

There is no doubt that there are still farmers who grossly underpay their workers and treat them with little respect. But these cases are a tiny minority. Skilled and loyal farm workers are a valuable commodity. If not out of common decency, most farmers treat their employees properly in order to prevent them from leaving and finding employment elsewhere. A successful commercial farmer, just like any other sensible employer, knows that a good relationship with his work force is essential to productivity.

Stories abound of violent farm attacks where nothing was stolen, suggesting murder and assault were the motives. The statistics don't support this being a trend. There is no clear explanation for the extreme violence often used during attacks on farms. Perhaps one explanation is that attackers have more time than with other attacks.

South Africa's farmers are generally excellent agriculturalists and are critical to food security and stability and employment on the 'Platteland'. We need to care about their safety and give them special protection because of their vulnerability. But we should oppose the efforts of some to turn attacks on farms into propaganda and a rallying point for right-wingers. Even otherwise sensible parties and lobby groups like Freedom Front Plus and AfriForum should be called to account when they resort to hyperbole in their campaigns against farm attacks.

The stark reality is that whites are generally the most unlikely part of South African society to get murdered, raped or assaulted. Young black men make up the biggest single category of victims of violence. An analysis of the crime statistics in the Western Cape is a good example of national trends.

According to a report by the provincial community safety department, the province had the third highest murder rate in the country—43.4 victims per 100 000 people—between April 2011 and March 2012.

Most murder victims lived in the city's black townships. Eighty-seven percent of the victims were male. Seventy percent of those killed tested positive for alcohol. Crime is a cancer eating away at our society. We need to understand exactly how it manifests itself if we want to treat it effectively.

Open Letter to President Zuma   *Stephen Price*

13 October 2012

Dear President Zuma

It's two years to the day when Gareth Cliff, a local media celebrity, wrote an open letter to you. It caused quite a stir at the time. And as I was thinking about what I was going to say to the Class of 2012 of my school, his letter came to mind. As I re-read it, I realised it was about time for another one. Not quite as controversial perhaps but nevertheless another open letter borne out of my desire to see the 200 matrics that we're about to send you, fulfil their dreams in a positive, dynamic South Africa.

My name is Stephen Price. I am the Principal of Bergvliet High School here in the Western Cape. Some would describe this school as a 'former Model C school' . . . . a description generally used to justify why other schools are underperforming. But that is another discussion.

You see, right now I am addressing close on 1000 teachers, parents and pupils at the Valedictory Service of the Class of 2012 of my school. It is a special occasion, full of excitement and expectation, of joy and sadness, of hope and trepidation, and it will be a day for them to remember. Their last official day of school. I'd like to tell you a little bit about them. But, before I do, consider this.

For the past 12 years or so every single person in this hall has been working towards this one goal; their educators, their families and themselves. And in the past 5 years it has been our mission at Bergvliet High to develop in these young people, a revival of respect, a unity of purpose, a spirit of participation and more importantly, a sense of hope. Values we believe that will stand them in good stead in the 'big wide world' out there; values that we should be seeing in the leaders of our country.

In Gareth's letter he outlined various suggestions that he believed you needed to pay urgent attention to. Sadly you, and our Government, have not responded with anything resembling leadership and we have lurched from one crisis to another over the past 24 months. I believe that many of Gareth's suggestions are still valid, notwithstanding the crudity of his delivery at times. But I share his deep sense of frustration because, like him, I believe in the future of this country and our youth.

What follows is what my staff and I have taught our 200 matrics at Bergvliet High and I would venture you and our Government could do with a few lessons in this regard. Let me tell you what we have done.

A Revival of Respect – we have taught these youngsters about our shared heritage, about our country, about each other, about the value of treating others with respect, about being proud of who they are and about loyalty and integrity. But this is what we were up against from you and our Government, our elected leaders—continuing rampant corruption, fraud, self-enrichment, misuse of public funds, the appointment of family and supporters regardless of ability, the manipulation of the justice system by convicted criminals—Shaik, Selebi come to mind and finally the massacre at Marikana. You let us down at every turn. You did not care. You lacked leadership. But most importantly you have undermined everything we tried to teach our young charges. Our Government has not, under your leadership, developed a revival of respect. Well, we are sending you 200 young South Africans who know what respect is, who know the value of others, who are proud of where they come from, who are proud of this country and who are loyal, passionate and honest. My request to you is that you show them the respect they deserve. They might be young but they are citizens of this country and they will be our leaders one day. Take them but don't mess them around. Provide them with opportunity—they will create the jobs you need—we taught them how. Respect them sir. I do.

A Unity of Purpose—my staff have taught our matrics to work together, to understand that each of them has a different and unique role to play in achieving the common goal, that without a vision people will perish, that if we all pull in different directions we will never achieve anything and that our strength is in the whole not the individual. Again you and our Government have let us down. We have watched in dismay as the unions, the factions within the Government, the personal agendas of our elected leaders and influential individuals, have dragged the people of this country further apart, ever deeper into a pit of despair and ever backward and away from the vision that we all bought into in 1994. Why did you do that? Is the Alliance more important than the future of our matrics? Is Mr Malema so important that he can do and say what he wants and, by doing so, undermines any unity of purpose? Is it all 'just politics'? Is the culture of entitlement that prevails amongst our people and fostered by union, alliance and populist leaders, worth more than the value of hard work? Again we are sending you 200 young South Africans who know the value of hard work, of having a vision and working towards it and who understand that in order to achieve the vision they have to work side by side, shoulder to shoulder with each other. We are giving you 200 young South African eager to be a part of the solution. Please use every single one of them. I personally recommend them. They won't let you down. They will work hard. I know.

A Spirit of Participation – my staff have worked above and beyond the call of duty to provide every opportunity for our children. Clubs, societies, community service, sport, art, music, drama, endurance, debating, quizzes, National Olympiads, culture, recycling, continuing education, incoming and outgoing tours, exposure to exchange students from Germany, USA, Reunion, Canada, Australia, China and the UK, refugees from French speaking Africa and a myriad of extracurricular courses on project management, philosophy, engineering, design, music and art to name but a few. Every one of our students has had equal opportunity to be part of a vibrant 21st century South African school and the benefits have been incredible. Sportsmanship, empathy, understanding, comradeship, connection, health and wellness, competition, talent, strength, intellectual growth, stamina, love of learning, service to others, understanding the needs of others over self, leadership, courage, passion . . . I could go on and on. But what example do you set? Instead of building up, you break down. Lack of school sport structures, bureaucratic interference in performing schools, constant changes to curriculum, lack of text books, lack of community infrastructure and your lip service to policy that outlines wonderful aims and objectives. We couldn't wait for you to deliver. So we did it ourselves. Our parents got involved, paid their school fees, supported our teachers, gave them benefits that you should have provided and this allowed my staff to give more and more. Do I hear the Hadedas shouting 'former Model C school' at this point? Probably . . . but that's your fault I'm afraid. You've not done enough to raise the level of involvement in education. We witness the collapse of the Eastern Cape Education Dept., Limpopo and instead of solutions we have officials avoiding accountability, scurrying for cover and making excuses.

But here's a thought. We have just produced 200 hundred young South Africans that are not afraid of rolling up their sleeves and getting involved. We've taught them the value of participation. Put them into work programmes . . . Helen might be able to help you in this regard . . . into learnerships . . . we have 6 trainee teachers permanently stationed at our school . . . into sport and teaching, into apprenticeships, into corporate South Africa and I can guarantee you things will start to happen. But don't delay as many of them are looking to opportunities across the ocean and we need them here, you need them here. Tell them you want them to stay. I would.

And finally Mr President . . . I've always wanted to say that . . . A Sense of Hope. Hope—not in the sense of wishful thinking, not simply in the sense of a positive attitude, of being optimistic without reason but rather hope in the sense of confident expectation based on a solid foundation. That's what we've given our children at Bergvliet High. We've given them something to strive for, to look forward to, a vision, a better life for all . . . sound familiar? Why then does my DUX scholar, scoring over 90% in all her subjects, not get accepted into UCT or Stellenbosch for medicine? Why are her hopes being dashed? They should be knocking down the door to enrol her. Not your fault I hear you say . . . nothing to do with you. I'm sorry sir but it has everything to do with you. Gareth Cliff said *"India and China are churning out new, brilliant, qualified people at a rate that makes us look like losers. South Africa has a proud history of innovation, pioneering and genius. This is the only way we can advance our society and economy beyond merely coping."* She IS one of these people that Gareth is describing . . . and, believe it or not, we have 199 more like her. We are giving them all to you. Give them HOPE . . . because my staff have nurtured, grown and developed this hope in our youngsters. Do everything in your power to make it happen. They are ready and waiting and keen as mustard. Stop focusing on Mangaung. We have 200 matrics that deserve your attention. And they deserve it now . . . not after Mangaung.

Thank you for reading this (I hope you do) and I quote Gareth again to end off.

"We know who we are now, we care about our future—and so should you."

Kind regards, Stephen Price, Principal

Mr President, you should lead by example

18 October 2012   *Clem Sunter*

I have just read the following paragraph on *News24*: "Zuma also called on senior officers in business and government to freeze salary increases and bonuses for the next year as a 'strong commitment to build an equitable economy'."

I totally support the sentiment, but the president has to be the first in line by announcing what sacrifices he is personally going to make in order to get the show on the road. Genuine leadership is about action, not words. I wrote the following in an article after Warren Buffet called for the US government to get serious about *shared sacrifice*: "Coincidentally, I have been saying the same for some time that Barack Obama should be leading from the front by taking a pay cut himself. He should insist that members of Congress do the same."

For a start, I find it amazing how many members of government are allowed to travel business class on SAA. The other day, I remember seeing a prominent SACP individual in business class on his way to Cape Town when just on the other side of the curtain in economy sat the ambassador of one of those western capitalistic nations he so often derides. The ambassador told me that budgetary considerations now meant that all his diplomatic staff had to travel in the back of the plane.

As for hotels, the appalling stories in the press of senior government officials booking penthouse suites in the best hotels in London, New York and everywhere in South Africa make you wonder how such extravagance can be tolerated in these economic hard times. Sometimes the rooms are not even used. Ordinary folks now stay in budget hotels or bed and breakfasts to cut down the cost of travel.

Moreover, this belief that there is an endless stream of taxpayers' money swelling state coffers extends to flashy cars and bodyguards. Why is it that even at provincial and local government level, senior employees are allowed to drive top-of-the-line models? I drive a 10-year-old Mini on trips around town and a Land Rover Discovery with the wheel on the back if I am going on holiday.

Blue light convoys and bodyguards are yet another example of total excess. Please give me one other country in the world where the leader of the ruling party's youth wing travels around in a convoy with a troop of bodyguards. Not even in Russia. Is South Africa so spectacularly dangerous that every single minister and every single senior party official has to be afforded the level of personal protection that they are given? I remember in Anglo American that the only person who had a bodyguard was Harry Oppenheimer, who successfully evaded him when he wanted to walk by himself to the barber in Commissioner Street.

We can widen the list of items to be trimmed to residences, conferences, overseas trips, the quality of whisky, you name it. The fact is that for a party that espouses left-wing ideology and calls for measures to narrow the gap between the haves and the have-nots, there is an Orwellian contradiction between the sacrifices being demanded of others and the sacrifices being made by the party itself. "Some people are more equal than others" is the perception held by many members of the public.

Nevertheless, I shall heed the President's call. I solemnly promise that I will not put up my fees for my speaking engagements in 2013. Now I want to know what you are going to do, Mr President.

A Paralysed Citizenry: When did we Give Up?

19 October 2012   *Motheo Mtimkulu*

The South African news stream has been markedly negative over the last couple of months and if we're being completely honest, most reports post the 52nd National Conference of the *African National Congress* (ANC) held in Polokwane in 2007 have been of the distressing variety. Yet gauging by the reactions of the citizenry at large one could not be blamed for thinking that all is hunky-dory.

Most if not all of the ills that have now so suddenly and completely engulfed our nation can be attributed to a single moment in time, 21 September 2008 at 19:30. We stood idly by, batting not as much as an eyelid as the leadership of the ANC dictated to the populace that the sitting President, President Mbeki, would resign with immediate effect. We were now on a slippery slope to a leadership drunk with power as it quickly realised that when a nation's people are so disconnected from the political reality of the day, they can easily be manipulated.

We feign surprise when the ANC bulldozes over our State institutions with impunity, when its leadership blatantly shows disregard for the rule of law or when our country loses billions of Rand in unauthorised, irregular, fruitless and wasteful expenditure. Yet aside from the constant armchair moaning and groaning and the occasional discussion with friends and family about *"how this country is going to the dogs"*, we as citizens have delegated our hard won right to be active in the political processes of the day in a hope that the bad times are temporary and the good times will roll again. What then if, as a result of our citizenry paralysis, we are dragged so deep into the abyss that the good times never return?

In the 1964 film *The Best Man,* directed by *Franklin J. Schaffner* with a screenplay by *Gore Vidal* the sitting President of the United States, President Art Hockstader, says the following to William Russell:

> *"Power is not a toy we give to good children. It is a weapon.*
> *Because if you don't fight, the job is not for you.*
> *And it never will be."*

Social contracts the World over have always dictated that governments are mandated with power by the people in order to serve and fight for the people. It would appear that the leadership of the ANC has this notion misconstrued as it has used that power as a weapon to fight against the people in an effort to serve themselves. If this is how the ANC leadership wish to run this country then in the words of President Hockstader, "The job is not for you. And it never will be."

We as citizens need to awaken to the fact that South Africa's politics have long shifted from ideological issues, those who wish to convince you otherwise simply want to maintain the status quo. We have been told that it is inevitable that President Zuma will preside over the ANC until 2017 and run the country until 2019 and we accept it as if it were ordained as such. Have we forgotten that a political revolution is possible by simply voting in the best interests of the nation and not along party or patronage lines come 2014?

What will it take for **ALL** of us to stand up and voice our utter disgust at the current state of affairs where our nation (a nation that has been used as a case study at the Kennedy School of Government at Harvard University on how to successfully carry out political transition) is viewed as one suffering from chronic failures of judgment, bereft of intellectual substance and losing sharpness on crucial policy issues. Julius Malema, service delivery protests (a term that has now become entrenched in the lexicon of the average South African), mining strikes which culminated with Marikana, the ratings agency downgrades, the R 5 billion SAA bailout, Nkandlagate and severe inequality evidenced by general social disunity are all symptoms of a greater cancer. A cancer which if left unattended will become malignant and eventually annihilate our country as we know it, leaving it a shell of its former self.

The days ahead look terribly bleak unless South African's once again can find their voice and rise up together with that united voice and say enough is enough. No political party will be able to get the message across as poignantly as a *"Gatvol"* population. Events in Syria and the rest of the Arab World should not be dismissed as freak occurrences that can never be repeated elsewhere, but they should be looked at as lessons of how a leadership that is addicted to attaining, maintaining and consolidating power can in a very short space of time utterly devastate what were once relatively prosperous nations. The emperor isn't wearing any clothes but no one seems ready to call him naked. Let me be the first.

With Apologies to Paul whom I tried to locate, as I responded to his letter in the media . . . .

Email to My ex South African friend in Aussie

25 October 2012   *Paul*

Hi Jeff, Hope all is well with you guys. I will drop you a line later with the family news but I would first like to respond to the email you sent me attaching an article by Clem Sunter which seemed to concern you about us here in South Africa.

You also sent me an article last year by Moletsi Mbeki warning about the danger of an "Arab Spring" in South Africa. I often get emails like this from "concerned friends" worried about us which is sweet of you guys. Of course we are concerned. Some worrying things have happened but we have been through and survived much worse in much more volatile environments. Including the Boer War, two World Wars, Apartheid, the Rindapest, Ge Korsten and Die Antwoord!

However for as long as I can remember there have always been people who think SA has 5 years left before we go over the cliff. No change from when I was at school in the sixties. The 5 years went down to a few months at times in the eighties! But it seems the people who are the most worried live far from the cliff in places like Toronto, Auckland, London and other wet and cold places. Also from

St Ives and Rose Bay in Sydney, Dallas and Europe and other "safe places" that are in the grips of the Global Financial Crisis, which by the way is quite scary. Many of them have survived decades of rolling "5 years left" since they left South Africa. So maybe they will be right one day!

My message is, please don't stress about us in South Africa. We are fine. We are cool. We know we live in the most beautiful country in the world inhabited by the warm and vibrant people. There are more people here with smiles on their faces than any country I have ever been to! Young people are returning in droves with skills and a positive attitude. Collectively we bumble along and stuff many things up while letting off a hell of a lot of steam (have you heard of a chap called Julius Malema?). Yet in between South Africans do some amazing things like win a few gold medals, big golf tournaments and cricket and rugby matches. The South Africans I know get off their butts and do things to build our country rather than whinge from a position of comfort. We actively participate in projects that improve the lot of underprivileged communities. I would not trade for anything last Saturday in a hall full of 1500 African teachers singing at the top of their voices and demonstrating their commitment to improving education in their communities.

We have our challenges and surprises. The standard deviation of our emotions are set at MAX. You are never just a "little bit happy" or a "little bit sad". At one moment you can be "off the scale" pissed off or frustrated or sad or worried or fearful or depressed. The next moment you're "off the scale" exhilarated, or enchanted, or inspired, or humbled by a kind deed, or surprised by something beautiful. It makes life interesting and worth living. After all why do we have emotions?

We also have passionate debates about the future of SA, helped of course by red wine which you must taste again because it is getting better every year! Clem makes a great contribution to the debate as do others like Moletsi Mbeki. Russell Loubser the ex-head of the JSE made a feisty speech the other day that has whipped up emotions. Up to MAX on the emotions meter of the ANC Youth League whose campaign for nationalisation of the mines was attributed to people who have IQ' s equal to room temperature. South African politics has always been volatile, we have opinions that could not be further apart and it evokes emotion on a massive scale. Interesting and stimulating for those that want to take it seriously but noise in the system to me.

Fortunately we are rid of Apartheid that would definitely have pushed us over the cliff. These are the birth pangs of a new and unpredictable democracy. So buckle up and enjoy the ride and contribute! That is the message I convey to South Africans.

Sad as it is, it is true that the South African Diaspora has a largely negative influence on confidence in South Africa. It would not be a problem if their fretting about how long we will last before we go over the cliff was merely a reflection of their concern for us, their friends and family. The problem is that it does impact foreign investment which is important for economic growth. A person that is thinking of coming to visit or investing is often put off by listening wide eyed at the stories of people who have gapped it. As you know I own Ellerman House that hosts many foreign visitors and I have never, EVER, met anyone who has visited for the first time without being blown away by the beauty of the country and the warmth of the people. It is not for nothing that South Africa has the highest ratio of repeat visitors of all long haul destinations.

So, Jeff, how can I help you stop stressing out about us? Maybe best is that you get exposed to some articles and web sites that give a more balanced and uplifting perspective of South Africa. I have attached some links below that you may find interesting. The two websites are SA The Good News and The Homecoming Revolution, both have stories that will make you feel better. The article is by a young Jewish lady Martine Schaffer that I work with and admire greatly.

I will sum up my feelings about South Africa with a quote from Joanne Fedler's book *When Hungry—Eat* that Martine also quotes. Joanne emigrated to Australia in early 2000. "South Africa is a place of spirit-distorting paradox, a land with a bipolar disorder that swings you from joy to despair in the space of a heartbeat. It twists your arm behind your back and ties your sanity in a knot. It bullies you until you've forged your opinion on politics, crime, AIDS, the state of the roads, the economy or the politicians. It's not for the wishy washy or the fence sitters. It demands you know who you are and what you stand for. It keeps you fit, on your toes and looking over your shoulder. It steals your purse and holds your soul ransom. As much as I was, at times, on the edge of sanity living there, I was also stimulated, driven and felt bungy-jumpingly alive. The shades of happiness and fear mottled. I knew that leaving, like chemotherapy, would kill off the best things in my life as well as the worst."

So please don't worry and if you get a chance put in a good word for us. All the best.
http://www.homecomingrevolution.co.za/blog/

My Spontaneous Response *Eve Hemming*

26 October 2012

Hello to Paul. I would love to see Jeff's response please.

I live in Auckland, where I have resided for the past 4 plus years. I can assure you that almost every 'Saffa' that ever left SA holds her very close to their hearts; possibly with the exception of those (some whom I know), who left when their fathers, mothers, siblings or children were murdered or violated . . .

I'm in the process of writing a book and the gaping paradox unfolds—the folk back home and the migratory population. One cannot really see things from the migrants' perspective unless one, too, has walked their brave, tough and amazing journey. It is the most profound and courageous thing I have ever done; to leave so much that I revered; my life, treasured family members who opted to stay, my footprints, my entire infrastructure and roots ripped from my gut.

It is a hard road. It takes time and immense strength to fully immerse oneself in a new life as a mature *tabular rasa* being, with a new slate to the alien world. It is the crossing of the metaphorical Rubicon . . . and the sense of liberation is astounding, as is the sense of loss acute. It encompasses a far wider spectrum of emotions than one could ever start to imagine; the highs and the lows are way more poignant than I ever experienced at home. In the latter years (in SA) all the colours and the joy were muted and subdued by a growing awareness of so many tragic scenarios. And before anyone makes a judgement call; I left SA at the age of 58, having worked at the coal face, uplifting disabled, disadvantaged and underprivileged people my entire life, and was passionate about *ubunthu*. And believe it or not, people out of Africa also go around cleaning wounds, helping beggars and orphans . . . we do not walk away from our passion for humanity. We do not turn our back on life. We merely seek a place where we hope our children's offspring will have more opportunities and will live to tell the tale.

It astounds me that every South African seems to live contentedly until a member of their family becomes a statistic. Even if it's the neighbour that becomes a statistic in a body bag, it does not seem close enough to deter the delirium of those in Africa; joyful under its balmy warmth and its wild beauty . . .

None of us can predict when the 5 years truly does become 5 years and if it ever will. But the farmers in Zimbabwe suffered to the extreme and their time did finally run out. None of us has a crystal ball. It is up to each individual to stay or leave, care and share. It really is as simple as that. And the stayers can't really point fingers at the goers nor visa verse. As none of us are walking in the others' shoes. Namaste. Eve
http://www.homecomingrevolution.co.za/blog

Book Reviews & Excerpts

Cry, The Beloved Country   *Alan Paton, 1948*

"There is a lovely road that runs from Ixopo into the hills. These hills are grass-covered and rolling, and they are lovely beyond any singing of it. The road climbs seven miles into them, to Carisbrooke; and from there, if there is no mist, you look down on one of the fairest valleys of Africa . . ."

Thus commences Alan Paton's book, which was published in New York in 1948. It enjoyed success worldwide, but was banned in South Africa. (Interestingly enough, the copy which I have—now yellowed with the binding torn, was a gift to my mother in South Africa, and is dated 1948.) The separatist National Party came into power four months after the book was published. Paton's book was a social objection against the culturally defined South African society, which was on the verge of the birth of apartheid. Paton illustrates how the system in South Africa creates suffering for all cultures; he alludes to the Europeans suffering due to the criminal activities of the Africans, and the Africans suffering due to the disintegration of their tribal structures, leading to the decay of their moral fibre. Fear becomes an underlying theme . . .

"Cry, the beloved country, for the unborn child that is the inheritor of our fear. Let him not love the earth too deeply. Let him not laugh too gladly when the water runs through his fingers, nor stand too silent when the setting sun makes red the *veld* with fire. Let him not be too moved when the birds of his land are singing, nor give too much of his heart to a mountain or a valley. For fear will rob him of all if he gives too much."

Ironically fear remains a predominant argument and topic in the current South African society some sixty five years later. Paton's concluding paragraph reflects his unfaltering vision of emancipation for all South Africans.

"For it is the dawn that has come, as it has come for a thousand centuries, never failing. But when the dawn will come, of our emancipation, from the fear of bondage and the bondage of fear, why that is the secret."

Long Walk to Freedom   *Nelson Mandela, 1994*

"Apart from life, a strong constitution, and an abiding connection to the Trembu royal house, the only thing my father bestowed upon me at birth was a name, Rolihlahla. In Xhosa, Rolihlahla literally means 'pulling the branch of a tree', but its colloquial meaning more accurately would be 'troublemaker.' I do not believe that names are destiny or that my father somehow divined my future, but in later years, friends and relatives would ascribe to my birth name the many storms I have both caused and weathered . . . ." This is the opening paragraph of Mandela's autobiography in which he shares this epic journey in search of political freedom from the oppression of apartheid for the African people of South Africa.

This great political leader, born on 18th July 1918, now in the winter of his life, has lead an extraordinary life; from political activist and prisoner to an international hero, winner of The Nobel Peace Prize and after his victorious release in 1990, after twenty seven years in prison, became the President of South Africa. Mandela was head of the African National Congress and head of the anti-apartheid movement. Mandela, fondly called 'Madiba' has been the focal point of a gripping saga, being instrumental in shifting South Africa towards a multicultural government, majority rule and the same emancipation alluded to by Alan Paton in 1948. Madiba is highly respected for being instrumental in his fight for equality and human rights, for his victory of optimism above desperation and bitterness. Mandela epitomises forgiveness and that faith can combat evil. He is also seen as a controversial figure by people who refer to him as a 'terrorist'.

He concludes his book, "I have walked that long road to freedom. I have tried not to falter; I have made missteps, along the way. But I have discovered the secret that after climbing a great hill, one only finds that there are many more hills to climb. I have taken a moment here to rest, to steal a view of the glorious vista that surrounds me, to look back on the distance I have come. But I can rest only for a moment, for that freedom comes responsibilities, and I dare not linger, for my walk is not yet ended."

'As I walked out the door toward my freedom I knew that if I did not leave all the anger, hatred and bitterness behind that I would still be in prison.' Quote—Nelson Mandela on his release from prison after 27 years.

Andre' Brink on Country Of My Skull
by Antjie Krog, 1998

Andre' Brink believes that it would be futile to try and understand the New South Africa without the Truth and Reconciliation Commission. He adds that it would be irresponsible to attempt to understand the Commission without reading *Country of my Skull*. It is a book every person seeking answers thus needs to read.

It is a non-fiction book based on the findings of the South African *Truth and Reconciliation Commission* (TRC). It is primarily an analysis of the Commission's potential and its effects on *Post-Apartheid South Africa*.

The book includes a collection of accounts from the TRC hearings, with testimonies of the appalling human rights violations, as a result of the struggle against Apartheid. Furthermore, the book explores and analyses the political and moral philosophy established by the TRC.

Krog analytically reflects on and analyses her own life as a white Afrikaner radio journalist who finds herself grappling with her country's violent past and how covering the TRC impacted her personal life.

Poems—Farewells, Migration, Memories—

Poetry is a deal of joy and pain and wonder, with a dash of the dictionary.

Kahlil Gibran

Poetry & Prose

Let us depart! *Robert Southey*

Let us depart! the universal sun
Confines not to one land his blessed beams;
Nor is man rooted, like a tree, whose seed,
the winds on some ungenial soil have cast there,
where it cannot prosper.

Africa *Eve Hemming*

Africa—the wild continent . . .
The wild place that runs free in the wind;
Won't permit shackles. A law unto itself.
Don't put me in a tight lidded box.
Let me fly!
Free me from any preconceived ideas or man-made visions, clocks, ideologies.
Don't smother me with your audacity.
Don't plunder my inner guts or my outer rampant growth with your greed.
Let my vines sprawl

Irreligiously and sacrilegiously—to smother your order.
Let my roots fight oppressive tarmac!
Let the underbelly of my growth be free to sprawl in thirsty, greedy, fecund profusion.
Let my creatures roam in statuesque splendour free from barbaric men with guns.
Let my rocky outcrops, my dust, majestic storms, my red soul be unleashed . . .
Let my aridity and heat and antiquity bask, unfettered.
No one owns Africa. It belongs to no one.
Let it be what it is.

To Me   *Carol Blignaut April 2012*

When the world is our Oyster
Give thanks, Take it, and embrace it as our own.
Never to grieve for the land left behind,
As it is not behind, but within
This glorious world that is ours.
With love, Carol

For An Exile

When we feel ourselves in exile, longing for our homeland, living in a place where no one seems to truly know us, it may be difficult at times to imagine this ever being otherwise. And yet as we awaken, new tendrils of life begin to reach out, searching the landscape for those who are emerging from their own cocoon, those whose metamorphosis leaves them glowing with the colors of indigo, violet, fuchsia, and gold, matching our own soul embers.

Poet, philosopher, theologian, and teacher John O'Donohue wrote of this process in his "blessing," "For an Exile." *To Bless This Space Between Us.*

May the eyes of your heart open, "to see and celebrate the new life, for which you sacrificed everything."

For An Exile
John O'Donohue (1956–2008)

When you dream, it is always home.
You are there among your own,
The rhythm of their voices rising like song
Your blood would sing through any dark.

Then you awake to find yourself listening
To the sounds of traffic in another land.
For a moment your whole body recoils
At the strange emptiness of where you are.

This country is cold to your voice.
It is still a place without echoes.
Nothing of yours has happened here.

No one knows you,
The language slows you,
The thick accent smothers your presence.

You sound foreign to yourself;
Their eyes reflect how strange you seem
When seen across a cold distance
That has no bridge to carry
The charisma in which your friends
Delight at home.

Though your work here is hard,
It brings relief, helps your mind
In returning to the small
Bounties of your absence.

Evening is without protection;
Your room waits,
Ready to take you
Back like some convict
Who is afraid
Of the life outside.

The things you brought from home
Look back at you; out of place here
They take on lonely power.

You cringe at the thought
That someone from home
Might see you now here,
In this unsheltered room.
Now is the time to hold faithful
To your dream, to understand
That this is an interim time
Full of awkward disconnection.

Gradually you will come to find
Your way to friends who will open
Doors into a new belonging.

Your heart will brighten
With new discovery,
Your presence will unclench
And find ease,
Letting your substance
And promise be seen.

Slowly, a new world will open for you.
The eyes of your heart, refined
By this desert time, will be free
To see and celebrate the new life
For which you sacrificed everything.

I said goodbye to my daughter today   *Janine Egan*

I said goodbye to my daughter today.
Whilst my head celebrates my heart,
heavily draped in lead, has descended
to the soles of my feet—
And every step I take, each heavy tread
bruises and tears that broken heart.
Ah, the sacrifice of love cannot be

more defined than this . . .
To love enough to let go is surely
to love too much?

I said goodbye to my daughter today.
My misery is the reward of my own success—
my shameless cajoling, my relentless urging.
Be brave, be safe, be free—
the blame for that inculcated mantra
lies with me.
Mea culpa, I am the author of
this rheumy tale, and a well of sadness
is the price.

I said goodbye to my daughter today.
Unconditional love matched by
uncompromised trust has led to this.
No more will I be the first call
of comfort and nurture;
my tenure has come to an end.
The time to give wings has just begun,
be brave, be safe, be free . . .
"Go", I said . . .
And now she's gone.

I say goodbye and do my best not to cry *Lynette James*

Walk straight ahead and get on the jet, that will take me to place I have not seen yet.
Dare not turn around or make a sound, but leave my heart on your dear, dear, ground ~ oh Africa.
How can it be, that this fate has come upon me, that this dear land I now must flee?

The past of forefathers I did not know, has made it such that I now must go.
Why oh why is it now an eye for an eye?
Sins of the fathers be not mine.
Forgiveness, please . . . . it is about time.
Let's join together and ride the weather. Oh Africa . . .
My beloved land . . . I extend my hand.

Just a little heartfelt poem. I am very homesick today. Lynette James

Africa—Now that I'm Gone . . .   *Eve Hemming*

I used to think of you in
Aching bold colours –
Red, vermilion and magenta
Cutting into my heart with a
Sharp purple violet void.

Now I think of you
In softer hues;
Stone washed blue and indigo, blended
With warming ochre's, gold's and greens.

They sneak in to
Remind me.

This Drug Called Africa   *Dave Farrell*

Its hallucination of promise
And highs of falsehood

Violence and corruption a side effect
Death its inevitable outcome

Sickness contaminating
Forlorn hopes of change

Withdrawals racking our very being
Cold sweats repelling foreign body

Rendering immunity defunct
Inviting infection without cure

Futures seen through blooded eyes
Self-infliction the scourge

Self pity the result
Self help the answer

This drug called Africa.

My tears I cry for Africa

Rene' Turner

Years gone by, my memories abide.
A beautiful land, my forefathers pride,
Beauty and splendor, with a spirit unique,
Lush river valleys through passes and creeks,

Mountain escarpments, winelands and game,
The big five itself, the pride of our land,
I hear the cries, that cold, dreaded sound.
Where is the joy that once was found?

How sad it is, what change has brought.
Can peace be found, among this wrought?
My heart cries out in pain and fears . . .
for what might be . . . I shed my tears.

Man destroys and kills the sights,
that once was built for every life
How sad it is to view this now,
peace before, with love I vow.

My heart cries out, Lord heal my land.
Protect it from the sinners' hand.
Has evil come to claim with scorn?
Lord spare my herd, and safe from harm.

If change could come and peace could be,
Lord will I see, my land set free?
But by your grace Oh mighty God,
please heal my land, South Africa.

New Beginnings   *Dave Farrell*

The black ocean surges in the darkness
Crashing her waves upon the land
Hissing in retreat only to gather again
The skies a myriad of sparkling eyes gaze downward
Bemused by the anger of her age old sister
The old man, retired before the breaking of dawn
Cold air biting the soft flesh of my face

The lifeless beachfront whistles a sorrowful tune
All have taken refuge from the winter night
Trance like I watch and wait in anticipation
For what I cannot tell
Perhaps for life's next move
Surreal suspended animation prevails

The sky wakens and the ocean illuminates
Heavenly light appearing from everywhere
Colours replacing monochrome voids
Sparkling blues and greens with dancing white horses
Tranquillity subdues the turmoil

The lure of hope for the new day
She washes all remnants of days past
Along with the footprints of my very existence
The mist from her breathe settles on my lips
As a soft salty kiss

She grooms herself before the deluge of impending humanity
The excess of modernization degrading her timeless beauty
Commercialism mocking her integrity
Neon her new garish jewellery

No wish to witness the onslaught
I turn away
Replacing her comforting smell
With the stench of burning fossil fuel
Consumed by the very teeming masses I wish to avoid.

Africa Smiled   *Bridget Dore*

Africa smiled
A little
When you left.
"We know you,"
Africa said,
"We have seen
And watched you,
We can learn
To live
Without you,

But
We know
We needn't
Yet."

And Africa smiled
A little
When you left.
"You cannot
Leave Africa,"
Africa said.
"It is always with you,
There inside your head.
Our rivers run
In currents
In the swirl
Of your thumbprints;
Our drumbeats
Counting out your pulse,
Our coastline,
The silhouette of your soul."

SCATTERLINGS—A TAPESTRY OF AFRI-EXPAT TALES

So Africa smiled
A little
When you left.
"We are in you,"
Africa said.
"You have not
Left us,
Yet."

Love Poem—Kaaapse Style

Clementine, oh, sous of mine,
Ek smaak you stukkend, say you'll combine.
You're my morning, my sunshine, my moon and my stars,
You're my air freshener from the OK Bazaars;
You're my beaded love-letter, my breeze in the night,
You're my coffee, my Cremora, my Blitz firelight.
You're my Crime-Stop, my Tracker, you're my AZT,
My pap, Mrs. Ball's chutney, my Nando's for free.
You're my lambchop, my dewdrop, my partner in crime,
My chillie, my pepper, my vetkoek sublime.

The list is just endless and this isn't all,
You're my Lotto jackpot, my dop and my zol.
You're my 4X4 when the road is so hilly,
You're the Floro margarine that butters my mielie,
I smaak you, my poppie, so please be my wife,
'cause, Babe, you're the Tomato Sauce on the slap chips of life
Author Unknown

South African all-time favourite Traditional Recipes and Memories

A chapter on traditional and favourite South African recipes has been incorporated, as once a migrant, I became aware of how much South Africans talk about food and recipes and that it's a pivotal part of one's culture which one takes with one to one's new land.

It got me thinking of how many Southern African immigrants I'd met who bewailed the fact that they had gained several kilograms after emigrating. It heightened my awareness of how food is so central to one's culture and that we also eat as an emotional form of comfort. The combination leads to Saffas cooking up the proverbial storm with their *potjies, braais, bobotie, biltong* making, *koeksusters* and *vetkoek*—all traditional fattening comfort foods!

I asked Saffas to supply their trusted, loved and favourite handed down recipes for you to enjoy. Some are metric and some are Imperial measures just the way they were, to add to the nostalgia of old handed down favourites from yellowed food stained recipe books from *ouma* (grandma). Thank you to all the contributors. I wish you all hours of pleasurable cooking, baking and eating everyone. *Geniet*! (Enjoy).

Packing tea cups
Eve Hemming

When we moved home in NZ after two years, I hauled out a disused New Zealand Herald and wrapped a tea-cup in a page—not any old teacup, but a French designer Longchamp cup in a caramel cream whirly design reminiscent of the late 60's; part of the dinner

416

service wedding gift from years ago. They came from Nagels, (in Pietermaritzburg, SA), which later became The Hub.

I started crying when Ant said—"I wonder how many times you've wrapped that cup." And I counted twelve times—my entire married life flooding through my mind; extracted from the spider-web swamped labyrinths. I cried, not only because forty years had erroneously slipped through my fingers like water escaping from a running tap; not just because I felt that they were lost, irretrievable years to return to and reconstruct, but also because the tea cup's future remained unconvincingly tenuous.

The first time the tea cup was wrapped was to move from our first home—a modest *rondavel* (circular thatched abode with a conical roof), decorated with bath towel curtains, where we'd animatedly ripped open our wedding gifts. I was nineteen. The tea cup remained unused. There was no place for guests to drink tea in a bohemian dwelling with no table. A later wrapping was due to relocating from a one to a two-bed roomed flat, when our first baby joined our family ranks. The tea cup remained unused. There was no time for special occasion tea parties when life revolved around feeds, sleepless nights and nappy changes.

The tea cup and its set came out of the confines of the cupboard and into functional use in our various homes in KZN—including bastardised Victoriana, a rambling Midlands Meander country thatch, (where we ran a Sunday meander restaurant, with roast lamb cooked with tomato, onion, garlic, rosemary and feta cheese, and Eric Clapton CDs setting the tone) suburban modernistic, a converted post office in Winterskloof, and an original wattle and daub clad home with a kitchen burner and ball and claw footed bath. Mostly interesting homes with impressive views. Places to drink tea under the African sun. Meaningful moments. Moments that became those years I cried about last night.

Thereafter the teacup went bubble wrapped in a box in an outsized container. It must have sweated in its wrapping in the dark bowels across the ocean, first docking at Port Louis, followed by Sydney before arriving at Auckland harbour. We traced the tea cup and all our worldly possessions on the Internet from our empty home in Auckland. We even went to the harbour and gazed at a thousand containers, where omnipotent cranes bent their heads on a Sunday.

Joyfully its destination was reached. The container was unpacked and a trillion boxes delivered to our doorstep by NZ Van Lines, where some amiable Jonah Lomu type blokes with tattoo festooned muscles, carried our furniture and the boxes, including my tea cup, in. I joyfully opened the box and the bubble wrap contents to find my symbolic cup, which by then was running over.

And last night I wrapped it again—this time to move to a cosier rental home a kilometre away as the NZ duck flies. But why so sad on this momentous journey to yet another characterful home—this one an authentic Kiwi wooden multi-levelled home, where my cup will once more be unwrapped?

The sadness this evoked is for all the lost moments I didn't sufficiently or abundantly embrace—the teas I sipped unfocused, the company I kept maybe insincerely, the people my life, paved with good intentions, meant to, but didn't invite to sip tea before emigrating from Africa.

More poignantly the sadness was for the terrible loss of family teas, (with grandchildren spilling from their tumblers, and teddy bear's picnics . . .) . . . evaporated into this vacuum created by distance.

My mother was a staunch fan of the institution of tea drinkers. I also missed her because the association I have of tea has motherliness about it. I miss not being that type of mother, because I was always 'too busy' being the perennial student and full-on professional career woman. Mothers should find the time to sip tea with anyone old, sad, ill or lonely.

And musing about who can come over and sip tea from the Longchamp cup one fine Auckland day. *First Published in 2010—The Witness*

Food and supermarkets make for memories of South Africa!

Food, glorious food . . . .
25 January 2012   *Anne Morkel, Toronto, Canada*
                                  Blog: *morkels.wordpress.com*

It had been a rough day, the icy wind had been blowing, the ironing was piled up in the laundry and the job hunting escapade had not been fruitful. How do I comfort myself in times like this? I reach for the FOOD . . . . But not just any food, it has to be food that conjures up the comfort of the familiar.

My familiar foods have passed the test of time and have been savoured without boredom coming into play. Now we all know that the concept of time is relative to one's age. So if I had the urge to comfort myself with a familiar food that had passed the relevant criteria, it would have to hail from South Africa! The comfort of Ouma rusks with a cup of hot tea after a long day of teaching or a packet of salty chips as a meal in a bag when time is of the essence. My mouth just watered at the mere thought of these simple comfort foods.

That was it, I had to satisfy my stomach and calm my jaded being. I reversed out of the garage and chased down the road to my wonderful find of 2 weeks prior . . . the South African shop. There was no sighing as I pushed this trolley and the memories of trying to do this 'job' as fast as I could were in the distant folds of my cortex. I pushed my tiny trolley around the isles and drank in all things familiar . . . boerewors, rusks, Oros juice and Romany Creams to name a few. The cheerful shopkeeper rang up my goods and as I handed over my dollars I thought about how important it is to keep things constant when one is dealing with change. If it means a 10 kilometer drive for a bottle of mayonnaise and a packet of biltong, so be it. We all cope in different ways and for us as a family, our South African foods and treats put a spring in our step when the going gets tough.

My Grandmother came to Africa, and I leave . . . but we chat over soup   *Karen de Villiers, London, UK*

We are waiting for the snow to fall. Every Saturday morning I go to the Organic Farmer's market to get my celery. The only bunches still with leaves on for my Ouma's soup. It is imperative to use the leaves, without them, it would not taste like history. Also like to buy organic meat, English cider, pears and the first, baby born Daffodils.

I know the heat from the apartment will coax them open. The park is still silver with frost and I can hear the geese discussing the coming snow—they know, the lake is frozen in places. Time for soup. I make soup. I make time to make soup. It is my therapy. And today I just needed to feel my *Ouma* and my mother close. We are connected by our Dutch vegetable soup.

Back in my Ouma's house in winter, I could smell the celery fumes rising up from the bubbling liquid. Watching her carefully grate the potatoes, the onions, the carrots. Scooping with huge hands the colours from the cutting board to add to the pot before boiling the Rookwurst which would go in last. Hollandse kos, while she poured more tea and told me about her arrival in South Africa as a young bride, one suitcase,

419

to spend her life with a man she barely knew and never to see her mother again. Back then I did not really understand, only remember feeling so safe in that kitchen, her peppering the sentences with Dutch words and wiping her hands on her apron. My mum chatted back, taking over without being asked—telling me how my *Oupa* cycled from Kroonstad to Lindley every week for work, returning home for two days on the weekend. When he did there would be soup and Mocha cake, his favourites.

When my Ouma died, my childhood home smelt of celery in the winter time. Men would watch rugby by the fire while we chatted in the kitchen, repeating the ritual without recipe or thought. Mom and Dad had no intention of going anywhere, still living in the same town they were born in, but mom would still chat in Dutch sometimes, just to keep it up.

And now I make our Dutch vegetable soup. It is my time to chat to Ouma in my head—to think about how I really understand what it must have been like now. Now that I have left the land of my birth, my roots to start a new life. Will I settle? Will I have the choice to return which she did not?

But when things are so different, when what you knew and what you planned are nothing to what you are now, food is a fond memory. I think she made her soup to calm her down and take her back. My mum did the same and now here I am, carrying on the tradition.

Just before dark, we walked in this bitter cold to the small South African shop in Southfields. Choose the chips, the biltong, the sweetie marshmallow mice. There is rugby on. Snuck in the Tex, the Tempo and the Romany creams. The men will watch while I chat to *Ouma* and mom, making our soup in the kitchen. Miss you my special ladies.

The Funky Table *Eve Hemming*

I'm in the supermarket aisle to grab a few of those basic necessities of life. Music emanates from somewhere near the ceiling that's reminiscent of 'home' which makes my eyes sting . . .

A combo of music and supermarkets just gets me going and tends to bring those inner floodgates close to the surface. I bite my lip and feel a hardness in my breath.

Food is part of the institution of the soul. The body's fuel. The hearth of the family. Supermarketing is associated with fine family fare and celebratory or sometimes maudlin gatherings. And the table becomes the epicentre of all these happenings . . . Ours was called 'The Funky Table'—I'd purchased it in 1993 in a second hand furniture shop in what was then called Commercial Road. I could swear it had been a prison table—long, narrow, a morbid dead grey, with a few rough antediluvian nails dangerously protruding and a foot rest worn down by many shoes rubbing against it. Basically it was bloody buggered. I proudly got it delivered to our home, much to everyone's disgust. 'Lunatic mum' my kids probably thought.

We acquired custom made benches to use at the table, comfortably seating 14. The next 15 years we shared meals and functions at Funky, with a rich, diverse selection of family and friends around our now cheerful green Funky Table in a spacious sunflower yellow rag-painted Funky Room. We celebrated significant birthdays, a wedding luncheon, my Mum's funeral tea, a couple of hens' parties and baby showers, my 50th birthday dinner and various grand-kiddie's parties, plus their messy painting, playdough and baking activities. Some sort of esoteric chats were also held at the green table and creative fabric painting and decoupage workshops, plus 'swot-ins' when several of us in the family were studying.

The funky table moved with us from home to home, always the heart of the family. In our last home in South Africa it resided on the veranda, as it was too long to fit inside. It became worn, weathered, sanded down and repainted. It was adorned with hand painted fabrics, candles and glass jars bulging with hydrangeas. And many Christmas's were spent at the Funky Table, when it would be decorated with Christmas crackers, tinsel, silvered pine cones and St Joseph lilies. Add hefty food platters and old funky would creak and groan.

I often wondered where Funky had been before. I tried to visualise a gang of inmates seated round it in prison clothes, scoffing down fat slices of bread dunked into steaming broth with large gnarled hands. I suppose I was biased believing that Funky felt more contented being a jovial green, standing on our veranda, where my grandchildren played hide and seek under the table, sliding along its foot rest.

It was serendipitously a family conversation at Funky which triggered my decision to apply to work in New Zealand. We also had a last symbolic family candlelight supper at Funky; a big moon watching this unfolding. We've been residing here for the past two and a half years. Funky was bequeathed to our older son and his wife when we left SA. And when we return for holidays, we generally celebrate with a lekker *Braai* around Funky, next to their pool.

Here in Auckland, we miss what Funky emblemised for us. But, hey, we still have family and friends around in our home, but Funky's absence leaves a conspicuous gap, along with old mates and home nosh. Here Maoris traditionally have a *Hangi* (food, which is called *Kai*, cooked in an earth oven). And I still plan to master the art!

We entertain our Asian, British, Aussie and Kiwi colleagues and neighbours, combined with 'Saffa' family and friends. Food includes tasty local boerewors and biltong, my home cooked *Bobotie,* and of course Mrs Ball's chutney, combined with sushi, Chinese, Indian, Malaysian, Korean, Indonesian, European and 'Kiwiana' foods. Adapting has made life exciting and interesting . . .

But my eyes still sting when I'm trolley-pushing to purchase items for a function, knowing there's no Funky Table to share meals at with mates and family back in 'Good old *Maritzburgh*'. Especially when Johnny Clegg's *'Scatterlings of Africa'* wafts down the supermarket aisles. 'Well JA no fine', (or as the Kiwis say, 'Sweet As') . . . then I'm allowed to have a teeny snivel.

First published in The Witness

Soups and Starters

Butternut Soup   *Supplied by Jeanne Herringer*

3 Large onions—sliced
3 Potatoes—cubed
1kg Butternut Squash
1L Chicken stock (can use Vegetable stock)
1 tsp. Cumin
1 tsp. Cinnamon powder
2 Tablespoons margarine
Black pepper

Sauté onions in 2 Tablespoons margarine. Add potatoes and butternut. Add 1 litre stock. Add 1 tsp. Cumin and 1 tsp. Cinnamon powder. Cook till soft. Liquidise. Serve by adding a swirl of cream (optional).

(This soup freezes well).

Home-Made Cape Fish Soup

4 cups (1 litre) water
Head and bones of one fish
1 bay leaf
5 peppercorns
2 t (10 ml) salt
2 T (30 ml) butter
2 medium onions, chopped
1 t (5 ml) curry powder (medium or strong, defending on preference)
2 t (10 ml) turmeric
2 T (30 ml) flour
2 t (10 ml) sugar
2 carrots grated
2 ripe tomatoes, skinned and chopped
250g cubed fish
1 T (15 ml) lemon juice
2 T (30 ml) cream
2 cups (500 ml) cooked rice
¼ cup (62, 5 ml) parsley, chopped

Boil the fish head and bones in the water with the bay leaf, peppercorns and salt for 20 minutes. Strain and discard the bones. Sauté the onion in the butter. Turn the heat down. Add the curry and turmeric and fry lightly to develop flavour. Add the flour and sugar, carrots, tomatoes and fish liquid.

Add the cubed fish then simmer slowly for 20 minutes. Add the lemon juice and the cream. Taste and adjust the seasoning. Dish 4 spoonful's of cooked rice into each soup bowl. Ladle the soup over and add the parsley. Enjoy an economical meal-n-one!

Zimbabwean Chicken and Vegetable Soup

Ingredients
1 tablespoon olive oil
1 onion, diced
4 cups vegetable stock, divided
1/2 cup peanut butter
2 cups canned diced tomatoes, with juices

1/4 teaspoon crushed red pepper flakes, or more to taste
1 cup finely chopped cabbage
1 cup chopped sweet potato
1 cup peeled and chopped carrot
1 cup peeled and chopped turnip
1 cup chopped okra
1 cup chopped cooked chicken, or to taste

Method

Heat the olive oil over medium heat in a large soup pot; cook and stir the onion in the hot oil until translucent, about 5 minutes. Whisk 1/2 cup of vegetable stock and the peanut butter into the onions until the mixture is smooth. Beat in remaining vegetable stock, diced tomatoes with their liquid, and crushed red pepper flakes; bring to a boil, reduce heat to medium low, and cook at a simmer for 30 minutes, stirring occasionally.

Stir in the cabbage, sweet potato, carrot, and turnip; simmer, stirring occasionally, until the vegetables are tender, about 30 more minutes. Stir in the okra and chicken and simmer until the okra is tender, about 30 additional minutes.

Chicken Liver Pate'

250 g Chicken Livers
60 ml chicken stock
2 large onions, sliced
Salt to taste
60 ml Brandy or Sherry
30 ml chopped parsley
Pinch of sugar
Pinch of mustard powder
1 ml mixed herbs

Fry sliced onions in a little butter until transparent. Add chicken livers, chopped parsley and bay leaves, pepper, salt and sugar, mixed herbs and stock. Simmer for ten minutes. Add Brandy/sherry and pour into containers. Garnish with bay leaves. Pour clarified butter over the top.

Snoek Pate' *Supplied by Suzanne du Toit*

1 Kg Smoked Snoek (remove bones & flake)
150 g margarine
250 ml beaten cream
Black pepper
300 ml dry white wine
Grated rind & juice of 1 lemon
Dash of vodka

Mix *snoek*, wine and butter in a blender to a paste. Add a little of each of the other ingredients at a time. Fold in cream. Chill well. This freezes well. Defrost in fridge for 6 hours.

Fish Dishes

Pickled Fish *Supplied by Sheena Hayes*

3 lbs. fish fillets
2 large onions
2 cups vinegar
2 cups water
3 T sugar
2 T curry powder
2-4 T cornflour
1/2 tsp. salt
1/4 tsp. pepper bay leaves and peppercorns

Fry fish (remove skin and bones) put aside. Slice onions into rings.
Add vinegar and simmer. Thicken vinegar with cornflour and curry powder.
(Mix with water). Add sugar and 2nd seasoning.
Cook until thick and onions soft. Pour over fish.

Haddock Kedgeree

750g Haddock
2 Rashers Bacon
125 g Butter

15ml Chopped Parsley
1 Hard Boiled Egg
60g Mushrooms
45ml Uncooked Rice
Salt and Pepper
190ml Milk

Boil haddock and remove water. Boil rice. Peel and chop the hardboiled egg. Flake fish and put into casserole dish. Add all the ingredients except the rice. Bake in a hot oven. Add the cooked rice and blend in with a fork.

Tuna Pie   *Supplied by Theresa Van Der Merwe*

2 Tins tuna
1 tin condensed mushroom soup
1 large packet salt and vinegar chips
Onion chopped

Crush chips, mix all other ingredients together in a bowl, fill tin of soup with milk and mix together with the rest, place in an oven proof dish, sprinkle cheese on the top and put it in the oven for at least half an hour or more. Very *lekker!*

Crustless Tuna Tart   *Supplied by Jeanne Herringer*

½ cup grated cheese
2 eggs
2 Tablespoons self-raising flour
1 cup milk
1 can tuna
Sliced onion
Sliced green pepper
Salt and pepper to taste

Line a greased dish with tuna, onion & green pepper.
Mix all remaining ingredients together (except the cheese) & pour over the filling.
Sprinkle cheese on top & bake at 180 degrees for approx. 25 minutes.

Braised Snoek

1 T (15 ml) oil
1 T (15 ml) butter
2 onions, sliced
2 potatoes, diced
4 ripe tomatoes, skinned and chopped
½ 2 (2,5ml) sugar
Pinch of chilli powder or cayenne pepper
250g smoked snoek, skinned, deboned and flaked
A little sour cream if available.

Sauté the sliced onion in the oil and butter mixture. Add the diced potatoes and stir-fry until golden. Add tomatoes, sugar and chilli. Simmer gently until the potatoes are cooked. Add snoek and heat through. Season to taste. Stir in a little of the cream. Garnish with lemon wedges and chopped parsley. Serve on a bed of white tossed rice garnished with parsley and a green salad on the side.

Chicken & Meat Dishes

Liqui Fruit Chicken   *Supplied by Claire Gifford*

1 Pkt. Mushroom Soup
250ml Apricot Liqui Fruit Juice
1 small tin of Apricots

Chop apricots into little pieces and mix together with soup powder and juice. Pour over chicken pieces and bake in oven at 180 until cooked.

Good old fashioned Chicken Pie

1 chicken, carved into portions
1 large onion
1 cup (250 ml) chicken stock
½ cup (125 ml) dry white wine
1 bay leaf
4 pinches of all spice

Pinch of grated nutmeg
Black pepper
1 T (15 ml) sago
1 T (15 ml) butter
1 egg yolk
Juice of ½ lemon
2 hard-boiled eggs, quartered
100 g cooked ham, diced
Flaky or sour cream pastry.

Sauté onion in a large saucepan. Add skinned and deboned chicken portions, rock, wine and spices. Simmer for 40 minutes. When cooked remove the stock. Add the sago to the stock. Simmer gently until the starch is cooked. Add butter, egg yolk and lemon juice to the sauce. Simmer but don't boil else the egg will curdle. Add diced hard-boiled egg, diced ham and the chicken to the sauce. Spoon the mixture into a pie dish.

Easy Tomato—Chutney Chicken　　*Supplied by Jeanne Herringer*

Chicken pieces
Brown onion soup
½ cup tomato sauce
½ cup Mrs. Balls Chutney
1 cup water

Coat chicken pieces with the brown onion soup powder. Put a little oil in a pan and brown the chicken pieces. Mix tomato sauce, chutney and water together and pour over the chicken.
Cook until chicken is tender—stir sauce and coat chicken during cooking.
Allow to cool. Then top with pastry and bake for about 40 minutes at 220' until the pastry is beautifully crisp and browned.

Frikkadels—in a flash!　　*Supplied by Theresa Nothard*

500g Mince
1 Egg
1 cup White breadcrumbs
1 Grated onion
½ tsp. Nutmeg chopped parsley

Salt and pepper
Sprinkle of mixed herbs and barbeque spice
Good shake of Worcester sauce

Mix all the ingredients together, roll into balls and shallow fry in oil.

Sosaties (Cape Malay Kebabs)

Can be made with chicken breasts, firm fish or lamb.
Ingredients

500g lamb, cut into 25mm cubes
2 large onions, one sliced into rings, the other chopped finely
50ml olive or cooking oil
4 cloves of peeled and crushed garlic
one tablespoon of curry powder
a teaspoon of turmeric
a tablespoon of brown sugar
4 crushed bay leaves
One tablespoon of lemon juice, plus two lemon cut into small wedges
120ml of meat stock
125g packet of dried apricots
One green pepper cut into blocks the same size as the meat cubes
A good blob of butter
Wooden skewer sticks.

Place the meat in a non-metal bowl with the bay leaves at the bottom. Heat the butter in a saucepan and sauté the chopped onion, garlic & curry powder for a few minutes.

Add the turmeric, lemon and meat stock, bring to the boil. As soon as the marinade comes to the boil, pour it over the meat. Allow to cool and place in fridge overnight. When ready to cook skewer the meat, apricots, green pepper & onion rings onto the sticks.

Pour the marinade into a saucepan, add a blob of butter and salt and pepper to taste, bring to the boil and serve warm with the sosaties and lemon wedges.

To prepare the sosaties you can either grill them under a very hot grill for about 10 minutes, or braai them over very hot coals, turning them as you go along.

Serve with the lemon wedges. For side dishes make a bowl of fluffy white rice, potato salad, baked potato or small jacket potatoes & crispy bread to soak up the sauce.

To spice up and burn your mouth, add additional garlic and crushed chillies, crushed curry leaves and a sprinkling of peri-peri powder to the marinade. Have a cold beer handy to extinguish the flames in your mouth!

Jeandre's Bobotie   *Supplied by Leigh Dalton*

500 grams mince meat
2 or 3 onions
2 slices of bread
1 cup milk
2 eggs
1T mild curry powder
1 t hot curry powder
2t salt
½ t pepper
1½ T sugar
½ T Turmeric
2 T vinegar
1 cup raisins
3 T chutney or apricot jam

Preheat oven to 180°. Fry the onion until brown, add the meat and fry until cooked.

Soak the bread in milk, then press the excess milk out and crush with a fork.

Mix all the ingredients except one egg and the pressed out milk. Place in oiled dish and bake at 180° for 40 minutes. Remove from oven, Mix the milk and egg, pour over meat and return to oven for 15 minutes. Serve with rice and chutney.

Bobotie Chicken Potjie   *Supplied by Andreas Senger*

Sauce

30 ml curry powder
40 ml sugar
10 ml salt
2,5 ml pepper
12 ml turmeric
50 ml vinegar/juice of one lemon
40 ml chutney
125 ml pitted raisins or craisins (dried cranberries) (optional).
150 ml cream

Meat

1 kg skinned chicken thighs
1 onion
Potatoes (baby or normal)—enough for everyone—microwave for 7 minutes on 80%
Power.

Marinade chicken thighs in mixture for 20–30 minutes.
Heat 15ml oil in the pot, brown the onion.
Add the meat with bobotie sauce
Add raisins / craisins
Add potatoes
Cook slowly while enjoying a beer or glass of wine until everything is cooked.

Vegetables

1 kg frozen mixed vegetables—chunky/winter mix or the other with carrots, peas and corn 1 cup grated cheese (Tasty works the best)

If you have chunky / winter mixed vegetables steam it until cooked
Place in an ovenproof dish and sprinkle with Maggie Three cheese recipe mix
Grate some cheese and sprinkle over veggies.
Place in a preheated oven to melt the cheese until crunchy.

Otherwise add veggies to the pot.

Please note that it is the first time we ever made it. Never heard of it before either. Shows how versatile a potjie really is. It was great. I'm going to make it again with some tweaks here and there.

Andreas Senger—a versatile Saffa in NZ!

Traditional Potjiekos

Ingredients
50 ml cooking oil
250g carrots
250g cauliflower
500g beef, diced
450–550 ml of sauce

Wash everything thoroughly with soap and water before you start cooking, *including your hands* , as you probably will be handling some of the food. Normal hygiene rules apply when working with food so stick to them.

Today's "potjie" is not *'traditional'* in the sense that we will not be using an open fire, outside on the ground neither will we be using traditional ingredients like game meat *("wildsvleis" in Afrikaans)*. We will however be using the traditional method with ingredients that should be readily available anywhere in the world.

Easy Boerewors Recipe   *Supplied by Mano G. Thanos*

2 pounds of ground beef
1 pound of ground pork
2 tablespoons ground coriander
1 tablespoon kosher salt half a tablespoon ground black pepper half a tablespoon ground nutmeg
1/4 of a tablespoon ground cloves
1/4 of a cup red wine vinegar

Mix all together well, form patties and sauté or grill to doneness. Cut open some hearty rolls and put Mrs. Ball's chutney on one side, then put the grilled Boerewors patties on the other side. Close both sides, open your mouth and take a BIG chomp!! Enjoy!

Gesan's Easy As 1-2-3 Curry Recipe   *Supplied by Gesan Naidoo*

Dry Ingredients

1 tsp. each of: Coriander seeds, Fennel seeds, cumin seeds
6 whole cloves, 3-4 cardamom pods, 2-3 pieces of cinnamon sticks, 1 or 2
star anise

Dry Spices
1 tsp. Garam masala, ½ tsp. turmeric powder, 1-2 tsp. of chilli powder
(masala) add more if you want it hot. 1 tsp. crushed garlic, ginger and chillies
(add more depending on flavour)

500g meat or chicken diced into about 2cm . . . . here again not fixed
depending on personal size choice.*   *   * Vegetarians can used potatoes,
mixed veggies, peas, chick peas and diced eggplant etc.
2 Tbsp. vegetable oil/ olive oil
1 medium onion chopped
I can chop/diced tomatoes
1 or 2 bay leaves

Vegetables optional depending on what you like; either potatoes only
or potatoes and peas, or mixed veg. only or peas only. Use any other veg.
depending on personal taste.

2 cube potatoes, 1 cup mixed vegetables, 1 cup peas, Fresh coriander chopped
or dry coriander.

Heat oil in saucepan until hot, add the dry ingredients and fry until aromatic
1-2 minutes, careful not to burn. Add in the dry spices and stir fry for 1-2
minutes to bring out flavour again be careful not to burn these spices. Add in
the onion, garlic, ginger and crushed chillies, cook until onion is translucent
and keep on low heat. Once onion is cooked add meat and stir fry until meat
is evenly brown and sealed. Add in the tin of tomatoes, bay leaves, bring to the
boil. Then simmer. (30mins-1 hr. depending on the type of meat) At this stage,
it all depends what vegetables you are adding. Use discretion here when to add
these vegetable, potatoes needs more time than the likes of the frozen veg.

If the sauce becomes too thick or dry add water slowly and stir, this will depend on how thick you want your sauce to be. When the meat is nearly cooked you can sprinkle another 1tsp of garam masala over the top and a few sprigs of fresh coriander or dry coriander.

Cook rice as per normal, basmati, jasmine or ordinary long grain rice. (You can add 1tsp of turmeric powder to the ordinary long grain rice add colour when cooking)

Once the curry is being served you can sprinkle a few sprigs of fresh coriander.

To make Breyani

Cook curry as per above minus the potatoes (you can buy pkt. of dry Breyani spice mix)
Cook rice as per normal, basmati, jasmine or ordinary long grain rice. (You can add 1tsp of turmeric powder to the ordinary long grain rice add colour when cooking)
Cook brown lentils separately—1—½ cups
Extra
Fry cube potatoes to crisp the outside (soft inside) set aside
Fry one onion ½ rings until golden brown, set aside
Assembling the Breyani
In a large oven proof dish the rice and curry need to be layered.
Rice, curry, sprinkle a few potatoes and fried onion.
Continue until all the ingredients are used.
The top of the dish should have a few potatoes and onions sprinkled on and garnish with fresh coriander.
NB if you have saffron a few strands can go into the curry and or rice.
Serve hot and enjoy!!!
Gesan Naidoo—NZ Indian Master Chef . . . yeah right!

Natal Beef Curry

1 KG Stewing Steak, cubed
2 Onions, sliced
1 Small Piece Raw Ginger
2 Green Chillies, chopped
500 ml stock

5ml Coriander
5 Cloves
5ml Lemon Juice
12,5ml Chutney
25ml Oil
200 Dried Apricots, soaked
1 Clove Garlic, crushed
1 urinal, diced
12,5ml Curry Powder
5ml Turmeric
Stick of Cinnamon
1 Small Tin Tomato Puree
12,5ml Brown Sugar
200ml Yoghurt
Salt to taste

Fry onions and garlic in oil till soft. Remove from pan then fry cubed meat until browned. Add all other ingredients except sugar, chutney and yoghurt. Simmer for 1 ½—2 hours, stirring occasionally. Add remaining ingredients just before serving. (Have plenty of wine to serve with this curry if your guests aren't used to a Natal Curry!)

Oxtail Casserole   *Supplied by Cheryl Benecke*

Serves 4-6
4 to 5 lbs. oxtails
Salt 7 freshly ground black pepper
¼ cup flour
2 tablespoons olive oil
1 large onion chopped
2 carrots, chopped into half moons
2 stalks chopped celery
3 tablespoons chopped fresh thyme
4 cloves garlic, peeled and finely chopped
¼ cup tomato paste
1 (750ml) bottle dry red wine
2 cups beef broth
1 (15 ounce) can diced tomatoes, with juice
2 bay leaves

8 ounces button mushrooms
8 ounces pearl onions
8 ounces baby potatoes
2 tablespoons red wine vinegar

Wash and dry the oxtails. Add the meat to a large bowl and season with salt and pepper, to taste. Toss the meat in the flour until lightly coated. Add the olive oil to a large pot over medium heat. Brown the oxtails on all sides, until well browned. Transfer the meat to a plate. Add the onions, carrots, celery, thyme and garlic to the pot and sauté until the onions are tender and beginning to brown, about 5 minutes. Season with salt and pepper, to taste. Stir in the tomato paste and mix well. Deglaze the pot with the bottle of red wine and stir up all the browned bits on the bottom of the pan. Stir in the broth, tomatoes with their juices and the bay leaves. Add the browned oxtails into the pot along with the accumulated juices that may have collected on the plate. Bring the casserole to a slight boil cover with a tightly fitted lid and place the pot in a 325' preheated oven. Cook for about 2 hours, remove pot carefully and add the pearl onions, button mushrooms and baby potatoes. Replace lid and cook for a further 1 1/2 hours or until the oxtails are tender and falling off the bone. Skim off the excess fat. Add wine vinegar, mix and taste for seasoning. Serve with rice and favourite veggies. Enjoy!!

Tomato Bredie

Ingredients
1 kg beef or shoulder of mutton
2 T (30ml) oil
1 T (15ml) butter
2 t (10ml) sea salt
½ t (2,5ml) freshly ground black pepper
2 onions, chopped
6 ripe red tomatoes (or 1 x 400g tin whole tomatoes)
1 x 70 g tin tomato paste
1 t (5ml) sugar
¼ t (1ml) chilli powder
½ t (2,5ml) paprika
3 gloves garlic, crushed
1 t (2,5 ml) paprika
3 cloves garlic, crushed

1 t (5 ml) mixed herbs
1 ½ cups (375 ml) chicken stock
3 potatoes, diced
1 T (15 ml) flour

Cube the meat. Heat the oil/butter mixture in a big, heavy-bottomed saucepan until the butter discolours. Add the meat in batches and stir-fry until brown. Remove each batch with a slotted spoon and keep aside. Season the browned meat with salt and pepper.

Brown the onions in the remaining oil. When golden, soft and glazed, add the tomatoes, tomato paste, sugar, chilli, paprika, garlic, herbs, water and stock cube. Bring to a slow simmering boil. Add the prepared meat. Simmer the bredie very slowly for 2 hours. Add the cubed potatoes and continue simmering for another half an hour. Thicken the gravy with a little potato flour mixed with water. The bredie improves with keeping. Prepare a day in advance and leave to mature in the refrigerator. Reheat and serve with fluffy steamed rice to which a handful of chopped parsley has been added.

Accompaniments

Stywe Pap (microwave) *Supplied by Carole Venecourt*

3 cups boiling water
1 cup mealie meal
1 teaspoon salt

Method

Use I large Pyrex mixing bowl or 2lt microwave bowl—place the salt & mealie meal in the container. Pour in water while stirring with wooden spoon.
Cover partially with plastic wrap. (Leaving opening for steam to escape.)
Cook on 50 % medium power for 5 minutes and then stir.
Cover again and cook for 15 minutes on 30% defrost, stirring every 5 minutes.
Lastly stir in 1 Tablespoon of butter.

For Krummel Pap (Putu Pap) (microwave)

1 ½ cups boiling water
2 cups mealie meal
¾ teaspoon salt

Follow direction for the Stywe Pap, but use a two-pronged fork for mixing throughout.

Translation—Stywe pap—thick porridge
Krummel pap—crumbed porridge

South Africans enjoy this as an accompaniment at a braaivleis (barbeque).

Beer Marinade for a Braai (Barbeque)

600ml Beer
2 Onions, grated
90ml Sugar
Black pepper
Grated Rind 1 lemon
250ml Salad Oil
5ml Salt
Cayenne pepper
80ml Iced Water

Mix all ingredients together and brush over the meat as it cooks, or soak meat in marinade overnight before cooking.

Mieliemeel   *Supplied by Denise Nel*

Sout na smaak, vir die pap
Suiker na smaak
Botter
Water(hoeveelheid word bepaal deur hoeveel mense moet kos kry.)
1 blik sweetcorn
Olie vir braai
1 ui, fyngekap
1 pakkie sampione in skywe gesny

1 pakkie spek in blokkies resny
1 x 500 ml vars room.

Maak 'n stywe pap met sout en water, roer botter en suiker in dat die pap 'n soeterige smaak het an lekker smeerbaar maar nie pap nie. Braai in 'n pan due ui en sampione met 'n bietjie olie. Voeg spek by en braai tot bros. Voeg sweetcorn by en laastens die room. Smeer 'n bak met 'n lag pap en dan 'n lag sous . . . so twee lae en rasper hope kaas boo or en bak in die oond tot kaas verkleur.

Chilli Bite Recipe   *Supplied by Gesan Naidoo*

Ingredients
1 cup spinach chopped (fresh)
1 large onion, slice thinly (half-moon)
2 cups chick pea flour (obtainable from Asian stores) chopped fresh coriander (1/2 cup use discretion)
1 or 2 red/green chilli finely chopped depending on how spicy and hot you want it
1 Tbsp. cumin power
1 Tbsp. coriander powder salt & pepper to taste
1 cup plain yoghurt
1/2 cup water

Mix all the ingredients together into a soft dough consistency. Drop tablespoonful's mixture into hot oil and deep fry until golden brown. When ready chilli bites will float to the top.
Enjoy on its own while hot or serve with a dip/chutney. Do not be afraid to experiment by adding curry powder (masala), other spices, sweet corn etc.

Bunny Chow   *Supplied By Gesan Naidoo*

Curried mince cooked and flavoured to perfection
1 x uncut loaf of bread cut into halves or quarters.
Hollow out the soft white filling, then spoon in the curry into the hollow bread.
Top with the soft white filling.
Any salad can be served as an accompaniment, either on top or as a side.

Gesan's Sambals

Ingredients
1 tomato deseeded and finely diced
1 white onion finely diced green chillies (deseeded) finely diced (the no# depends on how much heat you want)
1 tablespoon mint leaves finely chopped
2 tsp. cooking oil (discretion to be used)
1 tablespoon vinegar (discretion to be used) salt and pepper to taste
1 teaspoon sugar . . .

Mix all together in a bowl, serve as side or on top of curry in bunny chow.

Gesan's Favourite Raita

1 large unpeeled English hothouse cucumber, halved, seeded, coarsely grated
2 cups plain yoghurt
1/4 cup (packed) chopped fresh mint
1 teaspoon ground cumin
1/4 teaspoon plus pinch of cayenne pepper salt to taste, (pinch)

Samoosas—Indian Appetizer

Ingredients:
For the crust:
All-purpose Flour—1 1/2 cups
Salt—3/4 tsp.
Ajwain (Carrom Seeds)—1/4 tsp.
Oil—2 Tbsp.
Lemon/Lime Juice—1 Tbsp.
Water—1/4 cup + 2 Tbsp.

For the filling:
Potatoes—1 1/2 lbs., boiled, peeled and cubed
Whole Coriander Seeds—1 tsp.
Fennel Seeds – 1 tsp.
Salt—to taste
Garam Masala—1/2 tsp.
Dry Mango Powder—1/2 tsp.

Sugar—1/2 tsp.
Cilantro (Coriander Leaves)—10 sprigs, chopped
Ginger/Green Chilli—1 Tbsp., minced
Lime/Lemon Juice—to taste
Oil—2 Tbsp.
Cumin Seeds—1/2 tsp.
Asafoetida – 1/8 tsp.
Frozen Green Peas—1/2 cup

Method

1. Soak Coriander Seeds and Fennel Seeds in a few tablespoons of warm water and keep aside.
2. In a bowl, mix All-purpose flour, Salt and Ajwain.
3. Add 2 Tbsp. Oil and mix until all the oil is well incorporated into the flour.
4. Add Lemon/Lime Juice and Water and knead into a smooth firm dough. Wrap in plastic wrap and let it rest for 20 minutes.
5. To the boiled Potatoes, add Salt, Garam Masala, Dry Mango Powder, Sugar, Cilantro, Ginger/Green Chilli, Lemon Juice, and the drained Coriander/Fennel Seeds. Mix well.
6. Heat Oil in a pan on medium heat.
7. Add Cumin Seeds, Asafoetida and Green Peas. Cook for 1-2 minutes until peas are tender.
8. Add Potato mixture and cook for a few minutes until heated through. Keep aside to cool to room temperature.
9. Divide Dough into small portions (slightly bigger than a golf ball).
10. Roll out each portion into a thin oval shape.
11. Cut the oval down the centre to make two semi-ovals.
12. Lift one side of the flat edge and brush plain water on it. Lift the opposite side and overlap the two edges to form a cone shape. Press the seams gently to seal.
13. Stuff the Potato mixture into the cone. Brush water around the top edge and seal shut.
14. Deep fry until golden.
15. Serve hot with *Tamarind Chutney, Mint Chutney* or Ketchup.

Salads, Vegetables & Vegetarian

Natal Salad

6 Bananas sliced
125ml Cooking Oil
30ml Brown Sugar
10ml Salt
125ml Vinegar
Juice ½ lemon

Mix together and store in fridge till required. If the mayonnaise is too thick, it can be thinned with cream, lemon juice or vinegar.

3 Bean Salad   *Supplied by Claire Gifford*

1 Tin Baked Beans
1 Tin Butter Beans
1 Tin French sliced Green Beans
1 Tspn. Dried Sweet Basil
3 Tspns. Sugar
30ml Oil
30ml Vinegar

Mix together and eat!

Fancy Baked Beans   *Supplied by Claire Gifford*

'Very yummy and passed on to me by a very dear friend, Gail Leeds who also left SA with her family and now lives in the UK'

1 Tin of Baked Beans or more if needed
Chopped Capsicum—Green Pepper
Chopped Onion
Dollop of Mayo
Swish of Worcester Sauce

Pinch of Curry Powder

Sauté onion and capsicum, add beans, heat through and add Mayo, Worcester sauce and curry. Great with a braai (bbq).

Potato Fritters

4-5 Medium Potatoes
1 egg
5ml Baking Powder
1 Onion, grated
30ml Flour

Grate the potatoes, mix with the remaining ingredients together and drop spoonfuls of the combined ingredients into hot oil and cook until golden brown.

Waldorf Salad

2 medium red delicious apples (about 2 to 2 1/2 cups cubed)
2 Granny Smith apples, cored and diced
1 tablespoon sugar
1 teaspoon lemon juice
1 dash salt
1 cup thinly sliced celery
1/2 cup chopped pecan nuts
1 teaspoon curry powder
1 teaspoon sugar
Pinch salt
1/4 cup mayonnaise
1/2 cup whipping cream, whipped
mixed salad greens

Preparation—Wash apples; core and cut into 1/2-inch cubes. Do not peel. Sprinkle cubed apples with sugar, lemon juice and salt. Add celery and nuts. Fold mayonnaise into whipped cream. Fold mayonnaise mixture gently into apple mixture. Waldorf salad is served on mixed salad greens.

Tuna/ pasta salad (hot or cold dish)   *Supplied by Michelle Cancino*
This is my own personal favourite for bbq/snacks'.
(makes 6 generous helpings, or more)

Boil small pasta shells till almost done, drain. Finely chop half an onion and whole green pepper into tiny blocks, and fair bit of cheese. Open tin of tuna chunks (I like oily one, others prefer in water). Open tin of sweet corn, in creamy sauce (I like Koo brand). Add all ingredients together with cooked & drained pasta in very large dish. Add spices for taste (pinch salt). Add mayonnaise and chutney for extra flavour, with sprinkle parsley for colour. Serve cold at any bbq, and warm up left over's next day until cheese is melted

Pasta Salad   *Supplied by Jeanne Herringer*

½ cup white vinegar
½ cup olive oil
1 ½ cups white sugar
1 cup tomato sauce (preferably All Gold)
3tsps curry powder
Bacon
Onion
Carrot
Baby peas
Small pasta shells

Method
Cook pasta until done. Fry bacon & cut. Chop onion & fry till soft.
Mix vinegar, oil, sugar, tomato sauce & curry powder together—mix well until sugar has dissolved. Grate raw carrot and add to sauce. Stir in the onion, bacon and peas. Mix together with the pasta. * It's best to make the salad the day before so that the flavours blend well.

CousCous—for the weekend braai

"Prepare couscous as directed. Mix everything together. Done!"
It really is THAT easy. You can basically add anything you like —olives, flaked almonds, fried mushrooms, bacon . . . . anything you choose!

Ingredients
1 box flavoured couscous (garlic or Parmesan), cooked as per instructions on the box
1 can chickpeas
1 red bell pepper, finely chopped
1/2 onion, chopped
1 tomato, chopped
1/4 cup fresh parsley leaves, chopped
1/2 cup crumbled feta cheese
Salt and freshly ground black pepper
1/4 cup olive oil
2 to 3 limes, juiced

Toss all the ingredients with the olive oil and lime juice, to taste in a large bowl.

Pumpkin Fritters   *Supplied by Cheryl Benecke*

(for 12-15 fritters)
2 cups cooked pumpkin, drained
½ cup flour
½ teaspoon salt
1 teaspoon ground cinnamon
2 teaspoons baking powder
2 tablespoons brown sugar
2 large eggs
Oil
Cinnamon sugar

Place all dry ingredients in a mixer, including pumpkin. Mix well. Add the eggs, and mix well until a thick batter forms. If the batter is too thick, add a tiny amount of milk. If by chance it's runny, add more flour. Use a non-stick pan, heat a little oil in the pan, using medium to high heat. Scoop up heaped tablespoons of batter and drop into the pan. To test if ready, press very lightly on the fritters. When done, they will tend to spring back. Sprinkle with lots of cinnamon sugar on both sides while still warm. Enjoy!

Potatoes in sweet and sour cream

6 large potatoes, peeled
2 eggs
½ cup (125 ml) cream
½ cup (125 ml) sour cream
½ t (2, 5 ml) salt
Pinch of pepper and nutmeg.

Parboil the potatoes for ten minutes. Slice into rounds and arrange in an oven—proof dish. Beat the eggs, sour cream and seasoning together. Pour over the sliced potatoes. Bake in a moderate oven at 180' for 40 minutes or until cooked and golden brown. with grated cheese over them to form a "skilletjie" before being served. Also ideal as a side dish with meat or *wors*, and can easily be prepared on the BBQ. Goes well with an Auslese type fruity wine!

Lekker SA Rice Salad   *Supplied by Marjolyn Rombouts*

Cook yellow or brown rice and let it cool. Cut in cubes—onions, tomatoes, green, yellow and red peppers & slice spring onions. Cut tin peaches into pieces. Add salt, oil and vinegar to taste plus curry. Then, Mrs Balls Chutney mixed with mayo. Also yummy with chopped nuts and raisins added. *Gooi in 'n bak en wag vir die boeries en choppies. Geniet*!

Vegetable Pie

Crust
2 cloves garlic
2 Tablespoons chopped parsley
4Tablespoons butter
2 cups whole-wheat breadcrumbs

Filling
3 Tablespoons olive oil
3 leeks, sliced
200 grams sliced mushrooms
3 grated carrots
Pinch salt
1 teaspoon sugar

5 ml mixed herbs
1 Tablespoon lemon juice

Topping
¾ cup yoghurt
1 teaspoon custard powder
1 egg
½ cup grated cheese
Pinch salt
Pinch cayenne pepper

Sauté garlic and parsley in butter. Add bread crumbs. Mix well. Line ovenproof dish with mixture. Heat oil and fry leeks until soft. Add mushrooms and celery and sauté. Add grated carrot. Season with salt, sugar, herbs and lemon juice. Dish filling into crust and smooth top with spoon. Mix custard powder with a little yoghurt to form a paste and add remaining ingredients. Pour over vegetable mixture. Bake at 190' for 35 minutes until golden brown.

Samp and Beans (Umngqusho)

This is a traditional African recipe. The samp and beans are commonly soaked overnight.

Ingredients
2 cups samp
3 cups black-eyed or sugar beans
1 onion
3 potatoes
1 large tomato
2-3 tablespoons olive oil
Salt to taste
1-2 teaspoons curry powder

Mix and wash samp and beans. Put them in a large pot with 6 cups water and cook until they start to soften. Check every half hour or so and add water if required. Once the samp and beans have simmered for a few hours and are almost done, drain some water off and add the vegetables, oil, salt and seasoning. Cook the remainder of time it takes until soft. (another half hour.)

Breads, Rusks and Savoury Tarts

Mielie Bread   *Supplied by Claire Gifford*

1 Cup Mielie Meal
1 Cup Flour
2 tspns. Baking Powder
2 Eggs
½ Cup Sugar
½ Cup Milk
Salt
1 Tin Sweetcorn (410gm)

Mix altogether, place in greased pan and bake for +—45 minutes at 180.

Nutty Banana Bread   *Supplied by Jeanne Herringer*
(Preparation time: 15 minutes)
(Baking time: 45-60 minutes)

180g butter/margarine
300ml (1 ¼ cup) sugar
3 eggs
600ml (2 ½ cups) flour
7ml (1 ½ tsp.) baking powder
1ml (¼ tsp.) salt
1 small can (165g) nestle evaporated milk
5ml (1 tsp.) bicarbonate of soda
5ml (1 tsp.) vanilla essence
250ml (1 cup) mashed banana
160ml (2/3 cup) chopped pecan nuts

Preheat oven to 180C. Line with wax paper and then grease 2 large loaf pans
(22x11cm)

Cream butter and sugar together in a bowl, and then lightly beat in the eggs
Mix together ideal milk, bicarbonate of soda and vanilla. Sift flour, baking
powder and salt together and mix into the butter and sugar alternately with
the ideal mixture.

Stir in the bananas and the nuts. Pour into prepared pans and bake for 45-60 minutes, until golden brown. Allow to cool before serving. (This cake freezes well)

Buttermilk Rusks   *Supplied by Jacqueline Holliday Yallup*

1cup bran
500g margarine
2 kg self-raising flour
1cup flour
15ml baking powder
5ml salt
3 eggs
500ml buttermilk
450ml sugar

Sift all the dry ingredients together.
Work in the margarine with the fingertips.
Once well worked in.
Beat the eggs into the buttermilk and add to the flour mixture.
Roll into balls and place into greased loaf pan.
Place each ball tightly together.
Bake at 180oC for 50-55 min.
Once cooked remove from pan and break at joints with a folk.
Each ball will break into 4.
Place on tray and place in warmer draw for about 5-6 hours to dry out.

Bran Coconut Rusks   *Supplied by Theresa Nothard*

1kg Self-Raising Flour
10ml Baking Powder
5ml Salt
500g margarine (Wooden Spoon is what I use—soften in micro but don't allow to become runny)
1 tsp. vanilla essence
3 eggs
2x500ml Bran
125ml Sultanas
125ml Sunflower seeds / chopped nuts
500ml Buttermilk

375ml White sugar
125ml Coconut

Line a baking pan (I use my oven roasting pan) with baking paper. Preheat oven to 180. Sift flour, B.P and salt together. Using your fingers, rub the marg. into the mixture. Add bran, sultanas, raisins, coconut and sunflower seeds/nuts. Add the buttermilk, eggs, vanilla essence and sugar. Mix with your hands till the mixture combines into a smooth dough. Smooth the dough into the pan using a spatula. Dipping the spatula in water helps to smooth it out nicely.

Cut it with the edge of the spatula or knife before placing in the oven. Bake at 180 for 60 minutes or until done. Allow to cool and remove from pan. Further cut the rusks, place onto racks/baking trays and place in the oven set at 120 for 3-4 hours or until the rusks are hard to the touch. Sit back, relax and dip a rusk!

Sweetcorn Tart   *Supplied by Jeanne Herringer*

1 Can Cream style sweetcorn—I use the Oak make
60ml Flour (standard)
60ml melted margarine
60ml sugar—I used brown sugar
15ml Baking powder
4 Eggs

Mix it all together with electric beater, pour in greased oven dish and bake at 180 for about an hour. I usually leave it in until it's a golden brown colour.

Treats

Tea biscuits (soetkoekies) *Supplied by Anita Dutton*

125 g soft butter/margarine
375 ml sugar
2 extra-large eggs
5 ml vanilla essence
750 ml flour
15 ml baking powder
4 ml nutmeg
1 ml salt

Cream the butter and sugar together. Add the eggs and vanilla essence and beat well. Sieve the flour, baking powder, nutmeg en salt over the creamed butter and egg mixture and mix well till you have a soft dough. Cover the dough and leave in fridge for 30 min. Roll the dough out on floured surface, take cookie cutter and press forms. Bake at 180 degrees for 8–10 minutes.

Vetkoek *Supplied by Denise Du Plooy King*

500ml luke warm water
10ml sugar
10ml dry yeast
5 x 250ml cups of flour
10ml salt
25 ml oil.

Stir sugar into water and add yeast. Let sit for 20 minutes approx.
Throw the rest of the stuff in and knead thoroughly. Leave it in a warm place for about an hour. Cover it with a greased sheet. Roll into vetkoek shape and leave for another 20 minutes. I usually leave it for longer before putting it in shapes. The dough comes out allot better. It also halves very well because this amount makes about 20 vetkoeke . . .

Vetkoek

Supplied by Yolandi Janse van Rensburg

500ml lou water (2k)
2 t suiker
2 t droegis, gelyk
5 k meelblom
10 ml sout (2 t)
25 ml olie (2 e)

Roer suiker in lou water en gooi gis by.
Laat rys tot gis bo dryf.
Sif meelblom en sout saam.
Voeg olie by gis, meng met meelblom en knie goed.
Laat rys vir 50 min.
Maak op in vetkoeke.
Plaas op oliegesmeerde blad.
Sit plastiek oor en laat weer vir 20 min rys.
Bak in warm olie tot bruin.
Ek laat dit deeg 1ste keer rys en knie dan af en laat 2de keer rys. Dan maak ek vetkoeke op uit bak soos ek hulle bak. Baie makliker en werk goed.

Lamingtons

Supplied by Theresa Nothard

1 cup margarine
½ cup milk
Pinch salt
3 cups flour
4 eggs
2 cups sugar
2 teaspoons baking powder
1 teaspoon vanilla essence

Pre-heat oven to 180.

Beat marg. and sugar together till light and creamy. Add eggs and beat well. Sift dry ingredients into the mixture and mix well. Stir in milk and vanilla essence. Put mixture into a square or rectangular ovenproof dish that has been greased and lined. Bake till top is light golden brown and skewer comes out clean. When cool, cut into squares and dip into sauce, then coat with coconut.

Sauce
1½ cups water
1 tablespoon margarine
4 tablespoons cocoa
3 cups sugar

Mix the cocoa with the water and sugar and stir over a low heat until melted. Add the marg. Bring to almost boiling point. Remove from the heat and keep the sauce lukewarm whilst coating the cake squares. Very messy but very yummy!

Flapjacks   *Supplied by Theresa Nothard*

1 cup flour
30ml Sugar
10ml Baking Powder
1 egg
15ml oil
125ml milk

Mix dry ingredients together and gradually add the wet ingredients. Whisk to a smooth consistency. Drop spoonful's into a warm pan. I double this recipe and it is enough for the 4 of us.

Peanut Butter Biscuits   *Supplied by Jeanne Herringer*

½ cup butter, or marg.
½ cup peanut butter
½ cup white sugar
½ cup brown sugar
1 tsp. vanilla essence
1 egg
1 ¾ cups flour
1 tsp. baking powder
½ tsp. bicarbonate of soda
½ tsp. salt

Cream butter or shortening and peanut butter well together. Add sugar gradually and beat until light and fluffy. Beat egg lightly with fork and add

to creamed mixture with vanilla essence. Lastly add sifted dry ingredients, kneading into a smooth pliable dough. Roll into small pieces of dough (1 tsp.) into balls between floured hands. Place onto a greased baking sheet. Press flat with floured fork.
Bake at 375 (180) for 12-15 minutes until golden brown.

South African Crunchies   *Supplied by Sheena Hayes*

180 grams Butter
1 teaspoon bicarb. of soda
1 cup flour
1 cup desiccated coconut
1 tablespoon golden syrup
2 cups oats
1 cup white sugar

Melt butter, syrup, bicarb. of soda on gentle heat. Add oats, flour, sugar, coconut. Pat into greased tin until flat. Bake 180 C 5 min. Switch off oven and leave in oven for 20 minutes. Remove and cut into squares.

My Mum's Afghan Recipe (Joan Macaskill)
My favourite biscuits as a child and still now!   *Eve Hemming*

7 ozs. margarine	3 ozs. castor sugar
7 ozs. flour	3 ozs. Post Toasties
1 oz. cocoa	1 level teaspoon baking powder
Pinch salt	1 teaspoon vanilla essence

Cream marg. and sugar; add vanilla, then sieved flour, cocoa, salt and BP. Lastly add the Post Toasties. Put small balls in patty pan and bake in moderate oven for ½ hour. Once cool top with butter icing & Walnuts (or Smarties for kids' parties.) (Leave plenty in the bowl for the kids to scrape and nibble before washing the mixing bowl . . .)

Romany Creams   *Supplied by Ozzie Forsyth*

250g butter/margarine
250 ml [1 cup] castor sugar
625 ml [2 1/2 cups] desiccated coconut

500 ml [2cups] flour
50 ml cocoa
5 ml [1teaspoon] baking powder pinch of salt
1/2 slab [50 g] plain milk chocolate, broken up in bits

Preheat oven to 180 deg. C. [350 deg. F] Grease 2 baking pans. Beat butter till light and creamy. Gradually add castor sugar bit-by-bit while beating the butter. Add coconut and stir in thoroughly. Sift flour, cocoa, baking powder, and salt. Mix in well. Then 'knead' in mixture so that all the ingredients 'stick' together.

Roll little 'balls' of the mixture [1 teaspoon in size]—place on baking sheet and press down very slightly. Bake for 10–12 minutes.

Melt chocolate in a glass bowl placed over a saucepan of boiling water [or in microwave]—then sandwich two biscuits together. Leave to allow chocolate to set. Store in airtight container. Makes about 3 1/2 dozen biscuits. [double]

Sweets

Milk Tartlets *Supplied by Jeanne Herringer*

Sweet Biscuit Pastry
125g Margarine or butter
125ml Sugar
Egg, lightly beaten
500ml Flour, sifted
5ml Baking powder
1ml Salt

Cream sugar & margarine (butter) until light and fluffy.
Beat in egg then stir in sifted dry ingredients.
Knead lightly & chill for ½ hours.
Roll out and line cupcake tins.
Blind bake for 10–15 minutes at 200*C.

Milk Tart Filling

½ l Milk
40 ml Margarine or butter
20ml Flour
4ml Vanilla essence
50ml Sugar
12ml Cornflour
20ml Custard powder
Egg, extra large

Boil milk & butter. Mix eggs, sugar, cornflour, custard powder, flour & vanilla essence together well. Add a little hot milk to mixture. Mix then add rest & mix well.
Cook until the mixture thickens (+—1 minute in the microwave). Fill tart shells when cool.

Amarula Malva   *Supplied by Janene Magson*

5ml vinegar
2 extra-large eggs
250ml Castor sugar
15ml Smooth apricot jam
310ml Flour
5ml Bicarbonate of soda
Pinch of salt
30gr butter
125ml milk

Sauce
250ml cream
100gr butter
125ml sugar
100ml Amarula Cream Liqueur (Canterbury Crème is more economical and tastes as good.)

Beat together the eggs and castor sugar until light & fluffy.
Mix in jam. Sift dry ingredients.
Melt butter and mix with milk and vinegar

Alternately add milk mixture with dry ingredients to egg mixture and mix well

Pour into a greased 2litre ovenproof dish and bake at 180° for 30-40 minutes

Remove from oven.

For the Sauce

Mix together all ingredients except liqueur and bring to boil

Remove from heat and add liqueur or hot water

Pour over hot pudding—until all is absorbed.

Malva Pudding   *Supplied by Theresa Van Der Merwe*

250ml Sugar

1 egg

15ml softening butter

60ml apricot Jam

250ml flour

5ml bicarb.

1ml salt

250ml milk

10ml brown vinegar

10ml vanilla essence sauce

250ml cream

100g butter

125g sugar

160ml hot water

Preheat oven to 180 deg. C. Beat sugar, egg, butter and jam until fully and pale. Sieve dry ingredients and mix in milk, vinegar and vanilla. Fold into egg mixture. Spoon into a dish and bake for 45minutes.

Sauce

Heat all ingredients together in a saucepan until butter has melted pour over hot pudding with cream. Let it soak in and enjoy!

Bread and butter pudding

Ingredients
2 ripe bananas, peels removed
2 tsp. bourbon or brandy
2 tsp. Demerara or light brown sugar
1 tsp. vanilla extract
1 handful walnuts (or pecan nuts), roughly chopped
Double thick cream, for serving
2 oven-proof ramekins
1 baking tray
1 sheet tinfoil, doubled over, to fit the baking tray

Pre-heat your braai to the highest setting and line the baking tray with the tinfoil.
Slice the bananas and put the equivalent of 1 banana into each ramekin.
Then divide the remaining ingredients between the ramekins, place on your lined baking tray and then onto your braai.
Grill and cook for about 10 minutes, until golden and bubbling.
Serve as soon as possible with the double thick cream (or vanilla ice cream).
*If you would prefer not to use brandy, substitute this with about 1 Tbsp. of fresh orange juice and a drizzle of honey. h*ttp://www.food24.com/Recipes: Sarah Graham courtesy of The SA Magazine*

Five Minute Chocolate Coffee Mug Cake!

4 tablespoons flour
4 tablespoons sugar
2 tablespoons cocoa
1 egg
3 tablespoons milk
3 tablespoons oil
3 tablespoons chocolate chips (optional)
A small splash of vanilla essence
1 large coffee mug

Add dry ingredients to your largest mug and mix well. Add the egg and mix thoroughly. Pour in the milk and oil and mix well. Add the chocolate chips, vanilla essence, then mix again.

Place the mug in the microwave and cook for 3 minutes at 1000 watts 9high. The cake will rise over the top of the mug, but don't be alarmed!
Allow to cool a little, and tip out onto a plate. Eat!—This can serve 2 if you want to feel slightly virtuous. And why is this most dangerous cake recipe in the world?
Because now you are only 5 minutes away from a chocolate cake at any time of the day or night.

Melkkos   *Supplied by Claire Gifford*

100 grams Flour
15 ml Marge
2 ml Salt
1 litre Milk
Cinnamon and Sugar

Using a big 2 litre size bowl—heat milk till boiling point in the microwave.
Mix flour and salt and rub in marg. to form crumbs.
Add all of mixture to milk and stir with a whisk to form little lumps.
Microwave again for about 3 to 4 minutes—mixing a few times.
Pour into bowls and serve with the cinnamon and sugar.

Warm Syrup Koeksisters   *Supplied by Franda Zondach*

"I don't know where it came from originally, but I got it from my Mum's old recipe book. The book is falling apart, and it's filled with flour and oil stains, but all the best and fail proof recipes live in there!"

Syrup
500g (625ml) white sugar
250ml water
12.5ml lemon juice
5ml vanilla essence

Dough
200g (375ml) flour
22ml baking powder
1ml salt
20g (25ml) butter

150ml milk one bottle oil (for deep frying)

Join sugar and water in a deep pot and heat over low heat till boiling. Stir every now and then till sugar is totally dissolved.

When the syrup reaches boiling point, boil it for 7 to 8 minutes slowly. Don't boil it too fast otherwise it will become too thick. Take pot off from heat and add lemon juice and vanilla essence. Keep separate until needed.

Sieve the flour, baking powder and salt together. Rub the butter with your fingers into the flour mixture until totally combined. Add the milk with a mixing spoon till a dough is formed.

Roll out the dough on a flour dusted surface till it is about 5mm thick. Now cut it in strips and fold the koeksisters.

Heat the oil in a pot until it is pretty hot. Place 3 to 4 koeksisters at a time in there, and fry it until it is golden brown on both sides. Take them out immediately and throw them in the pot with the syrup. When the koeksister absorbs some of the syrup you can take it out.

Bar One Cheesecake   *Supplied by Maria Chinn*
This yummy cheesecake recipe was sent to me by one of my friends in SA!

Chocolate base
250g chocolate coated digestive biscuits
150g melted butter
2 tablespoons brown sugar
20g extra butter

Filling
300ml cream
50g milk chocolate (chopped finely)
3 teaspoons gelatine
60ml water
500g cream cheese
110g castor sugar
120g Bar One, chopped finely

1. Blend biscuits into breadcrumbs and add butter to combine. Press biscuit mixture into a 20cm tin (bottom and sides or just bottom). Cover and refrigerate till firm.

2. Combine brown sugar with the 20g extra butter and 2tbs cream in small saucepan, heat on low until sugar dissolves to make butterscotch sauce.
3. Combine chocolate and 2 tablespoons of cream in small saucepan and stir over low heat until chocolate melts to make chocolate sauce.
4. Sprinkle gelatine over water in a small bowl over simmering water. Stir until gelatine dissolves. Cool for 5 minutes.
5. Beat cheese and castor sugar in medium bowl until smooth. Beat remaining cream in another bowl until soft peaks form. Stir slightly warm gelatine into cheese mixture and add in Bar-One and fold in cream.
6. Pour half cheese mixture into prepared tin and drizzle half butterscotch and half chocolate sauce over cheese mixture. Repeat the process with remaining cheese mixture and sauces.
7. Cover and refrigerate for at least three hours or until set but best to make the day before.

Peppermint Caramel Fridge Tart   *Supplied by Jeanne Herringer*

350ml Fresh Cream
1 tin Caramel Treat
2 Peppermint Crisps—grated
1pkt Tennis Biscuits

Whip cream until stiff

Add caramel and almost all of the peppermint crisp into cream & beat until just blended

Place a layer of tennis biscuits in base of dish
Pour ½ mixture on top
Add another layer of biscuits
Pour over rest of mixture
Sprinkle remaining peppermint crisp on top
Seal & refrigerate

Cremora Tart   *Supplied by Jeanne Herringer*
It's not inside its on top!

1 packet Marie biscuits
2 cups Cremora (dry powder)
I cup water
1 tin condensed milk
½ cup lemon juice

Press crushed Marie biscuits (mixed with marg.) into dish. Place in the fridge until the filling is completed.

Mix Cremora & water & beat until thickish.
Add condensed milk & lemon juice.
Place on top of biscuit base.

Creamy Custard   *Supplied by Theresa Nothard*

1 litre Boiling water
½ tin Condensed milk
6 tsp. Sugar
6 dessertspoons Custard powder

Put water in a pot. Mix the custard powder and sugar together with a little water to make a paste. Stir the condensed milk into the water, slowly adding the custard powder and sugar mixture, stirring continuously. Bring to the boil and pour into a jug. I prefer to stir all the time to avoid it sticking to the bottom of the pot. To prevent a "skin" from forming on the top of the custard, sprinkle a little sugar on top while still hot.

Tameletjie   *Supplied by Claire Gifford*
A favourite we used to make as kids!

Melt some marg. / butter in a pan. Add a heap of sugar. Mix and heat until sugar melts and starts to bubble, slowly turning brown. Pour onto a tray, wait until it sets and becomes brittle. Break into pieces.

My late Mum-in-Law Margot Hemming's Honeycomb Cream Pudding
(That I was useless at making and is my husband's favourite!)   *Eve Hemming*

Into 3 cups milk and 1 cup sugar put 3 teaspoons gelatine and stir until dissolved. Stir in yolks of 3 eggs and allow to boil up once. Add 3 egg whites (beaten & stiff).

Add flavouring—vanilla or brandy. Allow to set.

Vanessa Ritter's famous Vodka Christmas Cake

Once again this year, I've had requests for my Vodka Christmas Cake recipe, so here goes. Please save your copy, as I'm beginning to get tired of typing this up each year! (I made mine this morning!!!) 1 cup sugar, 1 tspn. baking powder, 1 cup water, 1 tsp. salt, 1 cup brown sugar, Lemon juice, 4 large eggs, Nuts, 1 . . . bottle Vodka, 2 cups dried fruit.

Sample a cup of Vodka to check quality. Take a large bowl, check the Vodka again to be sure it is of the highest quality then Repeat. Turn on the electric mixer. Beat one cup of butter in a large fluffy bowl. Add 1 teaspoon of sugar. Beat again. At this point, it is best to make sure the Vodka is still OK. Try another cup just in case. Turn off the mixerer thingy. Break 2 eegs and add to the bowl and chuck in the cup of dried fruit. Pick the fruit up off the floor, wash it and put it in the bowl a piece at a time trying to count it. Mix on the turner. If the fried druit getas stuck in the beaterers, just pry it loose with a drewscriver. Sample the Vodka to test for tonsisticity. Next, sift 2 cups of salt, or something. Check the Vodka. Now shit shift the lemon juice and strain your nuts. Add one table. Add a spoon of sugar, or *somefink*. Whatever you can find. Greash the oven. Turn the cake tin 360 degrees and try not to fall over. Don't forget to beat off the turner. Finally, throw the bowl through the window. Finish the Vodka and wipe the counter with the cat.

Epilogue

Yesterday is but today's memory, and tomorrow is today's dream
—Kahlil Gibran

Why hold onto just one life
Why hold on to just one life
Till it is filthy and threadbare?
The sun dies eternally
And wastes a thousand lives each instant.
God has decreed a life for you
And He will give another,
Then another and another.
Rumi—Persia 13th Century

My yesterdays are endless memories, like a previous life. My today's unfold, sometimes expectedly and sometimes with surprise. My tomorrows remain unknown. In the depth of pain, I am able to honour that moment, knowing that it, too, will pass. Can I feel whole again I muse? I think not. I'm ripped from Africa, or was it ripped from me with its beguiling secrets? It's blood-lust history? Africa's wildness, unfettered deepness and harshness draws one back, not three dimensionally, as the Africa we ideologically hold onto does not exist . . . but always in the soul. That madness, the wild open unharnessed spaces, the vastness of a place without defined boundaries beckons one into its honey trap.

For me it is Africa's unyoked, almost reckless wildness for which I yearn; it's a place that tries to set us free—to run with the wind—yet paradoxically and tragically it's a place where we are barred and shackled to survive its relentless madness and mayhem . . .

In Janet Bray Attwood and Chris Attwood's book *The Passion Test*, they refer to the fact that, "We're all on the same highway." I liked that.

They argue that quantum physicists would state that the differences which humans perceive, start to cease to exist from the vantage point of one "unified, unchanging field of life, from which all the diversity and change we perceive arises." It is our field of consciousness which gives rise to whom we are and who we become. But beyond that, as humanity across the vast planet, we are all interconnected. It is in our connectivity with others and in knowing ourselves that we are better able to move towards a sense of harmony and acceptance, so that we are able to fulfil some purpose in our existence and to feel a degree of fulfilment.

The authors interviewed an esteemed quantum physicist, Dr John Hagelin, who said, "The most important key and happiness in my life is experiencing unbounded awareness." For Dr Hagelin, this refers to the spirituality within himself and its connection with the 'unified field' . . . (Which he alludes to as 'the universal intelligence that governs the universe.')

For Dr Hegler he finds joy and creativity as well as a connection to nature, success and health in his life. This is my wish for you; to have that connectivity with yourself and your world, wherever it may be, and to permit your connection to Africa to strengthen rather than confine you.

We are travellers
On a cosmic journey,
Stardust,
Swirling and dancing
In the eddies
And whirlpools of infinity.
Life is eternal.
We have stopped for a moment
To encounter each other,
To meet, to love, to share.
This is a precious moment.
It is a little parenthesis in eternity.

—Paulo Coelho

In writing this book, and reading others' contributions, I have felt some of that sense of healing; of joy, creativity and fulfilment, as well as a profound connection between humanity past and present, in Africa and abroad. I thank those who have touched my life for that. I have discovered while collating this book that I have learnt far more about people, the human psyche and myself than I imagined possible. I have learnt about human tenacity, stubbornness, pride, audacity, courage, recklessness, folly, fear, faith, strength, pain, loss and love among other emotions and character traits. Writing this book and gathering people's profound tales to add to the book have both been unequivocally humbling.

I have learnt about the full spectrum; "When our neighbours were subjected to a carjacking at gunpoint, we couldn't simply up and move to a better part of town. This was the better part of town." (from David Bennun's *Tick Bite Fever*) to people who seem to opt to suppress or withhold feelings of fear and make the decision to not move from either the worst or the best part of town . . . . When nearing the conclusion of my book, a man communicated with me and told me of his wife's horrific rape ordeal less than 100 metres from their home while she was out on a morning jog in the Northern suburbs of Johannesburg. Despite this ghastly ordeal, they elected not to leave South Africa. She continues to jog along the same route in the morning where she was brutally attacked and violated. Is it insanity, foolishness or inflexibility? Is it denial or courage? Only they can make that judgement call. His only comment to me was that it's a tragedy that people of common roots aren't able to accept one another's choices, which can lead to bitterness. The man said that if it wasn't for his wife's incredible strength he'd have fallen apart. He added that her faith and her mind are so strong that afterwards she could compare the violent act to someone merely sticking their finger in her ear. She was able to reduce it "to unemotive and inconsequential body parts." They decided, even though they have two daughters, that they would not permit one man's 'brief insanity' to disrupt their own relationship or their affinity for their country . . .

This left me aghast for a few days as I tried to distil and digest this story. It made me ponder long and hard about faith, hope, strength, resilience, obstinacy and more. It made me wonder where one draws the line between irresponsibility and passion. Is there a beginning? Is there an end? Is there a continuum about humanity and its responses? What is a normal response; what is valiant and what is madness? How long is a piece of string and when is enough 'enough'? Through all these stories and Scatterlings, it has galvanised for me how individualistic we all are and that truly we each have to travel our own chosen path. It has made me view the African Diaspora, whether rooted at home or flung like seeds in the wind, as a people made of mettle.

It is in leaving Africa that I have found the true meaning of Africa. It is that incomprehensible place that has an unmarshalled prowess like the call of the Fish Eagle; strong, magnificent, with a melodic, yet doleful cry. It is in leaving Africa, that I have been freed to love her; to yearn from my state of dichotomy.

What does the future hold? Who has a crystal ball? All I can add is that one should 'Never say never'; whether to staying, leaving or returning to Southern Africa! It will stay there waiting and beckoning, tantalising and possibly betraying. Some things remain answered . . .

"The threshold and the hearth are mythic spaces. Each has sacred and ceremonial aspects in the history of our myth. To cross the threshold is to enter another world—whether the one on the inside or the one on the outside—and we can never be really sure what is on the other side of the door until we open it." Jeanette Winterson.

Leaving Africa . . . . Eve 2012

Even now I wake some days,
my heart with broken glass shards cutting into it,
silvery blue sharp jagged pieces,
wispy long razor slivers in my mind's eye.
Tears are close, chest heaving, the trigger in my heart . . .
the searing reality of my shrapnelled soul, my arms outstretched—

One hand touching the antiquity of my Freestate Koppies,
caressing my childhood Cumulous nimbus clouds,
gathering golden wheat ears,
kissing the laughing sunbeams
feeling red earth between my toes,
softly brushing my wizened finger tips on my lost
family's faces . . .

The other hand touching Aotearoa's form,
as it emerges triumphantly from a subterranean dark ocean;
My fingers trailing aimlessly in silky azure,
exploring new found shells, silvery ferns,
holding my husband's hand,
gratefully holding our family here.

Smiling, praying, crying, breathing.
It is the way it is.

References

Bennun, David *Tick Bite Fever.* United Kingdom: Edbury Press, 2003

Bhugra, Deinesh & Becker, Matthew *Cultural Psychiatry, Institute of Psychiatry.* De Crespigny Park, London, UK, February 2005. Department of Psychiatry, Southern California Permanente Medical Group, San Diego, CA, USA.

Botha, Ted and Baxter Jenni *The Expat Confessions.* New York and Australia: Jented Publishing, 2005

Bray Attwood, Janet & Attwood, Chris *The Passion Test.* Sydney, Australia: Hachette Australia, 2007

Brink, Andre *On Antjie Krog's Country of my Skull.* Book Review, 1998

Burke, Lynn *The Consequences of Truth: Post-traumatic Stress in New South Africa.* South Africa in Transition-News-Top Story. http//journalism. berkeley.edu/projects/southafrica/news/traumaprinterfriendly.

Cliff, Gareth *Letter from Gareth Cliff to the SA Government.* 12th October 2010 *Belowthelion.co.za*

Coelho, Paulo *Life-Selected quotations.* London: Harper Collins, 2007

Deitz, Melissa *My life as a side effect. Living with depression.* Milson's Point, NSW Australia: Random House, 2004

Dooley, Mike *Infinite Possibilities.* New York: Atria Books, 2009

Du Plessis, Jan, Dr *South Africa: Detailed Analysis: 2010: Collapsing into a Failed State. http://macua.blogs.com/moambique_para_todos/2010/09/*

safrica-detailed-analysis-2010-collapsing-into-a-failed-state-41-.html.
Sunday 12 Sept 2010

Du Preez, Max *The sickening smell of 'revolution'.* News 24. 6 July 2011

Du Preez, Max *Understand the cancer of crime if you want to eradicate it.*
(My Tuesday column) 2012

Fox, Bronwyn *Working Through Panic—Your step to step Guide to Overcoming Panic/Anxiety Related Disorders.* Frenchs Forest, Australia: Pearson Education Australia Pty Ltd., 2001

Frankl, Viktor *Man's Search for Meaning.* Vienna, Austria: Verlag fur Jugend und, 1946 (Beacon Press, English translation)

Fuller, Alexandra *Don't let's Go to the Dogs Tonight.* New York: Random House, 2001

Fuller, Alexandra Fuller *Cocktail Hour Under the Tree of Forgetfulness.* New York: The Penguin Press, 2001

Gardiner, Jeremy *South Africans could do with a healthy dose of perspective.*

www.sagoodnews.co.za/newsletter, 09 November 2012

Gibran, Kahlil. *The Prophet.* London: Heinemann, 1970

Gibran, Kahlil Quotes, www.quotationspage/quotes/Kahlil Gibran

Gill, Sharon *From frying pan to fire?* 28 November 2011

Gill, Sharon *A South African at home—Home isn't where it used to be* 5th November 2011

Godsell, Bobby *Live without fear and help to make our land a better place.* 02 February 2012

Gordimer, Nadine *Telling Times Writing and Living.* 1954-2008, New York, London: W.W. Norton & Company, 2010

Harris, Paul *Email to My ex South African friend in Aussie.* *http://www.homecomingrevolution.co.za/blog/* 25 October 2012

Hemming, Eve *Painting the Soul—A Process of Empowerment.* Saarbrucken, Germany: Lambert Academic Publishing, 2011

Herman, Judith, M.D. *Trauma and Recovery—The aftermath of violence from domestic abuse to political terror.* New York: Perseus Book Group, 1997

Ignatieff, Michael *The Lesser Evil—Political Ethics in an Age of Terror.* Edinburgh: Edinburgh University Press Ltd., 2005

Ilardi Steve Dr *The Depression Cure.* London: Vermilion, 2010

Jemison, Elizabeth Lee *The Nazi Influence in the formation of apartheid in South Africa.* Canton: MA 02021 U.S.A., 2004

Kabta-Zinn, John *Coming to our sense—Healing ourselves and the world through mindfulness.* New York: Hyperion, 2005

Knott-Craig, Alan *Don't Panic! A book by South Africans for South Africans.* Johannesburg: Penguin Books, 2008

Krog, Antjie *Country of My Skull.* Johannesburg: Random House (Pty) Ltd., 2002

Mabaso, Vusi *Apartheid: The new and improved version—Growthpoint Organisation—Extraordinary People doing Exceptional things.* 29 October 2011

Mabaso, Vusi *The Tokoloshe.* News 24, 13 November 2011

Manassis, Katherina, MD, FRCPS & Levac, Anne Marie, RN, MN. *Helping your Teenager Beat Depression, A Problem-Solving Approach for Families.* USA: Woodbine House, 2004

Mandela, Nelson *Long Walk to Freedom.* New York, London: Little, Brown and Company, 1994

Masman, Karen. *Why Feeling Sad is no reason to be Happy.* Crow's Nest, NSW, Australia: Allen& Unwin, 2009

Matthews, Alex *On emigration from South Africa. www.huffingtonpost.com/alex-matthews/south-africa*, 12 September 2010

McGraw, Phil Dr *Real Life.* New York, London: Free Press, 2008

Ministry of Health, Refugee Health Care: *A handbook for health professionals.* Wellington, New Zealand: Ministry of Health, 2012

Moody, Raymond & Arcangel, Dianne *Life After Death, Finding Hope through Life After Life.* San Francisco: Harper, 1998

Mtimkulu, Motheo *A Paralysed Citizenry: When did we Give Up?* 19 October, 2012 News 24

Murphy, Alan, Armstrong, Kate et al *Southern Africa.* UK, USA: lonelyplanet.com, 2010

Paton, Alan *Cry the Beloved Country.* London: Jonathan Cape, 1948

Pennington, Steuart *Grasping the nettle—responding to the State of the Nation address. Newsletters—South Africa—The Good News,* Wednesday, 15 February 2012

Potter-Effron, Ron, M.S.W & Potter-Effron Pat, M.S. *Letting Go of Anger, The 100 most common anger styles and what to do about them.* Oaklin, CA, USA: Harbinger Publications, 1995

Price, Stephen *Open Letter to President Zuma.* News 24, 13 October 2012

Richard, Katie *Coping with Immigration Stress.* Sabona Magazine, 01 April 2007

Schoch, Richard *The Secrets of Happiness, Three Thousand Years of Searching for the Good Life.* New York: Scribner, 2006

Shuudi, Pashu *The way things are . . . in Africa.* The Namibia Sun, 24 March 2011

South Africa Tiger Books International, no date given.

Spellman, W.M. *Uncertain Identity, International Migration since 1945.* London: Reaktion Books, 2008

Sunter, Clem *Mr President, you should lead by example.* News 24, 18 October 2012

Sunter, Clem *Peace or war: It's your call.* News 24, 20 June 2012

The Witness, Pietermaritzburg, KZN, SA. *www.witness.co.za*

Winterson, Jeanette *Why Be Happy When You Could Be Normal?* London: Vintage Books, 2011

Worsnip, Michael *'Thirty-three out of one hundred'.* The Witness, 11 Jan 2012

Zille, Helen *Zuma's 'Giant Leap'—Off the cliff.* Helen Zille's weekly newsletter. SA Today. 1 July 2012

Internet references interspersed in the body of the text.

When you follow your bliss . . .
Doors will open where you will not have thought
There would be doors; and where
There wouldn't be a door for anyone else.
Joseph Campbell

Appendix

Topical Books—Southern Africa

Cry, The Beloved Country—Alan Paton, 1948

The Conservationist—Nadine Gordimer, 1974

A Question of Power—Bessie Head, 1974

A Dry White Season—Andre Brink, 1979

July's People—Nadine Gordimer, 1981

The Story of an African Farm—Olive Schreiner, 1983

Come and Hope with Me—Mongane Wally Serote, 1994

Long Walk to Freedom—Nelson Mandela, 1994

Tomorrow is Another Country—Alistair Sparks, 1996

Country Of My Skull—Antjie Krog, 1998

Disgrace—J.M. Coetzee, 1999

A Place Called Vatmaar—AHM Scholtz, 2001

Welcome to Our Hillbrow—Phaswane Mpe, 2002

Mukiwa: A White Boy in Africa—Peter Godwin, 2004

Politics in Southern Africa: Transition and Transformation, Gretchen Bauer & Scott D. Taylor, 2005

Mandela: A Critical Life—Tom Lodge, 2007

When a Crocodile Eats the Sun: A Memoir of Africa—Peter Godwin, 2008

Rainbow's End: A Memoir of Childhood, War and an African Farm—Lauren St. John, 2008

Mafeking Road and Other Stories—Herman Charles Bosman, 2008

Art and the End of Apartheid—John Peffer, 2009

Bring Me My Machine Gun: The Battle for the Soul of South Africa, from Mandela to Zuma—Alec Russell, 2009

Torn in the New SA—Living, Loving & Leaving South Africa—Bronwyn McIntosh, 2010

Shades of Exodus—Barry Levy, 2010

Should I Stay Or Should I Go? To Live In Or Leave South Africa (With André Brink, Kevin Bloom, Jacob Dlamini, Kerry Rogers, Liz Butler, Gillian Tucker, Sarah Britten, Sarah Penny, James Carolin, Barry Levy, Anne Townsend, Ian Macdonald, Daniel Ford, Louie Cowan, Ted Botha, Jenni Baxter & Tim Richman.)

The Fate of Africa: A History of the Continent Since Independence—Martin Meredith, 2011

The Fear: Robert Mugabe and the Martyrdom of Zimbabwe—Peter Godwin, 2011

Catastrophe: What Went Wrong in Zimbabwe?—Richard Bourne, 2011

Sometimes There is a Void: Memoirs of an Outsider—Zakes Mda, 2011

The Vase with the Many Coloured Marbles—Jacob Singer, 2011

The Locust Retribution—Alan Hancock, 2012

Saving Nelson Mandela: The Rivonia Trial and the Fate of South Africa (Pivotal Moments in World History)—Kenneth S. Broun, 2012

Mandela: In Celebration of a Great Life—Charlene Smith, 2012

CPSIA information can be obtained at www.ICGtesting.com
Printed in the USA
LVOW08s2010280813

350050LV00001B/303/P